John Ross Macduff

Brighter Than the Sun

John Ross Macduff

Brighter Than the Sun

ISBN/EAN: 9783337155780

Printed in Europe, USA, Canada, Australia, Japan

Cover: Foto ©Thomas Meinert / pixelio.de

More available books at **www.hansebooks.com**

BRIGHTER THAN THE SUN:

OR,

Christ the Light of the World.

A LIFE OF OUR LORD FOR THE YOUNG.

BY

J. R. MACDUFF, D.D.

WITH ILLUSTRATIONS BY A. ROWAN

"I am THE LIGHT OF THE WORLD." — *John* viii. 12.
"His countenance was as the Sun shineth in his strength." — *Rev.* i. 16.
"A light from heaven ABOVE THE BRIGHTNESS OF THE SUN." — *Acts* xxvi. 13.

> "Thou Sun of this great world, both eye and soul,
> Acknowledge HIM thy GREATER: sound His praise
> In thine eternal course; both when thou climb'st,
> And when high noon hast gained, and when thou fall'st."
> *Paradise Lost, Book V.*

> —— —— "his inferior flame
> A new enlightened World no more would need:
> He saw a GREATER SUN appear,
> Than his bright throne or burning axle-tree could bear."
> *Milton's Hymn on the Nativity.*

AMERICAN TRACT SOCIETY,
150 NASSAU STREET, NEW YORK.

PREFACE.

THIS is the only portion of the following pages addressed to those senior to the generality of my readers.

It is with the deepest reverence,—with a devout and prayerful sense of responsibility, that in any form a writer ventures to offer, in the permanent shape which authorship implies, THE LIFE of all lives. Nor is this responsibility in any degree lessened, rather is it deepened and intensified, when the attempt has special reference to the mind in its early and most receptive stage.

I think it only due to myself to say, that the present volume was commenced very many years ago. Its progress was retarded, and completion rendered impossible, by the engrossing calls of a busy sphere. Greater leisure has permitted me to revise with care what had been already written; and to resume, amid other studies, what remained in this simple rendering, of the ever new, and ever more wondrous Narrative.

Lives of Christ by Bishop Ellicott, Dr. Pressensé, Dr. Hanna, and Dr. Farrar, may be taken as modern representative volumes on the sacred theme, adapted for matured and cultured intellect,—for manhood and womanhood. "*The Wonderful Life*" (Henry S. King & Co.) may be regarded, and strongly recommended, as a similar representative volume for thoughtful youth. That by the authoress of "*Peep of Day*," is peerless in its own domain for child-learners. The present is designed as intermediate between the latter two; and it is hoped will thus occupy a peculiar, and still, so far as I know, unappropriated niche in the Human Temple that has sought to enshrine the Greatest Biography.[1]

My aim throughout has been to write, with studied simplicity, *a pictorial Life of the Saviour;* making it as vivid and attractive as I could to youthful nature. While, however, I speak of "studied simplicity," neither have I discarded the advice formerly given by one well competent to speak, that it was often a mistake in books for the young employing too juvenile language. I have endeavoured, in what follows, to accept the truth of the observation by avoiding both extremes.

One remark I would desire to make by way of caution. Nothing is more important in the treatment of such a theme, than to keep steadily and constantly before the young mind that it is a *Divine* Life which is under contemplation: that that Great and Glorious FIGURE moving in every page of the Gospels, is none other than "the Mystery of Godliness"—"GOD manifest in the flesh." Yet, while deprecating what may be called the painfully exclusive humanitarian views which are only too prevalent, alike in the pulpit and the press, I have not scrupled to give every prominence to the blessed complementary and coun-

---

[1] Though for a different class of readers, let me commend the excellent "*Lessons on our Lord's Life*," by Eugene Stock, a book specially valuable to Sunday-School Teachers.

terpart truth of Jesus, "*the Child born,*" and "*the Son given,*" as well as Jesus "*the Mighty God, and Everlasting Father.*" I have put no arrest, so far as was allowable, on the portrayal of the human feelings alike through Childhood, Boyhood, and Manhood; —or in picturing the lowliness of birth, and station, and employment. All this 'realistic' treatment is designed to make the youngest feel, that he or she had in CHRIST a Brother in their nature, and have now a Brother on the Throne. If at times, therefore, in any one turn of the narrative, the human element may seem to eclipse or dim the Divine, let those to whom my juvenile readers look for guidance be ready with the needful monition — never unseasonable — 'Remember, this Meek and Lowly Saviour is the Great Lord of all;—"*The Brightness of the Father's glory, and the express Image of His person.*"' Let those words, which have been embalmed through long ages in the creed of Christendom, ever be placed on the forefront of the marvellous Life-story—"I BELIEVE IN ONE LORD JESUS CHRIST, THE ONLY BEGOTTEN SON OF GOD—BEGOTTEN OF HIS FATHER BEFORE ALL WORLDS, GOD OF GOD, LIGHT OF LIGHTS, VERY GOD OF VERY GOD."

I have written, as already said, with "The Morning of Life" alone in my mind. But simplicity may be made the vehicle of thought and teaching to every diversity of age. With the growth of years we are taught, indeed, how nearly allied culture and simplicity are.

Before closing this Preface, let me advert, in a word, to another component part of the work. Despite frequently of much artistic power and ability, it must be allowed that there is often great sameness and repetition in what are familiarly known as "Bible Pictures." It has been my special aim, as well as that of the artist, to whose genius, and I may add, reverence for the scenes delineated, I am indebted,—to depart from this ordinary conventional treatment. Subjects have been purposely taken, different from those usually selected; and I think I can appeal both to young and old for an approving verdict, alike as to the vigour and freshness of the accompanying illustrations.

CONTENTS.

	PAGE
A FEW OPENING WORDS	1

Early Dawn.

I. AN ANGEL TELLS ABOUT HIS BIRTH	7
II. HE IS BORN IN BETHLEHEM	16
III. HE IS TAKEN UP TO THE TEMPLE	26
IV. WISE MEN FROM THE EAST VISIT HIM . . .	34
V. HEROD TRIES TO KILL HIM	41
VI. HE GOES DOWN INTO EGYPT	46

Morning.

VII. HE GOES TO NAZARETH, AND LIVES THERE . . .	55
VIII. HE IS TAKEN UP TO THE TEMPLE WHEN HE IS TWELVE YEARS OLD	64
IX. HIS FATHER AND MOTHER SEEK HIM SORROWING . .	72

Noontide.

X. HE GROWS UP TO MANHOOD AT NAZARETH . . .	81

Meridian Brightness.

XI. HE GOES TO THE JORDAN AND IS BAPTIZED . . .	95
XII. HE GOES TO THE MOUNT OF TEMPTATION . . .	108
XIII. HE RECEIVES HIS FIRST FOLLOWERS	112
XIV. HE TURNS WATER INTO WINE	117
XV. HE GOES FIRST TO THE LAKE, AND THEN TO THE PASSOVER	123
XVI. HE MEETS NICODEMUS, A JEWISH RULER . . .	132
XVII. HE MEETS A WOMAN OF SAMARIA AT JACOB'S WELL .	138
XVIII. HE CURES THE NOBLEMAN'S SON	146
XIX. HE HEALS THE LAME MAN AT THE POOL OF BETHESDA .	149
XX. HE IS AT NAZARETH AGAIN	156
XXI. HE TEACHES AT THE LAKE AND CALLS FOUR DISCIPLES	162
XXII. HOW HE SPENDS A SABBATH AT THE LAKE . . .	165

		PAGE
XXIII.	HE GOES UP A MOUNTAIN, AND AFTERWARDS CURES A LEPER	169
XXIV.	HE HEALS A SICK MAN OF THE PALSY, AND CALLS ANOTHER DISCIPLE	172
XXV.	HE PREACHES THE SERMON ON THE MOUNT, AND APPOINTS HIS TWELVE APOSTLES	176
XXVI.	HE CURES THE CENTURION'S SERVANT	180
XXVII.	HE GOES TO NAIN, AND RAISES THE WIDOW'S SON TO LIFE	183
XXVIII.	HE SAYS KIND WORDS TO A WOMAN WHO WAS A SINNER	187
XXIX.	HE SENDS A MESSAGE TO JOHN THE BAPTIST	192
XXX.	HE TEACHES BY PARABLES, AND THEN CROSSES THE LAKE IN A STORM	196
XXXI.	HE GOES TO GADARA, AND CURES THE MAN WITH THE LEGION OF DEVILS	201
XXXII.	HE CURES THE DAUGHTER OF JAIRUS	204
XXXIII.	HE HEARS OF JOHN THE BAPTIST'S DEATH	209
XXXIV.	HE FEEDS A CROWD OF FIVE THOUSAND	214

Gathering Clouds.

XXXV.	HE WALKS AT NIGHT ON THE STORMY LAKE	223
XXXVI.	HE PREACHES IN THE SYNAGOGUE AT CAPERNAUM	226
XXXVII.	HE GOES TO TYRE, SIDON, AND DECAPOLIS	230
XXXVIII.	HE RETURNS TO THE EAST OF THE LAKE	234
XXXIX.	HE GOES TO THE COASTS OF CESAREA PHILIPPI	236
XL.	HE IS CONFESSED BY HIS APOSTLES TO BE THE SON OF THE LIVING GOD	240
XLI.	HE ASCENDS THE MOUNT OF TRANSFIGURATION	244
XLII.	HE GOES TO THE FEAST OF TABERNACLES	252
XLIII.	HE CURES A BLIND MAN, AND DELIVERS THE PARABLE OF THE GOOD SHEPHERD	260
XLIV.	HE GOES TO GALILEE, AND SENDS OUT SEVENTY DISCIPLES	263
XLV.	HE DELIVERS THE MOST BEAUTIFUL OF ALL HIS PARABLES	266
XLVI.	HE GOES UP BY JERICHO TO BETHANY	271
XLVII.	HE ATTENDS THE FEAST OF DEDICATION, AND RETURNS TO PEREA	275

Evening Shadows.

XLVIII.	BEFORE HE LEAVES PEREA HE BLESSES LITTLE CHILDREN	281
XLIX.	HE HEARS OF THE DEATH OF LAZARUS, AND GOES TO BETHANY	283
L.	HE GOES TO THE TOWN OF EPHRAIM, AND THENCE TO JERICHO	291
LI.	HE PASSES THROUGH JERICHO, AND CURES BLIND BARTIMEUS	294

Gleams before Sunset.

		PAGE
LII.	HE IS ENTERTAINED AT A FEAST IN BETHANY	305
LIII.	HE CROSSES IN TRIUMPH THE MOUNT OF OLIVES	309
LIV.	HE WEEPS OVER JERUSALEM, AND THEN ENTERS THE CITY	314
LV.	HE FORETELLS THE DESTRUCTION OF THE TEMPLE, AND IS FURTHER BETRAYED BY JUDAS	317
LVI.	HE SENDS TWO OF HIS DISCIPLES TO MAKE READY THE PASSOVER	321
LVII.	HE EATS THE PASSOVER WITH HIS DISCIPLES	324

Night Watches.

LVIII.	HE SUFFERS IN THE GARDEN OF GETHSEMANE	333
LIX.	HE IS SEIZED BY A TROOP OF SOLDIERS	339
LX.	HE IS BROUGHT BEFORE ANNAS AND CAIAPHAS	342
LXI.	HE IS CRUELLY TREATED IN THE HOUSE OF CAIAPHAS, AND DENIED BY PETER	345
LXII.	HE IS TAKEN TO THE PALACE OF PILATE	348
LXIII.	HE APPEARS BEFORE PILATE AND HEROD	351
LXIV.	HE IS GIVEN UP BY PILATE TO BE CRUCIFIED	357

Midnight.

LXV.	HE IS TAKEN TO CALVARY	363
LXVI.	HIS SUFFERINGS ON THE CROSS BEGIN	367
LXVII.	HE PARDONS THE PENITENT THIEF, AND COMMENDS HIS MOTHER TO THE CARE OF JOHN	372
LXVIII.	HE SUFFERS AMID THE DARKNESS, AND AT LAST BOWS HIS HEAD IN DEATH	375
LXIX.	HE IS TAKEN DOWN FROM THE CROSS AND LAID IN A TOMB	379
LXX.	HIS TOMB IS WATCHED BY A GUARD OF SOLDIERS	384
LXXI.	HIS TOMB IS FOUND EMPTY BY THE HOLY WOMEN, AND VISITED BY PETER AND JOHN	387

The Great Sunrise.

LXXII.	HE REVEALS HIMSELF TO MARY MAGDALENE AND TO PETER	395
LXXIII.	HE JOINS THE TWO DISCIPLES ON THE WAY TO EMMAUS	400
LXXIV.	HE APPEARS TWICE TO THOSE GATHERED IN THE UPPER ROOM	405
LXXV.	HE SHOWS HIMSELF TO HIS DISCIPLES ON THE LAKE-SHORE	410
LXXVI.	HE MEETS FIVE HUNDRED BRETHREN ON A MOUNTAIN IN GALILEE	417

Dawn of Eternal Day.

LXXVII.	HE IS TAKEN UP TO HEAVEN IN A CLOUD	425

LIST OF ILLUSTRATIONS.

                                                                                                                         PAGE

THE TRANSFIGURATION—
"*And His face did shine as the sun*" (Matt. xvii. 2) . *Frontispiece*

THE SHEPHERDS OF BETHLEHEM—
"*And there were shepherds abiding in the fields*" (Luke ii. 8) . . 20

THE JOURNEY OF THE "WISE MEN"—
"*There came wise men from the East to Jerusalem*" (Matt. ii. 1) . . 35

SABBATH EVE AT NAZARETH—
"*He came to Nazareth, and was subject unto them*" (Luke ii. 51) . . 63

THE DIVINE YOUTH OF NAZARETH—
"*He was in the world, and the world was made by Him, and the world knew Him not*" (John i. 10) 86

JESUS IN THE WILDERNESS—
"*And was with the wild beasts*" (Mark i. 13) 109

THE POOL OF BETHESDA—
"*An angel went down at a certain season into the pool, and troubled the water*" (John v. 4) 151

JOHN THE BAPTIST IN PRISON—
"*John calling unto him two of his Disciples, sent them to Jesus*" (Luke vii. 19) 194

THE BLIND MAN AT BETHSAIDA—
"*He took the blind man by the hand, and led him out of the town*" (Mark viii. 23) 238

CARRYING THE GOLDEN PITCHER FROM THE POOL OF SILOAM—
"*With joy shall ye draw water out of the wells of salvation*" (Is. xii. 3) . 257

LAZARUS IS DEAD—
"*But Mary sat still in the house*" (John xii. 28) 287

THE CHILDREN IN THE TEMPLE—
"*The children crying in the Temple, and saying, Hosanna to the Son of David*" (Matt. xxi. 15) 316

THE TRAITOR BAND—
"*They went backward, and fell to the ground*" (John xviii. 6) . . 340

THE HOLY WOMEN AT THE CRUCIFIXION—
"*There were also women looking on afar off*" (Mark xv. 40) . . 364

ST. JOHN AND THE MOTHER OF JESUS—
"*And from that hour, that Disciple took her unto his own home*" (John xix. 27) 375

MORNING ON THE LAKE-SIDE—
"*When the morning was now come, Jesus stood on the shore*" . . 414

[The Drawings are engraved by Mr. Pearson, of Bolt Court, Fleet Street.]

A FEW OPENING WORDS.

TELL me, my young friends, what you think is beyond all comparison the most glorious object in the outer world? I am sure you will at once answer—

It is THE SUN.

Who can wonder that Chaldean and Persian, Assyrian and Phœnician, worshipped it? Who can wonder that altars were built all over the East to "the Sun-God,"—generally placed on the tops of the hills to catch the earliest morning rays? The Deity of Thebes, the old capital of Egypt, was called Amun-Ra, "The Sun." The Sun-emblem is still visible on the gateways of Karnac and Denderah. The first site of Egypt's ancient Temples I visited, with its solitary obelisk standing amid mounds of weeds, was at On, "The City of the Sun." The most splendid ruin I have ever seen is "The Temple of the Sun" at Baalbec. Some Oriental Kings wear a golden image of the "Kingly Orb" as the proudest badge of royalty, and take the name, as their proudest boast, of "Children of the Sun." Who that has travelled in Eastern deserts, or sailed in Eastern seas, can forget the Arab guide or boatman, spreading his mat on the pathless sand or on the deck of his vessel, and falling prostrate as he descries the first rim of gold in the far horizon? Who can forget how full the sacred poetry of the Bible is of the same "Ruler of the day"? Yes, how the Great God of all, who hath set His glory *above* the Heavens, is said to take these beams and to weave them into a beauteous vesture for Himself,—" Who covereth Thyself with LIGHT as with a garment?"

A

Many of you doubtless have watched that glowing Sun rising in the Eastern sky. Ere the ball of fire makes its appearance, one twinkling star after another has dimmed and paled away before it. The world gradually puts off its dark sable mantle, and clothes itself in a robe of brightness. Wreathes of mist and cloud rise slowly from hill and valley, and the birds wake up to their chorus of song.

> "Far eastward in the Heaven
> You see at last the sign,
> O'er the far purple mountain
> A single silver line.
>
> "It broadens and it deepens
> To a sea of red and gold,
> With clouds of rosy amber
> Around its glory rolled.
>
> "Till each pane of your window
> Is silvered o'er and o'er;
> And lines of golden arrows
> Lie on the dusky floor."

Still higher and yet higher is the steep ascent of the heavens climbed. "In them hath He set a tabernacle for the Sun, which is as a bridegroom coming out of his chamber, and rejoiceth as a strong man to run a race." Onwards still he continues his giant course, till he seems to pause overhead at noontide, perhaps in the calm, cloudless blue of a summer sky. Now begins the descent towards the west. Fleecy clouds may be gathering around him. These at times deepen as the shadows fall. Then comes sunset with its parting burst of radiance; farewell gleams tipping every rock and mountain, every stem and branch and leaf, with a ruddy glow. "His going forth has been from the one end of the heaven, and his circuit unto the other end of it, and there is nothing hid from the heat thereof." Most glorious of all, when this Monarch of the sky seems to lay down his head on a pillow of crimson and gold; or, when lost from view, he leaves behind him a trail of beautiful light.

A FEW OPENING WORDS. 3

This, young readers, is a picture and image in Outer Nature of what I am going to try feebly to describe in this book.

A far more glorious LIGHT even than that glorious Sun of the firmament is to occupy our thoughts. We are to gaze together with devout and wondering eyes on the true "SUN OF RIGHTEOUSNESS." We are to trace together His rising from early dawn, on through the morning of His sacred life, till we behold Him pouring noontide brightness over the world whose darkness He came to lighten, and whose souls He came to save. We are together to watch the clouds which gathered around Him towards evening. Then the gleams of heavenly Light which pierced the gloom of His awful setting, until "the shadow of death was turned into the morning." Finally, we shall see Him rise to set no more; vanishing from our sight behind the earthly horizon, only to shine amid the splendours of the Heavenly City. *"The Lamb is the* LIGHT *thereof."*

While we are thus occupied in what follows, gazing on One "BRIGHTER THAN THE SUN," let it be your prayer and mine, "*I beseech Thee, shew me* THY GLORY:" that so, in closing these pages, we may be able, with humble happy confidence, to take and make the words of the Great Apostle our own :—

"God, who commanded the light to shine out of darkness, hath shined in our hearts, to give THE LIGHT *of the knowledge of the glory of God in the face of* JESUS CHRIST" (2 Cor. iv. 6).

EARLY DAWN.

"WATCHMAN, WHAT OF THE NIGHT? WATCHMAN, WHAT OF THE NIGHT? THE WATCHMAN SAID, 'THE MORNING COMETH.'"—IS. XXI. 11, 12.

"THROUGH THE TENDER MERCY OF OUR GOD, WHEREBY THE DAYSPRING FROM ON HIGH HATH VISITED US."—LUKE I. 78.

"THE PEOPLE THAT WALKED IN DARKNESS HAVE SEEN A GREAT LIGHT: THEY THAT DWELL IN THE LAND OF THE SHADOW OF DEATH, UPON THEM HATH THE LIGHT SHINED."—IS. IX. 2.

"THE GENTILES SHALL COME TO THY LIGHT, AND KINGS TO THE BRIGHTNESS OF THY RISING."—IS. LX. 3.

"NOW THE BIRTH OF JESUS CHRIST WAS ON THIS WISE."—MATT. I. 18.

I.

An Angel tells about His Birth.

IN a lonely village among the hills of Galilee, this 'Sweet story of old' begins. There we watch the first streak of promised Day-break.

There are few places in the Holy Land which have more of a quiet beauty about them than NAZARETH. Though sadly changed from its older and better days, it still remains a pleasant and favoured nook in the great "fruit orchard," which we know Palestine once was. It still has its green valley, its clusters of fig, vine, olive, and almond trees, and its gardens fenced with hedges of prickly pear. Patches of white limestone-rock peep out here and there on the slopes; the fields are golden in their season with wheat and barley; and in the early spring and summer the grass looks gay with red and white daisies and anemones, blue lupins, and tulips. No wonder the flowers are so numerous, for the name "Nazareth" is supposed to mean "flowery." A very old writer, St. Jerome, calls it "The flower of Galilee." Another speaks of it as "a rose in the midst of leaves." This peaceful little spot with its encircling hills recalled more than one familiar scene among the mountainous districts of our own country,—only with a sun and climate that can ripen, what is an impossibility under northern skies, the grape, the melon, the orange, and the citron.

From several of these heights a goodly number of famous places spoken about in the Bible are visible. I wish you had been with me when I stood, one cloudless day in spring, on the highest summit above the town, where a pole was placed in the midst of a heap of stones close by a Moslem tomb. From it were visible in the distance, among others, four well-known hills of Scripture story, and yet they seemed, in that clear air, to be very near. Can you guess what they were?

There was Carmel with its bold front, which reminded me of the great Elijah and the prophets of Baal. There was round Gilboa, which seemed still to resound with David's touching lament over the death of Saul and Jonathan. There was dome-shaped Tabor with its clumps of oak; to English eyes so home and park like,—which recalled the prophetess Deborah and the warlike Barak. Higher than all, there was great Mount Hermon, with a snowy top like a white crown, looking a king among the other mountains:—while far to the right, washing the sands of the Bay of Acre, were the deep blue waters of the Mediterranean Sea, over whose waves apostles and missionaries sped ages ago, bearing with them from Palestine the message of salvation to the distant shores of Greece and Italy, Spain and Britain.

The eyes of ONE, "BRIGHTER" far than the bright sun which was that day shining on all these scenes of sacred interest,—One meek and lowly, yet Godlike and divine, of whom I am to speak in the following pages, must have often, often gazed on the sublime and varied prospect.

At the time of which I am going to tell you, this Highland Village was very much apart from the rest of the world. It must have looked then, as it does now, like a secluded bird's nest. No great highway or road led to it. No din of traffic was heard in its streets. No prophet like Isaiah, no Psalmist like David, had ever spoken about it or sung about it. While, not far off, camps had been pitched, the trumpet of war had sounded, and great armies had fought; no battle that we know of, ever raged on its slopes, no blood had ever stained its thymey fields. It appeared as if it were meant to be, as we know it did become, the home of some PRINCE OF PEACE. Josephus, the Jewish historian, speaks of a vast number of towns and villages in the Holy Land, but he never mentions *Nazareth*. In other cities of Galilee there were many rich men and traders, soldiers, and merchants, and nobles, who had splendid houses, with slaves and servants to attend upon them. But no proud Roman or Greek would have cared to live here. Even the roving Arab would not think it worth his while to come and pillage its houses of baked clay and its scanty crops. It was simply a retired country hamlet. Some of its villagers would look after flocks of goats and sheep,—others would train vines and olives to make wine and oil. Perhaps it did not own another shop or place of business save the One where a Carpenter worked, which has given it all its fame and glory. Its handful of peasants and farmers would possess in common at least one public building. Just as in our own land the Church-tower or spire is seen in the humblest of our villages, rising among clumps of elms and yews, so would the Synagogue of Nazareth, situated as all synagogues were, on the highest ground available, and built of unhewn stone, catch the eye,—half hidden amid the blossoms of the apple-trees, the tall tapering cypresses, or the leaves of the clustering vine. The cypresses form a prominent feature in the first glimpse of Nazareth at the present day.

As I went up the steep and narrow streets of the town, with their round stones and rough crossings, I wondered if the flat-roofed dwellings on either side were much the same as those which existed nearly nineteen hundred years ago. At all events, it must have been in a house very like one of those I saw, that a humble tradesman once dwelt, who earned his bread, just as honest working men in our country do, by the sweat of his brow. There was a beautiful young woman of Nazareth who lived near him, and who was soon to become his wife. Her name is one familiarly known in the homes of Britain,—familiarly known in the homes of Europe and America,—*Mary* or *Miriam* (the Hebrew *Miriam*, the Greek *Maria* or *Mariam*). The Hebrew name, I may just say in passing, was in the first instance taken from Miriam the sister of Moses. But at this particular time it had become more common than ever in Palestine because derived from another and different personage. Mary or Mariam was the name of the recently murdered wife of Herod : better known as Mariamne ;— a Queen, royal in every sense of the word; for she had the royalty of kingly or queenly descent, and the better royalty of a noble nature. The Jews passionately mourned her cruel fate, and they retained the memory of her many virtues in the names of their children.[1] We shall find as we proceed, that among the few females mentioned in the course of our Lord's life, no less than four of them had the name dear to so many English brothers and sisters.

The day I was leaving Nazareth, I saw outside the town a number of women gathered round the village well, with rows of coins twisted in their black hair and round their wrists. They wore on the back of their heads scarfs or handkerchiefs of all colours, yellow, red, and blue. They were busy drawing water in their pitchers from a large marble trough. This same young Mary would be often seen there at the same hour in the morning and at sunset, carrying her pitcher on her head or shoulder, and taking it home to her parents' house. The well is named after her—it is called "The well of the Virgin."

A great honour was in store for Mary, and for her future husband Joseph, poor and humble as they both were.

One day she was visited by an Angel. The Greek Church, by erecting a building over the spot, have supposed that he addressed her as she was in the act of drawing water at that Fountain. But I think it far more likely, in accordance with the belief of the Latin Christians at Nazareth, that he would appear to her in her own house. Although only a foolish tradition, and I mention it as such, I remember being taken, as all travellers are, to a grotto hung with silver lamps, under the Church of the Latin Convent, where the angel is said to have shewn himself to the Holy Virgin behind the rude pillar which supports the roof.

Gabriel was the name of the Divine messenger. He was the same who appeared four hundred years before to the Prophet Daniel in Babylon, and informed him about the coming of "*Messiah the Prince*." He called the lowly maiden by her name. He said—

"MARY, the Great God of Heaven has sent me to tell you that you are to be blessed above all the women that ever were on the

---

[1] See Dean Stanley's "Jewish Church," vol. iii. p. 429.

earth. You are to be the Mother of JESUS CHRIST, the world's Saviour."

Angels, as you know, had often before appeared to the Jews at different periods of their history. Angels came and spoke to Abraham in his tent door at Mamre. A band of Angels went up and down the ladder which Jacob saw in his Bethel dream. Angels had appeared to Moses, to Joshua, to Gideon, and many others. But their visits had not been so common in recent years. We might not have been astonished therefore, if Mary had at first been much troubled at seeing this bright visitant, and at hearing news so startling. Wonderful tidings indeed they were.

"*And the Angel said unto her, Fear not, Mary; for thou hast found favour with God. And, behold, thou shalt conceive in thy womb, and bring forth a son, and shall call his name JESUS. He shall be great, and shall be called the Son of the Highest; and the Lord God shall give unto Him the throne of His father David; and He shall reign over the house of Jacob for ever; and of His kingdom there shall be no end*" (Luke i. 30—33).

She was to be the mother of a King. He was to be Greater than David. He was to "*sit upon a throne*," not for a lifetime only, but "for ever." His name was to be "*The Son of the Highest*," and the Great God was to be His Father.

And yet I do not know if you were ever struck with the singular calmness and absence of much wonder with which Mary received the Angel's announcement. I have spoken of her and Joseph as lowly inmates of a cottage. But in another sense they were *not* lowly. They were aware of a fact that would have made many like them very proud, viz., that they both were "*of the house and lineage of David*." What does this mean? It means that though they had lost their worldly position and worldly wealth—though Joseph was nothing else but a humble artisan, and she a humble maiden, yet they were descended from the royal line; they were children of a royal race, the blood of the Shepherd King of Israel flowed in their veins. Knowing therefore, as they did, that the coming Messiah was to be "the Son of David"—"a rod out of the stem of Jesse, and a branch growing out of his roots," Mary might not be so astounded as other Jewish women would have been, when she was told of the high privilege in store for her,—that of giving birth to the promised Redeemer.

There have been instances occasionally in history where the children of monarchs have been found working as tradesmen, or toiling as slaves and servants, or even wandering about as beggars; those with whom they lived or laboured unconscious of their "royal lineage," till some apparent accident dragged them into notice and fame. A similar secret Joseph and Mary had now kept to themselves. Poverty and the lapse of time had made them exchange the grandeur of a palace for the walls of a very different home. The dwellers in that remote hamlet knew them only as fellow-villagers; the one at his workshop, the other at her household cares, plying her distaff or carrying her water-flagon from the fountain. Little did the neighbours dream that the Cedar Halls of David might have been their residence, and that the Crown of David was their splendid birthright. Mary's, however, was now to be a greater honour still than being heir of "Solomon in all his glory." She was chosen among the daughters of Abraham to be the Mother of "the Prince of the Kings of the earth."

When Mary saw the Angel and heard his announcement, "*She cast in her mind what manner of salutation this should be.*"

The good Angel calmed her spirit. She inferred at once that it was a Divine message, and she felt assured that all he had told her would come true. It is well for us, like Mary, simply to believe without question what God reveals to us by His servants in His Holy Word.

When people are in doubt and perplexity they often find it a relief to go and speak to a friend and ask advice. Even when the youngest amongst you have something upon their minds, they like to carry their troubles to their fathers and mothers or some other kind adviser.

Mary resolved to do this. She had a cousin called Elizabeth, who lived probably at Hebron, the ancient Mamre, where the good old Father of the Faithful lived and was buried. If not

Hebron, it was at all events a city close by, one of the thirteen towns which had been assigned to the Levites. Elizabeth's husband was an aged Priest, who took his regular turn in ministering in the Temple. The Angel had told Mary that Elizabeth was to be honoured too like herself; for she was to give birth to John the Baptist, the Morning Star who was to precede a "BRIGHTER THAN THE SUN."

I dare say it was the Angel who put the thought into Mary's mind to go to the distant home of her relative, and speak about the wonderful news which he had brought to her.

The only difficulty must have been the long, long journey for one so young to take. Hebron was between eighty and a hundred miles distant from Nazareth, far off in the wild hill country or highlands of Judah. It could be reached only by winding dusty roads. I cannot think Mary could have gone for these five days all alone. I think she must likely have accompanied, so far at least, some of the pilgrims going to one of the Feasts at Jerusalem. There are silly traditions too regarding her journey:—about lilies springing up and blooming in her path: about animals wild and tame gathering around her—the lion laying aside his ferocity, and in company with the meek lamb, keeping guard over her as she pursued her way. But we do not need such fancies as these. The great and good God she served would doubtless "give His Angels charge concerning her, to keep her in all her ways," shielding her from danger and fear, till she reached her destination.

We can think of her, one bright evening, when perhaps the sun was setting on the hills above Abraham's tomb, knocking at her cousin's door. Elizabeth would doubtless be much surprised to see her relative from Nazareth standing there. No sooner was the door opened than they were locked in one another's arms; and as each told the tale of wonder, they praised God for His great goodness. "*How is it*," exclaimed Elizabeth, at once shewing that she knew the vast honour in store for Mary, "*that the Mother of my Lord should come to me?*"

Mary, like one of the Prophetesses of Old Testament story, replied in the words of that hymn of devotion, worthy of a seraph's tongue, which millions on millions have since so loved to use,—

> "*My soul doth magnify the Lord,*
> *And my spirit hath rejoiced in God my Saviour.*
> *For He hath regarded the low estate of His handmaiden:*
> *For, behold, from henceforth all generations shall call me blessed.*
> *For He that is mighty hath done to me great things;*
> *And holy is His name.*
> *And His mercy is on them that fear Him from generation to generation.*
> *He hath shewed strength with His arm;*
> *He hath scattered the proud in the imagination of their hearts.*
> *He hath put down the mighty from their seats, and exalted them of low degree.*
> *He hath filled the hungry with good things;*
> *And the rich He hath sent empty away.*
> *He hath holpen His servant Israel, in remembrance of His mercy;*
> *As He spake to our fathers, to Abraham, and to His seed for ever.*"

What a beautiful song! It tells us how meek and trustful and humble Mary was. There is no pride nor boasting in her sayings. Words that were afterwards spoken from the top of a green hill not far from Nazareth were surely true of her,—"*Blessed are the poor in spirit, for theirs is the kingdom of heaven.*" She seems to think most of Jesus, not as her Son, nor as "He that is mighty," but as "the Saviour," and better still as "MY *Saviour.*" She felt that she herself was a poor sinner like all the rest of the world, and needed ONE to save her.

I should tell you that the world was, at this period, increasing in wickedness and crime. The Romans now ruled over its kingdoms. They were the mightiest nation that ever existed: mightier than Egypt, or Nineveh, or Babylon, or Tyre. The Mediterranean Sea has been called at this time "a Roman Lake;" the cities which bordered its shores with their wealth and commerce were all in the hands of the great Cæsar who swayed the Roman sceptre. But if it was the vastest of empires, it was also the most corrupt. The Jews, too, were not the holy people they once were, loving God and seeking to please Him. There was no longer a good King David or a righteous Hezekiah on the throne of Zion. They were more taken up about the colour of the fringes of their robes and the shape and breadth of their "frontlets;"—about outward rites, washings and observances, than about justice and truth, purity and mercy, love to God and charity to man. Happy exceptions, doubtless, there were, in the midst of this darkness and apostasy. Not a few devout spirits, tired and wearied with the earth's guilt, were exclaiming, " Oh! when will the Great Deliverer come? When will that blessed Messiah appear, who is to dry the world's tears, and heal its sad hearts and wipe away its sins?" When is "*the True Light*," THE SUN OF RIGHTEOUSNESS, to dispel all this deep darkness? A quaint old poet (Quarles) thus expresses the longing of many such weary souls,—

> "Will't ne'er be morning? Will that promised Light
> Ne'er break, and clear those clouds of night?
> Sweet Phosphor, bring the day,
> Whose conqu'ring ray
> May chase these fogs; Sweet Phosphor, bring the day!"

Or, in the words of another and better known poet, although with a higher meaning to his beautiful emblem:—these saintly, saddened, earnest hearts were like

> "An infant crying in the night;
> An infant crying for THE LIGHT;
> And with no language but a cry." *

Mary was the first to be told "He is indeed coming at last." Hers was the first "Morning Hymn" of welcome and joy, hailing the true "Light-Bringer" (*Phosphor*), "Brighter than the brightest:" —"*The darkness is past, and* THE TRUE LIGHT *now shineth.*"

I have just one remark to add. You have perhaps been saying to yourselves,—"How honoured was this lowly Mary of Nazareth!"

So, truly, she was. But I wish you to hear words which were spoken by Jesus long after. One day as He was talking to the

---

* Tennyson's " In Memoriam."

people, and when His mother and His brethren were standing outside desiring to speak with Him, one of His followers told Him of it, saying, "*Behold Thy Mother.*" The answer of Jesus as He turned round was,—"*Who is My Mother? and who are My Brethren?*" And then He pointed with His finger to those, young and old, who were near Him, and who He knew had holy hearts and gentle, loving, obedient lives; and He said, "*Behold, these are My Mother, these are My brethren. For all who do the will of My Father in heaven, the same is My mother, and My sister, and My brother.*"

Oh wondrous thought! that all who love and seek to please Him, may be called 'the brothers or sisters of the Great Redeemer.'

II.

He is Born in Bethlehem.

THE two cousins remained together for three months, and then Mary returned to Nazareth.

Often and often, I dare say, when she got to her own home again, she would say to herself, "How very wonderful it is that I should be chosen for so great an honour! I would have imagined, if the Great God is to appear on the earth and become Man, He will surely come in splendid state. His selected home will be a palace with gilded ceilings. A King will be His foster-father, a Queen His mother, and troops of Angels will attend upon Him."

We might have thought so too. We might have thought it would be with Him as with the fabled gods of Greece and Rome, who were said, when they descended to the world, to come down to a beautiful mountain called Olympus, ten thousand feet high, on whose broad summit Jupiter their king had his throne under a canopy of cloud. But "God's thoughts are not as our thoughts." This "Tree of Life" from the Paradise of Heaven is to grow up "a Tender Plant" in a remote valley of earth. The Angel sent to tell of His birth came, as we have seen, to a poor occupant of a poor dwelling, in a village so unknown as not to have so much as its name mentioned in the Old Testament at all. A young woman in humble life is to be the Mother of IMMANUEL. A carpenter, and carpenter's wife, are to carry in their arms THE SAVIOUR OF MANKIND!

In due time JESUS was born; but not at Nazareth. His birth-place was BETHLEHEM, a town about six miles from Jerusalem, perched on the top of a rocky ridge, with flat roofs and white walls, and a valley or meadow below it, not unlike the one of which I have told you in far-off Galilee.

It was among the cornfields of Bethlehem that Ruth, who afterwards became the wife of Boaz, gleaned among the reapers. It was the very same town close to which King David, a thousand years before, when he was a boy, kept his father's sheep, defending them from robbers and beasts of prey. Under the shade of these fig and olive trees he played his shepherd's pipe, made of the reeds gathered in the valley,—the flock he had in charge browsing on the hillsides around:—while among these farther limestone crags, overhung with tufts of the caper plant and rough with masses of prickly thorn, the shepherds thought with pride that they could still point to where the brave young stripling fought single-handed the bear and lion, and where he first used the sling that raised him to the throne of Israel. There, too, was "the Well at the Gate," where his heroes drew water, and from which he had often drank in his childhood.

Not so lovely, certainly, as Nazareth, yet the situation and surroundings of Bethlehem, from my remembrance of them, are striking and attractive. It may have lost its right to its old name of *Ephratah* (fruitful). But still it has its terraced gardens, and vineyards with clumps of varied trees on its sunny slopes. There is one grand view especially, at which the traveller can never tire looking, across to the mountains of Moab. With their strange flat tops, they seem like a great sapphire-wall built by giants. The Dead Sea is at their base. How my young readers

B

would delight to gather the red and blue flowers which in spring make these meadows around Bethlehem like a rich carpet! There is one pretty white one, too, among these. They call it "The Star of Bethlehem." You shall presently hear how it got that name.

How beautiful Bethlehem must have been in those olden days when its pastures were clothed with flocks, its valleys covered with corn, the little hills rejoicing on every side! Bethlehem means "The house of bread." That name was now to belong to it in a truer sense than ever; for it was about to give to a perishing world "THE BREAD OF LIFE."

But what, you will ask, has brought Mary and Joseph these long sixty miles from Nazareth?

Cæsar Augustus, the Roman Emperor, had ordered that a roll should be made up of all the people he ruled in his great kingdom. Mary's ancestors, and Joseph's also, belonged to the tribe of Judah, and had lived, not at Nazareth, but at Bethlehem. They were required to go there to give in their names to the officers appointed to take what is called a *Census*.

We can think of the journey of those two villagers of Galilee; Mary seated on an ass, with Joseph walking by her side, along the camel-track leading through the centre of the country. We can watch them as they approach Jerusalem by the Damascus Gate, passing through the narrow streets, and out again by the great Hebron or South entrance.

On reaching the town of Bethlehem (possibly at sunset), they would naturally make, as all travellers did, for the large village Inn or Khan. This, however, they found, on entering its archway, to be already thronged with a crowd, many of whom had come for the same purpose as themselves. They had no favour shewn them. Every recess at the sides of the courtyard was already occupied. Even the open court itself was taken possession of. Some had spread their quilts or rugs on the rough stones, and were sound asleep after a long journey. Piles of goods belonging to travelling merchants to or from Egypt were littered in other places. The rough voices of the men, the wrangling of those engaged in traffic, the chatter of the women and children, the trampling of horses as they stood tied by a ring to the wall, the jingling of bells on the mules and camels, must have been irksome in the extreme to these tired and weary Pilgrims from Nazareth.

There being thus no room for them in the Inn itself, and no private home or lodging to be procured, there is nothing left but to accept far ruder accommodation. Accordingly, they go to the stable of the Khan, a place strewn with fodder, where mules and asses and yokes of oxen are housed for the night. How strange for these descendants of Kings, who had been hailed by an Angel, to be treated thus as outcasts in the city of their fathers!

I have told you about the fields of Bethlehem in bright daytime, let us now turn our gaze upon them at night.

Only those who have been in Palestine know how bright the stars are in that Eastern sky. They look exactly, as the little child said, "like holes in the floor of heaven to let the glory shine through." On one such beautiful night, a number of Shepherds were gathered on the grassy slopes under the town, watching their flocks. The sun had gone down. The women, and youth, and children of the village had, some hours before, returned from David's Well with their pitchers of water. The air was so warm and balmy that the Shepherds did not require to take their sheep and goats inside the walls to fold them there. They remained out all night with them in the open meadows. Everything was quiet—that strange peaceful stillness which all have felt so specially at night in Palestine. The birds had folded their wings to sleep. There was no sound of water, as in our land, to break the silence. Nothing was heard but the occasional bleating of the flocks. Perhaps now and then the sound of voices came floating down from the village Inn on the rocky ridge, or the flash of a lamp was for a moment seen on one of the flat-roofed houses, only to be lost again in the darkness.

I cannot help thinking these Shepherds must have been pious men; that they loved the Great God who made the mountains and the valleys, and the bright stars that glittered in the sky above. I daresay they often met together on these hills, or in some hollow or cavern sheltered from the night wind, and by the light of their watchfires, or the clear moon, read together their ancient prophecies about JESUS, or sang together some of David's sweet Psalms about Him,—Psalms, many of which he had composed on the very slopes around them; or perhaps they would pray together that God would soon bring it all to pass, that they might see with their own eyes that Good Shepherd who was to "gather the lambs in His arms."

I should not wonder if, on this very night I speak of, they had been talking to one another very earnestly about the Hope of their nation. If you can picture them doing so, I wonder if something like this would be their converse.

One would say to his fellow, "To what place do you think will the Great Messiah first come? Will it be *Bethel*, where the Angels went up and down from the stony pillow of the Patriarch?"

Another perhaps would say, "Will it not rather be *Hebron*, the old capital of Palestine, where David was crowned King, and where the Fathers of our nation are buried?"

Another would possibly say, "Will it not rather be *Shiloh*, where the Ark of the covenant so long rested, and where the holiest child of Old Testament times ministered before the Lord?"

Another would perhaps say, "No: will it not more likely be *Jerusalem*, in whose Temple Jehovah has dwelt for ages; will not the old Shekinah-cloud come down again with a glory 'brighter than the sun;' will not the children of Zion be the first to be 'joyful in their King'?"

Or we may suppose yet another of that band of watchers saying, "Nay, I am sure, when He comes, it will be to none of these. It will rather far be to our own Bethlehem. For did not the prophet Micah, seven hundred years ago, speak of *Bethlehem* by name as the birthplace of Him who was to be 'Ruler in Israel'? He said that though it was a very little city, it was to become a very great and famous one, because ONE was to arise in it who had lived from all eternity as the Great God" (Micah v. 2).

Then they would wonder, too, *how* He would come. Would He come as a full-grown man, without knowing anything of the

"*And there were shepherds abiding in the fields*" (Luke ii. 8)   (*opposite page 20*)

weakness and helplessness of infancy and childhood? Would He be seated on a bright cloud, a rainbow about His head? or would it be with chariots and horsemen around Him; or amid thunderings and lightnings such as were seen on Mount Sinai?

Though perhaps in a very different way from what the godly Shepherds may have expected, their hopes and prayers were on the eve of being answered.

In the midst of these quiet solitudes, a glorious Light in a moment fills the sky and brightens up all the valley. The stars, which a moment before had sparkled so beautifully, are dimmed and hidden with the strange splendour.

What can it be?

It is an Angel sent down from heaven with a message to these keepers of sheep.

We cannot wonder that they are at first struck with awe and terror. But the Angel spoke kindly to them. He said, "*Be not afraid: for I have good news for you; a very joyful message to you and to all mankind.*" He told them the good news. They were the gladdest tidings the world ever heard; that "a Saviour that day had been *born* in Bethlehem, who was '*Christ the Lord.*'" In answer to their inquiry where this Infant of Glory was to be seen and adored, did he reply that they would find Him with a crown on His head, jewels and precious gems on His dress, and for His couch a cradle of gold which Angels had borne on their wings from heaven and dropped on their way to the shining plains? did he speak of the queens of the earth nursing Him and singing His cradle-song?

No; they were informed that in a place built of rough stones they would find a poor child, wrapped in swaddling-bands and lying in a borrowed manger, amid the stamping of mules and horses, and the lowing of cattle.

Just as the Shepherds were listening to the story of His birth, a still brighter light filled the heavens, and a vast army of Angels, all white and glorious, appear in the sky. You may recall a verse of one of the best-known of the ancient Christmas carols,—

"Shepherds lay afield that night to keep their fleecy sheep;
Hosts of angels in their sight came down from heaven's steep.
Tidings! Tidings unto you! To you a child is born,
Purer than the drops of dew, and brighter than the morn."

That heavenly host sang a still older and better-known Christmas Hymn,—" GLORY TO GOD IN THE HIGHEST, AND ON EARTH PEACE, GOODWILL TO MEN."

Then all again was hushed. The strange music ceased; and the stars looked down as before from their silent thrones in the sky.

Beautifully does Milton thus write in his "Hymn on the Nativity,"—as the eyes of the blind poet gazed through their darkness on ONE "*Brighter than the Sun.*" I have quoted the lines in the titlepage; but here is the stanza in full:—

> "The stars with deep amaze
> Stand fix'd in steadfast gaze.
> The Sun himself withheld his wonted speed;
> And hid his face for shame,
> As his inferior flame
> The new enlighten'd world no more should need:
> He saw a GREATER SUN appear
> Than his bright throne or burning axle-tree could bear."

The Shepherds, I daresay, were for a moment dumb with amazement. But looking at one another, they said,—" Do not let us be afraid. Do not let us doubt the word of the Angels; or even wait for the morning light. Let us at once leave our sheep and go up the slope to Bethlehem, and see with our own eyes this wondrous sight."

So, no sooner have the last notes of the heavenly song died away in the darkness, than they proceeded up the ascent through the vineyards. We are told "they went with haste," taking the shortest footpath they could see to reach the city gate.

Continuing their way along the steep and narrow streets, they found it to be all true what the Angels had told them. They saw a dim light, fed with olive-oil, burning in the Inn stable, and Joseph and Mary seated by a manger.

Imagine what they must have felt, when, passing from stall to stall, their eyes first fell on the little infant Babe, lying in that rough wooden cradle, wrapped in the usual coarse blue material used for swaddling-bands! Mary seemed to have been afraid lest the animals around might trample on Him. So, with a mother's care and love, she had lifted Him for safety, and placed Him in one of the empty troughs from which the beasts of burden ate their food.

"Every fox had where to rest,
Every little bird its nest,
But the Great God the worlds who made
Had not where to lay His head!"

A great Painter you may have heard of, called Murillo, has more than once represented this scene. He has a beautiful and favourite idea in his pictures of "The Nativity." He makes the light which shines on the faces of the Shepherds not to come from any lamp hanging from the rafters, but from the face of the Holy Infant Child. The only authority which the famous artist had for his treatment of this sacred subject was from a false Gospel of the early ages, called "The Gospel of the Infancy," in which the grotto, dark in itself, is spoken of as being filled (strange that the very words are used which I have given as a name to this volume) with light "*Brighter than the Sun.*" But there was in this expressed, at all events, a touching truth;—not only that that Infant Child was THE LIGHT OF THE WORLD, but left, as He was, neglected and unowned, to be born in a lowly manger, "*The Light shineth in darkness, and the darkness comprehended it not.*"

I have seen the spot in Bethlehem which is supposed to be the birthplace of Jesus. It is a limestone cave, which is reached by a flight of steps. Sixteen lamps hang from the roof. A silver star is in the centre of a smaller grotto hollowed out from the bigger one; and the words are put in Latin, "IN THIS PLACE JESUS CHRIST WAS BORN OF THE VIRGIN MARY." Close by, also in the rock, there is pointed out the alleged situation of the manger-cradle. It is cased in white marble, and lamps with fragrant incense burn always before it night and day. Many pilgrims who visit the cave are seen to fall on their knees, and, with tears rolling down their cheeks, kiss the pavement. No one can possibly tell if this be really the true spot where the birth of Jesus took place. But while most others of what are called "sacred places" in Palestine cannot be relied on, I think we have strong ground to accept the truth of the tradition connected with this grotto.

At all events, none can enter the gates of Bethlehem, and walk up its long street, without saying to themselves, "Oh, how wonderful to think that, some way near, the Great Lord of Glory first appeared in the world as a feeble Child!"

I like to think that these Shepherds tending their sheep were the earliest worshippers of the New-born King; that it was to them the Herald Angels first sang the story and the song of grace.

Do you ask me why I like to think this?

It is because they were *poor* men. God wished thus to honour the poor in every age. Yes; let those who live in poor houses or cottages, and who work for their daily bread, remember that the first selected in Palestine and in the world to hear of the birth of Jesus, and who came to worship Him, were not those with great riches or clad in princely attire;—not the soldiers of Rome who in glittering armour paced the walls of Jerusalem; not Herod's courtiers or favourites in his splendid palace on Zion; not learned Rabbis and Priests and Scribes;—but men with shepherd's crooks and coarse clothing from the hills of Judah. The Bible is the Friend of the poor. These keepers of their flocks may have often sung together, in their lonely night-watches, words which one who knew these valleys well warbled in his latter days:—words which speak most truly of Him at whose infant cradle they were the first to kneel,—

> "*He shall deliver the needy when he crieth;*
> *The poor also, and him that hath no helper.*
> *He shall spare the poor and needy,*
> *And shall save the souls of the needy.*"—(Ps. lxxii. 12, 13.)

I have spoken of Bethlehem in connection with Boaz and Ruth and David. It may not be without interest to mention, that one writer has given some ingenious reasons for supposing that the Inn in which Jesus was born may have been the very house in which Boaz and Ruth had lived, which had descended to Jesse the father of David, and in which, therefore, the Sweet Singer of Israel had himself dwelt, when, as a little boy, he fed his father's flock.[1] It would take too long to explain the grounds which have led to this conclusion. We cannot be at all sure about it. But certainly it is interesting even the possibility that Mary, on reaching Bethlehem, had been directed to the home of her distant fathers and grandfathers, and that her Divine Child, the world's Great Redeemer, was born in the same spot where the gentle Moabitess had dwelt with princely Boaz, and whose walls had listened to David's earliest prayers.

One other remark will naturally close this portion of the Divine story. As little children among ourselves are baptized, and receive a name by which they are known all through their lives; so the Holy Child of Bethlehem, eight days after His birth, was circumcised according to the Jewish law, and called JESUS. Most of the proud rulers and kings and warriors of the world have distinguished themselves by high-sounding titles, such as "The Great," "The Grand," "The Wise," "The Mighty," "The Magnificent." The name "JESUS" has really a much more beautiful meaning than any of these. It is the Greek form of the Hebrew name *Joshua*, which means "The Help" or "Salvation of Jehovah," —("*the Saviour*"). It was in accordance with what the Angel told Joseph in a dream, "*Thou shalt call His name* JESUS, *for He shall* SAVE *His people from their sins.*"

Thus, then, the first faint flush of early morn, which we descried over the hills of Nazareth, has passed into sunrise. The first golden gleam of the All-glorious Orb is lighting up the pastoral valleys of Bethlehem,—and a rejoicing world can say— "THE DAYSPRING FROM ON HIGH HATH VISITED US."

---

[1] See Dixon's "Holy Land," p. 98.

III.

He is taken up to the Temple.

WHAT a beautiful building that is! It is pure and milk-white. So bright are its stones and rich its carvings, it seems like the work of angels. How its roof, covered with plates and spikes of gold, glows as if with fire!

There is a deep valley immediately beneath, with a stream flowing along a rocky channel; and on the other side a green mountain with three tops. The mountain is dotted over with clumps of trees. Many of the trees have knotted, twisted stems and grey leaves. Here and there are also tapering palms and dark cedars, with flocks of doves perched on their branches. There is the fig, too; and prettiest perhaps of all, specially in early spring, is the almond-tree, so rich in blossom, as if snow-flakes had just been showered upon it, and these had been turned into crimson.

Can you guess what mountain I mean?

That green hill is the *Mount of Olives;* the prevailing olive-tree gives it its name. That great pile fronting it, with its marble pillars and golden pinnacles, is *the Temple of Jerusalem.* It was magnificent in King Solomon's time, its first builder, but it is more so than ever now. How grand it must have been in the still morning, when the smoke went up from the huge altar of rough stones; or on the Festival Seasons, when, loud above the din of the streets close by, rose the blast of the silver trumpets and the music of the Temple-Psalms; when hundreds of sweet clear voices were heard singing, "*Oh, give thanks unto the Lord, for He is good, for His mercy endureth for ever!*"

Let us go and stand in the middle of its courts. The occasion of which I am now to speak is not a Great Feast day. There is no crowd. I can fancy I see Mary of Nazareth, the young mother we beheld six weeks ago seated by her Babe in the manger. She is attired in a humble dress, just like a peasant.

Yes, it is the same. We can follow her and Joseph and the Divine Infant in thought, as they leave home early that morning. I think I see them walking along the road from Bethlehem. They pass the tomb of Rachel, Jacob's loved wife; then Jerusalem bursts upon their sight, with Herod's Palace crowning the heights of Mount Zion. How peacefully and joyfully Mary gazes on the face of her little child as she carries Him in her arms! Her kind husband is at her side. He seems, now that we see him in broad daylight, much older than she. He also has something in his hands. It looks like two of the lovely white turtle-doves I have just spoken about, flocking round the cedar-trees or perched on their branches in the sun.

They approach God's Holy House, like most of the worshippers, by the eastern gate, called the Gate Shushan; the same gate through which often, in later years, He, who was now borne a feeble infant, used to enter with some lowly Galilean fishermen.

As this "going up to the Temple" will often occur in future pages, I may as well at once try briefly to describe to you its various courts, on the occasion of this first visit of Jesus.

He and His parents would pass through what were called "the cloisters," of which Herod, who planned them, seemed to have been specially proud. Indeed, I believe I am right in saying, there was nothing equal to these in any temple of the ancient world. As "the Tower of David" was "builded for an armoury, whereon there hung a thousand bucklers, all shields of mighty men" (Sol. Song iv. 4), or as the Temple of Victory in Rome was adorned with what were called 'trophies'—crowns and bracelets, vessels of gold and silver, swords and spears, helmets and battleaxes taken in war—so in front of these cloisters, we are told by the Jewish historian, were suspended similar spoils and weapons. The Infant Prince of Peace, He whose religion of peace is, one day at least, to cause men to "beat their swords into ploughshares and their spears into pruning-hooks," was now passing under the emblems of battle and conquest!

It was in this first outer court that a richly-carved stone screen, three cubits in height, was erected, on which letters were placed, both in Roman and Greek, forbidding any Gentile to go farther.

Continuing their way over the bright inlaid pavement, they came to what was not the least wonderful thing in the vast building—the centre gate which led into the inner court. It bore a name to which it was well entitled, " *The Gate Beautiful.*" Like many things in ancient times, it was also of great size, as well as of great beauty. Josephus tells it was forty cubits high, and could only be opened and shut with the help of twenty men. The other nine gates which led into this second court were covered with plates of gold and silver, but this one was made of Corinthian brass, richly carved, and shone with the brilliancy of the sun. Herod had placed over it the huge image of an eagle—the emblem of the power of Rome.

Passing yet along, they came to fifteen steps. These led to a still higher platform, called the Court of the Priests, in the centre of which was the Altar of Burnt-offering. Mary, Joseph, and the Child, after ascending this flight of steps, stood by the open rail at the entrance. Before them, rising beyond the altar, amid a throng of priests, was the Holy Place itself, its outside glittering with marble and gold. Of the inside they could see nothing, save perhaps the golden grape-clusters that hung from the vine adorning its cedar portico.

What has brought "The Holy Family" to the Temple, and what are they going to do there? I see other mothers carrying their infants, just as Mary does. Some fathers, like Joseph, have brought with them full-grown turtle-doves, some have young pigeons, others have a bleating lamb. But these gifts, whether doves, or pigeons, or lambs, are given into the hand of a priest clad in white robes, to be offered to God in sacrifice.

I think you would like me to explain more fully the meaning and purpose of this.

Every mother in Israel was required, forty days after her first boy-child was born, to take him into the Temple "and present him to the Lord." If the child's parents were rich, then they could afford to procure a lamb, and bring it as an offering. But if they were poor, and lived in humble homes, and had not money to pay for a lamb, then God graciously allowed them to bring instead "a pair of turtle-doves or two young pigeons." The father and mother of Jesus were too poor to get the better offering; they were glad therefore to present that which was not so costly. These two birds which Joseph was carrying by the side of the Holy Child tell you and me, my young readers, how poor Jesus was. His was the gift which was graciously provided for the humblest of the people—"*Though He was rich, yet for our sakes He became poor.*"

One priest takes the two doves. He offers them both in sacrifice "before the Lord" (Lev. xii. 7) on the Great Brazen Altar. Then another comes forward and receives the Divine Infant in his arms. He puts the question to Mary, "Is this your first-born son?" On Mary replying that He is so, the priest answers, "The Child being the first-born, belongs to the Lord: you cannot receive Him back unless you are willing to pay the redemption price. As it is written in the law, '*All the first-born of man among thy children shalt thou redeem.*'" Mary and Joseph were quite aware, in presenting the Holy Jesus, that this question would be put to them, and this redemption money demanded. Accordingly Joseph takes five shekels, which he has all ready, from his leathern girdle, and gives them to the officiating Levite. Each shekel was worth about half-a-crown of our money. On payment of the stipulated sum, the Heavenly Babe is replaced in Mary's hands.

How little does that priest imagine that this Infant of days is, in a sense which belongs to Him alone, "*the First-born and Prince of the Kings of the Earth*" (Rev. i. 5). It may be, had he and his fellow Levites known Who it was that had thus "suddenly come to His Temple" (Mal. iii. 1), they would have made its courts resound with the beautiful Song of Isaiah,—

> "*Unto us a Child is born,*
> *Unto us a Son is given;*
> *And the government shall be upon His shoulder:*
> *And His name shall be called*
> *Wonderful, Counseller, The Mighty God,*
> *The Everlasting Father,*
> *The Prince of Peace.*"—(ISA. ix. 6.)

There were others, however, then in the Temple who had been long waiting for that blissful moment, and eager to sing that song of welcome.

One was an aged worshipper whose name was *Simeon*. In all the pictures I have seen of him, he looks so calm and tranquil and joyful. So beautiful, too, with his long flowing silvery beard, and his eyes lifted up to heaven. Some have said that he was even now more than a hundred years old.

This man was honoured, because God had told him that he was sure, one day before he died, to see Jesus the Messiah, who was coming to "comfort Israel" (Luke ii. 25).

Thus was he living in constant expectation of hailing HIM who was 'Brighter than the Sun,' and the very promise of whose rising seemed to bless and enlighten the evening of a long life. He never gave up hope. I think I see him with tottering step, leaning on his staff, ascending morning after morning the Hill of Zion, as the traveller climbs the mountain or the sentinel his watchtower, to catch sight of the earliest beam;—saying to himself, "I wonder much if I shall see Him to-day?" Probably words often on his lips would be these,—

> "*My soul waiteth for the Lord*
> *More than they that watch for the morning:*
> *I say, more than they that watch for the morning.*"—(Ps. cxxx. 6.)

At that moment of which I have been speaking, when he saw Joseph and Mary and the Divine Babe first coming up the marble staircase which led into the Great Court, and then passing into the Court of Sacrifice, a voice seemed to say to him, "Simeon, 'the gladsome hour is at last come. The Infant carried by that humble carpenter's young wife is the promised Saviour of mankind. Go, take Him in your arms and bless Him'!"

Do you not almost suppose he would be inclined to say to himself, "Impossible! This little helpless Child cannot be the Messiah who has formed the subject of my lifelong prayers. I have been expecting a glorious King, this is only the first-born of a peasant of Galilee."

But Simeon never doubted God's word and God's guidance. I daresay at first he could scarce believe for very joy. But he went and took hold of the wondrous Infant, and, gazing on His face, he thanked and praised God, and said that he was now ready and pleased to leave the world. He had seen the glorious LIGHT which for years he had lived for and longed for.

I like to think of that kind old Patriarch with Jesus in his arms and salvation on his tongue. I don't imagine there was such a happy man in all the world. He could not resist thus giving vent to his joy,—

> "*Lord, now lettest Thou Thy servant depart in peace,*
> *According to Thy word:*
> *For mine eyes have seen Thy salvation,*
> *Which Thou hast prepared before the face of all people;*
> *A light to lighten the Gentiles,*
> *And the glory of Thy people Israel.*"—(LUKE ii. 29–32.)

The aged man then turned to Mary, and after bestowing upon her his blessing, and declaring that her Child was "Set for the fall and rising again of many in Israel," he added the words— "*Yea, a sword shall pierce through thy own soul also*" (Luke ii. 35). What did he mean by this?

At the end of this Book we shall find how truthfully his saying was fulfilled. The time was coming when, not very far from where Simeon now sang his beautiful song, Jesus was to be killed by wicked men. On one of the hillocks of that green valley (for there I think Calvary was), His enemies were to drive nails into His hands and feet and a rough iron spear into His side, and subject Him to the awful death of the cross. Mary would then be so grieved for her Divine Son, that, as Simeon tells her, it would be like "a sword" plunged into her own heart. She would not be likely to forget the aged worshipper's words. It may be from that very hour she often thought of them, and had some sad fear every now and then present with her as to the future. The saying of Simeon reminds me of some old lines in a Welsh book of prayer. The prayer is in the Welsh language, but I give it in the words of an English translator. It is somewhat remarkable that the Welsh peasants used in former times to repeat these lines daily along with their other devotions. They are about the sword piercing the heart of the Virgin Mother,—

> "'Mother, O Mother, tell me, art thou weeping?'
> The Infant Jesus asked, on Mary's breast.
> 'Nay, Child,' she answered, 'I am only sleeping,
> Though, vexed by many a thought, I cannot rest.'
> 'O Mother, tell me why thy heart is failing?'
> 'I see,' she said, 'a crown of prickly thorn,
> And Thee, my Child, upon the cross of wailing,
> All Heaven amazed at earth's ungrateful scorn.'"

But it was not old *men* alone, like Simeon, who were made happy by the thought that Jesus had come. Perhaps it was a happier thing still for Jewish *women*, and for all women, that such a Redeemer was born.

Before this kind and gracious Saviour appeared in the world, mothers and daughters were cruelly used and cruelly suffered. JESUS was the first to speak kind words to them, and to say (as we shall find him addressing the mother with the broken heart at Nain), "WEEP NOT."

I like to think that no sooner had aged Simeon given back to Mary her beloved Child, than at the same instant another aged worshipper—an aged woman, bent down with a load of years—came into the Temple. Her name was Anna. Her husband had died when she was very young. She was good and holy too. She loved much the courts of the Lord. She almost never left them. No sooner were the large cedar gates thrown open in early morning than she was seen to enter, and she only left when the last rays of the sun were lighting up the top of the Mount of Olives. Like Simeon she was fond of prayer. Her chiefest prayer, we may well believe, would be, like his, for the coming of the promised Jesus.

God again showed how He loves to answer His believing people. Her prayers are turned into praises, for she too gazes on the Divine Redeemer. In that hour of which we are now speaking, she seems to have gathered a cluster around her of those who were then worshipping in the Temple, and she told them through joyful tears the wonderful Story of grace.

Thus to an old man and an old woman was revealed what still was hidden from the knowledge of priests, and rulers, and learned Rabbis. Oh, how God always rewards simple faith and patience!

Can you remember a beautiful verse about these two Christian graces? Here it is:—" *That ye be not slothful, but followers of them who through faith and patience inherit the promises.*" Simeon and Anna were possessed of both. They had *Faith* (looking for Jesus). They had *Patience* (waiting for Jesus). Through that Faith and that Patience they came to inherit the greatest promise which the Great and Faithful Promiser had ever given to fallen man and a fallen world! " *Unto you that fear My name shall* THE SUN OF RIGHTEOUSNESS *arise.*" We hear no more after this about these two aged Temple-Saints. They appear like bright morning stars heralding the Day-dawn, and then they vanish from the firmament—lost in that better and BRIGHTER radiance.

We can only picture Joseph, Mary, and the Child, remaining perhaps under the cool stone pillars, or under the shade of the trees, till the heat of the day was over, and then going back again in the calm of the evening to their humble home in Bethlehem. I need not say they were no longer living now in the Inn. They must have taken up their abode in some other house in the Town of David.

C

IV.

Wise Men from the East Visit Him.

BUT there were other heralds already on their way, from remote Gentile lands, to do homage to this mysterious Infant, whom aged Simeon had recently sung of as "a LIGHT to lighten the GENTILES," as well as "the glory of God's people Israel." A strange silent messenger had been sent to tell of the Great Sunrise on the Hebrew mountains. Distant tongues were tuned to sing your best-known Christmas Hymn,—

> "*Hail the Heaven-born Prince of Peace!*
> *Hail the Sun of Righteousness!*
> *Light and life to all He brings,*
> *Ris'n with healing in His wings.*"

In the countries far east of Palestine and the Jordan there lived a number of men called "*Magi.*" They were greatly esteemed at the courts of Oriental kings. Daniel, you may remember, though no idolator, but, on the contrary, a faithful servant of the true God, could be known by no more illustrious name than "Chief of the governors over all the wise men of Babylon" (Dan. ii. 14). Many of them, however, unlike him, were "fire-worshippers." They paid religious homage to the sun and moon and the host of heaven. They had their watch-towers, corresponding to our observatories, along the banks of the Tigris and other Eastern rivers, to allow them to study the heavenly bodies. The stars seen in the skies of Chaldea, Media, and Persia were, I daresay, even more beautiful than those seen in Palestine.

One night some of these Magi, as they looked up to the firmament, observed a new star, brighter than the rest. Along with many others in Eastern countries, they expected at this period the coming of a Great King who was to rule over the whole world.

"There came wise men from the East to Jerusalem" (Matt. ii. 1). (opposite page 35)

found who was born "King of the Jews?" "*We have seen,*" they said, "*His star in the east, and are come to worship Him.*"

First to one and then to another they met on the streets the same earnest question was asked, "*Tell us where is He that is born King of the Jews?*"

How singular their appearance as well as their question must have been! I have seen, now and then, foreigners with turbans on their heads and curious dresses, walking along the streets of London or Edinburgh, and the people as they pass gazing upon them with wonder. How much stranger it must have been to the Jews in Jerusalem to see these richly-dressed men seated on the backs of their camels, with bracelets and nose-jewels, and to hear them in some broken Eastern tongue asking, as they move in a long line with noiseless tread through the streets, about the birth of a King of Judea! I am quite certain their appearance created a great stir in the city.

Surely they must have been very trusting and simple in their faith! They might naturally have expected all Jerusalem to be ringing with the news about the young King,—that the glorious tidings would be on every lip, and that crowds would be flocking to the place of His birth.

How different! No one seemed either to know or to care anything about the matter. Do the Magi turn their camels' heads at once towards the East and make for their own homes, vexed and displeased that their long journey has been in vain? No: they start again all alone in the direction of Bethlehem. They know that the God of heaven was speaking to them and guiding them by His own star. They were the first to breathe, at all events in their hearts, the beautiful invocation of a future hymn,—

> "Brightest and best of the Sons of the morning!
> Dawn on our darkness and lend us your aid;
> Star of the East, the horizon adorning!
> Guide where the Infant Redeemer is laid."

The great Lord in their case made His own promise true—"*Then shall we know if we follow on.*"

It is very likely they had rested at Jerusalem, during the day, after their long journey, and waited till evening before setting out again. At all events, from what is said in the Bible story, the bright star seems to have been withdrawn for a while from their view. I am sure they would be very sorry to lose the help of their heavenly light. But as they went a little farther on their road, how glad they were, probably as the sun was setting over the hills at their right, when it appeared once more above their heads!

I remember stopping at a well halfway between Jerusalem and Bethlehem, about which there is a curious tradition in connection with the star. I do not repeat the story as a true one, because it is not in the Bible, and we should be careful as to receiving anything which is not expressly written in the Word of God. But the tradition still believed by Christians in Bethlehem is this. These wise men, on losing sight of the star which had hitherto guided them from their own country to Jerusalem, were greatly vexed, for they did not know whether the road they pursued was the right one. They seated themselves by the brink of this well. But in stooping over it to get drink for themselves and their camels, they saw the missing star reflected low down in the water; and in looking up to the sky above them, there it was. They rose with glad hearts, and followed the silent guide in its silvery path. It passed right over the quivering palms at the gate of Bethlehem, then over the flat roofs of many of the houses, till it stood over the place where the young Child lay.

We may be sure the stranger worshippers lost no time in unloading their beasts of burden and taking out the valuable things they had brought with them, "gold, and frankincense, and myrrh." Gold from the mines of Ophir or from the beds of their rivers. Frankincense and myrrh—jars of fragrant gums and precious oils, resins extracted from the trees of Arabia or India—something perhaps resembling the "attar of roses," sold to this day in all the bazaars of the chief towns of Asia.

I should perhaps tell you, that tradition has been busy here too in giving alike the names and ages of these "Wise men;" or, as some call them, "Eastern Kings." One was Melchior, an old man with a silver beard. Another Belthazar, in full-grown manhood. The third Caspar, a youth. The three stages of human existence, the morning, meridian, and sunset of life, come to do homage to ONE " Brighter than the Sun !"

How strange it must have been for those used to splendid houses and hanging gardens and brilliant dresses in the East, to enter some lowly abode in the City of David, and find a humble man and woman bending over a little helpless Babe ! But these good travellers do not seem startled. They fall down before the Holy Child, their foreheads touching the floor. They strew their presents at His feet, and then return with rejoicing hearts to their far distant homes.

> " Saw you never in the twilight,
>   When the sun had left the skies,
> Up in heaven the clear stars shining,
>   Through the gloom like silver eyes ?
> So of old the wise men, watching,
>   Saw a little stranger star,
> And they knew the King was given,
>   And they followed it from far.
>
> " You have listened to the story,
>   How they crossed the desert wild,
> Journeyed on by plain and mountain,
>   Till they found the Holy Child.
> You may also seek His cradle,
>   There your heart's best treasures bring,
> Love, and Faith, and true Devotion,
>   For your Saviour-God, and King."

My young friends, I would like you to pause for a moment and recall the number and variety of worshippers the Infant Jesus had. Think of all, both in heaven and on earth, that had united to do Him homage !

I. There were the bright Angels sent to the plains of Bethlehem to tell of the Heavenly palace He had left.

II. There was the beautiful Star in the deep blue above, telling of the interest felt by silent nature and by far distant worlds in the Divine Child.

III. There was old Simeon and Anna, telling that grey-haired age was not ashamed to come and welcome "an Infant of Days" as the Lord and Saviour.

IV. There were the Wise Men of the East, Oriental princes—reminding of the rich and great, and noble and learned, who would in future feel honoured to own Him and adore Him. "*The Kings of Tarshish and of the Isles shall bring presents; the Kings of Seba and Sheba shall offer gifts.*"

V. There were the Shepherds from the hills of Judah, telling how He came to be the Friend of the poor, and simple, and unlearned;—those who have none of the world's wisdom, or the world's riches and splendours.

All seemed to unite in saying, "This 'Sun of Righteousness,' who has risen with healing in His beams, is like His type and image in the sky. He is to shine alike on all: on palace, and on cottage, on rich and on poor, on mighty and on lowly, on king and on beggar, on old and young, on age and on childhood." His glorious Name, which stands as a motto on the title-page of this Book, is not "I am the Star of Bethlehem," "I am the Golden Lamp of the Temple of Jerusalem," "I am the Light of Israel." No; "I AM THE LIGHT OF THE WORLD." Just as there are planets of different sizes and brilliancy, which circle round the central sun of our solar system, so do stars of diverse "magnitudes" revolve round this Great Centre of the spiritual universe.

I close this chapter with one thought that has special reference to those younger than the youngest portion of my youthful readers. "*How kind it was in Jesus to come in the form of a little Child!*"

He might have descended to earth all at once, like the fabled gods of the heathen, in the fulness and strength of perfect manhood; "THE LIGHT OF THE WORLD" might have had no day-spring, no early dawn, no streaks in the Eastern sky. He might have blazed forth suddenly in the brightness and lustre of His dazzling noontide glory. His countenance might have been "as the sun shineth in its strength" (Rev. i. 16). It would in one sense have been much more startling and impressive if He had never lain an unconscious babe on His mother's knee—never been borne helpless in her arms, or rocked by her in His cradle in infant slumbers, or had a child's lullaby sung over Him. He might have been created just as we believe the bright Angels in heaven to have been created. They never knew the lispings of infancy. They were made all at once to excel in strength. Without passing through any previous stages of being, their mighty wings were outstretched in messages of love, doing the will of God. Not so, however, was it with Jesus. As in the case of Moses in his little frail ark of bulrushes by the river's side, when the wail of an infant was borne to the ear of Pharaoh's daughter; so God seems to say to the lowly Mary of Nazareth, "*Take this* CHILD, *and nurse Him for Me.*"

Why was it so? There may be other reasons: but one assuredly was, that the very youngest might be able to say, 'Jesus was once as I am. Jesus knows my heart-sores and heart-aches, for He was once Himself a feeble Child. He once lay helpless in a manger-cradle. He rushed to pour out His sorrows and vexations in His mother's ears:—He lisped His prayers at His mother's knee. While grown-up people may best love His name "*Immanuel*, God with us," I best love His other name, "*The Holy* CHILD *Jesus.*"'

A good old Father of the Church who lived very long ago, whose name was Irenæus, has this sweet saying—"Jesus made childhood lovely" (and he might have added too, He made a childhood of *poverty* lovely), " by passing through it."

"Made like the sons of clay,
Thy matchless glories lay,
In form of feeble infancy concealed.
No pomp of outward sign
Proclaimed the Power Divine,
No earthly state the Heavenly Guest revealed.

"Thou didst not choose Thy home
Beneath a lordly dome;
No royal crown did wreath Thy infant brow;
Nor on a soft couch laid,
Nor in rich vest arrayed,
But with the poorest of the poor wert Thou."

V.

Herod tries to kill Him.

I HAVE just narrated the story of the Wise Men from the East coming to worship the meek and lowly Jesus.

I think you will not be surprised when I tell you who was the one person in Jerusalem who was very angry when he heard of their visit. It was King Herod. He was a miserable old man. You may say truly, in one respect he ought to have been a very happy man, for he was, in the earthly sense of the word, 'Great,' and made himself to be called so. He wore a crown, and had numbers of servants and slaves dressed in cloth of blue and crimson and gold to wait upon him, and soldiers in coats of brilliant armour to guard him. He had one vast palace with cedar-walls in Jerusalem, another at Jericho with delicious gardens,—groves of palm and balsam, and every lovely shrub and flower. Another, half-palace half-fortress, on a mountain (Je'bel Fureidis), which he called his "Paradise," and which was visible from many of the heights around Jerusalem. His youth had been one of rare promise. Even in outward appearance there were few like him,—with his finely-formed figure, his thoughtful countenance, his jet-black locks. Like another Absalom, he had stolen the hearts of many who were proud of his stately mien and fearless courage, alike in the battle and in the chase. He was famed, too, for higher qualities. He had a love for study. He had stored his mind with the learning of the age. He was passionately fond of art. No single king, perhaps, who ever lived, built more numerous or more splendid cities and towers, theatres and temples, than he. Possibly, if he had been under better training, he might have turned out at once a famous and a good man. But as he advanced in years, he became more and more a tyrant and despot, and "sold himself to work iniquity." The tiger or leopard, which when young can be stroked and caressed, comes, after tasting blood, to show the ferocity of its nature. So it was with Herod. He became like a savage wild beast in his old age. One dreadful crime made him bold to attempt another; and yet he had no sooner committed his enormities than he was often seized with remorse and horror. In a fit, half of jealousy half of sport, he had drowned, in one of the baths in his Jericho palace, his noble and beautiful brother-in-law, the Jewish High Priest, at the early age of eighteen. He had killed his wife, his three sons and uncle, besides other nobles and friends, and many, many hundreds of innocent subjects:—some with the sword, some by fire, some by prolonged torture; some were left to linger in chains, some were scourged to death with rods.

Well, when the news reached this wicked old King that Angels had been heard singing in the sky about a little Child born in Bethlehem; still more, when he heard about this bright silver lamp that had been hung in the heavens, guiding the Wise Men, he became greatly troubled. He had been told by some learned teachers in Jerusalem that the Jewish prophets, and specially their prophet Micah, had said that Bethlehem was the place where the promised King of the Jews was to be born. He must have known well, too, about Balaam's prophecy; for he was himself an Edomite, and as such he may perhaps have felt that he had no *right* to the crown of Judah. He feared that if all he had learnt were indeed true, a Child *born* in Judah might live to become his rival;—that by this Child he might lose his throne and be put out of his kingdom,—perhaps placed in chains in a dungeon, and at last killed.

The Magi seem to have been conducted to his presence. You can imagine the scene in the Cedar Palace I have spoken of: he would receive this Eastern embassy in great splendour,—perhaps in his state-room with its throne of ivory, sculptured lions flanking its marble steps, he himself wearing his purple robe, a collar of massive gold round his neck, and his sword-hilt sparkling with jewels. Herod, like most base natures, was a master in the art of cunning, or what is called 'duplicity.' He wished to give these Wise Men the impression that he was deeply interested in what had brought them from their distant homes. He told them to go to Bethlehem, and ask all about this kingly young Child, and bring him back word again, that he might drive out there in his royal chariot and worship him too.

We shall presently find he had very different thoughts in his vengeful and jealous heart. He was very angry that these Strangers had come not to worship *him*, but to worship the Babe of Nazareth peasants, and that they had left none of their golden gifts in his royal house.

What made him still more displeased was, when he found that they had gone away to their distant homes without coming to see him again, and tell him about the mysterious Infant: for God had warned these good men not to come back by Jerusalem.

Herod's will was always obeyed: but when he saw now that it was not, the blood rose to his cheeks and the fire flashed in his eye.

It is said in the Talmud that he gave instructions to have all the records of Jewish families destroyed, the registers of family births and family names which were kept in the Temple. Whether he did so or no we are not informed in the Bible narrative. It would have been an act of wanton mischief and cowardly fear—no more. But the Bible story *does* disclose to us a decree of the darkest and most selfish cruelty, which he proceeded quickly to put in force. He said, 'I will give orders that all the male children in Bethlehem, under two years of age, be slain with the sword.' He knew that if he did this, the Infant Jesus would be sure to be killed, and thus he would get rid of his fears. He gathers his captains and officers about him, and tells them of the horrible crime he has resolved upon. I daresay many of the manly and brave Roman soldiers who stood in his presence and listened to his dreadful injunctions would shudder at the thought of so many infant children cruelly perishing. A really brave heart always shrinks from hurting the poor or weak or innocent.

But they know well they could not resist the word of their angry master. He would doubtless take care to pick out the most hard-hearted he could find for the sad work. "Kill every one of them," would be his command; "let none be left."

Not only so, but you will observe the cruel order was not confined to the town of Bethlehem. It extended to what is called in the Gospel of St. Matthew its "coasts." What, you will ask, does 'coast' mean? for there was no sea—which the word 'coast' seems to imply—where the inland town of David was situated.

Coast, in the Bible, means "the district," with its hamlets and homesteads, lying all around. There were many such, nestling sweetly in the little valleys close by Bethlehem. Specially near Solomon's Gardens and Solomon's Pools, there would be terraced vineyards, having "lodges" or "watch-towers," with families living in them; while shepherd's homes and 'shielings' would be in the less cultivated spots.

You may imagine that company of murderers setting out from the gates of Jerusalem on their way to Bethlehem and its neighbourhood. Little does many a mother in that quiet and peaceful city and its peaceful coasts know what, in a brief hour, she will be called to witness and endure! In the town itself, and in these cottages and hamlets I have alluded to, perched on the hillsides in the midst of vineyards and olive-gardens, many little Hebrew boy-children were that morning seen, some lying peacefully by their mother's side in their cradles, others playing about their mother's feet, or climbing on their father's knee before he went out to work. A few were even beginning to be taught to lisp the name of their father's God, and to sing some hymns or psalms to His praise. Their parents, as they gazed on their innocent faces, would think of them with pride as growing up to manhood, and say of them, "This same shall comfort us."

Suddenly a wild shriek rises. These same mothers, who were seen so recently sitting at their distaffs and looking so happily on their lisping babes (or perhaps carrying them in their arms to the neighbouring fountain as they went to draw water), are now rushing about the streets and highways in frantic grief, wringing their hands, tearing their hair, beating their breasts, and crying out, "Oh, my child! my child!" They implore the soldiers to have mercy. "Spare him!" one is heard crying, "he is my only one; if you take him you take my all." "Spare him," another is heard saying, "he is my Benjamin, my best beloved; none are so dear to me as he!"

But all their pleadings, and tears, and cries are in vain. The iron-hearted assassins of Herod are deaf to the voice of affection. No house in these 'coasts' is without its trampled flower,—no mother without her dead son.

Oh, what a night of weeping that must have been! There was not so much as one infant boy left. I have told you of the tomb of Rachel, which was close by Bethlehem. So sad and bitter was the weeping of these Jewish women over their Innocents, that the sacred writer (in what is called 'a figure of speech'), describes this Mother of Israel as being roused from her grave; just as if she could not rest in peace when she listened to the crying babes and weeping parents. She said she could take no comfort: so terrible to her feeling heart was the scene of death! "*Rachel weeping for her children, and would not be comforted, because they are not*" (Matt. ii. 18).

Not unlikely the Burial-place of Bethlehem was nigh Rachel's tomb. If so, a number of little graves would be seen clustered around it, with flowers from the hillsides scattered on them by the hands of sorrowing mothers. The murdered Infants there slept that sleep which cruel Herod could never again disturb.

But we must not dwell more on so terrible a picture. Rather think of these Lambs of the flock, before sin had stained the white purity of their fleeces, being folded by the Good Shepherd beside the living fountains of waters : rather think of another Babe who came into the world, and grew up to manhood, just that He might say to these and all other weeping mothers, "Hush your wailings: dry your tears: '*for of such is the Kingdom of Heaven.*'" Rather think of shining Angels bearing these little children aloft on their wings to that happy place of which it is said, "There shall be no more crying" (Rev. xxi. 4).

> "*Around the Throne of God in heaven
> Ten thousand children stand,
> Whose sins are all through Christ forgiven,
> A holy, happy band,
> Singing glory, glory, glory!*"

You will however, be desirous of hearing now about Mary and the Infant Jesus. You remember aged Simeon spoke to her of "a sword" which was to "pierce through her own soul." Did he mean the sword of one of those fierce soldiers of Herod? Was she, too, made to tremble for the life and safety of her dear child?

No. He who has all events in His hand, kept this 'Lion Herod' in a chain. He would not suffer him to destroy 'the Lamb of God.'

I shall tell you next, how the precious Young life was preserved and rescued from danger.

VI.

He goes down into Egypt.

ANOTHER of these bright Angels, or perhaps the same who had already come to Mary, spoke to Joseph one night when he was asleep and dreaming. He seemed to say to him, 'Rise up from your couch. Do not wait another day. Take Mary and the young child; for Herod is seeking the Infant's life; and never stop till you come to the land of Egypt. There you will be away from the wiles of the jealous King. Remain there till I bring you word from God that it is safe to return.'

There was not a moment to be lost. Mary folded her mantle round her Infant so that He might not be seen. Joseph saddled his ass, and seating Mary and Jesus on it, he walked by their side.

They would probably pass through or near Hebron. Would Mary have time to "salute" her cousin Elizabeth? or would the Angel's message rather hasten them on?

Ere long they are pursuing their solitary way through the desert. They were already far on their journey when Herod's soldiers were marching from Jerusalem.

Egypt, you know, is a country far south of Palestine. It was then, and had been for some thousand years, a very great kingdom, with its rich fields and cities, and its vast Pyramids which are still among the wonders of the world. Often when the Jews were in want of food, or in danger from their enemies, they were in the habit of fleeing to this land; so that Joseph and Mary were not now doing anything strange in going there.

I daresay it would be at night when they commenced their pilgrimage, before any of the other villagers were awake. The moon and the stars might be shining when they went out by the gate of the city. Doubtless for many hours after starting, the parents of Jesus would be anxiously turning round at every height they reached, to see if Herod's horsemen were in pursuit.

Some old writers have absurd stories of their own devising about this journey of the Holy Family. They speak of birds following and brushing away with their long feathers the mark of footsteps on the sands, so that Herod's soldiers could not trace the fugitives. They speak of the wild beasts becoming tame before them, and beautiful flowers springing up at their feet, and the trees by the way bending down that they might pluck their fruits. These things are not true. But, in a far better sense, we may feel assured that the Great God would keep His beloved Son from lions, and wolves, and leopards, and every evil thing, and feed Him, as He had done Israel before in the wilderness, when He gave them manna from heaven.

I saw not long ago in North Italy, in perhaps the richest church in the world, this impressive picture. It was Joseph leading the ass on which Mary and the Child were seated. Lovely guardian angels with golden wings are represented flying behind, some near and some more distant. A still more beautiful idea of another painter is that of little cherubs gathering round the spot which Joseph and Mary have selected for their night's rest. These cherubs are gazing with wonder and adoration on the Heavenly Infant as He lies on His mother's lap. Doubtless the words of the sweet Psalmist of Israel, which I have already applied to the lowly Virgin, were equally true regarding her Holy Child,—"*He shall give His angels charge over Thee, to keep Thee in all Thy ways*" (Ps. xci. 11).

It was a very long journey. It would take three days at least to reach the borders of the land. They must have paused in the heat of the day, and rested under some of the juniper shrubs, or where a well of water could be found; and at night, after the sun had gone down in clouds of silver and gold, they would sleep under the bright stars till morning awoke them, and the desert dew glittered like diamonds. Perhaps Joseph and Mary, as they bent over the Divine Babe, may have sung that beautiful Psalm they both knew well,—

> "*The Lord is thy keeper:*
> *The Lord is thy shade upon thy right hand.*
> *The sun shall not smite thee by day,*
> *Nor the moon by night.*
> *The Lord shall preserve thee from all evil:*
> *He shall preserve thy soul.*
> *The Lord shall preserve thy going out and thy coming in*
> *From this time forth, and even for evermore.*"

How strange it must have been to these peasants of Galilee to be in the old country of the Pharaohs, although no king of the name of Pharaoh was ruling then! They would doubtless often think of how their Fathers dwelt here in the house of bondage. They would gaze with wonder on the Pyramids these Fathers had built, and on the mighty river Nile, compared to which their own Jordan was only a mountain rill. They would remember the story of Joseph, who, in that land of corn and plenty, became a famous Prince. They would perhaps think of the true Joseph whom they were now carrying in their arms, who was come, in a far higher sense than in the case of the Hebrew ruler, "to forgive His brethren," and to deliver the whole world from a much sadder slavery.

It is not likely that Joseph and Mary, simple dwellers in a village in the middle of Palestine, had ever been out of their native land. If so, this would be the first glimpse they got of a heathen country. They were brought up, like all Jews, with a hatred to idolatry. How they must have been shocked as they gazed on the monster idols which met their eyes wherever they turned;—pillared temples of enormous size, within which animals were worshipped, from the bull and cow, the dog and crocodile, to flies and mice : "*And changed the glory of the uncorruptible God into an image made like to corruptible man, and to birds, and four-footed beasts, and creeping things*" (Rom. i. 23).

Some years ago, when in Egypt, I sat on the spot, a few miles from Cairo, where it is said Joseph and Mary and the Child Jesus once were. No one can say whether this be the case or no; but I could not help gazing with great interest on the gnarled hollow trunk of that great sycamore, "the Virgin's tree," which marks the place, and whose branches are still believed by the ignorant native Christians to have miraculously bent down in order to form a leafy tent of shelter for the Holy Exiles. There is a well also close by, "Sitti Mariam" (of my Lady Mary), whose waters, the same simple souls allege, were drank by the Virgin. The thought, I repeat, was a solemn and hallowed one,— 'JESUS the Son of God *may* possibly have sat here on His Mother's knee, or nestled in her bosom!' I may add, the place referred to is adjoining those old ruins (I spoke of in the opening chapter), of a city once called On or Heliopolis, "the City of the Sun," the ancient college or university of Egypt, and where there was a famous Temple dedicated to the Sun, who was worshipped under the name of Osiris. More than likely it was at On where the old historian of Egypt, Herodotus, tells us he saw a vast image of a sacred cow. It had a purple mantle over its body; its neck and head were wreathed with plates of gold; and aromatic incense was burnt before it night and day. He specially notes that it had

D

"*a round golden sun between its horns.*" It is at all events interesting to think that He who was BRIGHTER THAN THE SUN, in His infant days may have lighted this Sun-city with "the brightness of His rising."

Joseph and Mary and the little Child did not require to remain long in Egypt. Cruel Herod died in a few weeks. You will not wonder to hear that a King who lived such a dreadful life of guilt and sin suffered a dreadful end of misery and pain. All his riches could procure him no relief. He was seized with a burning thirst. His body was covered with sores, and, like another of the same name, he was eaten of worms. The Bible speaks of "a worm that dieth not." That worm must have preyed on the wicked man's conscience. Doubtless the murder of those dear little children were among the thorns of his death pillow. God has said, " Be sure your sin will find you out." What mattered the golden coffin in which his body was laid, and the crown which still decked the departed man's brow? What mattered the gorgeous procession, which took seven days to reach his mountain burial-place? What though the towns and villages turned out by tens of thousands to see the glittering ranks of soldiers, and guards, and household slaves, wending along hill and dale, in the midst of which the purple bier was borne? What mattered the five hundred caskets of spices and perfume which five hundred incense-bearers scattered on his tomb? His name and memory came to be so hated, that the day of his death was kept among the Jews as a day of feasting and rejoicing. Yes, and we may feel assured that when called before the judgment-seat of the King of Kings, he will learn the truth of words spoken by a God who cannot lie: "*Know thou that for all these things God will bring thee into judgment*" (Eccles. xi. 9).

Had Joseph and Mary to wait for a long time before they heard of Herod's death? There were no posts or telegraphs in those days, as with us; and unless when special couriers were sent on swift horses or dromedaries, news travelled very slowly. The holy pair had doubtless that great love of home which was common to all Jews, and they would desire very much, so soon as it was safe, to retrace their steps. Swift as any telegraph message, word was brought to them. Again the Angel came as he promised, and told Joseph he might now return without danger. So he, Mary, and the Child left the land of Egypt without delay, and the saying of Hosea quoted in St. Matthew's Gospel was fulfilled, "*Out of Egypt have I called My Son.*"

Where, you ask, did they go? and what road did they take?

I cannot exactly tell you; but most likely they would travel by the ordinary camel-track along the coast, past the Philistine city of Gaza, with the bright blue waters of the Great Sea every now and then in view. How glad they would be when, after long miles of desert, they came in sight of the welcome hill-tops of Judah, with little towns crowning them,—the well-known circlets of terraced vineyards on their slopes, and flocks of sheep browsing in the hollows!

They went back, not to Bethlehem, but to their own dwelling in Nazareth. Joseph himself, perhaps, would have preferred going to Bethlehem. He must have loved Bethlehem as the birthplace of the Holy Child. He must have loved it when he thought of the Shepherds, and the song of the Angels, and the visit of the Wise Men. He must have loved it because it was so near Jerusalem and its Temple, with the Simeons and Annas and other good people there. He may have thought, too, "If Jesus is to be King of the Jews, it will be better for Him to dwell near the Holy City, rather than far away in the Highlands of Palestine."

But God's thoughts and wishes were better than his. Another very wicked King had come in Herod's place, and sat on Herod's throne. He had already murdered, not hundreds, but thousands of poor Jews. So, once more, Joseph was divinely warned in a dream, on the way from Egypt, not to go near Jerusalem, but to his old quiet home among the hills of Galilee.

Accordingly they continued their journey along the coast, through the beautiful Plain of Sharon, leaving the Damascus road as they turned round the base of Mount Carmel in the direction of Nazareth.

Do you not think it was better for other reasons that Jesus should not return to Bethlehem? It would have been sad to

His kind heart to remember that all the other babes of His own age had been killed, and that He alone remained. We never once again hear of Him, during His life on earth, being in Bethlehem. Those who are young—yes, and grown-up people too—like to visit the places where they were born; but we never read, even when He was a man, that He ever entered its gates.

MORNING.

"HE SHALL BE AS THE LIGHT OF THE MORNING WHEN THE SUN RISETH, EVEN A MORNING WITHOUT CLOUDS."—2 SAM. XXIII. 4.

"UNTO YOU THAT FEAR MY NAME SHALL THE SUN OF RIGHTEOUSNESS ARISE WITH HEALING IN HIS WINGS."—MAL. IV. 2.

"AND THE CHILD GREW AND WAXED STRONG IN SPIRIT, FILLED WITH WISDOM, AND THE GRACE OF GOD WAS UPON HIM."—LUKE II. 40.

VII.

He goes to Nazareth and lives there.

WE have hitherto watched *the early dawn* of the Great Sun of Righteousness. We pass now to the bright cloudless MORNING of that Divine and glorious life.

I can picture a beautiful day in spring, when two people, one of them carrying a little Child, were seen entering the Valley of Nazareth. We seem to know that valley well now, with its white limestone rocks and green hills and carpet of flowers.

Joseph and Mary were familiar with every turn in the road and with every face they met. But it is the first time the Holy Child had seen the place that was to be for so many long years His earthly home—the green nest where the heavenly Dove of Peace was to fold His spotless wings.

I see them passing through the lanes of the little hamlet, and unlocking the door of their humble home. Home has always a happy look, especially after having been some time away, or if troubles and anxieties have taken place during absence from it. They would therefore be very glad, I am sure, to rest after all the never-to-be-forgotten events of the past weeks, and specially after their more recent long journey from the land of Egypt.

I have no doubt you would like to know a great deal about this beautiful period in the life of JESUS. You would like to know how He lived, what He saw, and what He did, and what He learnt. But I can tell you almost nothing regarding all this. The Bible says much about Him when He was grown up, but very little indeed about his early life, either as an Infant, or when advanced from Childhood to Youth.

I can only think of Him as spending that childhood in the peaceful valley which was His home for nearly thirty years. And as I venture for a little to speak of that interesting period, let us devoutly fix our minds at the outset, on the amazing condescension of Him who was none other than "GOD *manifest in the flesh*," stooping to such lowliness, going through all the stages and experiences of human nature, and that, too, in its humblest station! Let us remember that while He was "very God of very God," He was also "very Man." He had the feelings and hopes, the joys and sorrows, of any other child. It was customary among the Jews to take their infant children to the Synagogue of the place, on the first return of their birthdays (what we would call the first "anniversary of their birth), and there receive a special blessing from the Rabbi. May we think of Mary and Joseph in this respect also "doing according to the custom of the law," and bringing the Holy Child to receive the wonted benediction? The writer who mentions this circumstance recalls how, thirty-two years later, that same Holy Child, when He came to be reverenced and esteemed by mothers in Israel as a Holy Rabbi, had young children brought to Him that He should *touch* them: And "*He laid His hands upon them and blessed them.*"[1]

When He was very young, I can, with reverence, think of Him sitting on His mother's lap, or playing at her feet, or learning to speak. I can think of Him, when a little older, going by her side to the village well, or assisting her to glean in the harvest field or to carry water to the thirsty reapers. I can think of Him, yet older still, helping with His own hands His father at His daily toil. Joseph, you already know, was the carpenter of the place: his house would be known by the trunks of unsawn trees piled around the door or in the little square courtyard common in Jewish dwellings. He would have his bench, perhaps, outside, with hammer and plane and saw lying upon it. All day long He would be busy making instruments of husbandry for the farmers, or wooden vessels and kneading-troughs for houses, or poles for pilgrim tents, or perhaps boats and oars for the not far distant Lake of Galilee. There is a strange tradition that He was a clumsy workman. This may only mean that, like other

---

[1] See Dr. Plumptre's interesting article "Synagogue," in *Bible Dictionary*.

native Jews, he gave himself to the commoner kinds of carpentry, such as I have indicated. The Greeks, who resided in the Greek and Roman cities, such as Sephoris and Tiberias, were what are called skilled artificers, "cunning workers" in gold and brass, marble and cedar-carving.

Every youth among the Jews was taught some trade that might be useful to him in after life. This was the case even with their greatest men, such as the celebrated teachers Hillel and Shammai; the one was a woodcutter and the other a carpenter. In the hills and pasture-grounds of the province of Cilicia in Asia Minor there were vast flocks of goats with long rugged fleeces. These fleeces were used for clothing. They were also weaved into strong canvas for the tents of that pastoral people. St. Paul, you may remember, learnt, when he was a boy at Tarsus, the trade of a maker of these goats-hair tents. It would be the same with Jesus. In this, as in other respects, He was "made like unto His brethren;"—He was brought up to His father's trade of carpentry.

But I think we can entertain some other and different thoughts about the early years of the Holy Child and Divine Youth of Nazareth. May we not think of Him as climbing the limestone heights around, among the thick groves of prickly thorn? (that same kind of thorn which His murderers at last twisted into a crown for His brow). Perhaps, while the other youths of the town, and among them His own cousins (children of Alpheus), were busy with riotous sports and play, they may have wondered how their young Companion preferred often being thus alone. He seemed to have some high thoughts they could not understand, and desired at times at least, like the brightest of the stars we see in the nightly heavens, to "dwell apart." Yet, too, they must have greatly loved Him. They had never seen Him angry or selfish or jealous. When they were tempted to do wrong, they saw that He never followed their bad example. When they quarrelled with each other, He never did. They had, perhaps, heard Him speak about some Great FATHER *in Heaven* whom He called "MY

Father." Perhaps in that clear still air they would often hear His young voice, far up the green hills, singing some sweet song of praise; or, if they had followed Him, it may be at early morn, they might have seen Him at times bending His knees amid the wild flowers, and as He looked above toward the blue of the bright sky, they might have listened to Him sending up a prayer to this Greater and better than Earthly Parent.

> " He took Him, where the Eastern heaven
> Glows with the sun serene,
> Where the strong wings to morning given
> Brood o'er a world serene.
>
> " And there He breathes His matin thought
> Of pure unconscious love,
> There tastes the dew of Angels, brought
> In silence from above."

All that is told about Him in the sacred narrative is in two short verses. "*The* CHILD *grew and waxed strong in spirit*" (Luke i. 80); also that "*He increased in wisdom and stature, and in favour with God and man*" (Luke ii. 52).

I cannot help thinking, young readers, that when Jesus was like you, He would specially love the carpet of rich colour which that Heavenly Father He served had spread all along these heights of the Valley of Nazareth:—so bright, as I have already described, with the blue iris, the sea-pink, the scarlet anemone, and the many-coloured tulip. He who said so sweetly afterwards, "*Consider the lilies how they grow*," must surely have often in His early days gazed with joy on these clusters of wild flowers which clothed the hillside, from the tall wild hollyhock to the modest daisy, as well as on the hedges of prickly pear with their great bunches of red blossom, which enclose now, as they would do then, the village gardens. He who spoke in future years of "the birds of the air," and the sparrows that are "not forgotten by God," would love to listen to the cooing of the doves in the summer morning amid the groves of fig, and olive, and palm; or to the murmur of the bee as, after sipping all day long the fragrant thyme, it winged its way to its rocky home when the sun was sinking to rest, and flooding all the valley with golden light; or to watch the flock of nimble gazelles bounding through the glades. In all these varied sights and sounds, all these varied pages of the book of nature, He would read in glowing letters the name of that same Father-God. He did not require, like Job, a mighty wind to help Him to see Jehovah, or, like Moses, a burning bush or the thunders and lightnings of Sinai. He beheld this Divine Father of heaven wherever He turned—in the street, at the fountain, on the hillside, in the workshop. Jacob could only call one place, but He could call every place PENIEL, for "*He saw God face to face.*"

I shall come afterwards to speak about all we know or can imagine regarding the outward face and form of Jesus. Meantime let us think of Him and picture Him with a heart pure and lovely. There was not so much as one spot or stain on it. He never gave His mother an unkind look. He never spoke to her an unkind word. He never cost her one moment of sorrow; He was always a bright sunbeam on her path. Other children, when they kneel down on their knees at night to their evening prayers, have many faults and sins to confess, and for which they have to ask forgiveness. Think of this ONE little Child of Nazareth, who, when He bent His knees in prayer to His Heavenly Father, had not so much as a single sin to own or a single fault to mourn. His words never were, "O my Father! blot this trespass I have committed to-day out of Thy book." No. His prayer was rather this—"O my Father! teach me to have more and more delight every day in doing Thy holy will, and in loving Thee perfectly. Prepare me for my great work in saving a lost world." He might well be named "Thy HOLY Child Jesus."

There are many questions about His childhood and early youth you might be tempted to ask, but which we should not be too curious to know; as the Holy Ghost, who taught and guided the writers of the Bible, has thrown no light upon them.

For instance, I think you may perhaps wonder whether Jesus in His boyhood years was ever at any school.

This, I repeat, I cannot tell; and for the reason I have just given, because the Bible tells us nothing about it. We know that at the time at which Jesus lived, the Jews were very particular about the education of the young. In all the principal towns and villages there were schools. Every village, indeed, that could number as many as twenty-five boys was obliged by the law to provide a schoolmaster, who generally acted also as *chazzan* or minister of the Synagogue. In Jerusalem alone there were no less than 394 schools. We may well believe that Nazareth was not behind other places in this respect. Some have thought it doubtful if the Divine Youth received any *public* instruction in His native town. They draw this inference from what the Jews said when they afterwards found Jesus teaching in the Temple and ministering to the people, " *How knoweth this man letters, having never learned?* " That is, 'who has never been taught by any master or Rabbi.' But whether he went with other children in Nazareth of his age to be educated or not, I believe the earthly school where He learnt most was at His father and mother's knee. They would teach Him, as was the case with most pious parents among the Jews, to repeat brief prayers; above all, they would instruct Him out of God's Holy Word, and He must have acquired by heart many portions of it, for in His after life He often quoted them. Just as it is with you, there would also, doubtless, be some parts that would be with Him special favourites. His young heart would beat, as has been the case with millions of youth in all ages, as He listened to the beautiful tale of Joseph, or to the story of piety and manliness of youthful David; or He would listen with deep interest to the description of Naaman the Syrian and the little Jewish maid, which we find Him afterwards quoting; or to the account of the holy childhood of Samuel, or to the great deeds of the great Elijah, or to the lovely songs and hymns of Isaiah.

A writer, well acquainted with Jewish customs, mentions the interesting fact that it was the practice to impress on a child's earliest memory some one particular verse of Sacred Scripture, what we would call "a birthday text." It was intended as a motto and watchword for it all its life, and was repeated in its daily prayers. The verse was selected in a singular way—from the Hebrew letter which either began or ended the young one's name. That verse was carried about as a sacred charm to the end of life. We reverently wonder what the holy saying was which formed the protecting promise and part of the daily prayer of the Divine Child of Nazareth;—taken from the first or last letter of the Hebrew name for Jesus or Joshua (יהושע). I doubt not it would prove to Him a source of solace, and joy, and strength in many an hour of deep sorrow, strong temptation, and fierce suffering. Further, among all the God-fearing families of Israel there was one special silent instructor which met the eye of young and old on every gate and doorway. Not only on the outside door, but occasionally at the opening of other chambers. It was called *Mesusah*. It was a piece or roll of framed parchment, containing the well-known words from Deuteronomy vi., beginning with "*Hear, O Israel, the Lord our God is one Lord*," &c. They were more to the Jew than the Creed and the Lord's Prayer are to the Christian, for they were considered the symbol and emblem of Jehovah's presence and protection. The house, without this framed writing, would have been deemed like the Hebrew dwelling in Egypt which was neglected to be sprinkled with the blood of the Paschal Lamb. Moreover, it is an interesting statement made in the Talmud, that children had small parchment rolls of their own, containing, along with other extracts, this same portion of their Holy Scriptures.[1] We can think, therefore, of the eye of the youthful Jesus very familiar with words which He did not require to learn, for they formed the truthful description of His whole life—"*Thou shalt love the Lord thy God with all thine heart, and with all thy soul, and with all thy might.*" Joseph and Mary would not be among those likely to disobey the injunction—" And

---

[1] See these, and other interesting particulars, in Dr. Edersheim's "Jewish Social Life."

ye shall teach them diligently to your children, speaking of them when thou sittest in thine house, and when thou walkest by the way, and when thou liest down, and when thou riseth up. And thou shalt write them upon the door-posts of thine house, and upon thy gates" (Deut. xi. 19, 20).

He would be *gradually* instructed, too, just as other children are, for He had no infant perfection. He was not in mere *semblance* a child, while in reality He had the mind of a full-grown man. No. He did not attain His knowledge of things miraculously. Truth would slowly dawn upon Him just as on any other infant or youth. This would be the case even in regard to ordinary outer objects. It would not, for example, be all at once, but by degrees that He would come to see the beauty of the flowers, or the glory of golden sunrise, or the tender crimson glow of sunset. He grew in observation and intellect and in feeling as He grew in stature. And just as earthly parents are the appointed instructors of their children, so with Him. Joseph and Mary would teach Him to lisp His first infant prayer, and to begin and end the day on His bended knees. If the youthful Timothy acquired the first lessons of a holy life as he played, a little boy, at the feet of "his grandmother Lois, and his mother Eunice," much more would Jesus drink in the first lessons of heavenly wisdom from the lips of the devout guardians of His early years. On the Sabbath, when the axe, and saw, and hammer of the other six days were laid aside, He would doubtless accompany His parents to the village Synagogue. In winter the Sabbath lamp of olive-oil would be lighted, or in the summer evening Joseph and Mary, ascending by the outside stair, would go and sit with their loved Child in the booth erected on the top of their house. There they would sing together some of the Psalms of their Shepherd-King: perhaps the one about "the green pastures and the still waters," and "the Valley of the Shadow of Death;" or it may be the one which celebrated the glories of the coming King as having "grace poured into His lips," and the royal sword girded on His thigh; or, yet again, that other which speaks of His dominion being "from sea to sea, and from the river unto

"*He came to Nazareth, and was subject unto them*" (Luke ii. 51) . (*opposite page* 63)

the ends of the earth." What a befitting "even-song" for the "Son of David" would be these sweet strains of His royal ancestor! They would remain out, it may be, till it was dark, and the sky became bright with stars sparkling like jewels in the crown of night. Mary would perhaps sing that beautiful Jewish hymn which spoke, though probably she did not know it, of the Youth who was then at her side—"*When I consider Thy heavens, the work of Thy fingers, the moon and the stars which Thou hast ordained; what is man that Thou art mindful of him, or the son of man that Thou visitest him?*" (Ps. viii. 3, 4). Yes! it was He who had made all these bright worlds in the sky, and who was Himself BRIGHTER than them all, who came down as the Babe of Bethlehem and the Boy of Nazareth, in order that He might save you and me!

Such, then, is a feeble picture of the early education and training of the Holy Child and the Divine Youth. It is necessary, however, to add, that though there was growth in wisdom, just as in every other child or youth, there was a training peculiar to Him alone, far other, far higher, than human. He had the Holy Spirit "given to Him without measure." "*The grace of God was with Him.*"

I must close this interesting period in the history of Jesus by recalling once more, for I cannot do it so well again, that lovely thought so comforting to the very youngest, that this Great Being lived once Himself a child-life, that He could remember, and that He remembers *now* on the throne, His infant years and infant home! He had a childhood and a boyhood, with its sunshine and shadow. It is true He never had tears to shed for sin, but I believe He had His little troubles and trials, the same as all of us. Yes; I can think of this Holy One with the tear of sorrow in His eye, rushing (just as childhood does among ourselves) to His mother, to bury His face in her bosom;—to have His brow stroked by her gentle hand, and to have these tears kissed away as He sank asleep in the couch by her side.

Young reader, while you bear always in your mind the remembrance that He was in very truth not only the Son of God, but *the Great God Himself,* 'by whom all things consist;' I would like you to think also much of what I have been saying regarding the beauty and loveliness of His *human* nature. With devout reverence I would ask you to take this Village Boy of Nazareth as your *example.* If you could only read of Him as the Divine *Man,* who rebuked the winds and hushed the waves, and cast out devils, and raised the dead, you might perhaps feel and say, "This Saviour can be an example to grown-up people, but He cannot be an example to me. This Saviour can understand the heart of grown-up people, but He cannot know mine."

Yes, He can. He does. I think one reason why He afterwards so gently and lovingly took up even little children in His arms, and laid His hands upon them and blessed them, and that they smiled fearless in His face, was just because He was once Himself even as they. He knew what it was to be loved and caressed by fond and pious parents. He knew all the tender thoughts that surround that happy word "Early Home"—the father's care and the mother's watchfulness. "*He knoweth our frame,*" can be lisped by the tongue of infancy and youth as well as by the lips of age. Oh, I am sure there is not one amongst us all who would like to miss from our Bibles and our memories this story of the sunny HOME OF NAZARETH!

VIII.

He is taken up to the Temple when He is twelve years old.

THERE is one beautiful story regarding Jesus while He was at Nazareth which I cannot pass over in silence.

All the fathers and young men of Palestine were in the habit of going at least once a year to Jerusalem, to keep one of the great feasts. They had done so at the command of God for many hundred years.

The women were not by the law required to accompany them, but Mary seems to have so liked to attend, that she went regularly every year with her husband, leaving Jesus behind. It was not till a Jewish boy or youth reached the age of thirteen, that he was also allowed to join his parents in keeping the Passover. At that age he became what was called " *Bar Mizvah,*" " a Child of the Law."

But how is this ? Jesus is not thirteen, but only twelve ; and yet, a year earlier than others, He prepares to go up to the solemn assembly in Jerusalem. We can only take it as a beautiful evidence that He has so grown in " wisdom," and (in the truest and holiest sense of the word) " piety," that His parents could not resist his ardent wish to " appear before God." A Psalm dear to every Jew, may have been often heard on His lips :—those who were daily witnesses to the purity and loveliness of His life could not refuse to gratify its devout aspiration—" *How amiable are Thy Tabernacles, O Lord of Hosts ! My soul longeth, yea, even fainteth for the Courts of the Lord.*"

You, doubtless, remember what this Feast of the Passover was, and when it was appointed ?

It was instituted by God to call to mind that never-to-be-forgotten night when all the first-born in the land of Egypt died, and when only those houses of the Israelites which were sprinkled with the blood of the slain Lamb were " *passed-over* " by the destroying angel. Hence it was called " the Feast of the *Passing over.*"

The Feast itself took place at the most delightful time of the year in the Holy Land. Spring is a lovely season at home ; but I think, from what I saw, it is still lovelier there. The orchards are filled with blossom ; the vine and the fig are clad in their early bright verdure. The olive leaf has its silver lining, and the grass, which at the close of the year is browned and blighted with the summer and autumn sun, looks green as an emerald. A great deal of rain has fallen, the dust on the roads is laid, and everything is refreshed.

Where the highways needed it, they were repaired. If any

F.

stones or branches of trees impeded the busy thoroughfares, they were removed or cut down. "Prepare ye the way of the people; cast up, cast up the highway; gather out the stones" (Isa. lxii. 10).

What a happy occasion these festival gatherings must have been! I should think they would be the happiest hours of a young life, thus journeying through the valleys of Palestine to see for the first time the City of the Great King. I daresay the youths in their distant homes would think much of all the sacred pleasure in store for them. Many months beforehand they would count the days till the joyful moment came, when what was called the 'Caravan,' with its crowd of pilgrims, was ready.

The 'Caravan' is well known at the present day to all who have visited Palestine and Syria. People for safety travel, not singly, or in families, but in companies. I never can forget the sight of these caravans wending their way along the desolate tracks: mules with panniers carrying provisions or merchandise; occasionally camels more heavily laden with tent poles and furniture. The men with rough wooden shoes, some with girdles round their waists, are walking—the women and children seated on horses or asses; while the varied colours of their eastern dresses make all the brighter picture contrasted with the barrenness around. There seems to have been an equal necessity for thus travelling in companies in the time of Jesus. Wayfarers were then exposed to what St. Paul afterwards speaks of as his experience elsewhere—"Perils of robbers, perils of the wilderness, and perils of false brethren." The wandering Arab tribes—the Sons of Ishmael—had, according to the prophecy, "their hand against every man." They were ready to pounce down upon and plunder every lonely unprotected traveller. Specially perilous was it to traverse the country alone at night. And, although that was not a frequent occurrence, the vast numbers who came to Jerusalem by way of the Jordan Valley were subject to the attacks of wild beasts as well as to those of the Bedawin of the desert. The wolf had his den on the adjoining mountains, and the lion his lair amid the tall reeds and rushes of the border river. But when a considerable number of pilgrims travelled together, they could, by lighting fires round their encampment, and keeping watch by turns, protect themselves against all plunderers.

It would surely be a glad time then, to the youthful Passover *Pilgrim of Nazareth*, as the day drew nigh when the village caravan would start on its way to the City of Solemnities. Every place on the journey, too, would be so new to Him. In order to avoid the heat of the day, the festal companies often travelled by night. The full Passover moon shone upon them. There were some of the Psalms of the Great Singer or Singers of Israel, they loved then specially to use ; indeed, which were set apart to be employed in going up to the feasts. You have doubtless noted many Psalms towards the close of the Psalter called "Songs of Degrees," or "Songs of the going up." These are supposed by many to have been sung by the Pilgrims at the different stages on the way. They made the roads and valleys through which they passed resound with these "songs in the night."

We can follow in thought Joseph and Mary and Jesus along the steep road which leads out of Nazareth. It is at present one of the roughest mule paths in Palestine; but I remember in passing along, how sure I felt that it must have been trodden again and again by the footsteps of Jesus, as it is the only possible approach to the plain of Esdraelon,—the only possible outlet from the enclosed dale to the south, while the northern road is by a zig-zag path across one of the surrounding hills. After descending this rocky gorge, they would cross the great flat plain where Barak and Sisera fought. It would then, doubtless, be well cultivated, though now only covered with coarse grass and thistles. They would pass by the foot of the Hill of Samaria with its glittering houses, which the prophet speaks of as "a crown." If Nazareth were beautiful, more beautiful still was the Valley of Shechem through which they next continued their journey, with its song of birds and music of streams. They might "rest at noon" by Jacob's Well, and drink perhaps of the cool water; then on, past Shiloh and Bethel, and other holy spots and holy names. As they paused every now and then to light their fires and cook their meals, the younger travellers would gather the fuel, or bring water from the springs close by, and then, rising up refreshed, all would begin again their anthems and hosannahs.

It would be on the fourth or fifth day they obtained the first glimpse of "the mountains round about Jerusalem." Perhaps, as summit after summit disclosed themselves at early sunrise, just as the birds in the thickets around were waking up to melody, so would they sing their well-known 'Song of degrees,' "*I will lift mine eyes unto the hills from whence cometh my help, my help cometh from the Lord who made heaven and earth.*" Then at last, when the longing wish of their hearts was fulfilled, and they saw straight before them the City of the Great King, old and young, with branches of palm and olive and myrtle in their hands, would be heard joining together in the most joyous psalm of the pilgrims, "*Our feet shall stand within Thy gates, O Jerusalem!*"

Yes, there Jerusalem was, close by, with its vast walls and towers, its gates and Temple, and deep valley with the brook Kedron; and more striking in its way, perhaps, than any of these, all the face of the green Mount of Olives, was, on that occasion, covered with tents and booths,—some made of cloth and canvas, others of twisted branches and leaves. The citizens of Jerusalem were proverbial for their hospitality on that occasion. Their houses were freely thrown open to strangers; and if the interiors of the dwellings were full, mats were spread on the roofs to serve as beds and couches. Pilgrims indeed did not require to knock and solicit for quarters. An embroidered cloth suspended from the door formed the silent signal that there was still room and welcome within. But yet, despite of this, the ordinary houses were quite unable to contain the vast numbers who crowded up to the Feast. So, temporary leafy dwellings, such as I have spoken of, had to be erected for the accommodation of the rest of the Pilgrims. Perhaps Joseph and Mary and the young Jesus lived, during the week, in one of these humble huts made of branches of trees. They would go down, it may be, to the Pool of En-rogel or Siloam to fill their jars and skins with water, or they would buy bread and fruit from those who had stalls under two large cedar trees, which, we are told, grew near the top of the hill.

I think, my young readers, it is an impressive incident in the Divine life I am now describing to you; JESUS among that company going up to that spring Feast! His youthful feet trod these roads; His youthful voice sang these songs; His youthful heart would leap, just like that of the others, for joy, as He got the first sight of the Holy City, and saw, perhaps, the cloud of incense rising up from the Temple into the blue sky. It was His Father's house—the house His feet were so often in future years to cross, and whose doom He was yet so bitterly to bewail. His mother, surely, would be very happy as, hand in hand, they went up the steep path and entered together the Courts of Zion. You remember the last time they were there together. It was nearly twelve years before, when old Simeon held the Infant Saviour up in his arms and blessed Him. Jesus had not probably seen any other church or temple except the humble synagogue at Nazareth. How He must have gazed with a boy's wonder at all He beheld and all He heard! The white garments of the priests; the loud anthems of the singers, in which the sweet voices of the youthful Levites—even children—blended with the deep notes of their elders; the clashing of the cymbals and the clear tones of the trumpets; the gates of cedar and brass and gold and the pillars of pure white marble.

Think of Him, going up perhaps alone at daybreak to watch the earliest beam as it broke over Mount Olivet and struck on the golden lamp above the porch—the signal for the commencing services of the day! The trumpets pealing loud over city and valley and hill; and immediately after, the silver cloud from the morning altar gleaming in the light of the rising sun!

I have sometimes thought, too, though we are not told, that at this same festival season, some other honoured youths may have gone up in that same company with Jesus, and that they may have met unconsciously among the crowds on Mount Olivet, or in the Temple;—some young fishermen boys from a fishing village on the Lake of Tiberias. Perhaps, too, a dark-eyed Pilgrim from

Tarsus, who was one day to be struck down on his way to Damascus, by "a light above the brightness of the sun." That "LIGHT"—their future Lord and Master—was, all unknown to them, in their midst.

We are not told anything as to how Joseph, Mary, and Jesus kept the Feast. It was about two o'clock in the afternoon of the fourteenth day of the month Abib, that a long blast was heard of the silver trumpets in the courts of the Temple, intimating that the services had commenced. This was answered by a clash of cymbals, a blowing of horns, and a shout of Psalms all through the crowded lanes and streets. Not in the city alone, but in a wave of song it floated through the waiting multitudes, from the tents in the Kedron Valley up to the very summit of the Mount of Olives; and the procession, or rather the thousands of family processions, began to move in the direction of Mount Moriah. How strange to think of Jesus going up to the Temple at the side of His reputed Father! the latter carrying "a lamb without blemish" on his shoulders. How strange to think of Him gazing on that lamb as it was slaughtered! It was the first time in His young life He had seen a sacrifice offered;—the first time He had heard the bleating cries, and watched the struggles of the innocent victim. The blood of that slain lamb flowed direct from the wound which the knife had made into a golden vessel, and was handed to a row of Priests to be sprinkled at the base of the Altar of Burnt-offering. Was He allowed to behold in all this a significant type and picture of His own future sufferings, when His own precious blood—that of "a Lamb without blemish and without spot," was to be poured out for sinful man;—"the blood of sprinkling" which was yet to speak better things than that of all the two hundred thousand lambs that were often slain at every Passover in Jerusalem? We cannot tell.

In the evening, when the stars came out in the sky, the Feast began. Several families generally met together under one roof, or under the canvas of one tent. We shall come afterwards to read how Jesus celebrated this same Festival of the "Passing-over" before He suffered. We can only think of that 'Holy

Family,' now perhaps in company with a number of their friends from Nazareth (there were never fewer than ten at the Paschal Supper), reclining on benches around a table, on which was served the Lamb roasted whole. There were also placed on a side table thin cakes of unleavened bread, a platter filled with bitter herbs, a dish of thick sauce in which everything they partook of was to be dipped, and a goblet of red wine for "the four cups," the last of which was "the cup of blessing." The place of meeting was often decked with flowers and filled with their perfume. Who can tell but in the present case, some of these may have been gathered by holy hands on the hills of Nazareth, or from the wayside meadows on the road to Jerusalem? There was a remarkable incident in the course of the celebration. One of the young ones, if not the very youngest, of the company, was selected to ask the question, "*What mean ye by this service?*" In answer to which the Father or presiding guest rehearsed, in brief, the nation's history, and specially the story of the Bondage in Egypt, which the bitter herbs were designed to recall, and the sprinkling of the blood of the lamb on the night of deliverance. Is it not possible, is it not most likely, that Joseph himself would occupy the chief seat at the table, and that He who put that question was none other than the Holy Child Jesus? We can think of the little company singing together what was called "the Hallel." This consisted of a few appointed Psalms which were deemed best suited for the sacred occasion, specially the beautiful one hundred and eighteenth, from which the following are a few verses,—

> "Oh, give thanks unto the Lord; for He is good,
> Because His mercy endureth for ever:
> Let Israel now say,
> That His mercy endureth for ever.
>
> "The voice of rejoicing and salvation
> Is in the tabernacles of the righteous:
> The right hand of the Lord doeth valiantly.
>
> "This is the day which the Lord hath made,
> We will rejoice and be glad in it.

> Save now, I beseech thee, O Lord,
> O Lord, I beseech Thee send now prosperity;
> Blessed be he that cometh in the name of the Lord!"

With the exception of Joseph and Mary, who treasured in their hearts the mighty secret, little did the others present think that the blessing they implored was actually resting on the head of a Young Pilgrim, who at that very hour was with them at the table; who was eating the Paschal Lamb, and singing the Paschal Song, and putting to His lips the cup of sacred remembrance! "Surely the Lord was in that place, and they knew it not." It was His blood that was to avert the Destroying Angel, and bring all His true people safe to the Heavenly Canaan. Do you remember how St. Paul in after years speaks of Jesus being the true Paschal Sacrifice, whose blood is sprinkled on the lintels and door-posts of every heart, young and old? *"Christ our Passover is sacrificed for us"* (1 Cor. v. 7).

IX.

His Father and Mother seek Him sorrowing.

But the happiest times and happiest meetings in this world must come to an end. The Feast of the Passover has closed. Joseph and Mary seem not only to have kept the special Feast day, but to have remained all the seven days which followed it, and which were called "the days of unleavened bread." The caravan Pilgrims make ready to go back again to Nazareth.

There were very large bands of these Pilgrims at the close of the Feast, sometimes amounting to several hundreds at a time. Joseph and Mary had probably seen, or at least never doubted, that Jesus had joined the crowd. There is always great bustle and confusion in the East in starting on a journey. The taking down the tents, collecting the baggage, piling and securing it on the backs of mules and asses, is not the simple matter which such a journey is with us. Joseph and Mary may at the moment have been so taken up with these necessary arrangements for the start homewards, that they may have omitted to make sure that Jesus was among them. They felt quite certain, however, that He would appear at their encampment at sundown. It is thought by some that the boys and youths kept together in a small company by themselves, and that His parents would feel satisfied that their dear Son was all safe and happy among His young companions, or perhaps with His cousins. They paused for the night, probably, at Beeroth, known to travellers still, alike for its copious fountain and as being the first usual halting-place on the northern road.

Their tents had been erected, the pitchers of water had been drawn from the adjoining spring, the faggots for the camp-fire had been gathered and lighted, all was in readiness for the last meal of the day previous to the night's repose, when Joseph and Mary discover that Jesus is still missing! They go first "among their kinsfolk and acquaintance,"—that is, to the tents in the large encampment occupied by their relatives and neighbours from Nazareth. Jesus may be so engrossed in the company of friends He loved, speaking and hearing about the Feast and its holy services, that He may have forgotten how the hours had passed, and that the sun had already set. But tent after tent is searched in vain. They looked all about for Him, and could not find Him. They would grieve and reproach themselves that they had allowed Him to go out of their sight. They felt sure that He was so loving and devoted and obedient, and so considerate of their wishes, that He would not Himself have given needless trouble and distress by wandering away from them. I wonder if Mary would think again about Simeon's 'sword'?

She and Joseph could not help knowing that there were, as I have already told you, many robbers and lawless men at that time going about the country, who might have seized Him, and made Him a slave, just as Joseph was by the Ishmaelites long long before. Cruel Herod we saw had tried to kill Jesus in Bethlehem. Perhaps the king who came after Herod, and who had already shown his tyrant nature, will now attempt to do the same. I have no doubt the sorrow-stricken Mother had very little sleep that night, thinking of her loved One, and dreading lest any evil had befallen Him. Any parent would be concerned about a lost and missing child. But Joseph and Mary had a far higher and deeper cause for their anxiety. They knew the secret of His birth, and the greatness of the trust that had been committed to them. So anxious were they both, that though they had to leave the fellowship of their friends, they resolve to go back alone next day all the way to Jerusalem and try to discover Him.

As they meet company after company, they would eagerly inquire if the lost One was in their midst. A whole day they spent seeking Him, but they could not find Him. On the third day, tired and weary with the sleepless nights, the glaring sun, and the dusty roads, they go perhaps first to the part of the Mount of Olives where the people from Galilee were in the habit of pitching their tents. But He is not there. Then they go up the steps to the Temple. Can He be there?

Yes. In going into one of its halls in the outer court, or court of the Gentiles, there He is. He is seated in the midst of some learned Teachers.

These Teachers were in the habit of having what would be called among us 'Lecture-rooms'—free or open schools—where they invited all, old and young, to come and either listen to their instructions, or ask questions. Some have thought that among these Doctors of the law were two very famous Rabbis, who were the heads of the sacred school or college. Their names were Hillel and Shammai. Perhaps also Nicodemus, of whom we shall by-and-by hear; and the learned scholar Gamaliel, at whose feet young Saul of Tarsus sat.

They are all gazing on Jesus with wonder, listening to His words. They had never heard before such wisdom proceeding from the lips of youth: They were saying in amazement, one to another, " Who can this thoughtful young pupil be?" How searching are

His questions! How marvellously versed in Moses and the Prophets! Where can such bright intelligence be found in half heathen Galilee? The word used in the original Greek is far stronger than that in our English version. It means "they were very greatly astonished."

I think too, they would be all the more astonished when they saw that He was not, like many young persons, asking questions merely for admiration, and in order to be thought knowing and clever and wise. They saw that He was meek and lowly, docile and humble, and that all He said was from a simple desire to know the truth and to grow in wisdom.

It was a natural thing for the parents of Jesus to seek Him in the Temple Schools. He was one of those whom the Psalmist beautifully describes, "*whose delight is in the law of the Lord, and in His law doth He meditate day and night.*" During the eight days the Feast lasted, while others might be admiring the grandeur of the Temple and the splendour of its services, He may have preferred quietly resorting to these learned, and many of them devout, expounders of God's Holy Word and will. He could say as none other could—"Oh, how love I Thy law, it is my meditation all the day!"

His happy parents are so glad to see Him again. They are amazed to hear Him converse as He is doing with these great scholars. He is "*both hearing them, and asking them questions.*"

I have before me a well-known picture of "*Jesus in the Temple.*" I like to look upon it; it seems so true. There is a circle of Jewish teachers; some old, some young. There is one old and blind, with a white flowing beard, probably intended to represent Hillel, who, if present, must have been considerably upwards of a hundred years of age. All seem to turn towards the gentle yet noble-looking Boy of Nazareth, in the centre of the group, with His dress of white, striped with blue, and His eye so full of meaning and beauty. The birds of the Temple are flitting to and fro, or perched on some of the rich carved work of the chambers. His anxious parents have just found Him. I dare say they would be amazed to see Him so calm in the midst of these great men;—

a Child speaking to grey-headed teachers. His mother seems in the act of saying to Him, " *Son (Dear Child), why hast thou thus dealt with us? behold thy father and I have sought Thee sorrowing.*"

The painter of this remarkable picture seems to have caught up with singular truth what is conveyed in the original—that Mary whispered the gentle rebuke, so that it might not be heard by others, into the ear of her divine Son. " *Unto Him*, His mother said." Also he has wonderfully depicted the intense anguish which she felt, and which is not at all fully expressed in our English Bibles. It is far more than ' *sorrow*.' It is keen mental *torture*.

Jesus answered in words well worth remembering—words of divine import, that have the ring not of earth but of heaven in them. They come from deeper than the depths of His mere human soul. Many other gracious words proceeded out of His mouth, but these are the first we are told about in the Gospels: —"*And he said unto them, How is it that ye sought me? wist ye not that I must be about my Father's business?* (Luke ii. 49).

Perhaps you were expecting that this kind, devoted, obedient Son, the pattern to all young persons, would say with a tear in His eye as He listened to the reproof from His best earthly friend, " I grieve that I should have pained you so, or cost you one hour or one moment of anxiety or uneasiness. Such you may feel sure will never happen again." No. The language of this meek and lowly Boy is the reverse. It is the assertion of a lofty claim which He seems astonished they had failed to own. The glorious rays of the Sun of Righteousness, or rather of One " Brighter than the Sun," hitherto hidden amid morning clouds, suddenly burst forth. He had tenderly obeyed and loved a father and mother on earth, but now He tells them that though He loves them still as much as ever, and will strive to please them as much as ever, that His Father in Heaven He must honour above all others. Yes, even *above* them. He has come on earth to do that Heavenly Father's will and finish His work. The wondrous fact of His being 'God manifest in the flesh,' would seem from this time to have opened more fully upon Him. What a strange feeling it must be to a prince, the eldest son of a sovereign, when he first begins to take in the thought that he is the heir of the throne and will one day wear a crown and be called king. Similar, but far more wondrous, must have been the feelings of Jesus now! "*Thy father and I,*" Mary had just said to Him. "No," said He, "I have now dawning upon me a far grander truth, I have another, and far Greater Father, whose 'Will' I have come on earth to do. I know that I am Son of the King of kings, the Prince of the kings of the earth. A glory is mine which belongs to no earthly king. My heavenly Father will yet glorify Me with His ownself, with the glory which I had with Him before the world was." The very Temple where He stood, with its glorious courts and songs of praise and ceaseless services (earth's truest picture of Heaven), must have woke up in His Divine Mind wondrous thoughts of a past that never had a beginning. Could it fail vividly to bring before Him "the Building of God, the House not made with hands, eternal in the heavens?"

Jesus leaves the Temple-court at the call of His parents, and they take their journey to Galilee.

NOONTIDE.

"AND THE LIGHT SHINETH IN DARKNESS, AND THE DARKNESS COMPREHENDED IT NOT."—JOHN I. 5.

"I WAIT FOR THE LORD, MY SOUL DOTH WAIT, AND IN HIS WORD DO I HOPE. MY SOUL WAITETH FOR THE LORD MORE THAN THEY THAT WATCH FOR THE MORNING; I SAY, MORE THAN THEY THAT WATCH FOR THE MORNING."—PS. CXXX. 5, 6.

"THE PATH OF THE JUST IS AS THE SHINING LIGHT, THAT SHINETH MORE AND MORE UNTO THE PERFECT DAY."—PROV. IV. 18.

"AND HE WENT DOWN WITH THEM AND CAME TO NAZARETH, AND WAS SUBJECT UNTO THEM. . . . AND JESUS INCREASED IN WISDOM AND STATURE, AND IN FAVOUR WITH GOD AND MAN."—LUKE II. 51, 52.

X.

He grows up to Manhood at Nazareth.

THE Sunrise and bright Morning of the Divine Life are now merging into NOONTIDE—those still, peaceful hours which precede the burden and heat of the day.

Did the meeting with the Doctors and great men of the Temple make Jesus proud? Did the dawning conviction that He was the Son of God and the Messiah of Israel make Him keep aloof from the ordinary work of the world or the ordinary duties of life? Did it make Him love less His home and His calling and His relatives and friends at Nazareth?

No, He was just as "meek and lowly in heart" as He was before. All that we are at this time told about Him is, that along with His parents, "*He went down, and came to Nazareth, and was subject unto them*" (Luke ii. 51). He seemed quite willing to exchange the splendour of the Temple Courts for the humble cottage of Galilee.

Does it not only lead us the more to wonder at His condescension? What! He who was now fully alive to the fact that He was not really the Son of Joseph; He who was beginning to have the awful consciousness that He was the anointed Jesus, the Great God in human nature; might we not have expected to hear Him speaking no longer with the voice of an obedient Son, but with the authority of a Master: not asking His parents what He should do; telling them rather, with a commanding tone, what *they* should do; changing, in fact, places with them, and usurping authority over them? But no such thing. Oh, what a beautiful example for youth, this Heavenly, heaven-born Child—obedient, dutiful, loving, submissive as ever—looking up still with fond filial reverence and devotion to those who stood to Him in the most sacred of earthly relations, "*He was subject unto them.*" Subject too, I may add, to Mary, not as she is sometimes falsely represented as "the Queen of Heaven" with the moon at her feet, and a cluster of stars round her brow, but Mary the lowly mother of a lowly earthly home!

I believe Joseph must have died soon after this. If so, it is probable that the first tears of bereavement which the Holy Saviour shed, would be over the grave of one who had proved so good and kind to Him. A great painter has touchingly represented the former laying his head on the bosom of Jesus at the moment of his death. Some have maintained that "the brethren and sisters" who are spoken of (Matt. xiii. 55, 56) were Joseph's children by a former marriage, and that they may all have lived together in the same house. But, as I have already said, we have strong grounds for supposing, following the opinion of Jerome and many others since his time, that they were rather the first cousins of Christ: so that we may think of the Home at Nazareth in connection only with Him. We can certainly conclude that He would continue still at His trade in order to support His widowed mother.

I like to dwell on this picture of Jesus before He began His great public work, being a comfort to her who had loved Him so long and so tenderly; speaking dutiful words to her, and doing little acts of kindness for her. Yes, I like much to imagine Him thus, for whole eighteen years (more than half of all the time He spent on earth) living in this quiet dwelling among the green hills, while good and gentle to every one, devoted specially to His best earthly friend. As the Christian poet says—

> "A Son that never did amiss,
> That never shamed His mother's kiss,
> Nor crossed her fondest prayer."

How honoured Nazareth was in being for so long the earthly home of the Lord of glory! How honoured, too, the working-man in every town and every village on earth who earns his bread by the sweat of his brow, that the Saviour of the world—the great 'Son of the Highest'—came and lived, not in halls of splendour, but toiled as a carpenter in a poor village! Do you not remember what some of His townsmen said about Him afterwards, one Sabbath when He was teaching them? In the 6th chapter of Mark and 3d verse, we read that they asked, with words and looks of scorn, "*Is not this* THE *Carpenter?*" (not "the Carpenter's *Son*," which was said of Him at another time, but THE *Carpenter*).

Oh what a strange wonderful thought! Jesus (and Jesus knowing, too, who He was, and what He had come on earth to do) for about twenty years led the simple life of a tradesman among the peasants of Syria, shaping planks and oars, and preparing timber for floor and roof and lattice, the drops of labour standing on His brow!

Justin Martyr, a writer of the first age of Christianity, specially mentions His "making ploughs and yokes for oxen."

Does He not wish to teach all, young and old, that it is a good thing to work, and that it is a bad thing to be idle. I was reading a book not long ago, on "The Dignity of Labour." Jesus, by His life of employment at Nazareth, wrote, surely in golden letters, the brightest and best page in that book. Never need any boy or girl be ashamed of a humble and lowly occupation, when they know that JESUS, at one time, stooped to do rough common work.

And I would like you farther to note that He continued in the trade He had been brought up to, and was contented and happy in it. There are many who would like to be in some other place and lot than God has given to them. Not so the Divine Son of Mary. He did not say to His mother, "I dislike all this hard labour and toil in this hot dusty street. Knowing my future high destiny, I should like to go back to the Temple and to live with the Doctors and Rabbis there, and join in the solemn worship. I would feel far more than I can ever do here, that I am in my Father's House, and about my Father's business. Or, if that be impossible, I should like better some other trade. I should like to be a shepherd, like David; to go out with the flock and climb these beautiful hills all day long; or under some spreading tree, or by some joyous brook, warble sacred strains on the shepherd's pipe. I should like thus to live in the Great Sanctuary of Nature, among the wild flowers, and feel the cooling breeze fanning my temples. Anything rather than this dull ungenial workshop."

No, He felt that the Heavenly Father He loved had placed Him there, and in this, as in everything else, He sought to do His Father's will.

Jesus was called afterwards, "The Man of Sorrows." But these must have been happy years to Him in Nazareth, loving His Father in heaven, and being gracious and considerate to all about Him.

We are not told of the many kind things He doubtless said, and the many kind deeds He doubtless often performed. You may be sure there would be, in or around the town, beggars like blind Bartimeus, and rows of lepers stretching out their hands and crying for help. There would be boys and girls who had lost their fathers, or who could point to the grave of a dead brother or sister. There would be mothers weeping bitterly over their children.

Is it likely that, with the love that glowed in His bosom, He would look on these broken hearts and not try to bind them up? John in his Gospel says that there were so many kind and gracious things Jesus did, and so many kind and loving words Jesus spoke, that He supposed "all the world could not contain the books that would be written about them." I think many of these books, had they been written, would have been taken up with the sayings and the doings of these holy years in Nazareth. I have seen often how one dear little child could make a home of much suffering and sadness, happy with its bright face, and joyous smile; or as it printed its kisses on the cheek of pain. What a joyous, peaceful home, that must have been where the pure, bright, sinless Saviour was. Never a hard word, never a cold look, never an evil thought, never a movement of wayward self-will, or trace of sullen temper, or stormy passion: anticipating His mother's wishes, wiping away her tears, and telling her of "His Father, and her Father, of His God, and her God." Surely, as Jesus, tired with the day's toil, flung Himself on His bed at night to sleep, the bright seraphs from Heaven must have liked to come unseen to that couch and home of love! Nazareth would be like what Bethel and its dreamer was, long, long before, with the ladder on which glorious angels went up and down. His own after prayer, never perfectly fulfilled in the case of any other human being, had its answer in that holy life, " *Thy will be done on earth as it is done in heaven.*"

You may imagine, too, how happy Mary must have been to have had such a Son! How glad she would be to minister to Him! Any time He needed to go a little way from home, to some of the neighbouring towns or hamlets,—to Cana or Nain, Endor or Capernaum, how pleased she would be, as she was seated in her porch at her distaff, to watch Him coming in the distance! How glad to lift the latch of her door and welcome Him in; to have the floor of her cottage swept; the bath ready for His weary feet; and, perhaps, the cluster of wild flowers from the great garden of nature He loved so well!

There was a feeling which must have been quite peculiar to her regarding her Divine Son. All other mothers have not only the sad fear present with them, that their children may be tempted in an evil hour to fall into sin; but another mournful thought also at times hangs over them, that death may early take their loved ones away. Not only did Mary know that the pure and spotless Jesus could never fall into temptation and never grieve her by wrong-doing, but she knew that His holy life was shielded from early death,—that He could not be removed from her, until the great work was done for which His Father had sent Him into the world. One dark cloud of a parent's heart was thus absent from her dwelling.

In describing His Boyhood, I have previously pictured to you His going up all alone to the familiar hills around His home. In His after life, as we shall come to find, He often liked to go to "solitary places apart:" especially to the green mountains round the Lake of Tiberias where, away from everybody, He prayed to His great and kind Father. He must often have done the same now. When the day's work was over, He would love by these little water-courses to ascend the breezy hills around Nazareth and speak face to face with God.

I have sometimes thought, also, that a number of striking images which Jesus used in His teaching in after life, may have been gathered during those quiet years in His Galilean home.

Do you ask me what I mean?

Well, do you remember one story He tells about *a Shepherd* going away on the hills, after a wandering sheep, never resting till he had recovered it, and 'when he had found it,' he carried it upon his shoulders, and brought it back safe to the fold? Jesus, whether now or in earlier boyhood, may have seen some such shepherd, as the daylight was fading on the hills of Galilee. The fold was low down in the valley, and the flock of sheep were lying peacefully on their green pastures. But that shepherd heard a lost sheep bleating far up among the rocks. He thought of the sharp flints that would cut its feet, and the night-winds that would howl around it, and the wild beasts that might devour it; so, with his crook in his hand, he was seen mounting from rock to rock, and from hill to hill, crossing a stream here and some rough stones there. He never heeded the darkness of night, nor the howl of the wolf, nor the sword of the robber. Perhaps early the next morning, from some thyme-covered height to which the Divine Youth had gone for meditation and prayer, that shepherd was seen coming down the opposite hill slope, and calling out to those who were watching him from below—" *Rejoice with me, for I have found my sheep which was lost* " (Luke xv. 3–6).

Or do you remember another story, about a man who " built his house upon the sand ; " and about another man who " built his house on the rock ? " On an autumn evening when He was on the slope of one of these hills above the village, Jesus may have seen some one with spade and axe, plane and saw and hammer, erecting a cottage for himself. But the man, thus busy, had made choice of a wrong piece of ground. If he had been wise he would have cut down some vines that were trailing over a hard

"He was in the world, and the world was made by Him, and the world knew Him not." John i. 10.

page 86

bit of rock, and built his house securely there; but he had never thought of a storm coming on, or rain washing his work away; so he foolishly built his house on the loose sand, and made the house itself of soft clay. All at once, the black clouds gathered over the hills—there was not a rift where blue could be seen in the sky. The thunder rolled; heavy torrents of rain fell; and, rushing along the hill slope in great wild streams, they carried the sand and moist earth away: the clay dwelling came down, and was a mass of ruin. Whereas his neighbour, who had begun to build at the very same time, either raised his new cottage on a foundation of big stones, or he had dug deep till he came to the solid limestone. When the same storm broke in the sky, and the little rills, swollen into rivulets, came foaming down, they did no harm to the man's house *"for it was founded upon a Rock"* (Matt. vii. 24-27).

Or to take another of these nature-pictures. For many days or weeks in autumn, there had only been a little red in the morning sky just about sunrise; the rest of the day or days it was wet and misty and gloomy. But one evening Jesus may have been on the top of the cliff above Nazareth, watching a beautiful sunset towards the distant shores of Tyre, over the Mediterranean Sea. The sky all at once broke, and became aglow; the fleecy clouds were tinged with ruby; the very fringe of yellow sand on the seaside seemed of a fiery colour, as it caught the tint of the heavens. The sun seemed as if he went asleep on a pillow of crimson, with crimson curtains around him. Then, when that sun had gone down, and the glow had faded, out came clusters of bright stars in the clear blue sky; and the next morning when Jesus awoke, not a dank mist or drizzling rain but a golden light was streaming through the lattice,—this continuing day after day for many weeks together. Might it not be when He called to mind afterwards some such picture as this that He said *" When it is evening, ye say, it will be fair weather; for the sky is red: and in the morning, it will be foul weather to-day; for the sky is red and lowring"* (Matt. xvi. 2, 3).

These and similar other scenes; the flash of the lightning

—the roll of the thunder—the bursting of the green buds in spring—the woman losing her piece of money, and with lighted candle sweeping the house till she found it—the games of the children in the open market-place, or by the village fountain, may possibly now have come at different times before the eyes of Jesus; He stored them in His mind and made use of them afterwards in teaching the people.

This, young reader, has been the description of a bright and happy Youth and Manhood. Yet I cannot close this chapter without telling you that, happy as that home was, Jesus had His trials to bear. His own kinsmen, these same brethren and cousins, seemed to be jealous of Him, and some of the people of the village were rough and rude to Him. He is spoken of in the Song of Solomon, as "*a lily among thorns.*" How true! This beautiful snow-white Lily, from the Garden of Heaven, grew up in the earthly valley of Nazareth. But wicked people, like those hard and prickly thorns so often to be seen in Palestine,—harsh and cruel friends, hated Him for His goodness, and spoke unkindly to Him. He would perhaps have felt it His duty, when He saw them acting unjustly or dishonestly, or when He heard them uttering harsh, or impure, or malicious words, to raise His protest, —bravely yet graciously to tell them of their faults;—and just because of the faithfulness of His reproofs they would treat Him with unfeeling severity.

Yet I am quite sure of this, that He would not pay them back with the same. The thorn might pierce or the clouds might darken, but the Lily lost none of its whiteness or purity. I think I hear Him saying only one thing in return for all their harshness. It was the same beautiful utterance which came from His lips long after,—"*Father, forgive them, for they know not what they do.*"

It would be unfair, however, not to add, that with others in Nazareth it was doubtless different. Goodness and gentleness and meekness in the eyes of those whose good opinion is worth having, are always attractive. Love begets love in generous natures. "Why does everybody love you?" was the question put to Philip Doddridge's daughter. The reply was, " Because I love everybody." It must have been so in a higher sense with Jesus. Among the best of His companions and fellow-villagers He could not fail to be a favourite. He "increased in favour," we read, not only with God, but with man. The word " increased " would seem to denote that even those who were disposed at first to be unkind to Him, had their envy and jealousy disarmed as they became more and more familiar with His gracious character,—as they marked His growing intelligence—His unselfish ways—His stainless purity in thought, word, and deed. They saw in His very countenance, in His eye, and in His smile, the index of the lofty loving soul within. So that we may believe that the coldness and reserve shown for a time by many towards Him, were gradually exchanged for esteem and admiration.

This, at all events, we do know, that whatever was the case with man, " *He increased in favour with* GOD " (Luke ii. 52). This may seem at first a strange thing to say. If Jesus were the quite Perfect, Holy, Loving One we have represented Him to be —without so much as a flaw or speck of sin or frailty in His nature—how could He be said to 'grow' or 'increase' in favour? Is it possible for a thing or a Being that is *perfect* to increase in perfection?

I answer by giving you an illustration from the emblem of the lily, which we have just employed. Some of you may have seen, not the common Lily of the Valley, but one of those magnificent plants which the gardener regards as the pride of his hothouse, called the Lily of Japan, or the Lily of the Nile. When the pure virgin white leaves are beginning to open, the natural exclamation is " How perfectly beautiful!" There is no spot or blemish upon them to mar their early loveliness. But day by day, as the petals grow and expand, the singular beauty of the flower becomes more and more manifest. It is viewed with increasing interest. That beauty was in one sense 'perfect,' when the pure new-born white bud was resting in its earliest cradle of long green leaves. But what was the perfection of this bud, compared to that of the large massive cup to which it grew (more delicate than the finest porcelain) poised on its tall and graceful stem. Jesus was spoken of as " growing up before God as a tender plant." This " Plant of Renown " was really and truly *perfect* at His birth as " the Holy Child Jesus." But as the lovely graces of His human nature became more manifest day by day,—the white leaves of gentleness and meekness, unselfishness and submission,—might not that true " Lily of the Valley " (Sol. Song ii. 1) be said to " increase in favour with God " ? God " saw the light that it was good " at early dawn ; but He regarded it with a deeper complacency as it shone " more and more unto the *perfect day*." The Dayspring of childhood deepened into youth—the tender Morning light of youth deepened into the full Noontide glory of manhood, till His holy soul, like His countenance, described in after years, was " as the sun shineth in his strength."

Thus, then, had the Meek and Lowly Jesus lived for thirty years a life of seclusion and silence, without any signs, by miracle or otherwise, of the Divinity which was within Him, or of the greatness which was yet to be revealed. His human body was the sacred sanctuary in which Deity dwelt. The silence of these years reminds us of what is said of the Temple of Jerusalem, which was a type of Him—" *There was neither hammer nor axe, nor any tool of iron, heard in the house while it was in building* " (1 Kings vi. 7).

> " No workman's steel, no pond'rous axes rung,
> Like some tall palm the noiseless fabric sprung."

And yet, all the greatness and glory and pomp of the world, were nothing in real interest to what these thirty years had witnessed in that quiet Village of Galilee. Rome had risen to the height of her splendour. She bore the proud eagle on her standards. That eagle may be said to have winged its flight to every region of the globe, and planted its iron claws on the prostrate nations. But what was that bird of Roman conquest and victory compared to the Divine Dove of Peace that was nestling, unknown and unheeded, amid the rock-cliffs of Nazareth? The eagle carried nothing on its rushing wings but terror and death. The Dove from the Ark of Heaven was to carry the olive branch to the remotest bounds of the earth and to the latest ages of time.

MERIDIAN BRIGHTNESS.

"THEN SPAKE JESUS UNTO THEM, SAYING, 'I AM THE LIGHT OF THE WORLD: HE THAT FOLLOWETH ME SHALL NOT WALK IN DARKNESS, BUT SHALL HAVE THE LIGHT OF LIFE.'"—JOHN VIII. 12.

"IN THEM HATH HE SET A TABERNACLE FOR THE SUN; WHICH IS AS A BRIDEGROOM COMING OUT OF HIS CHAMBER, AND REJOICETH AS A STRONG MAN TO RUN A RACE. HIS GOING FORTH IS FROM THE END OF THE HEAVEN, AND HIS CIRCUIT UNTO THE ENDS OF IT: AND THERE IS NOTHING HID FROM THE HEAT THEREOF."—PS. XIX. 4-6.

"AT MID-DAY, O KING, I SAW IN THE WAY A LIGHT FROM HEAVEN, ABOVE THE BRIGHTNESS OF THE SUN, SHINING ROUND ABOUT ME."—ACTS XXVI. 13.

"WHEN THE FULNESS OF THE TIME WAS COME, GOD SENT FORTH HIS SON."—GAL. IV. 4.

"AND JESUS HIMSELF BEGAN TO BE ABOUT THIRTY YEARS OF AGE."—LUKE III. 23

XI.

He goes to the Jordan and is Baptized.

JESUS leaves His home to begin His public ministry.

To use the words of a great German writer (Schlegel), " we have traced the obscure rise of an almost imperceptible point of Light from which the whole modern world was to spring." We have now to watch the Sun of Righteousness coming forth " as a Bridegroom out of His chamber ; " ascending above the hills of Judah and Galilee, and gradually attaining His MERIDIAN glory and strength.

He left Nazareth ; but not to forget it. It is surely a touching thought that *the Saviour remembers Nazareth in Heaven!* He said to Paul when the persecutor was struck down by a light " above the brightness of the sun," " I AM JESUS OF *Nazareth.*"

This may not be an unsuitable place for a few remarks on a subject in which most, if not all, of my young readers will naturally feel interested : I mean the outward appearance of Christ, now that He had attained to manhood.

I cannot, however, give you any reliable information. The sacred narrative, as we have seen, tells us that He had increased, not only " in Wisdom," but " in Stature." It tells us no more. There are some baseless traditions about pictures and statues of Jesus made in the time of the Apostles. Among other legends is one that His portrait was painted by St. Luke, the writer of the third Gospel. The most famous of these alleged pictures dates to the fourth century. It is known as that of Edessa, and is specially mentioned by a devout Father of the Church, John of Damascus. Though a few of the early Christian writers entertain a different view, it may, perhaps, be lawful for us to take our ideal impression of the Divine Human countenance from this representation. It shows the Lord " in the bloom of youthful power and beauty, with high and open forehead, clear eyes, parted hair, and an auburn beard." He is otherwise described as being, like His Virgin mother, pale, with an expression that betokened wisdom, majesty, and meekness,—His hazel-coloured hair flowing over His shoulders. We know well, there are many people truly loving and beloved, who have no beauty of countenance; and we know, on the other hand, that there are those who have outer beauty of face who are without the far higher beauty of goodness and gentleness and kindness. But do not all these ideas, which seem to have been followed by the religious painters of the Middle Ages, accord with the slight touches which are given in the Holy Bible, as well as with what our sanctified thoughts picture Him to have been. "*His head is as the most fine gold*" (Sol. Song v. 11); "*His countenance is as Lebanon, excellent as the cedars*" (verse 15). No two things among the Hebrews formed such types of beauty, as the fine gold of Ophir and the cedar-trees of Mount Lebanon. He is spoken of farther as "*The King in His beauty,*" "*Fairer than the children of men,*" "*Full of grace and truth,*" "*The chiefest among ten thousand . . . altogether lovely.*" Of Him who was "BRIGHTER THAN THE SUN," St. Jerome says, "The majesty of Godhead shone in His face."

At the time we have now reached, Jesus was thirty years old. It was the age among the Jews when the young Scribes got the sanction of their Rabbis to go out and teach. These aged instructors were then wont to lay their hands on their successors and say, "I admit thee to the chair of the Scribe." Thirty years had passed since the angels had sung His birth-song, and the Wise men had been guided to His manger by the silver lamp in the starry heavens. His mother then was a Young maiden of Galilee: now she was the Matron of middle life. Her countenance would be marked with lines of deep anxiety and care.

Perhaps the thought may occur, were any of the Shepherds of the Plains of Bethlehem still alive who had been guided to His manger-cradle? If so, must they not have wondered at hearing nothing more of the wondrous life of the Divine Babe? Would not the anthem of the Heavenly host thirty years ago, by this time appear to have been a mere vision which they had mistaken for a reality? May we not, however, suppose that some among them would still cling to the firm belief that the hour of His "showing unto Israel" was only delayed, and that the Dayspring from on high would in God's own time surely visit them? Perhaps, again and again, at night, when out with their flocks in the same fields, they may have listened for some new songburst from the starry sky! Yes, you humble, trusting, faithful watchers on the hills of Judah! hope on, and trust on; for He whom you have so long served is about to fulfil His own promise—"*The Lord is good unto them that wait for Him.*" They would, perhaps, remember the words of one of their own prophets—"*For the vision is yet for an appointed time, but at the end it shall speak, and not lie: though it tarry, wait for it; because it will surely come, it will not tarry*" (Hab. ii. 3). "*Unto you that fear my name* SHALL THE SUN OF RIGHTEOUSNESS *arise.*"

Zacharias and Elisabeth, Simeon and Anna, must now have been in their graves. To them had only been given the privilege of seeing the Early Dawn, not the glories of the Risen Sun.

An officer named Pontius Pilate was now Governor of Judea.

That is always a sad day when any youth among ourselves bids farewell for the first time to his father and mother's home. His parents and brothers and sisters never forget the hour they follow him down the road till he is lost from their sight, or as they receive a last wave of his hand when the vessel is leaving the pier, taking him away to a far country.

With all reverence we say, it could not be different at present with Mary and Jesus. Her Divine Son indeed was no longer a Youth, but He had never till now finally quitted the roof under which He had been so long nurtured. Oh how could that loving mother help feeling, and feeling deeply, when He, who had been far kinder to her than all earthly relations or friends, was about to leave her? He had put aside for ever the workshop and tools;—cleared away the last planks of pine and cedar; and with His scrip and sandals and pilgrim staff, He prepares for what they both well knew was, so far as "a Home" is concerned, His farewell to Nazareth.

Many a day would she think of the empty seat at the table—the silent bench, the absent footstep, the withdrawn voice. But the Heavenly "Father's business" was more to Him and to her than any earthly parent's love. I think I hear mother and Son exchanging with one another the word which at such times was common among the Jews, but they would say it now with more than wonted tenderness—" *Peace be with thee ;* " or, as on the old fields of Boaz, " *The Lord be with* THEE "—" *The Lord bless* THEE ! " I think I see Mary mounting the outside stair leading to the housetop, and there watching Jesus, proceeding first along the winding streets, then up the ascending foot-road,—His form growing less and less, till it was lost from her sight in the distant valley. Perhaps she would, through her tears, call to mind her own divine song and anew sing it, " *My soul doth magnify the Lord, and my spirit hath rejoiced in God my Saviour.*"

When Jesus left Nazareth it was winter (the time of our month of February), when the trees were in early bud, and the young corn was showing its first green. Sometimes there are heavy rains at that season, but sometimes, too, the days are bright with sunshine and even warm.

Whither does He go?

There is a great valley in the Holy Land of a very remarkable kind. It is like a deep seam or fissure cleft in the middle of the country. Through this strange narrow valley a swift river rushes (which you know well by name), with rocks and trees, sandbanks and hills, on each side of it. It is the Valley of the Jordan. The river, " The Descender " as it may well be called from the number of its falls and rapids, is fed first of all by the melting snows of giant Hermon. It enters the reedy Lake Merom. Then passing through the Sea of Tiberias, of which you will hear more by-and-by, it flows, after many turnings, through jungles of tamarisk and willow into the Dead Sea. The shores of this sea are naked and dreary and barren. I have seen great logs and branches of wood brought down by the rapid stream, lying on the beach, quite white with the salt, and very bitter when put to the lips. It is extremely hot all around; the hottest air I ever breathed was there. There is neither cloud nor shadow, but a fierce fiery dazzling glare. No wonder, however, it is so stifling, for this "Asphaltite Lake" is no less than 1300 feet below the level of the ocean.

Somewhere in the Jordan Valley, and at some open place on the banks of the river, was a ford called Bethabara, which means "the House of Passage." On its eastern side, at this time, a great crowd gathered day after day. They were collected from all parts of the land. Numbers seem especially to have come from Jerusalem by the dreary, rugged road which led down to Jericho, and where the man of the Gospel parable fell among thieves. All kinds of people, too, seemed to be among the assemblage: old and young, rich and poor, fathers and children, soldiers with helmets on their heads and swords dangling at their sides: wild Arabs with their spears, and shepherds with their crooks: sailors from Joppa: fishermen from the Sea of Galilee: ragged beggars from the streets and waysides: peasants from their vineyards: tradesmen from their workshops: mothers with little infants in their arms.

What do you think has taken them there; or who do you suppose they have gone all that way to see and to hear?

It is the great Prophet of the Desert, the famous JOHN THE BAPTIST. There had been no "Seer" among the Jews for 400 years: not since the days of Malachi. We need not wonder, then, when a prophet was said again to have appeared, that there was a mighty stir throughout the land, and that many came long distances to listen to this new 'voice crying in the wilderness.'

John was the son of Elisabeth, Mary's cousin; the same cousin she went to see at Hebron. He must have been six months older than Jesus. I believe both John's father and mother were now dead. He was, therefore, an orphan; he had neither parents, nor brother nor sister. If he had wished, he might have become a priest like his father, wore the priestly garments, offered sacrifices and burned incense. But he chose to serve God in the great Temple of Nature, rather than in the Temple of Jerusalem.

Let me tell you something more about him. His face was browned with the sun. Long shaggy hair, which had not been cut for thirty years, hung down his back. He did not wear even the cloak striped with blue which the poorest peasants possessed. A coarse rough camel's hide was flung over his shoulders, and tied round his waist. That girdle was often made of linen and wrought with thread of gold and silver; but a piece of untanned leather—a rope of skin—was all that fastened John's clothing. So wild and strange did he appear to some, that they thought he must be mad and possessed with a demon;—"they say he hath a devil" (Matt. xi. 18). He was a man who cared nothing at all about comfort. Although, as a child, he had lived among the smiling vineyards of Hebron, near where the famous grapes of Eschol grew, he had now no house to live in—no one to spread his couch, or cook his food. He ate the wild fruits and roots gathered in the woods around, and the wild honey which the bees had stored in holes of the rock. The only animal sustenance he allowed himself (if we can call it so) was locusts. These, however, I may tell you, formed no uncommon or strange meal to the children of the desert. Locusts prepared for food, steeped in brine and dried in the sun, find, indeed, their way at this day to the bazaars and markets of many Eastern cities, and are there purchased by the poor. The traveller Burckhardt tells us he had himself seen "locust shops" in some Arabian towns. More than that, in one of the Nineveh marbles, locusts are represented as being carried by servants to the royal table, though, doubtless, served up under a more dainty form than the desert fare of the Baptist. He dwelt, likely, in some hut made of leaves, or, perhaps, in one of the caves which were common there. Josephus speaks of a man of the name of Banus with whom he himself lived for three years in the same wilderness. This hermit's manner of life may describe to us what John's was. "He used no other clothing than grew upon trees; and had no other food except that which grew of its own accord; and bathed himself often in cold water, both by day and night." The Baptist,

I need hardly say, was very brave. There were lions and leopards and hyenas, down in some places of the Jordan jungle, among the tall canes which line its banks, but their roaring during these long nights did not frighten him. He made his couch and pillow the turf. The swift Jordan, with its thicket of reeds, was at his side, and the beautiful clear bright stars were above him. He was all alone in these hours of darkness. And yet he felt he was not alone, for the Great God of Abraham was with him. Having the fear of this good and gracious Jehovah, he had no other fear. You remember Solomon says, " The righteous are bold as a lion " (Prov. xxviii. 1). And when the gloom of the night was over, and the sun again shone out on the white cliffs of the river, he would go forth from his leafy dwelling, in order to speak all day long to the vast crowds who were waiting for him. I may just further remark that it must have been somewhere amid the mysterious mountains behind, that the man so like him in character—the great Elijah—went up to heaven in his chariot of fire.

What was the subject of the Baptist's address? It was about the sins of those who had come to hear him. But observe, his appeals were not about sin in general. He spoke to each individually about their own particular faults and failings,—the servant, the soldier, the Publican, the Pharisee, the Sadducee. He cried aloud over and over again, with the fire of truth and earnestness in his eye, " REPENT, REPENT." He spoke of " *the wrath to come*," and told them to flee from it.

He might well thus preach to those present, yes, and millions beyond hearing of his voice; for as I previously told you, never perhaps were the inhabitants of the world more wicked than they were then : kings and queens and princes; priests and nobles; masters and servants; I fear even youth and children. And the worst was, that people such as many of those John was addressing, did not *feel* how sinful they were. Their hearts were as hard and rocky as the stones of the Jordan lying at their feet. The Baptist, who had been brought up by a holy mother, was glad to get away from the towns and cities where this evil and wickedness specially abounded. He could bear a cheerless hut, and the cold night, and the dewy grass, and the winter rain; but he could not bear to live among those whose lives were lives of iniquity. I have just said, he was a bold man and not given to tears, but I almost think, from the strong words used, that he must have wept at times now, as he spoke of this evil that was around him, and which he hated so much.

He tried to make those he exhorted sorry for their faults. Perhaps, at the moment he was speaking, he heard, in the dense forests around him, the ringing axe of the woodman cutting down a dead tree or lopping its branches. He told them that the nation of the Jews—once "a holy nation," had become like useless trees about to be levelled to the ground, and cast into the fire.

That crowd, on the patches of green grass by the river side, never took their eyes for a moment off the speaker. With what silence they all listened! Look at yon soldier. He is trembling as he never did before in the hour of battle! Look at yon shepherd! so interested is he, he has almost forgotten the flock of sheep he had just brought across the river, and was driving to the Temple for sacrifices. Look at yon Publican!—the collector of the Roman taxes—how his conscience is roused within him as the speaker brings to his remembrance his greed and lying, his cheating and oppression. Look at yon old man and these young men too—the tears are starting to their eyes, as he speaks of *the fan* and *the axe*, *the chaff* and *the burning*.

"*What shall I do?*" cried one. "*What shall we do?*" cried a group of others. It will remind you, perhaps, of another scene in a future year, when a gaoler, with a flaming torch in his hand, sprang into the cell of two chained prisoners, and called out, in deep agony of soul,—"*Sirs! what must I do to be saved?*" (Acts xvi. 30).

But John told the stricken listeners around him joyful news also. When he lifted up his voice, and cried "*Repent! Repent!*" he added, "*The Kingdom of Heaven is at hand.*" The river that rolled by had been, several times in the past, the silent spectator of the Power of God: and it would ere long, "see greater things than these." The Dead Sea—the Sea of Death—with its sullen waters, was within sight of where John stood. But he came to proclaim '*The Life;*' to reveal to thirsty souls the Fountain of Living waters. "*In* HIM *was life, and the Life was* THE LIGHT *of men.*" Oh happy tidings for many heavy, weary, broken hearts that were listening to him! So stirring were the Baptist's words, and so famous had he become throughout all the land, that a great number began to wonder whether he was not himself, either the Prophet Elijah come to life again, or else the promised Messiah! 'Can this,' they said to one another, 'be Elias? or, better still, can he be the Great King at last arrived to destroy the hated Roman and set up the throne of King David, and live in the palace of Zion?' "*All men mused in their hearts of John, whether he were the Christ or not.*"

John was so humble, he could not bear the thought of being thus mistaken for either; and especially mistaken for Jesus. He tells them, 'No! You must not for a moment think that I am He.' He came indeed "in the spirit and power of Elias." But you remember in the "Drama of the desert," when that Prophet beheld from his cave 'the earthquake, and the wind, and the fire;'—these were only to prepare him for listening to "the still small voice." So it was with John. His preaching was the thunder and storm, preceding the calm and the brightness. "He was the Prophet of the Highest." He was only a night-watchman sent to rouse the sleepers, and announce the Risen SUN. Or, to use his own more forcible comparison, when they pressed him, and said 'Tell us, then, who you are?' he answered that he was only like one who ran before and told the people of another 'Mightier than he,' who was coming.

I remember, when in Cairo, seeing some finely-formed black Nubian boys, running before the carriages of the nobles and rich men. They held a long silver wand in their hands as they cleared the way in the crowded streets. John likens himself to such a runner; his voice calling out and "preparing the way of the Lord." He was only the Servant and Herald of the Great King;

not the King himself. "*Behold*," said God by His servant Malachi, "*I will send my messenger, and he shall prepare Thy way before Thee.*" John tells the crowd around him that there was One at hand, "the latchet of whose shoes he was not worthy to stoop down and unloose." Beautiful indeed is his humility! I have often seen in the Alps, in early morning (and there is no sight in nature grander), the snowy peaks tinted with gold, before the orb of the sun is seen. So bright are these pinnacles, you might almost mistake them for the sun itself. But not so. They only tell that the sun is close at hand, and that he will soon be seen. John was like these flaming mountain tops, catching the glow of the coming SUN. "*He was not that Light: but was sent to bear witness of that Light. That was* THE TRUE LIGHT *which lighteth every man that cometh into the world.*" "John," says Augustine, "was *a* light enlightened, but not the Enlightening Life in himself." He who was 'Brighter than the sun,' was about to baptize (if such a figure can be used) with His own divine radiance. "*He shall baptize you with the Holy Ghost and with* FIRE."

Look now, at this great and good Prophet! He is, perhaps, standing on a ledge of rock near the edge of the river, possibly on one of the stepping-stones of the ford. The river at this time of the year must have been full, after the winter rains, and the water would, doubtless, be as I saw it; not clear as we are apt to think the stream of the Jordan to be, but thick, muddy, and yellow with the soil brought down from the hills. First one and then another of those who have been listening to him draw near. They plunge in, and then go on shore again. He baptizes them in the Jordan, after they have "confessed their sins." Their submitting to the baptism of water, was an outward sign or token that they were not only ready to confess their sins, but to forsake them. John by this outward act taught them the great truth, that just as water washes and makes clean the body, so God likes nothing so much as the pure white heart; and that unless they had these clean hearts, they could not be ready to welcome the Great Messiah.

Did all the crowd thus confess their sins and have the sacramental water poured on their heads?

No. Some were very proud and haughty. They said to John, 'We have no need to confess anything. We do not require this water baptism of yours. We are not blind heathen Gentiles, seeking admission among the Holy Nation. We are the chosen people. "We have Abraham for our Father." We are "children of the Covenant."'

John tells them, in his own plain, earnest way, that being the children of Abraham, and having the Patriarch's blood in their veins, will be of no avail without holy hearts and holy lives. "Do *works*," says he, "*meet for repentance.*" He points to the large stones in the channel of the river or lining its shore, and he says, 'If you refuse to be holy and loving and good;—if you will not make your hearts ready to receive the coming King, God is able from these dumb rocks and stones to raise up those who will glorify His Son, and who will be called His children. He can make the very stones cry out "*Hosannah to the Son of David!*"'

But who is this approaching from the crowd towards the stream? He does not look different from the others. They take no notice of Him. They make no way for Him. He is a young man in plain peasants' dress.

It is none other than the meek and lowly JESUS! He has made out His journey from far off Nazareth. If the others do not know Him, that Man of God standing on the ledge of rock does.

The mother of the Baptist had, doubtless, often told him in their house at Hebron about his own earthly relative, the Child of Nazareth: about His wondrous birth, unlike all others: about the songs of the Angels in the Plains of Bethlehem: about His holy and beautiful young life.

I do not know if we have any reason to suppose that John and Jesus, though cousins, had often met before. They may have done so at the Passover or other Feasts. But Nazareth and Hebron were otherwise far distant. God would, however, seem at this moment to have flashed, in all its fulness, the great truth on John's soul—that the long-wished-for moment had come, and that he was in the presence of his Great Lord. The Satellite felt and owned the glory of the Parent SUN!

When Jesus comes forward and asks the Baptist to sprinkle water on His head, or to dip Him in the stream, the rough-clad Preacher starts back and says, "No; I am not worthy to baptize Thee. I have rather need to be baptized at Thy hands!"

John had just been speaking in loud, stern tones to the guilty, hard-hearted sinners flocking around. But at the sight of his divine Redeemer his voice becomes low and soft, sweet and tender as that of a little child.

Jesus would not let him say 'No.' He said, "*Let it be so now; I must fulfil all righteousness.*"

There is something surely very wonderful, very touching, about this humility of the Saviour. At the baptism of a royal prince on earth, what preparations are made. The event is announced weeks before. When the day arrives, crowds line the way to cathedral or chapel. Under a fretted roof, and with a gush of music, the marble font or golden basin is surrounded by a privileged throng, and the solemn rite dispensed. How different with the Prince of the Kings of the Earth! No crowds of interested spectators line the river banks. No gorgeous rites take place in Zion's Temple. No purple robe or kingly badge mark Him out from the multitude. He dips His foot in the rushing river, just like the others, a Pilgrim among pilgrims, unnoted and unknown. "*He was in the world, and the world was made by Him, and the world knew Him not!*"

Just as John and He were together coming up out of the water, and as the drops of the stream were trickling down the head of the Saviour, there seemed to be a rift or opening in the heavens above them. Jesus, we are specially told, was at the moment '*praying.*' The Holy Spirit, in the form of a dove, comes down and hovers over the head of Him who had just been baptized, or perhaps alights upon it; and far up in the deep blue sky a voice seemed to speak. They listened. It was the voice of God the Father; the same Father with whom Jesus had often held communion on the hills of Nazareth. I do not know whether the crowd listened to the voice. I think likely it was meant only for John. At all events, he heard it saying, "*This is* MY BELOVED SON, *in whom I am well pleased.*"

The Divine Father speaks, the Divine Son prays, the Divine Spirit descends in visible shape. It is the Blessed Trinity revealed in the opening act of the great ministry. The Holy Three in One in covenant for the world's salvation.

Some who read these words may be ready to ask, and I do not wonder, 'Was it not a very strange thing for the Holy Jesus to be baptized at all? We thought that baptism was only for a sinner; that it spoke of the need of having sin washed away, and of the heart being made clean? This could not surely be in any sense true of the Saviour. How could He who never transgressed require to be dealt with just as the vilest and basest of that crowd at the Jordan, and to have the water of the river sprinkled on His sacred head?'

I have already given you the reply of Jesus Himself, when John seems to have felt the same astonishment. But I have another answer. Jesus, although He had no sins of His own, came into the world in the sinner's room and in the sinner's stead. He took your iniquities and mine upon Him. Holy and harmless Himself, He was reckoned and dealt with in the eye of the law as if He had been a sinner. I do not know any better reply to your question than the words of the Apostle Paul, which you will find in 2 Cor. v. 21. He would almost seem, as he wrote them, to have been looking at Jesus standing in the channel of the Jordan and receiving a sinner's rite at a sinner's hands. "*For He hath made Him to be sin for us, who knew no sin; that we might be made the righteousness of God in Him.*"

XII.

He goes to the Mount of Temptation.

A MYSTERIOUS cloud gathers around THE SUN OF RIGHTEOUSNESS just when beginning to shine in His meridian brightness. It reminds us of a verse in Isaiah, "*The sun shall be darkened in his going forth*" (Isa. xiii. 10).

Immediately after the Baptism of Jesus, perhaps before there had been time for the great news to be whispered through the crowd, He silently withdraws Himself. Whither can He have gone? Now that His Father has proclaimed Him to be "His Beloved Son:" can it be to Jerusalem to be proclaimed on Mount Zion King of the Jews?

No. It is *to be tempted of the devil* for forty days in the wilderness!

I cannot exactly tell you to what particular place He resorted. I remember when on the banks of the river Jordan, and looking up to the hills both on the right and on the left, I felt sure it must have been to one or other side He went. If it was to the left, which is perhaps the more likely, oh, in what an arid cheerless desolate desert He had lived! It is all white with limestone, and has very little of anything green in it, save some stunted bushes. I do not think there is such wild and bleak scenery in the world. Even the ruts or channels in the hillsides, where you expect to see water, are dry, and filled up with big stones and burning sand.

The "Palestine Explorers" have not long ago visited this '*Quarantana*,' as it is called, or in Arabic '*Kuruntul*.' They describe the view from the highest part as magnificent. The Jordan and its great plain; the mountains beyond; the Dead Sea and the Wilderness of Judea, round to the Mount of Olives.

How Jesus spent that awful time we are not told. Probably

"*And was with the wild beasts*" (Mark i. 13)

in mountain caves or holes of the rocks. There were no roads, no houses, no human voice to cheer the solitude—no fold of a shepherd, because no flocks could live on such blighted pastures, —no sound of stream, no hum of insect, or song of bird.

St. Mark tells us that "*He was with the wild beasts.*"—(Mark i. 13.) It is plain, however, that, wild and fierce as their natures were, they did not harm Him. They rather seem, as in our opposite picture, to have lain submissive at His feet, as if they had felt He was not their foe, but their Friend.

You may recall one of childhood's favourite stories, whether it be truth or fable, of "*Androcles and the Lion,*" or "*The power of kindness.*" This gentle, yet brave fugitive, who had escaped from human oppressors, was said to have extracted a thorn from the foot of a lion he found one day writhing in agony in the depths of the forest into which he himself had taken refuge. Thus instantly relieved of pain, the savage animal seemed to forget its wild instincts, and gradually became the companion of the lonely man's solitude. Months after, so the tale farther narrates, Androcles, captured by his foes, was taken to the arena to be torn by wild beasts. A monster, selected for the cruel sport, bounded into the amphitheatre. But instead, as the gazing crowd expected, of seeing him rend the victim in pieces, he crouched at the feet of his old benefactor, and licked his naked body in silent token of gratitude.

I may add a similar anecdote of recent date. On the woody top of Tabor, another hill in the Holy Land, a Russian hermit, not many years ago, lived in a cave. He was a kind and good man. One winter day a panther, with beautiful spots on its skin, came close to his secluded home. He looked fondly at it without manifesting fear, and threw it a piece of bread. It soon became quite tame. Ever after the panther lived with him; and the graceful creature was seen wherever the hermit went, keeping by his side, or following him like a dog all over the mountain.[1] If this were the result of such treatment by ordinary mortals, I

---

[1] See "Egyptian Sepulchres and Syrian Shrines," vol. ii. p. 59.

can quite believe how the wild animals in the Judean desert would show no fury of any sort to the only sinless One, the Kindest of the kind,—" Holy, *Harmless.*" At all events, in the case of a Greater than Daniel, God would shut every lion's mouth so that they might not hurt His dear Son.

But I have already told you of a far worse enemy He had to contend with, than even the fiercest lions and wolves. It was the Arch-enemy of God and man. Satan was allowed to meet Jesus in that stony desert and to *tempt* Him. The same dark spirit who had caused Adam and Eve to fall from their happy state in Eden, came and used all his wiles to make the Second Adam sin.

We know not in what shape the devil appeared. Whether as a wayworn pilgrim; or as a hermit from one of the caves around; or in demon-form, as a prince of darkness; or in the guise of a heavenly visitant—an angel of light. But what hours these must have been! He who was all Pure meeting him who was all impure. He who was all Light meeting him who was all darkness!

It would take too long to describe the succession of wicked thoughts the great adversary sought to put into the heart of the Holy One. I would, however, like to make three remarks about these temptations.

First, Satan did all he could to shake Jesus' trust in God, and make Him doubt his Father's love.

Just think of some one coming to you, who love your earthly father much, and seek to please him in every way you can; imagine some such wicked person trying to get you to distrust him—to doubt his care, and to do what you know would be quite contrary to his wishes. More than this: putting words into your father's lips which he never said, and perhaps offering you rich and beautiful presents and bribes if you would do something that would displease and dishonour the parent you reverence.

Such, but in a far more dreadful form, were the awful temptations which Satan offered to Jesus to forget and forsake and distrust that Better than the best of all earthly parents, the Father who had been so gracious to Him; and to whom on the other hand He had been so dutiful and obedient.

The *second* thing I would note is, that he chose for his terrible assault what he knew would be the time of Jesus' greatest bodily weakness. It was at the *close* of the forty days' fast, when the Son of God was hungry and faint and weary. For you must remember all that time Jesus had tasted nothing. There was no Brook Cherith to slake His thirst; no ravens, as in the case of the lonely Prophet of a former age, to fetch Him bread, morning and evening.

And the *third* thing I would like to point out is, that the Saviour in His replies quotes in every case *a verse of Scripture.* He fought the Great enemy of mankind with "*the Sword of the Spirit, which is the Word of God.*" Not only so—but it is well worthy of note that all His answers are from that special portion of the Book of Deuteronomy which, as I have previously explained, Jewish children were in the habit of learning by heart. Reminding us surely what a good thing it is to have the words of the Holy Bible so laid up in our memories, that when the hour of temptation comes, we may be ready, as Jesus was, to meet every assault with a Bible weapon. Three times Jesus was tempted; and three times over He says, "No, I shall not do what you bid Me; for "It is written"! "*It is written!*" "IT IS WRITTEN."

Though the Prince of this world came, he found nothing in Him. Jesus loved His Father too much to listen to the Evil One. The Tempter saw how vain it was to try and make Him sin. There are spots on the sun; but there were no spots in the holy human nature of Him who is "BRIGHTER THAN THE SUN." So the devil left Him at last, and went away to his own wicked abode, among his own wicked spirits, those "wandering stars to whom is reserved the blackness of darkness for ever."

Then, we are told, angels came and ministered unto Jesus. They would likely bring Him food to eat and water to drink. They would spread a couch of repose in the lonely desert, and hover over it as He slept, and comfort Him above all things with the thought, that He had done His Heavenly Father's will.

How glad the Holy Son of God would be when He came down at last from those white jagged rocks to the Plain of Jordan, and was once more close to His loved friend and earthly relative John the Baptist!

You see, young readers, how soon in His public life Jesus was sent to the school of trial and temptation. Perhaps you may recall a verse which speaks about these lessons which were taught Him of suffering and endurance,—you will find it in Hebrews v. 8. *"Though He were a Son, yet learned He obedience by the things which He suffered."* These few dark clouds, however, so far from dimming, rather increased the glory of the Divine Sun of Righteousness. Just as after an Alpine thunder-storm the air is cleared, and the hidden sun shines forth brighter than ever in its sky of cloudless blue.

In my next I shall tell you what John said about his Lord, and how others were brought to call Him *Master*, before He returned again to Galilee.

XIII.

He receives His first followers.

ONE day in the month of March, when John was addressing the crowd of anxious inquirers in the desert, he saw of a sudden the same Holy Being whom he had baptized in Jordan six weeks before, coming in the direction where he stood. The Baptist in a moment paused in his discourse. Questions had been pouring in upon him from the excited sin-stricken multitude;—" What shall we do?" " Where shall we go with the burden of our sins?" " Who can save us from the wrath to come?" In a moment an answer is revealed to him and to them; and pointing with his finger, he exclaimed—"*Behold the Lamb of God, which taketh away the sin of the world!*"

The next day also, John again beheld Jesus "as He walked," and repeated the very same words. The paschal lambs were ere long to be killed in Jerusalem. Perhaps a flock of them, as has been suggested, were coming across the river at the moment he was speaking. He tells the people, 'Here is the true *Passover Lamb*, who is to be slain for all mankind!'

On this second occasion there were two disciples among others who heard the Teacher's words. These two, we have good reason to believe, had for sometime attached themselves to John, coming and going frequently from their Galilean home to his secluded meeting-place in the desert, and were prepared by him for welcoming the promised Messiah. The one was a middle-aged man; the other was a good deal younger, probably four or five years junior to the Baptist, and to a Greater than he. They were two fishermen from the Sea of Galilee. They had left their boats and their nets once more, that they might hear the Prophet of the desert. The names of these two fishermen were Andrew and John. The last was the same who received from his Lord the appellation "Boanergos," which means "Son of thunder," and who came afterwards to be known by the more beautiful title, "*The Disciple whom Jesus loved.*"

The Baptist would seem to have addressed them alone, apart from the multitude. When they heard him speak of "*the Lamb of God*," and when the Saviour was pointed out to them, they said to one another, 'Let us follow Him.'

With what reverent steps they must have done so! They would wonder what Jesus would say. Would He take any notice of them, or would He forbid them thus to intrude upon Him?

Jesus heard them coming up behind Him. He turned round and asked what they wished.

He looked worn and weary, His face was pale with the forty days' fast. But they saw at once, from His kind look, that He was not displeased at their thus tracking His steps. They called Him '*Rabbi*,' and inquired where He lived.

"Come and see," were the first words they heard from the lips of Him who "spake as never man spake." So they went along with Him in silence.

We are not told where the dwelling of Jesus was. He must have had shelter of some kind for the night. Having been in Palestine, at that very season of the year, I know that in the end of March the nights are cold, and the dews heavy. Jesus may have lived in some hut made of green boughs, or in one of the canvas tents still to be seen near the Jordan, covered with a rough blanket. Be this as it may, at all events, the two fishermen accompany Him at four o'clock in the afternoon.

Neither can I tell you how long they were with the Divine Saviour that spring evening. I dare say they waited late. Perhaps the moon and stars were shining on the white rocks and the foaming river when they returned back. Neither of them, doubtless, slept much that night, thinking of the wonderful meeting and the wonderful talk they had had.

The younger of these two visitors afterwards wrote much that was beautiful about Jesus. In all the ancient paintings we have of this beloved Disciple, he is represented with the eagle at his side or at his feet. Why was this selected as his emblem? Because, like the eagle, he seems ever to be soaring on the wings of divine love, till lost in the radiance and glory of Him who is 'Brighter than the Sun.' This night would give him the first impression of what he so often in future years wrote about and spoke about. This scene on the banks of the Jordan would rise up often before him like a bright vision. "THE WORD *was made flesh and dwelt among us (and we beheld His* GLORY—*the glory as of the only Begotten of the Father*), *full of grace and truth.*" In these reflected *sunbeams*, his path from that hour was as the shining light—shining more and more unto the perfect day!

Next morning, Andrew (the elder of the two) hurried to his brother. That brother's name was Simon; he too was by occupation a fisherman on the great lake of Palestine. Andrew said to him, "I have indeed joyful news for you. He who was yesterday pointed to by John as 'the Lamb of God,' is none other than the true Messiah. Come and see Him and speak to Him just as we have done."

Simon, perhaps after a little hesitation, accompanied Andrew and saw Jesus. Jesus spoke very kindly to him also. He told him that in due time his name would be changed from '*Simon*' to '*Cephas.*' The word 'Cephas' means *a stone*. His future Lord and Master doubtless foresaw, that though Simon would occasionally prove not like a rock, but rather like a shaking reed, yet that as he grew older he would become more and more firm, steadfast, and rock-like, showing high qualities of courage and endurance, specially towards the end of his active life. Peter lived with his wife and his wife's mother in a house by the lake side in Galilee.

All these three, Andrew, John, and Peter, became the disciples of Jesus.

On the day following, the Saviour, crossing the ford of the river, went back again to Galilee. He took three days on the journey, thus travelling about thirty miles each day. His road would probably lie, first through the wild rocky passes of the Jordan Valley, afterwards through the plain of Jezreel or Esdraelon already described, then as richly cultivated as it is now desert and waste. When He had left Nazareth spring was hardly beginning; but now the whole land would be gay with its rich carpet of flowers. The green ears of wheat and barley would be bending on their stalks, and every fig and olive-grove they passed would be filled with the sweet song of birds. He takes along with Him these three happy disciples. Other two also join them.

The name of one of the two new followers was Philip, a fellow villager and fisherman of Bethsaida. But he also feels so joyous in the presence and with the converse of the Heavenly Teacher, that he hastened to tell the glad news to his friend Nathanael, whom they would seem to have accidentally met on the way. The good and holy among the Jews were frequently in the habit, beneath the leafy screen of trees in their gardens, or on the roadside as they journeyed, of reading the Scriptures and saying their mid-day prayers with their faces towards Jerusalem. Nathanael (or Bartholomew as he is afterwards called), seems to have been thus engaged under the shade of a fig-tree, the coolest of all resorts in the East, when his friend Philip found him and conducted him to the presence of Jesus. Who knows, but at the moment he might have been reading about the promised Messiah and praying for His coming.

> "In his own pleasant fig-tree's shade,
>   Which by his household fountain grew,
> When at noonday his prayer he made,
>   To know God better than he knew.
>
> Oh happy hours of heavenward thought;
>   How richly crowned! how well improved;
> In musing o'er the Law he taught,
>   In waiting for the Lord he loved." [1]

Jesus, either when He reached, or when He got near His old abode at Nazareth, is told that His mother Mary was not at home. She had gone to a mountain village not far away, named Cana. There are two sites which dispute the claim to be called the ancient Cana. I remember looking down upon one of them in crossing the hills from Nazareth,—a cluster of huts among some straggling fig and olive trees.

Nathanael was a native of Cana. He would, I doubt not, be glad when he heard the Divine Teacher was going there. It is not unlikely that he invited Jesus and His other four friends to go and stay with him in his house. He must have been a kind, open, honest man, with none of the pretence and deceit which is so common in the world. You remember what Jesus said of him at his first approach.

"Behold an Israelite indeed, in whom is no guile!"

At first Nathanael did not seem disposed to own Christ as Messiah; or indeed as anything great or divine. He knew, from being a neighbour, that Nazareth was a very wicked place. Many of its villagers had a bad name. "Can any good thing," he said,

---

[1] "The Christian Year."

"come out of Nazareth?" But Jesus set aside his doubts and prejudices by proving to him that He was more than human. While yet afar off, seated or kneeling under his fig-tree, the all-seeing eye of the Son of God had rested upon him.

"*Whence knowest thou me?*" said the guileless man to the Peasant Teacher, standing before him.

"*Before that Philip called thee, when thou wast under the fig-tree I saw thee.*"

"*Rabbi,*" he replied with all his heart, "*Thou art the Son of God. Thou art the King of Israel.*"

> "The veil is raised; who runs may read,
> By its own light the truth is seen,
> And soon the Israelite indeed
> Bows down t' adore the Nazarene!"

XIV.

He Turns Water into Wine.

CANA was bright and gay the day on which Jesus reached it. He found His mother and His cousins in another house in the village, where a marriage was about to take place. Surely she would be very happy to meet her dear Son again, after being away nearly two months. And yet, I cannot help thinking, she would see in His countenance, more than she had ever done before, the traces of weariness and pain; she would have the truth more strongly forced on her, that though, unlike others, not born a sinner, like others, He was born to be a sufferer; yes, "The Man of Sorrows." Perhaps He told her not a word about His forty days' lonely exile, and of being with wild beasts in the wilderness, and about meeting a worse than any roaring lion of the desert. But she must have guessed from His pale face and sunken eye that

He had been passing through some time of fierce trial. The "sword," which aged Simeon spoke of, may have again pierced through her heart.

The master of the house to which they went, being a neighbour of Nathanael, asked Jesus and His disciples to go to the marriage.

The sun would just be setting over the brow of Mount Carmel: for it was at sunset such ceremonies began among the Jews. They were times of great joy. Friends came from a long distance; and they had a feast every day for a whole week in the house where the marriage took place. On the marriage-day itself there was music and dancing. It was kept very like May-day in England. Even children had their gay dresses on. They were prettily wreathed with flowers, and followed the torchlight procession with merry songs, or playing their little flutes.

Jesus works His first miracle at that marriage feast.

Probably the household among whom the festivities took place were poor, and they had not been able to lay in much provision for their table. When Jesus and His five disciples, whom they had not expected to swell their numbers, came in, they found that they would not have enough wine for all. Indeed, some of the cups were standing empty. Probably they would have required to go a long distance before they could secure a new supply. Mary, the mother of Jesus, saw that the people of the house were uneasy about this shortcoming. Now, whenever Mary was in any trouble in her cottage-home at Nazareth, she used always to go and tell her loved Son. She does so now. She took Him aside and simply said to Him, '*They have no wine.*' I think she expected that Jesus would work a miracle; for she immediately after whispered to the servants, "*Whatever He tells you to do, do it at once.*"

There were six stone jars standing in a row, either at the door or at the front of the house. These jars were put there to allow the guests, as they came in, to dip their hands in the water with which they were filled. It was always the custom among the Jews, in coming off a journey, when the hands and face were covered with dust, to plunge them in water; or else there was a servant waiting to draw from the large stone pitchers into a smaller cup or flagon, and pour it on the hands. It would have been deemed unkind in any owner of a house if he had not vessels thus filled and ready for his visitors. While it would have been thought equally rude for any of his friends to sit down to eat without this washing having taken place. I may add that the same custom was common in the Jewish Churches, or Synagogues, of having at the door basins filled with water. It would have been considered wrong for a Jew to have gone in, and heard the law read and the Psalms sung, if he had not first dipped his hands in the trough at the entrance.

These large jars, then, at the marriage-feast in Cana, had served their intended purpose in refreshing the guests. They were emptied of their contents. Jesus told the servants of the house to go to the village fountain and fill them anew with water up to the top. They did as He bade them. They must have wondered much what the object was in thus hurrying to and fro with their brimming pitchers. Asking, however, no questions, but in accordance with still farther instructions given them by the Stranger guest, they took out the contents in smaller goblets and carried it to the master of the feast.

What a wonder he sees! The pure water in the flagons has been turned into red wine; not into common wine, but the costliest and best. And such a quantity too! Enough not for that night, but for many a day to come. Each one of the jars is supposed to have held twenty gallons. How amazed they would all be! I think many of the guests would be ready to say in the very words of Nathanael, "*Thou art the Son of God!*"

One there present would very specially rejoice. You doubtless know who I mean? Yes, the Mother of Jesus would surely say to herself, 'I have believed all along in what the Angel Gabriel told me. I have hitherto kept it locked up in my heart as a wondrous secret. But now I *see* it to be true. The name of the Child that was born of me may surely well be called "*Wonderful.*"'

How quietly, too, has Jesus performed His miracle! No show,

or noise, or parade. A heathen writer said: "The gods work in silence." This was true now regarding Him who was "God manifest in the flesh." In that mighty work, and in its silent working, the sacred writer truly says, "He *manifested forth* His glory (John ii. 11). The word is a striking one, and could not be more appropriate to the name I have given to this section of my volume, "*Meridian brightness.*" The "BRIGHTER THAN THE SUN" 'burst forth' all at once over Cana in His noontide splendour. But like His type in the firmament, He makes His presence and glory known by the blessing He silently imparts.

The contrast has often been pointed out between the first miracle of *Jesus* and the first miracle of *Moses*. Moses, in a time of trouble, changed the water of the Nile into blood: Jesus at a time and a feast of joy, turns water into wine. It is a picture of the difference between the Law and the Gospel—the Law with its images of terror, the Gospel with its symbols of grace and love.

Are any of my young readers astonished to hear that Jesus, whom I have just spoken of as "a Man of Sorrows," was present at a bright scene with songs and flowers and wine?

I do not wonder at all. By being at this gathering among the peasants of Galilee, He would tell us that He wishes to make this world of ours happy, and the very humblest people in it happy. By turning the water into wine, He sanctifies all God's gracious gifts, and converts the common things of life into rich blessings. He did not come to make the earth gloomy and dull and sad. He did not come to teach people to despise the gladness of family life and the joy of family meetings. He came to teach them to be happy in the midst of their everyday work, and to set value on that little but sweet and loving word "*Home.*" He is pleased to hear the chime of the marriage-bell, the song of the reaper in his field, the ringing laugh of children at their play. Yes; I would like you to note this, for many there are who, by their mournful faces, would make you think there should be no joy in the world at all. Jesus does not teach us so. It should never be forgotten that it was not at a death-bed, or at a funeral, His first great work of power was performed, but at a village festival—a house where there was singing, and playing upon the pipe and tabret; and where every face was lighted up with sunshine.

Yes, He surely wished, by this picture of happiness, to show what He came into our world to do. It was to turn its sadness into mirth,—its sighs into songs;—the black muddy water of sin into the red sparkling wine of joy. He would turn, if people would only hear His voice and do His will, what is often made a gloomy earth into a happy heaven. That Great SUN was placed in the moral firmament, to pour BRIGHTNESS over the face of the globe. He is set "to rule," not the murky night, but the gladsome day.

Some of the disciples, coming fresh from the teaching of John the Baptist, would perhaps think it very strange to see Jesus making the scene of His first miracle a joyous marriage-feast: above all, making His first miracle the turning of water into wine. John, being what was called a *Nazarite*, never tasted wine. He fasted and lived apart from all mirth. He had no home ties. He never would go to a feast. He would have felt himself very much out of his place at a marriage-supper with a wedding garment on. So different such a scene would be to him from his home in the forest, with his camel-hair blanket and his food of locusts and wild honey. But much as we love and admire the noble character of John—so brave and honest, so earnest and self-forgetful—Jesus' character and Jesus' manner of living were truer and better still. Men were not designed by God to live all alone in cells and caves, in woods and deserts, but rather to mix among their fellows, to do their part in the world's work—to love and to be loved. Jesus in *His* ways of life showed what was the brightest, the noblest, the best manner of existence: viz., to mingle with all that was innocently happy in the world, and yet never to allow the shadow of sin to darken His path. He felt, and He would have His disciples to feel, that He and they could be about the "Father's business" even amid the greetings and smiles and joyousness of a wedding. And He would have *you* to know, that you may look for His presence and blessing in the play-ground and around the cheery fireside, as well as when you are kneeling at your bedsides or seated in the House of God.

I would like you to note what the disciples at Cana *did* really feel when they saw their Master present at this feast. Were they startled or surprised or displeased? No, we are specially told by St. John (chap. ii. 11), that "*His disciples believed on Him.*" As His presence carried sunshine into the marriage banquet, so it seems to have carried the sunshine of increased love into the hearts of His few followers.

Nathanael would possibly remain after this for a little time at his house in the village; but it is likely the other four disciples would return to Bethsaida, and resume their nets and fishing. They would, with joyous faces, tell their friends all that they had seen and heard; and when they put on their rough coats at sunset to go out on the Lake, how they would love to speak to one another all night long about the Lamb of God; about the miracle of the wine at Cana, and of His conversation with them as they walked by His side! How wonderful, yet how meek He was! how kindly He had spoken! how gentle He looked!

They had now become the disciples of Jesus. Little did they think then, that ere long they would be honoured by becoming His chief friends. He was to love them,—yes, these poor humble fishermen, He was to love as brothers; and they were soon to call Him, in a way they could not now dream of, their *good and gracious* MASTER.

XV.

He goes first to the Lake and then to the Passover.

JESUS, His mother, and probably His disciples, went down from Cana to the Sea of Tiberias.

The road by which they would travel is one of the bleakest in Palestine. They must often afterwards have followed it in going through Galilee to Samaria. I remember when I took the same journey how bare the fields were, with no prominent hills around. I may, perhaps, except one mountain to the left, with two crooked tops like the horns of an animal; owing to which it is called by the name of "The Horns of Hattin." This is the height on which Jesus is supposed to have delivered His well-known sermon called "The Sermon on the Mount." A little way farther on, a point is reached from which the first glimpse is obtained of the great sheet of water deep down below. There are some purple-looking hills far beyond; and away to the north one very large mountain whose top is white with snow. No one can mistake Mount Hermon. Jesus knew it well from the heights above Nazareth, for it towered like a giant above all the others.

That half blue, half green water beneath, is "*The Sea of Galilee;*" sometimes called "*The Sea of Tiberias;*" sometimes called the "*Lake of Gennesaret.*" I shall, after this, call it simply by the name of "THE LAKE."

There is no sea or lake in all the world so interesting and so sacred as this. On its shores most of the disciples were born and reared. More than all, Jesus lived longer periods by this lakeside than in any other place in the Holy Land. He seemed to have a special love for it. He liked the simple ways of its people; the boatmen and fishermen, the peasants and cottagers, the woodmen and vine-dressers, the artizans and shepherds. How often He used to pray in the hollows or on the top of its soft green hills! How often He used to wander in meditation up these wooded craggy dells, fringed with flowers, in which He saw the beauty of His Father's hand, and amid the flocks of birds from which He drew the lesson of His Father's care and love. On that mountain, with the two peaks I have just spoken of, He preached; on that beautiful beach, with its lovely silver-like shells, He used often to land with His disciples; on these little sparkling waves the boat used to rock from which He taught the people as they stood or sat on the shore. On yonder distant mountain of Safed, crowned with buildings, is the "city set on an hill," to which, probably, He afterwards referred in His great Discourse. As is mentioned by the Talmud, it formed one of the beacon-stations on whose summit signal-fires were lighted,—the Jewish way of telegraphing the appearance of the new moon, not only throughout their own land, but to their brethren of the dispersion as far as the Euphrates.

What a changed scene Gennesaret is now! At the time Jesus was on earth it was like the more beautiful of our Italian Lakes —Como or Maggiore—in the wondrous life of city and village and hamlet—of palace, villa, and garden which lined its shores. Its very name, indeed, has been said to be derived from two Hebrew words, *gener sarim*, " Gardens of the Princes." There were at least nine Roman and Greek cities which could there be counted. Capernaum, Bethsaida, Chorazin, Tiberias, Tarichea, and others. It was like a ring of emerald set with sparkling stones. But all are gone now. I had to force my way among tall reeds and thorn-bushes to reach a few fallen pillars and rubbish, thought to be the remains of Capernaum. Chorazin can hardly be traced. Bethsaida, the home of Peter and Andrew, James and John, is marked by a flat-roofed mill, the wheels of which are turned by water rushing from the hills above. Tiberias alone is left, but it is a town so filthy and ruinous that one is glad to keep outside its walls. There are still a few Arab traders who bring articles for sale from the looms and bazaars of Damascus: you may still see them gathered, with their loaded camels, around a well called "The Spring of the Fig-tree." How different, however, from the old times, when a broad-paved road, like those still seen in Italy, was often thronged by Egyptian merchants with their balm and spices, and bales of clothing: or when on the bosom of the Lake itself, ships and boats of all sizes were seen bringing their goods to the Port of Capernaum on their way to the markets of the south. Josephus, the historian, speaks in his own day of a hundred and thirty war ships, where there are only now two poor, clumsy, leaking boats! He tells of the surrounding hills (now so drear and desolate), being cultivated to the very top, reminding us of the gardens and homesteads of the Vaudois of Piedmont, climbing far up the sides of their giant Alps. There is nothing, indeed, left of grand and fertile Gennesaret, except those things which time cannot change:—its rippling waters, its lovely beach, its green and grey mountains, its red and white flowers,—the lupin, the salvia, the yellow crocus, the purple hyacinth, the pink and crimson anemone, and the green oleander: its birds, with blue, yellow, and white wings: or the little bright-eyed tortoise which I often saw plunging into the rocky pools, or hiding in the reeds close to the shore.

Yes, and there is one other memory which lives longer still, and which no ages can destroy. It is the beautiful thought, present at every turn of its creeks and bays, 'JESUS *must have been here!*' On these waters He sailed; these pearly sands His footsteps trode;—on these same flowers, which He spoke of as lovelier than Solomon's kingly robe, His eyes fell. These hills were the altars where He prayed to His Father, and where the moon and the stars listened to their Maker's voice!

I have thought it well to tell you these things about the Lake now, as we shall often find the Saviour coming to it; and I should like you to have a vivid picture impressed on your minds of the spot which He selected as His chief abode when He was in the world.

Do you ask me was there any particular city or village which Jesus more specially made His home when He lived there?

He seems to have resided very much, if not always, at *Capernaum;* in the house, too, of His disciple Peter. How honoured Peter and Peter's family were in having such a Guest! Very likely it was only a small dwelling. Perhaps a few fig and olive trees grew in front of it. A vine may have spread its green leaves over the lattice to screen it from the fierce sun; and the graceful tassels of the caper plants (what Solomon called the hyssop), may have been seen hanging over its wall. But however small and humble, surely no house in all the earth at that time was so worthy of the name of a 'PALACE,' because HE lived in it who was "the King of kings!"

Jesus did not at present remain long at the Lake. The Passover was near at hand. A great multitude of people were already flocking from the north. After a few days spent at Capernaum, He and His disciples would seem to have joined the pilgrims and to have gone up to the Feast.

Vast numbers of these intending worshippers were doubtless assembling in one or more of the towns on the lake-side. Some had come (by the coast cities of Tyre and Sidon), from Asia Minor and the shores of the Mediterranean. Others, by the great camel-road across Mount Hermon from Damascus, bringing pilgrims from the region watered by the Tigris and Euphrates, and from the nearer valleys of the Lebanon. This is the first time we have heard of Jesus being in Jerusalem since "He was twelve years old." We can follow Him now in thought in His present journey, past the village of Magdala and the walls of Tiberias, by the western side of the Lake. Crossing "Jacob's Bridge," the caravan would proceed along the east side of the sultry valley of the Jordan. Indeed it would pursue a portion at least of the same route which Jesus and His disciples had trodden only a few days before, after parting with the Baptist. They had left the region of fruit and corn-field behind on the lake-side. But the wild flowers still sprinkled the precipices with their varied hues, and the little dells were musical with the streams fed by the latter rains. As they continued their route, they came to richer pasture lands, dotted over with clumps of oak and alive with sheep and cattle. On their left was a hilly country which had many stirring memories. No Israelite could pass without recalling at

one place the heroic and touching story of Jephthah the Gileadite;
—at another, the youthful home of the great Elijah;—at another,
the scene of King David's sad and lonely exile, where he sang
some of his most plaintive Psalms: where the good old chief
Barzillai the Gileadite, had the highland dwelling he valued more
than palace walls, and nigh to which he slept in a grave " beside
his father and his mother." Recrossing the Jordan at one of its
southern fords, the burning cliffs which frown over the sullen
waters of the Dead Sea would come in view;—then possibly a
gleam of the leaden lake itself. Passing by Jericho, of which I
have already spoken, and to which we shall refer more hereafter,
the band of brother worshippers would ascend through the Wady
Kelt—the grandest gorge in South Palestine—up towards the
City of Solemnities. The dreary, silent wilderness would ring
with Psalms: each glaring precipice of white limestone would
echo back the Paschal songs. At last Jerusalem is in sight. It
is approached now in a different direction from that which we
have supposed was taken, eighteen years before, by the caravan
from Nazareth, and affords a far more impressive view. From
the shoulder of Olivet the whole city would in a moment open
out before them in a vision of beauty and splendour which had
no equal at that time on the earth. The gardens would be seen
blossoming within the gates. The very hyssop would have its
vernal freshness on the olden walls, the green mingling with the
white of the marble and the gleam of the golden pinnacles. The
slopes of the Mount of Olives, as before described, would be
thronged with pilgrim-tents, and resounding with the buzz of many
thousand voices. The great deep trench of the Kedron Valley
lay between. Well has it been said " Never had a city such
natural bulwarks "—the types of a nobler and surer defence—"As
the mountains are round about Jerusalem, so the Lord is round
about His people from henceforth even for ever."

We have nothing in modern times at all like these gatherings
at the Passover. The nearest assemblages to them I can think
of, are those at the great Exhibitions which have been held,
during the last twenty years, in some of the principal cities of

Europe and America; which began with our own first Crystal Palace, and which brought together multitudes not only from all parts of Great Britain but from every quarter of the globe, even as far as China and Japan. The difference between the two was this—that the Passover, unlike these others, was a *sacred* gathering, made up of Jews alone, who came not to a great show for mere pleasure and instruction, but in order to keep a holy feast and to worship their Fathers' God. But it was *like* the others in the great crowd assembled from every part of the Holy Land, as well as from many other distant cities and countries outside Palestine, to which Jews had gone for purposes of trade. It was like the others in the varied dresses worn, the different languages that were spoken, the difficulty of getting house-room and lodging. The city swarmed like an enormous bee-hive.

When Jesus and His disciples reached Jerusalem, He went to the Temple.

He had already begun His great public work. He had been publicly baptized; He had performed His first miracle; He had chosen His first disciples. And now it was well that in going up to the capital city, He should do so not merely as a Jew to keep a national feast, but as the King of the Jews and the Messiah of the nation to display His power; or, as we have found John calling it, to "manifest forth His glory," and proclaim His kingdom.

If I have likened the Passover to one of the great modern Exhibitions, I think I may in this other respect, with reverence, compare it to a spectacle of a different kind of more recent occurrence. I refer to the mighty gathering in India, when vast multitudes—kings, princes, rulers, subjects, all assembled in the old city of Delhi to hear our beloved Queen proclaimed Empress of that enormous country. Jesus is from this time about to declare His Kingship and Sovereignty over the hearts of men. But, alas! the farther resemblance between the two cases fails: for no royal shout arose to welcome Him, no trumpets of fame sounded His praise—"*He came unto His own, and His own received Him not!*"

MERIDIAN BRIGHTNESS.

Our Queen is herself called by the Hindoos "The *Star* of India," and she confers a "*Star*" as the Eastern badge of honour. But He who is Brighter than the brightest "morning star" "*shone in the darkness, and the darkness comprehended Him not.*"

On entering the courts of the Temple, the first kingly act of Jesus was a noble one. We have seen how, all through childhood, youth, and manhood, He had loved His Father's name and sought to do His Father's business. His first deed—we may call it His first miracle in Jerusalem—is to defend the honour of His Father's house. On what occasion could this be more effectually and impressively performed, than when the crowds I have spoken of had come together for this sacred holiday.

He was made sad when He saw a multitude gathered in the holy courts, who were converting them into a place of gain, with noise and wrangling and confusion.

You who have never been in Eastern towns cannot believe what a loud din is made in the bazaars where articles are sold; very different from our quiet shops and markets at home.

Jesus would not have minded the noise, if these traders had put up their booths and stalls in the streets, or on the green grass of the Mount of Olives. But He could not bear to see "His Father's House" turned into a place of business;—stall-keepers selling, with fierce and boisterous tones, offerings for the Temple service. Where the Court of the Gentiles was—on either side of that "Beautiful Gate of the Temple" I have formerly described—there were erections made for cattle-dealers and poultry-merchants. Lambs were bleating, oxen were lowing, pigeons were cooing under the cedar-roofs and marble pillars. In one booth there were cages of turtle-doves: in another a row of young pigeons. There is a man who is doing his best to cheat a customer in the sale of a kid or lamb. There is another who, after loud altercation and squabbling, is leading away by a halter an ox he has just purchased. In the Court of the Women, too, there were tables on which were placed chests and piles of silver coin, with the greedy grasping changers of money standing behind them. These were giving Roman and Greek coins of copper and brass, which had often heathen images upon them, in exchange for half-shekel Jewish ones of silver, one of which each Pilgrim had to pay as a charge for the altar. The money-changers, utterly forgetful of the holy ground on which they were standing, were only intent on making the most of their opportunity—taking advantage of the strangers who brought with them foreign coin—also of the humble peasants and country-people, who, in their simplicity, could be so easily cheated. On other stalls there would likely be dresses and garments,—what are still called "*Caftans*" and "*Abbas*,"—coverings for the head, and striped cloaks of red and blue. There would be ear-rings and bracelets; there might even be some of those beads, shells, and flowers which are sold to this day in front of the Holy Sepulchre in Jerusalem, and of the Church of the Nativity at Bethlehem.

The sellers, I need not tell you, had no love for God, or for His Temple. They only wanted to make money, and to drive the best bargain they could. What an abuse of these sacred places! All these foul sights, foul odours, and distracting sounds mingling with the smoke of holy sacrifice, the fumes of holy incense, and the sound of holy Psalms. Well might the Great Lord of the Temple say in the words of the Prophet Samuel to King Saul—"*What meaneth then this bleating of the sheep in mine ears, and the lowing of the oxen which I hear?*" (1 Sam. xv. 14).

And yet, to show that we Christians have no right to be severer on the conduct of the Jews than upon our own, you will wonder, when I mention in passing, that in the time of King James I., the principal church in our country—the great cathedral of St. Paul's in London—was quite as bad as the Temple of Jerusalem in that early age. A large portion of it was filled with booths; it was turned into a fair. The English hucksters had not even the excuse of the Jews, that many of the things were for the Temple service. Goldsmiths had shops or stalls for rings and bracelets. Toymen had their toys; owners of poultry had their hen-coops; even dogs were chained to the wooden benches, or lay crouching at the base of the church-pillars, for sale. I tell you this, that you may be thankful we live in times when God's name and God's house are had in greater reverence. It would shock all good people to see such things now.

But to return to the Court of the Gentiles at Jerusalem.

Jesus greatly disliked such a scene as I have described. He knew and felt that He was Lord of the Temple, that its holy courts did not belong to these shameless sellers, but to His heavenly Father. It was intended to be "a House of Prayer," and it was turned into a house of gain. How could the Priests pray? how could the sweet Psalms be sung amid that sea of hoarse voices, the noise of herdsmen and cattle?

What did Jesus do?

He saw some hempen string—fragments of rope and halters—lying on the floor. He took these in His hand, or, as others suppose, some of the grass or rushes which formed the litter of the cattle, and made a whip of them. Then, not in wrath (for that could not be) but in holy anger, and jealous for His Father's honour, He drove all out; herdsmen and their flocks, bird-sellers with their cages. "Take these things hence," said He. While, passing into the next court, the heaps of money were swept by Him to the ground and rolled amid the dust under the broken wooden tables. "*Make not,*" He exclaimed, "*My Father's house a place of buying and selling!*"

How could this single Man effect such a work? His disciples seemed only to look on. They gave Him no help. He had no sword; no battle-axe; no spear. A scourge of small cord, twisted together, and that, too, in the hands of, apparently, a humble peasant of Galilee, did it all!

I answer, it was the Divine power within Him, which performed what was little else than a miracle. It made that whip of cords to act like a legion of soldiers, and these few words of rebuke to fall like tones of thunder. It is said that the mere glance of the human eye can make the lion to cower in his lair or den. What must have been the glance of Him "whose eyes are as a flame of fire?" (Rev. i. 14). The bright sun which can warm and gladden with a gentle genial heat, can also burn up and scorch. "HIS *countenance was as* THE SUN *shineth in his* strength." "*Who can stand in Thy sight when once Thou art angry?*"

I wonder if you can recall a verse in one of the later Prophets, which speaks of this sudden coming of Christ to the Temple in Jerusalem? It is from the Book of Malachi (iii. 1): "*The Lord, whom ye seek, shall suddenly come to His temple, even the messenger of the covenant, whom ye delight in: behold, He shall come, saith the Lord of Hosts.*"

I think we have reason to believe (John ii. 23) that on this same occasion Jesus wrought some other miracles in the Temple-court, or at all events gave some other signs of His power, and added to the number of His disciples.

XVI.

He meets Nicodemus, a Jewish Ruler.

I CANNOT tell you where Jesus lived when He was at the Passover. Perhaps it was at Bethany. Or there is reason to surmise He had occasionally a home in an olive-farm on the Mount of Olives near the Garden of Gethsemane.

Wherever it was, one night, when the sun had set and both streets and roads were in darkness, a man is seen muffled in his long cloak or *Abbah*, screening himself from observation. He is evidently bent on an errand he wishes no one to know anything about. It is not, however, because he has committed some deed of guilt, which requires to be hidden from the light of day, that he thus hies him so stealthily along. No; it is a very different reason. He is one of the few better spirits among his countrymen who is eagerly seeking after truth. He is dissatisfied with those "who call evil good, and good evil—who put darkness for light, and light for darkness." Groping his way in that "twilight age of Judaism" after the True Light, he wistfully inquires of every new religious Teacher, "Watchman, what of the night?" It is that inquiry which is now impelling him to leave his own dwelling in Jerusalem, and to risk his name and reputation by seeking an audience with the young Prophet of Galilee.

Nicodemus was a rich ruler of the Jews, and must have been a well-known man. Jesus calls him "*a Master in Israel.*" He was one of the chiefs of the Sanhedrim. The Sanhedrim was the great national assembly of the Jews. To take a comparison from British courts, it was partly a church synod, partly a college, partly a house of parliament. It was made up of all the chief men in school, and church, and state. So that we can think of Nicodemus as alike a scholar, a church dignitary, and a noble.

You may remember what I said regarding the Shepherds of Bethlehem, that they represented the poor who in every age of the world would come to Jesus; also that the 'Wise men of the East' represented the rich and the great who would in future be numbered among His followers.

We have in Nicodemus one of the latter;—a Jew of power and influence and learning in Jerusalem. And while other proud Israelites scorned the lowly Prophet, it must have been a joy to the heart of the Saviour to welcome an "Anxious Inquirer," who rose superior to sect and party.

Nicodemus had heard of the teaching as well as of the miracles of Jesus. He resolves, at all hazards, to go and see Him; but waits till the bulk of the Passover crowd have repaired to their tents or houses.

Perhaps it was the evening of the same day on which Jesus cleared the Court of the Temple that Nicodemus went to Him. He wished to hear specially about that "*Kingdom of God,*" which the new Teacher was reported to be proclaiming. He would seem to have been humble and courteous and kind. He is not repelled by the lowly appearance and the peasant dress. He calls Jesus "*Rabbi,*" a title of dignity. He owns Him at once as "*a Teacher come from God:*" although no more than a *Teacher*. "No *man*," he said to Jesus, "can do these miracles that Thou doest *except God be with him.*" It is manifest he never dreamt of any connection between this lowly Galilean and the name "IMMANUEL," which being interpreted is "GOD *with us*" (Matt. i. 23).

What does Jesus say to him?

Nicodemus wished to know chiefly, as I have just remarked, about "the new Kingdom;"—partly, perhaps, also about the Kingdom of the blessed in heaven.

Does Jesus all at once answer his queries?

No. If Nicodemus expected to hear either about the earthly throne of Kingly Messiah—or about "the House Beautiful," "The Land Beulah," and "the Crystal city," he was disappointed. The Saviour brings him, as He does all pilgrims, outside the gate of the narrow way, and seating him there says—"*Except a man be born again he cannot see the Kingdom of God.*" He must enter the heavenly road by the gate of a new life. He must be "*born of the Spirit.*"

What did He mean by that?

It was just the old teaching of the faithful Baptist at the Jordan,—when he cried to the people to 'Repent;'—to leave off their old sins, and become new creatures. It was like being born a second time;—to become little children again—to have the old heart of sin quite changed into the new heart of holiness, purity, and love.

No wonder this Jewish Ruler marvelled. 'What!' he would say to himself. 'I, a chief Rabbi—a strict Pharisee, who have kept the law, paid all my tithes, attended every feast, been daily at the Temple, never eaten with my hands unwashed, and have had the fringe of my robe scrupulously adorned with sacred texts! Is all this to go for nothing? Have I to begin my religious life again? am I to reckon myself a sinner,—no better, or at least no nearer salvation, than any Gentile, or than the vilest Publican or beggar on the street?'

Jesus said to him, 'Yes, it is quite true; all outward rites and ceremonies, feasts and fasts, tithings and washings, are nothing without this inward change of heart and life.'

Nicodemus then naturally asks, "How am I to get this entirely new nature?"

To which Jesus replies, "It is got *by faith in Me*." And in explaining what this simple faith in Him means, He corrects the false ideas which he, in common with most of his countrymen, had about the promised Messiah, as a mere temporal Ruler and King. He unfolds to His hearer, with the greatness of divine authority combined with the gentleness of a friend, the great "Plan of Salvation." He gives him the coming story of His sufferings and death for the ransom of mankind. He speaks some beautiful words;—some of the most precious and comforting utterances in all the Bible. If they failed to touch the heart of his attentive listener at the time, they would at all events be laid up in his memory for some future occasion. Among these sayings is that sweet verse, a favourite with young and old, which brings into one little word of two letters what could not be exhausted by whole volumes—"*God so loved the world.*"

Jesus, in further explaining the "great mystery of godliness," selected from the Old Testament an incident with which the Jewish Ruler was, doubtless, very familiar. He told him that He—"*the Son of Man*"—"*the only Begotten Son of God*"—was to be "lifted up on the cross," as the serpent of brass had been lifted up by Moses in the wilderness; and that all who looked to Him would live and have their souls saved, just as the bitten Israelites were healed of their bodily wounds.

I think I must give you in full, the closing words of this midnight conversation. They surely come appropriately from the lips of Him to whom we have given the title in this volume, "Brighter than the Sun." Hear how He speaks of His own blessed LIGHT, and mourns over those who reject it. "*This is the condemnation, that* LIGHT *is come into the world, and men loved darkness rather than light, because their deeds were evil. For every one that doeth evil hateth the light, neither cometh to the light, lest his deeds should be reproved. But he that doeth truth cometh to* THE LIGHT" (John iii. 19, 20, 21). I dare say this earnest visitor remained far on in the night talking with Jesus; the moon and stars may have been shining when he came away.

How kind it was in the Divine Teacher, so patiently listening to his questions, so tenderly meeting his doubts and difficulties! We have every reason to believe Jesus stood much in need of rest after a day of labour and toil. But He willingly surrenders His night's repose in order to clear away the darkness from a perplexed mind.

I do not think we have any reason to suppose that on this occasion Nicodemus avowed himself to be a disciple. One thing, however, we know, he never forgot that first meeting. He was timid, and no wonder. His brother Rulers would have been very angry with him if they had known he had gone to the lowly Son of Mary, to converse about some new spiritual truths. But though Nicodemus was at present afraid to resort to the young Prophet of Nazareth in open day, by-and-by he became bold and courageous; for we shall find him, three years after, entering bravely Pilate's palace, and begging from the Roman Governor his dead Master's body. He "remembered the words of the Lord Jesus how He said"—"He that doeth truth, cometh to THE LIGHT."

Perhaps I may just mention, before leaving the story of Nicodemus, that as St. John is the only one of the sacred writers who mentions it, and as he gives all the incidents of the interview very minutely, it has been supposed that he may have himself been present. There is nothing improbable in the surmise. If so, he got from it the text and key-note of his future Epistles— the key-note of his own future life—"*God so* LOVED *the world!*"

After this, and at the close of the Passover, Jesus seems to have gone for some time to the north of Judea, and to have gathered round Him there a great number of followers.

The place where He went was called Ænon, or "the Springs." John the Baptist was baptizing there, because there was "much water." No one is quite sure as to the exact spot where Ænon was. It is supposed most probably to have been a small valley, about six miles from Jerusalem, opening from the Jordan (Wady Fârah), where there are still several pools and fountains, called by the Arabs at this day "The Valley of Delight." It would be a quieter place than the 'Ghor' of the Jordan itself, and not so hot.

At all events, people could stand under the shadow of the rocks, and be better screened from the sun.

Jesus seems to have remained there till near the end of the year, and then to have returned to the Lake.

An event at this time must have greatly distressed Him. His best and chiefest friend, the Baptist, had been seized by wicked Herod Antipas, and put into a dungeon on the shores of the Dead Sea. Jesus must have been all the sadder, because not only does He appear to have seen, at this time, a good deal of John,—speaking with him about "the Kingdom,"—but John had shown himself to be so good and kind and humble. Some of the Baptist's disciples had tried to make him jealous of Jesus, and, as rival Teachers, to set the one against the other. More people were flocking to hear Jesus than to hear John. "All men," they said, "come unto Him." But the latter, instead of being downcast or displeased, declared rather it was what made him most glad. Jesus was far greater than he. *He* was only "of the earth," a sinner like other people. Jesus was "from above." He had no power of his own. "A man," he said, "can receive nothing except it be given him from heaven." But that "Lamb of God," to whom he had borne witness, "cometh from above, and is above all" (John iii. 31). John seemed only to be proud about one thing; that he was allowed to call Jesus his "Friend," and to stand and hear Him. His brave unselfish words were—"HE *must increase, but I must decrease.*" John, like the day-star of Milton,

"Flamed in the forehead of the morning sky."

But the moment the Divine SUN appeared, the "Lesser Light" was content to pale away and be lost in His superior brightness. "He rejoiced greatly because of the Bridegroom's voice." *His* own name and fame (so thought, at least, this humble-minded man) would gradually decline; while the name of his adored and adorable "Friend," as predicted by the Psalmist King, would "endure for ever, and be continued long as" (yea longer than) "*the Sun.*"

We shall hear by-and-by more of the Morning Star, ere vanishing to shine in a more glorious firmament. But Jesus and John never met again till they met in the Heavenly Jerusalem.

XVII.

He meets a woman of Samaria at Jacob's Well.

WE have just seen THE SUN OF RIGHTEOUSNESS, in the case of Nicodemus, dispensing healing from His beams. In the story I am now to tell, we are called to behold a still more remarkable and beautiful instance of what divine grace can do,—that same all-glorious Sun giving " Light to one sitting in darkness and in the region and shadow of death."

Jesus leaves Judea on His way to the Lake, and takes the great northern road leading to Galilee: the same with which we are now familiar, as that by which He used to travel with the caravan from Nazareth on His way to the Feasts. It has been thought that He would not unlikely pause for the night at a spot amid the mountains of Ephraim well-known to travellers then, as it is a familiar resting-place still, although having the rather dreaded modern name of "The Robbers' Fountain." It is one of the places I vividly recall as a 'picture of beauty' after the bleak unlovely plains and hills of Judah. A fountain is always a refreshing sight in Palestine. But here, as most probably in the time of Christ also, the water comes trickling down amid rocks and verdure, bringing to mind familiar nooks at home, with moss and lichen, and trails of maiden-hair fern. While in the valley around, patches of bold rock peep out amid clumps of vine, olive, and fig.

We can, then, with probability think of Jesus being there, the first night of His journey, sleeping perhaps in one of the sheltered hollows close by, and waking up in the early dawn amid the singing of birds in the groves around, or amid the bleating of the flocks led out by their shepherds beside these 'green pastures and still waters.'

In the course of a few hours He and His disciples enter the old plain of Moreh, where Jacob, long ages before, came up from his encampment in the Jordan Valley (the "booths of Succoth") and dug a well for his cattle.

Did you ever think what is meant when, at the beginning of the fourth chapter of John, it is said "He must *needs* go through Samaria"?

The 'need,' or necessity, would seem to be this, that He had a soul to save. The Good Shepherd had a lost sheep to restore to the fold. The "Brighter than the Sun" had a wandering star to bring back to the orbit from which it had strayed. How precious is even one single soul, whether old or young, in the sight of Jesus! He might have reached Galilee by the nearer route along the Jordan Valley. But He hears the bleat of this sheep on the mountains of Samaria. He "leaves the ninety and nine" to "go after that which was lost!"

It was now the very middle of the day. The fierce rays of noontide were beating down upon His head, and when He reached the Well of the Patriarch, He was very weary and thirsty. So weary, indeed, that He flung Himself down on the stone parapet furrowed with the ropes by which the water was drawn up in pitchers, and rested 'thus' (or, as that means, "*the best way He could*"); while He sent His disciples into the town close by, to purchase a little bread and fruit for the afternoon meal. The strong fishermen of the Lake, used to days and nights of toil with their boats and nets, seem to have been able for longer journeys and to endure greater fatigue than their Master.

Tired however as Jesus was, He could hardly fail to be interested in the scene around Him.

There, in front, was the bare grey rocky hill of Ebal, and opposite it the better clothed hill Gerizim. From these two mountains the blessings and the curses of the law were proclaimed in Joshua's time;—while the whole camp of Israel in the valley below, where the Levites stood with the Ark, echoed back their

'AMEN." He would recall earlier memories; for Abraham as well as Jacob had built an altar close by, and the smoke of the first burnt-offerings—the types of His own great coming sacrifice—had ascended from that very well-side. Only a short way off towards the right, the good and kind Joseph was buried. His embalmed body was brought up all the way from Egypt through the desert, and placed there, at his own request, in its "parcel of ground."

There is no place in Palestine so little changed as this is. The hills and the vast plain—*El Mukhna* ('Vale of encampment')—with the green growing corn, Joseph's white tomb, and the same Well where Jesus sat. In our visit to the spot we hired an Arab to bring a long rope, and, letting down a bucket through the rough stones on the top, got up some of the water.

While Jesus was resting by this wayside well, He saw a woman from Sychar coming up with a pitcher.

I cannot help recalling, on the occasion of this same personal visit, that when within a few paces of the well, I said to the friend who was with me, "Look there!" What did we see? It was a woman at a little distance, coming from the adjoining village with a pitcher poised on her head "to draw water." Little did that Jewish peasant know all the sacred thoughts which she and her water-jar brought to our minds!

It was in early morning or late evening that most of the women in Palestine went, as they do still, to get their supply from the nearest well or fountain. How this woman came at *noon* I cannot tell. But it is evident the Saviour could not have spoken to her so plainly as He did, had she come at the most frequent hour, and had there been a crowd waiting.

The water, so cool and refreshing, was deep down in the well and could not be reached without a rope and a bucket. Jesus says to the woman,

"Will you give me some water to drink?"

"How can I give you water?" she replied, rudely and sternly. "You are a Jew, and I am a woman of Samaria." (A Jew, at ordinary times, would not for the world have drunk, however thirsty, out of a flagon used by a Samaritan, or eaten the loaf that was made by a Samaritan baker). "Jews," she added, "have no dealings with the Samaritans."

Jesus saw that she was full of what is called "prejudice." He saw, too, what was worse; for He read her heart, and knew that she had been a very wicked woman. He looked on her with an eye of pity. Seeking to convince her of her sin, He takes the well, by the edge of which He sat, to lead her to a far better than any earthly fountain: just as He had recently, in the case of Nicodemus, taken the noise of the wind sighing and rustling outside, swinging the branches and driving the clouds ("blowing where it listeth"), to explain the operations of the Divine Spirit. He told her that whoever drank of earthly streams would be sure to get thirsty again. He wished to show her that no human joys, however bright and sparkling, can quench the thirst of the soul. Whereas the water that He would give was "living water." Whosoever drank of *it*, would never, in all time to come, know what thirst was.

What, you ask, did He mean by this "living water"?

It was His own salvation: so full—so free; offered alike to the king and the beggar: to old and young, rich and poor! He calls that salvation, too, "a *gift*."

A gift is something which is not only free but, generally speaking, precious. You know, I daresay, how valued wells are in the East; and in no place are they prized more than in Palestine. A fountain is called "The *Eye* of the desert." So precious is water considered, that a traveller tells us when the water-carriers in some Eastern cities go about the streets selling it from a big jar fastened on their backs, they cry, "The gift of God! the gift of God!"[1] Perhaps it was to this familiar name Jesus makes so beautiful an allusion now. He says to the woman, "*Water is* A *gift of God*. But I wish to tell you of THE *gift of God*. I would

---

[1] Miss Whately's "Ragged Life in Egypt," quoted by Mr. Stock in his "Lessons."

like you to know that Divine Gift. I would like you to drink of that which quenches the thirst of the never-dying soul: and that for ever and ever." "Oh," said the gracious Speaker, yearning over this poor, ignorant, guilty sinner, "if thou only knewest THE GIFT of GOD!" (iv. 10). It reminds us of what He said so shortly before to Nicodemus—"God *so* loved the world that He GAVE" (iii. 16). On both occasions Jesus speaks of Himself as the *Gift* of the Father's love.

The woman began to see that He who spoke to her was no ordinary man. She began also to discover that it was of something far higher, purer, and better than about the well at their feet He was discoursing. She had already commenced to address Him with the word of respect. She called Him "Sir," and after that *a Prophet.*' She must have been struck with His patience, kindness, and earnestness.

And yet, she did not like to be spoken of as a sinner, and to be reminded of her evil ways.

She tried to turn away the conversation from herself; she tried to get the Stranger into a new discussion as to whether the Temple on Mount Gerizim, or on Mount Zion, was the holiest. She pointed up to the buildings on the hill close by, saying, "Our fathers worshipped on *this* mountain; I should like you to tell me whether it is best to worship here or in Jerusalem?"

Jesus answers her that the place where people assemble for religious purposes is nothing; whether it be a temple, or a church, or a room, or a hut, if they only worship the Great God in spirit and in truth. He looks to the heart, and not to the building.

Again she tries to divert Him from farther probing her conscience by starting yet another subject. She abruptly says, "*I know that Messiah cometh.* When *He* is come He will tell us fully about all these things."

Jesus at once replied—"*I that speak to thee am He.*"

In her joy and wonder she leaves her heavy pitcher of water behind, and, disappearing among the old olive-trees, makes her way to the city. She had issued from it a miserable sinner; she returns a joyful believer. On reaching the town, she went first to this neighbour, and then to that, saying, "Come with me to the Well! come and see one who '*has told me all things that ever I did!*' He knows all about me; about my past life, and my past sins; '*Is not this the Christ?*'" We may suppose her farther telling them, what at all events she must have deeply felt, that he had addressed her so kindly and tenderly. 'Instead of covering me with reproach and driving me to despair, He has spoken to me, yes even to *me*, of "*everlasting life*."' "He will not break"—He has not broken—" the bruised reed!"

Meanwhile Jesus has remained seated on the curbstone of the well, gazing around Him on the fields of living green—tender sprouting corn—waving all around. These fields—the ripening grain, the coming harvest—brought other realities to His mind. He had just reaped, in the case of that Samaritan woman, the "first fruit"—the first ripe sheaf of a great spiritual harvest: and His divine thoughts wander on to that Great day when the reaper angels would come with their sickles and lay at His feet the golden harvest of eternity. He sees "the fruit of the travail of His soul and is satisfied." He is filled with a holy, heavenly joy, like to "the joy in harvest and as men rejoice when they divide the spoil" (Isa. ix. 3).

By this time the disciples had returned from their errand into the town, carrying their loaves or cakes of bread, probably with some dried fruits, such as figs or raisins. They had laid these at their Master's side. They see how wan and weary He looks; for He has not broken fast since morning, to say nothing of the toilsome travel through the hot plain. And though they saw that He was silent and taken up with other thoughts, they could not help abruptly, yet very reverently addressing Him. "They prayed Him, saying, '*Master, eat.*'"

"I have meat to eat," said He, "that ye know not of."

They said to one another, 'Who can have given Him food in our absence?' We may imagine various thoughts occurring to them. Could some chance traveller have passed and given Him out of his scrip? or would He who turned the water into wine, have not got for Himself, by miracle, what could stay the cravings of hunger? Could the silver plumaged doves of Gerizim, like Elijah's ravens, not have fetched the needed supply? or could the angels that ministered to Him on the Mount of Temptation not have brought Him manna from heaven?

Poor dreamers! We cannot blame the ignorant woman for not understanding about "the living water," when the Lord's own disciples are so slow to comprehend the meaning of "living bread." [1]

But Jesus sets them right. He is not displeased. No, rather, His face beaming with joy as He thinks of the fields of immortal souls "white already to harvest," and of the glorious "harvest-home" of heaven, He says, "*My meat is to do the will of Him that sent Me, and to finish His work.*"

That must indeed have been a happy day and happy hour to Him. Rejected for months by the Jews, He is all at once welcomed by these simple-hearted Samaritans; for this woman was not only brought to love and serve Him herself, but a great number of people in the town where her home was, many of whom, we may suppose, had hearts as heavy and sins as many as her own, were led to own Him as the Messiah. We can think of them following her along the shady road;—the merchant from his bazaar, the artizan from his bench or his anvil, the scribe from his table under the palm-tree, the idler from his lounge in the market-place, perhaps the youth from school.

That mountain with the Temple on its top, was "the Mount of Blessing." The name was true in a higher sense than it ever was before. Jesus had spoken to the dwellers at its base of rich blessings they had never, till now, known anything of. They had learned from Him, among others, two precious truths—that God was their "*Father*," and that He was "*the Saviour of the world*" (John iv. 23, 42).[2]

---

[1] Augustine.

[2] The subject of this rich and interesting chapter, with its many spiritual lessons, I have endeavoured to treat in "Noontide at Sychar; or, The Story of Jacob's Well."

After remaining two whole days in Shechem, the Redeemer and His disciples go in the direction of the Lake, to take up their abode there. The voice of the good and holy John being now stilled in death, Jesus felt it would be well that He himself, more than He had yet done, should go forth and proclaim that "Kingdom of God" which His servant had so boldly and earnestly declared to be at hand. He resolved to begin, not among the learned in Jerusalem, but among the simple-minded villagers and peasants of Galilee.

So we can think of Him and His few followers proceeding through that loveliest of valleys, of which I have previously spoken, between "the Mountains of Blessing and Cursing." The valley would then be looking its best, as at that time of the year the rills, most of which are dry in summer, would be flowing. Even now eighty of these streams can be counted. If as beautiful then as it is at the present day (and doubtless it was), He who had an eye for all that was lovely in the outer world could not fail to rejoice in His own handiwork. Might He not recall words He had often heard in His old home at Nazareth as peculiarly suitable while traversing this wooded glen,—"*He sendeth the springs into the valleys, which run among the hills. They give drink to every beast of the field: the wild asses quench their thirst. By them shall the fowls of the heaven have their habitation, which sing among the branches*" (Ps. civ. 10–12). Passing by Samaria to the right—"The Crown of Pride," with its circlet of hills, they would cross the great battle plain which divides Samaria from North Galilee. Before reaching the Lake, Jesus once more visits *Cana.*

XVIII.

He Cures the Nobleman's Son.

CANA, with its pleasant gardens and olive groves, would not be a strange place to Jesus now. He would always be welcome there in the home of good Nathanael. Both old and young, too, of the villagers, who had met Him at the marriage-feast, could not fail to love Him. There must have been, however, more than love. They could not help feeling that they were in the presence of some Great Prophet sent from heaven. No mere man could have turned, as He had, the water of their well into wine. He is going presently to give them fresh proof of His divine power.

A nobleman in Capernaum had a son who was very ill of fever. All the doctors round the Lake had not been able to do him any good. His father, with a heavy heart, feared he was going to die. We are not told anything about the nobleman's history. It is very probable that, like most of those who were in the wicked court of Herod Antipas, he may have hitherto led a life of godlessness and sin. He would likely have all that the world could bestow to make him happy. But what now to him was his palatial house, full table, and gilded halls; his barges and galleys on the Lake, his troops of slaves, his honours at the Court? Death was threatening to draw a dark curtain over every joy he had. He would have given all his money and all his honours if that dear life were only spared. He begins, however, to fear the worst. The unseen enemy, who has been called "the King of Terrors and the Terror of Kings," is knocking loudly at his door.

Some one had told the nobleman that He who had done many mighty works in Judea, was now at Cana. He thought to himself, "Oh! if I only could see this Divine Teacher, perhaps He could do what no other earthly Physician can. He may be able to save me from so terrible a sorrow as the loss of my dear boy!"

Cana was five hours' ride, or twenty-six miles from the Lake. But he did not mind the distance. So, getting his horse saddled, he hastened across the bleak road, of which I have already told you. It would be warm and sheltered at that season by the Lake-side; but very likely the nobleman would have to face bitter winds, or even hail and snow, when he got into these dreary marshy uplands. What, however, does he care? He will bear any fatigue to get his loved one back again from the hand and the gates of death.

He will go himself, too; he will not trust the matter to any servant or messenger, although he had many such in his spacious house. In the course of that journey there would only be one word and one thought during its long hours on the father's heart and lips—"My child! my child!"

He reached the village of Cana about one o'clock in the day; and immediately sought for Jesus.

"Sir," was his request to the gracious Healer, "Come down:" —(he says "Come *down*," because his home on the Lake was so much lower than Cana), "Come down before my son is dead, and heal him."

Jesus at once said to him, "Do not fear: you may go home happy, for I will raise up your son for you." "*Go thy way, thy son liveth.*"

The Saviour wished to show that He did not need to be close to the bedsides of the sick and dying in order to heal them. He could do so at a distance quite as well.

The nobleman had great faith. He believed at once what had been said to him. There seemed to be something in the very look and way Jesus spoke, which made him put away his doubts. Indeed so assured is he of the restoration, that he is in no hurry to go home. If he had not thus been quite certain, we may be sure he would have ridden back at once to Capernaum, even though the night was dark, and the road dangerous with robbers. He seems to say to himself, 'I have Jesus' word for it, and I shall trust Him. When I go home to-morrow, I know I shall find my child well again.'

And sure enough, it was all true: for the next day the nobleman's household servants met him on the road and told him, "*Your son liveth.*"

It was exactly at the time, too, Jesus pronounced his cure.

I like to think of this "Jewish Peer" coming to Jesus. It again brings to mind what we recently noted in the case of Nicodemus, that Jesus came to cure and bless and save, not the poor only, but the rich and the titled, who would go to Him and tell Him of their wants. True, the Meek and Lowly One never cared about "going after great people." We never once read of Him entering within the kingly gates of Tiberias, or seeking the society of those in high worldly station—who wore gorgeous dresses or sat at luxurious tables, and had heaps of money. He far rather loved the poor. He was at home in a fisher's hut. He ate bread with publicans and sinners. It was the "common people" who "heard Him gladly." It was little children who smiled in His arms. But His gospel was designed for the rich and the noble as well as for the despised and humble.

How beautiful, I again say, was the faith of this father! How simply he trusted Jesus! He believed alike in the *instant* cure and the *distant* cure. He did not even say, like Nicodemus, "How can these things be?" He took Jesus at His word; and "*He had seen the end of the Lord; that the Lord is very pitiful, and of tender mercy*" (James v. 11). What a lesson for old and young is here! Just to believe and feel sure that what Christ promises is true, and will come all to pass.

This grateful nobleman, known well at Court, would carry the news of his son's healing to the gilded halls of Herod's "Golden House" (the name given to the palace in Tiberias), and among what are called 'the upper classes' all round the Lake. It is evident he himself became from that day a disciple and follower of the Redeemer. Some have thought that he was Chuza, "Herod's steward," or chief officer of Herod's household, mentioned in Luke viii. 3. If so, the grateful mother of the cured

boy is specially referred to in the same place. Her name is
Joanna. She is spoken of as one of "the Holy Women" in
higher life, who followed the footsteps of Christ, and gave to
the Master and His disciples of their substance.

At all events, the raising up of this noble's child would help
greatly to extend the fame of Him who had wrought the cure.
So that now, though only very lately an almost unknown tradesman in Nazareth, people began to point to Jesus as a Great
Prophet and Worker of Miracles. Some said more: that He was
none else than the Messiah Himself. The Kingdom He had
come to found had thus begun in good earnest; so that in words
spoken often regarding Him, "His fame could not be hid."

XIX.

He Heals the Lame Man at the Pool of Bethesda.

JESUS, after this, seems to have visited for a few weeks the Lake-
side, and then to have gone back to Jerusalem at the time of the
Feast of PURIM, which would be about the middle of our March.

What, you may ask, was the meaning and occasion of this
Festival?

I can, perhaps, answer you this all the better, because it was
the only Jewish feast at which I was present in Jerusalem. I
can never forget it. It took place, amid a great noise, in a
synagogue near "The Wailing Wall,"—a well-known spot in the
city, of which you may have heard, where the Jews go every
Friday to weep over the ruins of their old Temple.

The feast itself, let me tell you, first of all, was not deemed one
of the three Great ones; nor was it among those appointed by
Moses. It dates long after, from the time the Jews were living
in exile. Its design was to call to mind the successful pleading

of Queen Esther with her royal husband, for the Israelites who were doomed to death—also the story of wicked Haman, who had got the king to agree to so cruel and wholesale a murder. I remember well that evening, hearing "*the Book of Esther*" read. The reader stood on a desk or raised platform, in the centre of this poor dingy building, with its bare white walls. There were a goodly number of boys present, with sticks and clubs in their hands. It was soon evident what use they were going to make of these, for every time the hated name of *Haman* occurred, they hissed and howled and scraped with their feet; they beat the seats and floors, and anything in front of them, as if they were flogging the cruel and hard-hearted man; while old and young clapped their hands in approval, and joined in a loud blessing, when the name of *Mordecai* was mentioned. I afterwards bought, near the Jaffa Gate, an old parchment roll, very tattered and soiled, of "the Book of Esther," to keep me in mind of the feast, at which, doubtless, it must have been often read; also one of the sweet sugar-cakes with bright colours upon it, which, in accordance with ancient custom, are yearly baked for the same occasion. The Feast of Purim, I should, moreover, tell you, always was, and still is, a favourite one with the people. It was kept as a sort of holiday, with loud clanging music and dancing; something in the merry way of our own Gunpowder Plot fifty years ago.

You may, perhaps, ask, how did Jesus come to join an assemblage where He would be almost sure to see much He could not fail to dislike, and which, moreover, often amid scenes of riot, would call to mind an old story of hatred and revenge?

I think His main inducement must have been, because He knew that He would find a large crowd gathered together, from all the towns and villages round about. Many then and there would hear His words, who could not be reached at any other time. Like all His true ministers He "sowed beside all waters." He went wherever He thought He would do good. He never "pleased Himself." His happiness was to do His Father's will.

On the Sabbath-day He wrought a miracle at a well-known place in Jerusalem, called *The Pool of* BETHESDA. There were

"An angel went down at a certain season into the pool, and troubled the water." (John v. 4)

page 151

many such pools or reservoirs in or near the city; but the water-supply was much more abundant than it is now. Some streams, diverted from their natural courses for purposes of war as well as for household use, ran under the streets, and came bubbling up here and there in large tanks or cisterns which were (to use our English word) "rendered" with cement.

Bethesda was one of these. If it is the same that is pointed out at this day (*Birket-Israel*), it is situated immediately above the valley of the Kidron, near St. Stephen's Gate, and not very far from the site of the Temple. It is described in St. John's Gospel as being "near the sheep-market," or perhaps rather "the Sheep-Gate"—the gate through which the animals were driven which were intended for sacrifice. The pool was covered in on the top to shelter from the sun's rays and the winter rains, as in the piazzas of Italy; while it likely had also a marble seat all round the rim of the basin. A great crowd of sick people were always gathered here (for there seem to have been no hospitals in Jerusalem such as we have):—some old, some lame, some blind, some palsied: some were sitting on the balustrade; others, more helpless, were resting against it wrapt in their tattered blankets. I daresay all of them were very poor.

Oh, what a blessing health is! and how sad, on the other hand, when pain and disease, poverty and want, come together!

These crowds at the pool imagined there was a healing power in the water. The Jews believed in some Angel who came down now and then from heaven and stirred the fountain; and when the water was agitated, the first cripple who stepped in was certain to be cured. Theirs was something of the same credulity still to be found among people in Ireland and elsewhere, who are seen gathering round what are called "Holy Wells," to the waters of which they imagine an angel or saint has imparted healing virtues.

The Jewish legend in connection with Bethesda was certainly a more beautiful one than that which the modern Arab connects with another well-known fountain in the Valley of the Kidron, called "The Fountain of the Virgin." When he hears now and then a gurgling noise in its waters, he imagines that a dragon slumbers in the pool![1]

The name of this pool in Jerusalem, of which I am now to speak, was surely an appropriate one. *Bethesda* means "House of Mercy." Jesus was going now to make it still more so. He saw there, among the other frequenters, a man who had been lame for thirty-eight years.

Try to think what that statement implies. Thirty-eight years of pain! Thirty-eight years!—When Jesus was brought a little child to the Temple, that man was then a sufferer! When Jesus spent His happy childhood in Nazareth, and with fleet foot climbed its hills and plucked its wild-flowers, that man was then a sufferer! He had continued so till the present hour. He could hear the distant blast of the silver trumpets in the Temple, he could, year after year, listen to the tread and the shouts of the joyous pilgrims as they waved their palm-branches and sang their marching hymns. But he could not join, he could not follow them. *His* farthest journey was to creep from his cheerless home somewhere near, to this saddest of meeting-places.

For a long time (we are not told how long), day after day, this helpless creature had been "waiting for the troubling of the water." But he had no friendly arm to aid him. Always some nimbler foot than his got before him. He began more and more to fear that he would never be able to reach the pool. Perhaps he knew he had less chance now than usual, for a great number of lame and blind had come into town attracted by the Purim Feast, and were crowding round the fountain.

A Stranger comes up to him. The man is startled with the Stranger's appearance. He is not a Priest, nor a Scribe, nor a Pharisee. There is nothing in the colour of His dress nor in the shape and fringes of His robe to mark Him out from the rest of the Pilgrims. But He seems so loving and gentle and good. And what strikes the cripple is, that while the unpitying crowd are hurrying past, never bestowing so much as a passing look on

---

[1] See Dr. Porter's Palestine, vol. i. p. 140.

the circle of sufferers,—this Stranger stops, and of His own accord speaks to him.

I need not ask you to tell me who the Stranger is. It is the divine and gracious Physician. He notices the sufferer's pain-worn face. He speaks kindly to him. He inquires of him, "Wilt thou be made whole?"

"*Rabbi, I have no man, when the water is troubled, to put me into the pool.*"

Jesus meets his difficulty, by telling him to "*rise, take up his bed and walk.*"

What does the cripple answer? Does he say, 'Alas! that is quite impossible. I can hardly manage to creep, far less to put my feet to the ground'?

No! there is something in that *look* and that *word* which whispers to him '*Try.*'

He obeys. And what is the result?

He rises; folds up his rug; and, to the wonder of all present, walks away with it under his arm, or on his shoulder.

A bed in Palestine, you must remember, is a very different thing from an English one. It is not even a mattress, but only a thick quilt, which can be conveyed without difficulty from place to place, so that the carrying of his bed, even to this enfeebled cripple, would imply no great exertion. In the cottages or poor homes of Syria they are simply rolled or doubled up, and deposited during the day in a corner of the room.

What a glad occasion that must have been to one whose case had seemed so hopeless! I daresay some of you know how pleasant it is, after being laid up with illness for many weeks or months, to go out for the first time, on an early summer day, to inhale the fragrance of the hawthorn, or to pluck the wild-flowers in the dell, or to hear again the music of the brook and the song of birds? Similar, surely, must have been the feelings of that cripple as he went forth from his place and scene of long weariness and pain, healed and restored!

"Stop! stop!" the voices of some Pharisees close by are

heard exclaiming; "you must not do so. No one is allowed to carry his bed through the streets on the Sabbath-day!"

The cured cripple could only tell the truth; that He who had made him whole, had told him to do what they said was unlawful.

The Pharisees on that occasion were like many who have done great harm in the Church in every age. They were much taken up about feast-days and holy weeks,—about rites and fastings; about the length of their prayers, and the washing of their cups and platters. But while occupied about these and other comparative trifles, they paid little heed to better things. They would object, as they were doing now, to a sufferer being healed during the hours of the Sabbath. They would challenge a man lighting a fire, or boiling a pot, or plucking an ear of wheat on the Day of Rest.

You can imagine how very displeased they were, when they heard that Jesus had told this cripple to carry his bed through the streets on the Sabbath! We are told they would have killed Him at once if they could. They had not forgotten His driving the buyers and sellers out of the Temple; and His giving as a reason that that Temple was His own; just as He now said that the Sabbath was His own:—"*I am*," said He, "*the Lord of the Sabbath-day*." 'I have a right to do on it whatever is good for the bodies or the souls of men.'

Jesus seems to have been met by these angry Chief-Priests and Rabbis in one of the courts of the Temple, and called there to answer for this alleged daring outrage on the Sacred Day. He makes it the occasion of preaching, what we may call (next to His Sermon on the Mount, and on the Destruction of Jerusalem), the greatest and most powerful of His discourses. The sermon you can read for yourselves in the fifth chapter of St. John's Gospel. In it, as the Divine Son, He claims equal power, honour, and authority with the Divine Father. He proclaims Himself the Final Judge of the world;—at whose Omnipotent word the very graves were to give up their dead. We are not told what effect it produced on those who heard it. We may well believe that if these Jewish Rulers said nothing, they must have felt much. As we read in the case of a similar assembly (Acts vii. 54), in muffled rage they would "gnash upon Him with their teeth," and silently vow future vengeance.

What, however, of the healed man? He has followed the steps of his Divine Restorer. It is pleasant to think that, after taking up his bed and leaving it at his own house, he went up with a glad and grateful heart to the Temple to render praise for his recovery. He was probably too poor to afford a costly offering, or indeed any offering at all, except "the fruit of his lips." He would "sacrifice the sacrifice of *thanksgiving*, and call upon the Name of the Lord." A whole lifetime had probably elapsed since he last gazed on the evening cloud of incense and heard the 'Vesper hymn.' His heart would, doubtless, be touched with these long-forgotten sights and sounds; and Jesus, perhaps seeing his emotion, whispered to him a gracious word of warning—"*Behold thou art made whole: sin no more lest a worse thing come unto thee.*"

The Saviour does not seem, on this occasion, to have remained at Jerusalem to be present at the great Feast of the Passover which was near at hand. He knew that a vast number of friendly people from the Lake would be there, who might be tempted to say resentful words to the Jewish rulers because of their rudeness to *Him*. So, as He always loved peace, He resolved quietly to take His departure. Who knows but His secret visitor Nicodemus (who knew all about the rage of the Pharisees), would advise Him thus to leave the city? If He remained, a riot might take place during the Feast, in which swords might be drawn, and stones thrown; it might even be, people slain. But it was not by sword, or force, the Kingdom of God was to be spread.

Accordingly, He directs His steps towards His old home at Nazareth. He seems to have reached it before the end of the week.

XX.

He is at Nazareth again.

You may have seen, in these northern skies of ours, the bright sun of a bright summer day for a moment veiled or hidden by a passing cloud. It was so with THE SUN OF RIGHTEOUSNESS. He had now risen high in the firmament, with healing in His beams. But "earth-born clouds" are already floating across the heavens. One such we have just noted in the angry threats of the Pharisees in Jerusalem; another, from a more unlooked-for quarter, now presents itself to view.

I am sure you will be inclined to think and to say, 'Jesus will at least be happy once more at His own bright Nazareth home. There, He will be far from the jealousies of Jerusalem Jews. Old faces and friends will be around Him!' We can imagine Him walking along the well-known valley. It would now be, just as I saw it (before Easter), gay with flowers; the patches of green grass clasping the white limestone rocks, the fig-trees clad in their tender green, and the almonds sprinkled with their rich blossom.

There, too, rising on one of the heights, is the synagogue, within whose gates He used so often to worship—on whose familiar entrance, fruits, grapes, and flowers are rudely carved; while the hyssop is spreading faster every year on its side-walls of unhewn stone.

When a man who has performed some great deeds which have won him celebrity and renown (and perhaps made the world better and happier), returns to his native town, how proud his old fellow-citizens are to welcome him! They have flags flying from their windows, and arches of flowers spanning the streets: his name is on every lip. The villagers of Nazareth will surely all be glad to welcome Jesus back again. They will pleasantly remember, in former years, how very good and loving He was. They will be proud of Him, too; for they must have heard of His fame: about His turning water into wine at Cana, as well as other wonderful works. They must have learned also that He had gathered a number of disciples around Him, and was claiming to be none other than the promised Messiah. Perhaps there were some, who never entered the synagogue at other times, who had gone on the first Sabbath after He arrived, in hopes He might make some display of His miraculous power.

How familiar the village sanctuary looks to Him! The old alms-box at the door, into which He was wont, even in boyhood, to drop His little offering for God's poor. Its high platform and wooden desk brightly painted in red and blue; the sacred ark with silken veil behind, screening in its shelves the parchment rolls He had so often heard read, and at other times had so often seen carried round to be kissed or reverently touched by the worshippers, young and old! Standing, too, by themselves, are the empty cups for the wine, which on Sabbath eve He had, doubtless, often put to His own lips. There also is the bronze lamp of olive oil (*ner tamid*) always kept burning; and the eight-branched candlestick, which He was wont to see lighted on the great festivals of the year; near it is the chest filled with the simple musical instruments used on these special occasions. And yon Rabbi, too,—the old man on a high seat at the upper end,— he knows the young Prophet well. He remembers Him as the youth who was wont to come to the sacred services so regularly with Joseph :—sometimes bringing His lamp the previous evening to commence the sacred devotions of the week. He remembers how they used to sit together, while His mother Mary went beside the other women behind the lattice. He may have even first taught Him, as a boy, to read the Hebrew scroll He is about to take into His hand. Yes, and how glad will the worshippers be when they see Him not only entering their Tabernacle, but making His way straight to the raised platform close to the brazen candlestick.

How impressive for us to think of Him, whom we have well

called in these pages, "BRIGHTER THAN THE SUN," joining in the opening 'Benediction' of the '*Shema.*' Thousands on thousands of lips were repeating it that same moment in every synagogue throughout the land. It was a thanksgiving for LIGHT, and specially for the lights or luminaries of the outer creation,—dim reflections of Himself, the One glorious LIGHT OF LIFE. "Blessed be Thou, O Lord, King of the world, who formest THE LIGHT and createst the darkness; who maketh peace and createth everything; who in mercy givest *Light* to the earth and to those who dwell upon it, and in Thy goodness day by day and every day renewest the works of creation. Blessed be the Lord our God for the glory of His handiwork and for THE LIGHT-GIVING LIGHTS which He has made for His praise. Selah!—"Blessed be the Lord our God who hath formed THE LIGHTS."[1]

Do you suppose "Jesus of Nazareth" is much altered from what He used to be?

No. There is no change in His dress or appearance. He has neither on a white priestly garment—nor wears a royal robe: nor, on the other hand, is He clad like John the Baptist in a hide of camel's hair. He looks very much the same as they had known Him for many years.

You can think of Him unrolling the parchment which has been taken out of the sacred chest, and reading the *Haphtorah;* that is, the section or lesson out of the Prophets for that day. The portion, either appointed or specially selected by Him, contained those beautiful verses about the Spirit of the Lord anointing Him to speak words of kindness and comfort to the meek and poor, the lowly and broken-hearted.

> "*The Spirit of the Lord God is upon me;*
> *Because the Lord hath anointed me to preach good tidings unto the meek;*
> *He hath sent me to bind up the broken-hearted,*
> *To proclaim liberty to the captives,*
> *And the opening of the prison to them that are bound;*

---

[1] These various particulars have been gleaned from a number of reliable authorities.

*To proclaim the acceptable year of the Lord,
And the day of vengeance of our God;
To comfort all that mourn.*"—Isa. lxi. 1, 2.

After He had read these verses, and returned the roll to the officer who had charge of the ark, "*He sat down*" (always His habit in teaching), and then began to address the little assembly. Any one was allowed thus to speak who felt inclined to do so.

He preached just as is done in our churches still. He gave a short discourse on the portion of Sacred Scripture read. The Jews called the address "*Derash.*"

The congregation, unlike an English one, rose when He was speaking. You can imagine Him looking round with gleaming eye on those who were so familiar and so dear to Him. The sweet tones of the speaker's voice at once arrest the ears of all present. Every eye is for a time fixed steadily upon Him. No wonder; for He tells them the amazing truth, "*This day is this Scripture fulfilled in your ears!*"

What did He mean by this?

That it is of Himself the Great Prophet spoke, many centuries before: that it is HE who had come to open the eyes that are blind with sin, and to release the souls that are bound with worse than iron chains, and to proclaim with better than silver trumpets the true year of liberty—what the Jews called their *Jubilee.*

So far all was well. But by-and-by their earnest gaze begins to lessen:—gradually it turns into wrath and anger. They rose up vehemently against Him. Their eyes flash fire. First there would be a buzz and whispers; then they would make a shuffling noise, similar to what I have told you I heard on the mention of Haman's name at the Feast of Purim. They could not bear to hear Him calling Himself the Anointed One! What! the Youth they used to see sitting by His bench in their own streets, or carrying His mother's pitchers from the well:—Who, when He came before to the synagogue, used never to sit on the chief seats near the ark, but was content with the rough pews of wood among the humblest villagers! Is He now to be allowed to say that He is the Son of King David—the Messiah of the nation?

that Messiah whom they expected to sit on a glorious throne, and to free them from the fierce Romans!

No, no; they can listen to Him no longer.

They said one to another with scorn, "*Is not this Joseph's Son?*" He is not even a famous Teacher or Rabbi imbued with learning. Whence could He know letters? What right has He to call Himself Great? If He be Messiah, there would surely be signs both in heaven and in earth to betoken His majesty. But where is the crown upon His head? Where are the chariot and horses of the conqueror? Who are His attendants? Truly, they are not like Solomon's bodyguard, with their capes of Tyrian purple, and their hair covered with golden dust. They are only rough-speaking fishermen from the Lake-side!

Most displeased of all are these people of Nazareth, because He has done one wonderful thing in Cana, and another at Capernaum, and done nothing wonderful in His own early home. They said, "If He has really power to change water into the juice of the grape;—still more, if He has power to rebuke disease and sickness; if He can do a mighty work at a marriage-feast, and for a Jewish nobleman, and for a poor cripple, why will He not show something astounding in His own village and synagogue? Let Him perform some miracle or magical art before our own eyes, and then we shall believe Him."

He told them that He had a higher calling than merely to work miracles in His native village. That, as THE LIGHT OF THE WORLD, His "healing beams" were intended for heathen lands as well as for Palestine. He reminds them of God's kindness by the hands of the prophets Elijah and Elisha to the poor woman at Sidon, and to the leper warrior at Damascus, both of whom were Gentiles.

Their rage, upon this reference, knew no bounds. They could not deny the truth of both these stories of grace, because their own Bibles contained them. But they could not bear the thought of this Young Teacher recalling them to mind, and wishing them to believe that God would still give His blessing to the outside heathen: they would not tolerate His classing the Hebrew children with the Gentile "dogs." Their wrath breaks out like a flash of lightning from a black cloud. Anew they yelled, and shouted, and uttered their curses. They would not allow so false a Jew, as they thought Jesus was, to be a moment longer inside their sanctuary.

Nor was this all. They say to one another, He is unfit to live. Rising like one man, they drag Him in their mad passion from the place of worship. They hurry Him to a rock close to where the synagogue was, and threaten to hurl Him down its face. The anger of the Pharisees at their Feasts of Purim could be nothing to that of those enraged villagers. They would have carried out their base purpose, too, had Jesus been no more than man. What was one against so many? Alas for these ungrateful neighbours and townsmen! They had heard read that very morning, since the synagogue service began, the remarkable words of the daily prayer—"*Blessed be Thou, O Jehovah, who restoreth His Shechinah to Zion.*" The true Cloud of Glory was covering their Ark and Mercy-seat. But "this was their condemnation, they loved the darkness rather than THE LIGHT, because their deeds were evil."

There were, however, unseen legions of Angels round about Christ to protect Him from danger. His Heavenly Father would not suffer them to hurt Him. Accordingly, in some way, of which we are not told, He contrived to escape from the fierce and furious crowd; and while they were still gathered wrangling and threatening, He had passed unseen through the midst of them, and all alone pursued His way to the Lake.

I do not think, after this, Jesus ever went back to Nazareth again. In many ways this would be sad to His loving heart, as those know well who are obliged to leave the happy home of their childhood never more to see it. Nazareth was the spot where He first was conscious of an earthly father's care and a mother's love, where He had first seen the buds of early spring and the bright stars in the sky: above all, where the thoughts of the Great Father in Heaven first dawned upon Him, and of His own great work to save the world. These reflections may have been

L

in His mind now, as He crossed the ridge to the wild upland plain.

If Jesus was grieved at the conduct of the Jews in Jerusalem, sadder still, I think, He must have been at the savage rage of His own familiar friends at Nazareth. But He knew well that He had far more awful trials than these in store. So, looking to His Father-God, and remembering the many kind and loving hearts waiting to receive Him in the fishermen's hamlets at Gennesaret, He never pauses till He has reached its hot and sultry shores.

He seems to have taken up His abode—His new second home—in the house of Peter.

XXI.

He teaches at the Lake and calls Four Disciples.

THE beautiful words which the prophet Isaiah spake seven hundred years before, regarding "*the land of Zabulon and the land of Nephthalim,—Galilee of the Gentiles*" (Matt. iv. 15, 16), are now to be fulfilled.

They have a special meaning in connection with the name given to this volume—"*The people which sat in darkness saw* GREAT LIGHT, *and to them which sat in the region and shadow of death* LIGHT *is sprung up.*" Dark, half-heathen Galilee, and that portion of it especially "*by the way of the sea*" (that is, which lies by the Lake-side), is to have days and weeks and months of BRIGHTNESS and blessing it never knew before.

Jerusalem, nigh to which He was born, had rejected Jesus; Nazareth, in which He had been brought up, had rejected and threatened to kill Him. He now turns His steps to the shores of this great inland sea, to speak "the glad tidings" to its peasants and fishermen. Invading armies from Nineveh, Babylon, and Damascus, had wasted all these lands in former days. The Prince of Peace was now to make them rejoice and blossom as the rose.

The cure of the nobleman's sick boy at Capernaum had spread the fame of Jesus far and wide. The people living on the banks of the Lake were anxious to see for themselves this Young Prophet of Nazareth. They would like, too, to hear some of the gracious and kind words which came out of His lips.

So, when He came to live among them for a time, we are told they eagerly assembled around Him "*to hear the word of God.*" A great many among these would likely be plain working people. You have seen, I dare say, in our own towns, the labouring men pouring out at their breakfast or dinner hours from their workshops; and, if a crowd be collected on the street or road, they stop for a few moments to know what is going on. So may it have been with most of those who now gathered round the Great Teacher. They would most probably do so as they went either to or from the tanyards or shipyards, the potteries or dye-works, the fields and vineyards around. These tradesmen and fishermen of Lower Galilee were open and simple-minded, ready to listen to a religious instructor.

An interesting Gospel picture of these teachings of Jesus is now brought before us.

Four fishermen, Peter and Andrew, James and John, had been out all night with their boats. Tired and wearied they had just come to shore. Two of them were on the beach mending the broken parts of their nets; the other two were washing theirs, a little way out from the land, ridding them of the rack and weed they had collected as they were trailed through the water.

At that moment their Master appears. A crowd is following behind Him, which speedily becomes larger. The people are "pressing upon Him," as all crowds do, and jostling one another as they try to get as near to Jesus as they can.

He says to Peter, "Will you push ashore and let Me into your boat, that I may go out a little way, and speak to the multitude from it?"

Peter, as you know already, loved Jesus; so he was only too glad to do the bidding of his Master.

You can think, then, of the meek and lowly Saviour seated in Peter's boat, the crowd occupying the pebbly strand close by, or reclining in rows on the green turf, which was laved by the little waves of the Lake. There are shelves of smooth rock still to be seen in that very place. Some may have been seated on these also. The people gladly listened. It must have been pleasant to Jesus having such quiet and attentive hearers, after the cruel way He had been treated at Nazareth.

After He had finished speaking, and had Himself come on shore, He told Peter and his fellow-fishermen to push the boat out again from the bank, and let down their nets. Peter was always ready (sometimes too ready) with a reply. He said, 'It was no use to do so, for they had toiled the whole night—the time when fish were most easily caught—and they had not yet got a single one.' But he instantly thought to himself, 'Why should I not do what the Master bids me?' and then he adds, "*Lord, at Thy word* (because Thou tellest me to do so), *I shall let down the net.*"

So he took his oars, and made a circuit near the shore; the net dropping into the water from the back of his boat. Such a vast number of fish were taken, that the nets could not bear the strain. When they tried to pull them, they began to break. The fish were piled up on the little vessels, and the load was so great that even the boats were in danger of sinking.

This is what is known as the miracle of *The draught of Fishes.* It took place just before Jesus called His first four disciples. He wished to show these humble fishermen by this outward act, the new labours that were in store for them. He said to them, "*Follow Me, and I will make you fishers of men.*"

What did He mean by this?

It was that they were henceforth to be engaged in catching immortal souls; that they were to help Him in His great work of saving men. They were to let down the Gospel net in the world's wide sea of death, and bring very many alive to the shores of life.

They had, till this time, followed Him as friends and disciples. They were now, or at least very soon, to become His *Apostles;*—to forsake nets, and boats, and home comforts—to "*leave all and follow Him.*"

It would be hard for them,—and perhaps all the harder at that moment, to do this,—just when these heaps of captured fish, with their silvery scales, were lying before them; giving promise of money and profit they had never reaped before. For you must bear in mind that these simple boatmen were as yet untutored in the high things of the kingdom. They were in the lowest form in the school of Christ. They had as yet none of the deep spiritual insight they afterwards came to have. But ignorant and simple-minded as they were, it shows they were strong in their love and attachment to Jesus. They did not hesitate for a moment to obey His summons. We may be very sure of this, that they never repented giving up their pleasant sea-side home, and pleasant earthly calling, to become the servants and friends of so gracious and loving a Master.

XXII.

How He spends a Sabbath at the Lake.

ON the next Sabbath Jesus goes to "the White Synagogue" in Capernaum, where the people of the town were gathered for worship; just as in the cities and villages of Britain congregations assemble on Sunday morning.

We have strong grounds for supposing that the site of Capernaum is at a place now called "*Tel Hum.*" If this supposition be correct, the ruins are very sad and mournful. When there some years ago, we could only reach them by making our way, as best we could, through a jungle of tall reeds and thistles. Among the vast heap, however, are a few blocks of stone, to which I may afterwards more particularly refer, and which seem to have belonged to the synagogue of the place. It was probably, indeed, the very building which had been presented to the town by one we shall come by and by to speak about—" the Good Centurion," of whom the Jews said, "*He loveth our nation, and hath built us a synagogue.*" Be this, however, as it may, it is at all events to the synagogue of Capernaum that Jesus now resorts. Who knows but, perhaps, "the Good Centurion" may have himself been present. Perhaps, too, the nobleman with his healed son. Jairus, of whom we shall hear presently, may have been there also, as "a chief ruler," occupying one of the central high seats; while behind the screen or curtain in the gallery, his little daughter, whom the word of Jesus was so soon to raise to life, may have been seated as a worshipper.

As Jesus is there preaching to the great crowd of eager and attentive listeners, a voice is suddenly heard in the middle of the congregation. It is not a common voice. It is a wild shriek or scream, which startles all present. "*Let me alone,*" says a raving demoniac, as if half afraid to come near the Pure and Holy Being whom he hears speaking. Then he falls down in the middle of the synagogue, still crying aloud, while the people crowd round him.

The voice, indeed, is not the man's own. It is that of an evil spirit which is rending and tearing him.

The Divine Speaker, with a look and a command, casts this evil spirit out. The poor victim, it had so long tormented, stood up calm and peaceful and happy;—restored at once to his right mind. Jesus, truly, in the best sense of the word, had given "*liberty to the captive, and the opening of the prison to them that were bound.*"

The congregation, on dispersing, carried the news of what had taken place wherever they went. So that, alike among poor homes and in great houses, the reputation of the Wonder Worker still farther spread.

The cure of the demoniac was not the only miracle performed by Jesus that day. At this season of the year a good many people at the Lake-side were afflicted with fever. Among these was the mother of Peter's wife. She must have been very ill; for it is called "a great fever." Those who have lived recently in the Holy Land tell us that there are still frequent cases of the same complaint round the Lake in the spring and autumn months. Jesus came straight from the synagogue to Simon's house. It was likely about midday, after the forenoon service was over, when the Jewish dinner and the *siesta* or 'rest at noon' took place. The Gracious Healer again shows His power over the sick in the case of this sufferer. He stood over her, touched her with His hand, and "rebuked the fever." She gets instantly so well that she is able at once to go about the house. All other patients would have been weak and sickly for some time after. But the omnipotent word of Jesus made her able to resume her home duties just as if she had never been bedridden. So complete is the restoration, that she makes the meal ready for the Divine Guest and His followers, and waits upon them.

This, as well as the miracle in the synagogue, was reported all over the town. You have already seen how very strict the Jews were about the keeping of the Sabbath. They would not even permit their sick to be healed during its sacred hours. But as the holy day ended at six o'clock in the evening, whenever they saw the sun setting, numbers afflicted with disease were brought from every quarter of the city round the door of Peter's dwelling. It must have been a strange sight, in the beautiful calm of twilight, to see such a train of misery and distress; some bedridden, some cripples, some palsied, some fevered; some lepers, perhaps, on the outskirts of the crowd, not allowed to approach nearer, known by their hideous wail afar off; some possessed with demons, howling their wild cries.

The Divine Redeemer, however, makes the place another

Bethesda—another 'House of Mercy,' and "*He heals them all.*" One He gently touches; to another He gently speaks; to another a look is enough. The twilight is very short in these countries; much shorter than with us. Indeed, no sooner would the sun go down behind the hill of Hattin, than these crowds of diseased and sick would be left to line the dark streets of Capernaum. But the stars, and perhaps the moonlight, would guide the steps of the Great Physcian from sufferer to sufferer and from couch to couch; and if neither stars nor moon, torches nor candle were there, every woe-worn face would be clearly seen by Him, from whom the darkness cannot hide but the night shineth as the day, to whom the darkness and the light are both alike.

Oh, how many homes would thus be made glad on the Lake-side! Here a man, known but yesterday to his neighbours as blind, is seen coming along the highway; but he is blind no more: he needs no longer to be led—his sight is restored. Here, one who a few hours ago was a limping cripple, is observed walking without his crutches, for his limbs have been made strong. Here, a sickly boy, who in the morning was dying of fever, has the smile of health on his lips as he trudges by his happy mother's side. Here, one who left his house dumb, is now speaking to the wondering crowd of Him who had bestowed on him the gift of speech. Here is another: she is bowed down with the saddest of afflictions: she has laid her husband and her children in the grave: she has no earthly friend left. But He who had healed the bodies of others, has healed too her broken heart. With His kind and comforting words He has dried her tears, and said unto her "*Weep not.*"

How could these things fail to make the power of Jesus known and marvelled at, all round the country, and specially in Capernaum? His name would be in every house and on every lip. The next morning's sun had risen on a healed city, after a Sabbath never to be forgotten.

Though one name by which Christ is called is "*the Man of Sorrows,*" that Sabbath must surely have been among the occasions when "He *rejoiced* in spirit." Jesus was always glad when doing good; making people happy, and lifting the heavy load off burdened hearts. He had surely done so that day with His works of mercy, and His words of love.

XXIII.

He goes up a mountain, and afterwards cures a leper.

AFTER these long hours of constant toil how much Jesus would need a night of rest!

But when the heart has been made happy with anything during the day, it is not easy to close the eyes in slumber. After all the exciting events I have described, the Gracious Healer may have tried in vain to go to sleep and could not. At all events He left His couch; "*He rose,*" we are told, "*a great while before day.*"

The streets of Capernaum were at that early hour quiet and silent. He could hear nothing but the ripple of the waves on the Lake, or the splash of the fisherman's oars. And when He got outside the gates and began to climb the footpath up the hillside, no sound would break on the lonely mountains around, save, perhaps, the night-cry of the jackal, answered at a greater distance by the baying of the wolf.

He had strong reason, however, for rising thus early. He wished to ascend one of the hills which surround the Lake, in order that He might hold communion with His Heavenly Father. Jesus did not require to pray. Yet how He loved it! Early this same morning He would perhaps plead for the souls of those whose bodies He had so lately healed. I think I am not wrong in saying He would pray for all the world He came to save. Yes, young reader, we may believe He would pray, as He knelt on the green grass of that Galilee mountain, for you and for me. In that quiet and peaceful hour of devotion, too, He would receive strength for His own work and duties. An old writer calls prayer "a Golden Key to open the gates of the morning." Jesus used that golden key now. It is a beautiful thought, that when the people of the towns and villages beneath were still sunk in sleep, this Great High-Priest had gone up to the silent Temple of Nature, and unlocked with His golden key the Gates of Prayer!

He had not told His disciples and friends where He was going; but on discovering where He was, they climbed after Him to His retreat. We might have thought He would perhaps have resented their thus disturbing His hour of rest and prayer; but uttering no word of reproach or displeasure, He at once descends with them to the Lake-side; only, instead of returning to Capernaum, He prefers going among some of the other villages and cities round about—"*healing all manner of sickness and all manner of disease among the people.*"

The shores and the hillsides were so crowded with houses and hamlets, olive-yards and farm-yards, that Jesus would be always busy. The Jewish historian tells us there were two hundred and four cities and villages in Galilee alone, and most of these were on the Lake.

Among other suppliants for help, there is one who specially attracts our attention and rouses our sympathy. The case is in every respect dreadful and repulsive.

We have many diseases in our own country, but I do not think we have such a loathsome one as *leprosy.* Terrible in itself, it is one of those ailments which, when it once takes possession of the body, is incurable by human means;—those suffering from it never getting better—always getting worse. There are rows of lepers to this day who sit or crouch near one of the gates of Jerusalem, showing their sores to the passers-by. Their wasted fingers stretched out for alms, their croaking voices, swollen throats, and suffering look, I never can forget.

It was one of these wretched beings Jesus now met.

The poor miserable object, with torn dress, and head bare, fell down upon his face and cried, "*Lord, if Thou wilt, Thou canst make me clean.*"

He may have heard how Jesus had cured others, he would say to himself, "Oh! is it not possible He may cure *me?* Yet how can I get at Him; how can I dare venture to come near to Him, and cast myself at His feet."

Well he might say so—for, as I recently told you, any leper among the Jews was not only forbidden to go near his fellow-men, but had to warn them away with his piteous cry "*Unclean! Unclean!*" It was a sad life; rather it was a living death. Think how would you feel to be cut off from ever seeing your brothers or sisters or friends? away from human kindness—all people you meet looking strangely upon you? Amid these crowds, and crowded cities, the leper was as lonely as if the desert were his home. He heard, spring after spring, the joyous voices of young and old going up to Jerusalem, at the season of the Passover;—but there was no place for him in these glad companies—"the multitude that kept holiday." He could only weep silent tears when he "remembered Zion." Yes—I am quite sure, there were no more deplorable outcasts in all Galilee than these, one of whom now cries to Jesus for help; and who knew well, too, that there was no other physician in the world who could heal him, if this Prophet of Nazareth failed to do so. It was an appeal to one "BRIGHTER THAN THE SUN" to dispel the *outermost darkness* of human misery and despair!

Can you not picture the crowd opening up and making a broad lane for the poor suppliant, who was himself in terror lest he might touch them and infect them with his own awful disease?

You ask 'what will Jesus do? will He not be afraid like the others of coming close to all this foulness and misery?'

Not so. The Meek and Gentle, the Pure and the Holy One touches with His hand the impure and unholy and defiled. He speaks back the very words of the leper's earnest prayer, "*I will, be thou clean.*"

Instantly he was made whole. "*This poor man cried, and the Lord heard him, and saved him out of all his troubles.*"

XXIV.

He heals a man sick of the palsy, and calls another disciple.

THE next Sabbath Jesus came back once more to Capernaum.

Crowds came flocking round the house where He was; they were greater than ever. Many among these had doubtless been with Him during the week, and had beheld His mighty works.

See four men coming, carrying in a mat or quilt some living burden! It is evidently a new case for the kind and merciful Healer.

These are bearing a man, ill of the palsy, and are very desirous of approaching close to where Jesus was. The sufferer himself, we gather from the narrative, seems to have felt that he was a great sinner, and needed his soul to be healed as much as his body. He got four kind friends willing to render to him needed help. The press was so great that the doorway was blocked up. You can imagine the four sympathising men calling out to the crowd to make way and let them pass in. They soon see, however, that the attempt is hopeless. They are obliged to devise some other plan of getting through the throng. What do you think it is?

They take him first up the outside stair, and then let him down to the inner court where Jesus was. By removing some tiles or planks from the top of the roof they were able to do so. The cripple is gently lowered till he finds himself placed by the side of the Great Physician.

Oh, how kind Jesus always was and always is! We might have thought He would possibly not have liked to be thus disturbed in the midst of His preaching;—taking off the attention of His hearers as the noise was going on above Him. But once more He "pleased not Himself." He never refused to perform an act of pity and mercy on those stricken with sin or suffering.

The Saviour greatly commended their faith. But before curing the man of the palsy, He wished to perform the greater and more urgent cure. He said—" *Son, thy* SINS *are forgiven thee.*"

The Pharisees and Scribes present were very angry at this. There was a frown upon their brows as they shouted out, " *Who can forgive sins, but God only ?* "

Jesus wished to show that He *was* God. In order to prove His Deity and that He had " power to forgive sins," He proceeded next to heal the man's body as well as his soul. The cure of the soul, as I have just said, was by far the greater of the two; but He knew that the people would be more impressed when He added the miracle of bodily healing. " *Arise,*" He said, " *take up thy couch, and go into thine house.*"

The cured man sprang to his feet, took up his bed (that is the rug or carpet on which he lay), and, putting it on his shoulder, walked along quite restored through the wondering crowd. They willingly made way for him now. The words were whispered from ear to ear, " *We have seen strange things to-day.*"

The cripple went straight to his home " praising God ; " and many others who witnessed the miracle had a similar " new song put into their lips."

That same Sabbath, Jesus called another disciple, who was afterwards to be well known. It was *Matthew*, who wrote the Gospel in the Bible which bears his name, and which forms the first portion of the New Testament.

Matthew was " a Publican." The Publicans were a class very much hated. Their occupation was to collect the taxes:—taxes of all kinds;—on grain and cattle, on fruit oil and wine:— tolls on the highways and bridges, dues at the seaports. They were generally regarded as greedy and grasping and cheating. They ground down the population by compelling them to pay this money to the Roman Government, but a great part of it they took to themselves, and thus came to be rich in a dishonest way. They were mostly Jews by birth; but I need not say it was only the vilest among the people who would agree to accept the office of Publican. They were classed with murderers and robbers. You may, perhaps, remember that the hardest thing a proud Pharisee could say was, "*God, I thank Thee that I am not as this* PUBLICAN."

Yet even from this worst class of Israelites—men who had lost character, or rather who had no character to lose—Jesus is to choose one of His Apostles. He wishes to show what His grace can do in changing the heart and life, making those who were most selfish and debased to be generous and good and kind to all around them.

This man, who seems to have been known when he was a tax-gatherer by the name of Levi, was sitting at his gate or toll-bar at the sea-side, collecting the tribute at the port of Capernaum;—perhaps the dues charged on the fish caught in the Lake, and on the wood that was floated on rafts from its north and east sides. The Gracious Prophet of Galilee said to him, "*Follow me.*"

You will, perhaps, ask, was this the first time Matthew had seen Jesus?

I cannot tell. But I do not suppose it was. I think it likely he may have listened to one or more of His discourses. Some words from the lips of his future Lord may have gone like an arrow to his heart and made him ashamed of his wicked gains and love of money. They may have roused his sleeping conscience, and made him very unhappy as he continued at a trade which had so many temptations to evil.

When the Divine Saviour now comes to him and addresses him personally, he resolves in a moment to obey the invitation. "*He left all and followed Jesus.*"

What do you think was implied in that "*all*"?

All the bright future of his gains;—his bags of gold and heaps of silver—and successful roguery. He sees the gracious Face—he hears the gracious Word; and though, in days to come, his will be a homelier meal, a humbler dwelling, and a more despised Master than Cæsar,—yet to be with Jesus as disciple, is better to him than thousands of gold and silver.

Oh! what self-denial! willingly leaving everything he had,

that he might be the follower of Him who "had not where to lay His head!"

A well-known Christian poet, speaking of this very scene, thus describes the rays of blessing sent to his darkened soul by Him who is BRIGHTER THAN THE SUN—

> "These gracious words shed gladsome light
> On Mammon's gloomiest cells,
> As on some city's cheerless night
> The tide of sunrise swells,
> Till tower, and dome, and bridgeway proud
> Are mantled with a golden cloud."

Do you suppose Matthew ever was sorry at the resolution he made? No: I think even at the very moment when he was locking the door of his custom-house, and leaving it for ever, he could say, as he felt that 'golden cloud' mantling him,—"*Thou hast put gladness into my heart, more than in the time that their corn and their wine increased.*" He whose service he now entered, would seem to have changed the name of His new disciple from Levi to Matthew, which means "*the Gift of God.*" Would not Jesus in a better way make up for all his losses, by bestowing upon him the riches of His own love and presence? Would He not make true His own promise,—"*Manifold more (spiritual) good things in the present life; and in the world to come life everlasting*"?

> "Jesus, I my cross have taken,
> All to leave and follow Thee;
> Naked, poor, despised, forsaken,
> Thou from hence my all shalt be.
>
> "Perish every fond ambition,
> All I've sought, or hoped, or known,
> Yet how rich is my condition,
> God and Heaven are now my own!"

XXV.

He preaches the Sermon on the Mount, and appoints His Twelve Apostles.

There is a wild rugged valley which leads up from the fertile plain on the west of the Lake to that curious mountain with the double top I have already described—"*the Horns of Hattin.*"

We are not exactly told, but it is very likely it was on the summit of this grassy hill that Jesus preached what is called "THE SERMON ON THE MOUNT." I dare say all my young readers know it well, as it is generally one of the first parts of the Bible which is learnt by heart.

There is a level piece of ground where the great crowd might easily have gathered as they listened to the Divine Teacher. We can think of them seated devoutly in this lofty Sanctuary of Nature amid the early breath of flowers;—the fleecy clouds of morning resting on the near mountains, and giant Hermon uncovering his head white with snow.

Jesus had Himself spent the night in prayer in one of the quiet nooks around. And when the stars had vanished from the sky, and the golden sun was rising right before Him, making a molten pathway on the Lake, He came forth from His solitude to speak to the people. The assemblage seems to have been a very large one, gathered from all parts of the Holy Land, for the fame of the Prophet of Nazareth was daily increasing.

He sat down on the grass;—the same position, you remember, He assumed when preaching in the synagogue. His disciples would be close around Him; while the dense multitude would sit in rows along the slope of the hill or on the level piece of ground I have just spoken of.

I can well believe it was a very different sermon from what most of them expected to hear. Many came that morning thinking that Jesus was about to declare Himself the King they had long looked for;—the mighty Conqueror with "the sword girded on His thigh," His "right hand teaching Him terrible things." They may have expected Him to speak of His predicted greatness—of the future pomp and grandeur of His court, the favours He would bestow in the way of riches and honours on the children of Zion;—the blessedness of those who were to sit down at the banquets He would give, in which the tables would be laden with angels' food; jars of heavenly manna—gathered from the Gardens of Paradise.

How startled must they have been to hear from His lips that those who were to be thus "*blessed*," were rather the poor, the humble, the gentle, the meek, the penitent, the mourner: that the greatest man in His Kingdom was not he who would subdue with the sword, and overcome his Roman foe; but he who would conquer by kindness; who would love his enemy, and do good to the persons who hated him!

Among other encouraging and comforting things,—among other bright genial rays from One "BRIGHTER THAN THE SUN,"—He made a new revelation to them of the character of the Great God. It was different from that of any other religious Teacher or Prophet who had ever lived. He spake of Him as "a *Father*;"—as THEIR *Father!* He pointed to the little birds winging their flight from bush to bush on the mountain; He pointed to the grass and flowers which formed the carpet at their feet, and He said—"If God takes care of these tiny winged-creatures;—if He watches every spike of grass and every leaflet of these wild-flowers, how much more will He (as your *Father*) love you and watch over you and be kind to you." "You know what it is," He said, "to love your own children. It is a pleasure to you to give them gifts and presents. How much more pleased will the Great Parent above be, to give good things to the humblest and poorest member of His family! He who does not even forget the despised sparrow, will not forget you—the children of *your* FATHER *which is in Heaven!*"

Oh what a joyful world this would be, if young and old would

M

only receive the comfort and strive to obey the words which the Great Teacher uttered that early morning on Mount Hattin! "*If ye know these things,*" He said at another time, "*happy are ye if ye* DO *them.*"

It would seem from the Gospel story, that before preaching that wonderful sermon, He had invited a chosen few up to the very summit of the hill and spoken to them alone, apart from the crowd. These were the twelve disciples to whom He now gave the name of "Apostles."

It was a morning surely never to be forgotten by any of them, and never to be forgotten in the Christian Church. They were from that hour to be the Friends of Jesus; constantly with Him; with Him in His teachings in the streets and villages by day; with Him treading the hot and sultry highways of Judea and Galilee; with Him when the shades of evening fell; with Him when they sang their evening hymn or Psalm together; with Him as they lay in slumber on the dewy grass with nothing but their rough garments to protect them from the cold; with Him till the awful hour came when He was taken from them; when "the Shepherd was to be smitten, and the sheep scattered." When He was no longer on earth, but had gone from them to His heavenly Throne, these privileged twelve were to go in His name first throughout the Holy Land, and then to different countries of the world, making known the Great Salvation.

You will see from this, that in choosing His apostles, Jesus did not select wise and learned Rabbis and Scribes: men of note and influence like Nicodemus. He took them from the humbler ranks;—those engaged in the honest callings and trades of common life. He wished to show that there was nothing in the men who proclaimed the glad tidings. The power lay in the Divine truth they taught, and in the grace and might of the Holy Spirit.

He loved all these twelve, only one of them at last failed Him and betrayed Him. That was *Judas Iscariot* (or Judas of the village of Kerioth).

There were three of their number He loved best of all. When we have many choice friends we often pick out one or two among them whom we esteem the choicest. Jesus did the same. PETER, JAMES, and JOHN were those favoured with special tokens of His confidence—the innermost of the inner circle.

With all his faults, we shall find the Master had a marked regard for Peter. He liked him for his kindly, frank, affectionate, and at most times brave nature. This open-hearted Bethsaida fisherman you may remember not long ago said in addressing Jesus—"*Depart from me!*" Instead, however, of assenting to his request, you see his Lord rather selects him as one who in the future is *not* to be parted, but on the contrary to be very near and very dear to Him.

We know perhaps least about *James*. But he seems to have been a trustful and devoted follower too. Jesus called him 'a "child" or "son of thunder"' from his zeal and boldness. He was an earthly relative of Jesus, probably, as I have previously said His cousin. He at last died a martyr's death for the sake of the Lord he loved.

The last of the three was *John*. He too from his zeal was called 'a child of thunder.' But though he had much of the brave devoted hero in his nature, he had still more of tenderness and fervour and affection. We best know him by another name, "*the Disciple whom Jesus loved;*" and, we may add, *who loved Jesus*. We always think of John as likest his Lord in character. He was, I dare say, generally nearest Jesus in their journeys;—walking by His side; he would often sit next Him at meals and perhaps lean upon His bosom as at the last meal they had together. In the old pictures of this Apostle there is always an eagle represented at his feet. It was the appropriate emblem surely of him who loved ever to soar "SUNWARD" in the heaven of love;—who wrote again and again the three beautiful words, "*God is Love.*"

> "Much he asked in loving wonder,
> On Thy bosom leaning, Lord!
> In that 'secret place of thunder,'
> Answer kind didst Thou accord.

> Latest he, the warfare leaving,
> Landed on the eternal shore;
> And his witness we receiving
> Own Thee 'GOD' for evermore!"[1]

It must have been a comforting thing for Jesus to have such tried and trusted friends always with Him to share His anxieties and sorrows, and to cheer Him in doing His Great Father's will. The grandest orbs of heaven have their moons and planets and satellites. He who was "BRIGHTER THAN THE SUN" had these twelve attendant planets also, to circle around Him;—and to reflect the Light of their all-glorious Centre. You remember what the most loved of the Apostles saw, long afterwards, in vision? It was "that same Jesus" with a countenance "*as the Sun shineth in his strength*," holding a cluster of STARS in His right hand (Rev. i. 16).

The work of the Divine Teacher continued to prosper, and His miracles increased, as you will presently hear.

XXVI.

He cures the Centurion's Servant.

THAT same afternoon on which the Master had appointed His twelve Apostles, He returned to Capernaum by the rocky dell through which He had passed the previous evening. The modern name of this secluded gorge is "*The Valley of Doves*," so called from the number of wild pigeons which have their haunts now, as they probably also had then, in its rugged cliffs.

While on the way to "His own city" a number of Jews had come purposely to meet Jesus. They were the "Rulers of the Synagogue," and had evidently something urgent to say to Him.

---

[1] Keble's Miscellaneous Poems.

They had been sent with a message from a Roman soldier. This soldier was an officer of Herod's army stationed in the barracks at Capernaum, with a hundred men under his command. Though an alien by birth, instead of hating the Jews as most Romans did, "*he loved their nation.*" So much did he love it, that he had, as I told you sometime ago, built at his own expense a synagogue ("*the*" synagogue—the principal if not the only one of the town) in which his poorer fellow-citizens might worship the God of their Fathers. Gentile as he was, he had evidently been brought to own and worship the Jehovah of Israel, and to become by faith a child of Abraham. While a good and brave soldier, he refused to plunge into all the vices of Herod's wicked court. He rendered unto Cæsar the things that were Cæsar's: but he also rendered unto God the things that were God's.

He was kind to all around him. More than one of the words which Jesus had spoken that morning on the green hill of Hattin,—were true in his case. "*But love ye your enemies, and do good, and lend, hoping for nothing again; and your reward shall be great, and ye shall be the children of the Highest*" (Luke vi. 35). "*Blessed are the merciful, for they shall obtain mercy.*"

It was no kindness the centurion wished done by Jesus for himself; but he had a servant (a slave)—so St. Luke speaks of him—who was lying dangerously ill. He was racked with pain, "grievously tormented;" indeed ready to die; and his master begged earnestly that Jesus would come and heal him.

It is beautiful to read the officer's feelings towards his dying slave. "*He was dear to him,*" or as that word rather means, "highly valued." There were not many Roman soldiers I fear at that age of the world who would be thus kind to their slaves. These were often captives taken in war;—or, if not so, they were bought with money; and their masters thought they had a right to do with them just as they liked; in other words, they treated them very cruelly. But this good soldier thought and acted far otherwise. His dying slave had proved a faithful and trusty dependant in past years. The master will now change places with him.

Seated night and day at his couch he will be himself "as one that serveth."

Jesus at once said to the Elders of the Synagogue "*I will go.*"

He had nearly completed His purpose, and indeed, " was not now far from the house " when the good Centurion sent some of his other slaves with a new message. What was this ?

It was to say to Jesus not to trouble coming all the way; but just to " speak the word," as He had done in the case of the nobleman's son.

"Tell Him," was the message, "I am not worthy to ask so Holy a Teacher to come into my house, or under my roof. But just as I say to the soldier in my ranks or to the slave in my tent, 'go,' and the man does what I bid him; so, if the Good Physician only gives the command, that will be quite enough; my slave will be restored."

What humility this was in an officer of the proudest nation of the world, to utter such things of a companion of fishermen!

Doubtless, however, he must have known well about Jesus. More than likely he had listened to some of His teachings, and seen some of His miracles. Indeed, in that very synagogue which he had built, he may have witnessed (as we conjectured in a former chapter) the Prophet of Nazareth casting out the evil spirit. He could scarcely fail to have heard about the miraculous draught of fishes, about the crowds that had been cured after the Sabbath-sunset, above all, about the restoration of the nobleman's son. Some of these wondrous works must have convinced him of Christ's ability to heal;—that, lowly as in one sense Jesus was, He had mightier than "a band of soldiers under him;"—was " Captain of the Lord's host "—He was possessed of a power greater far than that of Roman legions or the Roman Cæsar. He who by a distant word could raise up a child—could surely in the same manner cure a poor bond-slave !

How pleased was the Divine Healer with the perfect trust reposed in Him by this half heathen ! He said, "*I have not found, no, not in Israel, such true faith as in this Roman soldier !*" What a beautiful testimony ! No, not among learned Scribes and

Doctors; not among rigid Pharisees with their rites and alms and fastings and prayers: no, not even in Peter, or James, or John, or in any of the loved band He had so lately chosen.

The officer might well be prouder of these words than of all the orders of merit which glittered on his breast; or than if he had gained a hundred battles; or been borne in a chariot of triumph from the *Campus Martius* to the Roman Capitol.

On the return of the servants to the house, they found the simple faith of the soldier suppliant duly rewarded. Their master was happily seated by the side of the lately dying but now reviving man's couch. Jesus had spoken the needed word. The slave was healed.

That Roman officer and his servant suggested a new thought to the Divine Physician. Jesus took the opportunity of revealing Himself as the Great SUN whose light was to "lighten the *Gentiles*:" "*And I say unto you, that many shall come from the east and west, and shall sit down with Abraham, and Isaac, and Jacob, in the kingdom of heaven*" (Matt. viii. 11).

XXVII.

He goes to Nain and raises the Widow's Son to life.

NEXT day, the Master along with His disciples and a multitude of followers seems to have gone much further away from the Lake. He crossed the mountains by the foot of Tabor—the graceful cone I have before described wooded with thorn and oak—and came down on the great plain of Esdraelon, which has been well called the golden granary of Palestine.

On the south-west slope of the hill "little Hermon," was a village called NAIN, reached by a steep and rocky pathway. The meaning of Nain is *beauty*, or *pleasantness;* and I do not wonder at the name, from the accounts given by those who have visited it, and gazed on the hill-views all around, with the wide "strath" below.

If Jesus left the Lake in early morning, He would reach Nain about sunset. I daresay the place itself must have been well known to Him, as it was only a few miles distant from Nazareth. As He drew near to it, He must have been very tired and weary.

> "His lips were pale
> With the noon's sultry heat. The beaded sweat
> Stood thickly on His brow; and on the worn
> And simple latchets of His sandals lay
> Thick the white dust of travel."

As He came nigh the gate of the little town, He and those with Him see another crowd in the distance. The mournful wail heard at the hour of sunset—the time the Jews were wont to bury—tells them a funeral is approaching.

A very sad procession it was. A mother had lost her dear and only son. His bier, or open coffin, was carried by some sympathising neighbours. There was no covering on the pale young face. The sun was setting in crimson clouds over the steeps of Mount Carmel. But *his* "Sun"—the Sun of his valued life—"had gone down while it was yet day."

With a breaking heart the fond parent was walking with other weeping female friends in front of the bier. Had it been in Judea, the hired minstrels, wailing their loud dirges, would have been foremost, and the true mourners would have been behind the dead. But a writer familiar with ancient Jewish customs informs us that it was different in Galilee. The mother preceded the company which was carrying her loved one to his rocky grave.

She was a Widow, too. The present was not her first sorrow. She had no husband to share her grief. Perhaps it was not very long since she had borne another bier along the same sad road to the same burial-ground. In doing so, her only remaining comfort may have been the thought of her dear boy being still spared. She would, perhaps, picture to herself the blessing he would be to her—cheering her lonely hours and kissing away her tears. She would say to herself, like Lamech, "This same shall comfort us."

But the Angel of Death had come and taken him, too, away. She was left all alone. The one surviving light of her dwelling was put out. Without husband, or daughter, or son, the future is very dark and dreary to her. A great number of the villagers followed the procession; some wearing sackcloth, some with rent garments, in token of sorrow. They evidently wish to show how much they felt for her affliction.

But there were others, not far off, who felt even more deeply for her. Little did that crowd of sympathising friends think that in the band of weary, dust-covered wayfarers from Capernaum now meeting them, there was ONE who could say, as no other could, "*Leave thy fatherless children; I will preserve them alive, and let thy widows trust in me.*"

Jesus, the tender-hearted Saviour, when He saw the gathering of mourners; above all, when He heard, loud above their wailing, the sobs of the *chief* mourner, "*He had compassion on her.*" His own heart, so full of pity, was stirred when he noted the tears streaming from her eyes. ·Instead, as would have been the usual custom for strangers in meeting such a funeral, of allowing the bier to pass, and then in silence to join the crowd, He who was sent to heal the broken-hearted went at once up to the foremost portion of the procession, and whispered into the widow's ear the words, "*Weep not.*"

> "Wake not, O mother, sounds of lamentation!
> Weep not, O widow! weep not hopelessly!
> Strong is Mine arm—the Bringer of Salvation;
> Strong is the Word of God to succour thee!"[1]

His disciples wonder what He is going to do. They have seen

---

[1] Heber.

Him perform many wonderful things. They have seen Him heal the sick, cure the palsied, open blind eyes, and cause the dumb tongues to speak. They have seen at His word the leper cleansed and devils cast out. But here is something He has never done yet. Can he raise up *the dead?* Can He put colour into those pale lips, and life into those dull closed eyes, and restore warmth to that chill body? He who is BRIGHTER THAN THE SUN has in many ways brought to hundreds "healing in His beams;" but can these beams pierce the gloomy abodes of Hades? Can He call on the Angel of Death to come back with the departed soul from the world of Spirits?

Yes. He *can.* He is "the Lord of *Life.*" He stopped the procession, touched the bier, and at one word of divine power, "*Young man, arise,*" the dead youth "*sat up and began to speak.*"

Oh! what must *she* have felt, when the well-known tones were again heard which she thought had been hushed for ever!

A shout of praise rose from the assembled crowd. They glorified God for sending so mighty a Prophet. All that He had previously done was nothing to this—unlocking the very gates of the grave, and making the dead to hear His voice and live. "*God,*" they exclaimed, "*hath visited His people.*"

What becomes of the young man? Like James and John, Peter and Matthew, does he from that hour leave all, and follow Jesus? The Great Restorer has given him the precious gift of life. May we not expect that Jesus will likely claim that life as His own, and enroll him forthwith among the number of his constant attendants?

No. That kind and gracious Saviour saw that the restored one's appropriate and appointed place was rather to go home, and be a comfort to a widowed heart. He could serve and love Jesus as well in discharging the tender duties of a son, as in doing the work of an apostle. He could be a "follower" of Christ as truly in the quiet cottage at Nain, as in "mission labour" in the cities of Judea or at the Lake-side in Galilee. And, therefore, it is beautifully added: "*He delivered him to his mother!*"

" March, march ! the pale procession swings
    With measured tramp and tread ;
Wo. wo ! yon gaping sepulchre
    Is calling for the dead.

And bitter is the wail that weeps
    The widow's only joy,
And vows to leave her broken heart
    Beside her gallant boy.

    .   .   .   .   .

Halt, halt !—a hand is on the bier,
    And life stirs in the shroud ;
Rise, rise ! and view the Man divine
    Who wakes thee midst the crowd.

Home, home ! to make that mother glad
    And recompense her tears ;
Home, home ! to give that Saviour-God
    A second lease of years." [1]

XXVIII.

He says kind words to a woman who was a sinner.

AFTER the wonderful miracle at *Nain*, Jesus, still with a crowd of loving followers, visits for some days the towns and villages round about, teaching all the time, and then going back to Capernaum.

A touching Gospel story comes in about this period, although I cannot tell you exactly the place where the event described occurred. Probably it must have been somewhere on the Lake-side.

It was in the house of a proud Pharisee, who bore a name that seemed common at that time,—*Simon*.

---

[1] Quoted in Dr. Hamilton's "Lessons from the Great Biography."

Jesus was invited to take His forenoon meal with him. We are not informed how it was this Pharisee came to ask the Saviour to go to his house. I dare say it was no more than the mere wish to see and to speak with One whose fame had become so great. It is evident, at all events, that it was no feeling of love or reverence for Jesus, which made him open his door to the Prophet of Galilee.

You may remember I told you, when speaking of the marriage at Cana, that the first thing the Jews were in the habit of offering to guests coming into their dwellings, was water to refresh them;—water for the hands, and a bath for the feet, and I may add, in the houses of the rich, ointment to put on the hair and beard. There were servants waiting, ready to do all this as the visitors one by one entered. While the master of the house, as a mark of honour, kissed any very special guest on both cheeks.

Simon may have known Jesus to have been a man of humble birth, who had for many years, in an obscure village, earned His bread by the sweat of His brow; and did not think it worth his pains to offer Him any one of these tokens of respect. At all events, after taking off His sandals at the door, and, as was the custom, leaving them there, Jesus went to His place; not sitting as we do, but reclining on a couch or sofa on a level with the table. His bare feet, still covered with the dust of the day's journey, were turned towards the door.

When He was thus reclining on one of these couches, a sinful woman, from some city on the Lake, stole behind Him unobserved, and crouched down at His feet. She, too, had, doubtless, listened to some of the teachings of Jesus. Perhaps she had heard something from His lips that had come home to her guilty heart; some word which had shown her the greatness of her sins, and led her to sigh after a holier and a better life. She may have, perhaps, been led to think of her happy home, when, in the innocence of childhood, she had played round her mother's knee; and how she had now broken that mother's heart. No sheep in all the fold was such a truant and wanderer as she was.

Sin always leads to suffering and sadness. She may have felt her sin like a heavy burden. Who knows but she may have listened, among many other gracious sayings from the mouth of Jesus, to that which told her where alone the heavy burden could be laid down and her soul find peace, " *Come unto Me, all ye that labour and are heavy laden, and I will give you rest.*" Oh it was just what she needed, REST for her weary spirit; she could not find it in her guilty life, or among her false and cruel friends. She said to herself, 'This is what I have been long seeking for! I am a weary one—none but God knows *how* weary! How I would like to go with my sore, torn, bleeding heart to that great and good Teacher! But will He receive me? Will He listen to the cry of such a lost one as I am? There may be other weary ones to whom He may give rest; but my burden I fear is too heavy, my sins are too crimson and scarlet.'

'I will try,' she said, 'I will haste me where I know He is gone,—to Simon's house. I will make the attempt there to get behind His couch, watch some moment when I can plead with Him, and ask if I can be forgiven the past, and live a better life for the future. I have heard others speaking of Him as "the Friend of sinners," I will make proof of it for myself!'

She does so at once.

According to the Eastern custom, the doors leading into the dining-hall were open. She steals in with some other stragglers, and weeps out, close at His feet, the tale of her sorrow. Again and again, perhaps, she tries to speak, but she cannot. The words tremble on her lips, and the hot tears chase one another down her cheeks. She feels as if it were impossible for one so vile, so guilty, to talk to one so pure and spotless as Jesus.

Yet what will a soul in earnest not do? A new thought occurs to her. She cannot *speak* to Him; but she will endeavour to tell Him by a silent act what she cannot do by words.

In the language of the touching story, "*She washes His feet with her tears.*" Then she takes the long tresses of her hair, which are falling over her brow and neck, and she wipes His feet with them. Nor is this all. She puts her hand in her bosom, and brings out a little jar or bottle. The bottle was white alabaster, full of costly ointment. She opens it, and pours it on the feet she had just kissed.

Oh how broken was her heart! Mary of Bethany at another time anointed with her box of ointment Jesus' *head*. But this sin-stricken woman feels she is not worthy to do this. The *feet* of the Holy One are all she dare touch.

Simon is very angry. In his proud soul he hated the very sight of this woman. If she had come to *his* couch and touched *his* feet, either with her hair or with her tears, he would have spurned her away. He has been watching all that she has done, without any pity in his cold nature. What cares *he* for these burning tears of grief and shame? "It is plain," he says (not aloud, but to himself), "that this Jesus is not the divine Prophet He is said to be. Were it so, He would have known what a guilty woman that is who has been bold enough to come near Him. He would have turned at once from her defiling touch."

The Meek and Lowly One saw what was working in the Pharisee's hard heart, and He told him a simple parable story. Having done so, He adds a rebuke. "Simon," He said, "do you see this woman? I came a way-worn traveller into your house. I left My sandals outside your door, thinking, when I entered, that one of your servants would have had the bath ready as a token of welcome. *She* has made up for the neglect with her tears: she has bathed my weary feet, and wiped them with her hair. You gave me no kiss, as one Jewish Rabbi is in the habit of giving to another; but ever since she crept behind the table, she has not ceased to kiss my feet. My head with common olive-oil, you did not anoint; but she, in the fulness of her devotion, has poured out the costliest gift she has."

Then He turns to the poor trembling one. Till now He had not spoken to her a word. He had allowed her in silence to urge her suit. But He who will not break the bruised reed, nor quench the smoking flax, says, with His kind, loving voice, "*Thy sins are forgiven thee; thy faith has saved thee; go in peace.*"

She *did* come weary, she *has* found rest! Just as you have seen the sun shining on the broken-down battered flower, and it lifts its drooping head all "dewy with nature's tear-drops;"—so He who is BRIGHTER than the brightest sun in the natural heavens—the true SUN OF RIGHTEOUSNESS—shone on her broken heart and raised it up again! The poor castaway is floated to the Rock of Ages; and she is there safe for ever! Perchance she would often, as she thought of Jesus and of that hour of mercy, repeat to herself the words of David's Psalm—" *He brought me up also out of an horrible pit, out of the miry clay, and set my feet upon a rock, and established my goings. And He hath put a new song in my mouth, even praise unto our God: many shall see it, and fear, and shall trust in the Lord*" (Ps. xl. 2, 3).

If Simon, and his other proud and haughty guests, who had seen all that took place, were silent, cold, and joyless—this I am sure of, there was joy in Heaven that day among the angels of God over that one sinner that repented. Yes, there was joy in the heart of ONE higher than angels. Jesus was saying, like the shepherd in His own parable, as He laid the wanderer on His shoulders, "*Rejoice with me, for I have found my sheep which was lost.*"

This whole story of grace and forgiveness seems thus to speak to us—

"Pilgrim! burdened with thy sin,
  Come the way to Zion's gate;
There, till mercy shut thee in,
  Knock, and weep, and watch, and wait.

"Knock—He knows the sinner's cry;
  Weep—He loves the mourner's tears;
Watch—for saving grace is nigh;
  Wait—till heavenly LIGHT appears."

XXIX.

He sends a message to John the Baptist.

I SHOULD like to tell you of another occurrence which took place about this time,—a message that came to Jesus, and the reply Jesus gave to it.

The sender of the message was one whom we have not heard of now for long—the good and devoted *John the Baptist*.

I have already mentioned that John had been shut up by Herod in a dungeon in the land of Moab. How changed to him must his present life have been, away from the cheerful light, away from the gray rocks, and flowers, and murmurs of the mountain bee; away from the singing of birds among the forests of terebinth and olive, that skirted his old desert home! The balmy winds no longer played on his shaggy locks; Jordan, with its wild music, no longer rushed at his side; the stars, like wakeful angels, no longer looked down on his leafy couch. He had a lake near him,—but its sullen surface was never broken with blue ripples. No fisherman's oars were heard on it in the moonlight—no fisherman's boat was moored on its briny shores. The very birds ceased their flight or hushed their songs over this "Sea of Death," as it was well named.

Think of him in that low-lying prison; its stifling heat, like that of a furnace,—rough iron chains dangling at his side, or fettering his limbs.

It would seem, from what we are told, that he was not altogether forbidden to converse with the few disciples who still remained faithful to him. But, doubtless, the faces he most frequently saw were very different from those of attached friends and followers. Stern gaolers who did not know what pity was; the soldiers of Herod—the sentinels of his dungeon—pacing outside with daggers slung by their side, and ready to use them if any attempt were made at flight. The hunted partridge on the mountains flying from place to place had a chance of escape. He had none.

Sad often are the results, both to mind and body, in the case of those doomed for days and weeks and months to such cheerless captivity. Their eyes get red in their sockets, their brain gets dizzy, their very souls become like the vaults where they are—full of gloomy horrors, almost driving them to madness and despair.

Can we wonder if some hard thoughts had come into John's mind as he lay at night, sleepless, tossing on his pallet of straw? Might he not say to himself, " Can I possibly have been deceived all this time? Can it be I have mistaken Jesus of Nazareth for the true Messiah? Oh, I wonder, can He really be ' the Lamb of God,' to whom I pointed so many of my disciples, who is to take away the sin of the world? Or can the Holy Dove I imagined I saw, and the Divine Voice I imagined I heard proclaiming Him to be God's ' Beloved Son,' be only false visions—airy dreams?"

John might thus further pursue his reflections: " Surely, if Jesus had been the Son of God, He would not leave me to pine and suffer in this dark fortress. If I have been told aright that He has been doing such wonders elsewhere, making the blind to see, and the dumb to speak, and the dead to live, why has He not come to the help of His old friend? Why has He not sent some kind angel to break these cruel iron bars, and so permit me to go back to my great mission of warning from the wrath to come, and to point sinners to Himself as the Saviour? If I have appeared, as He declared I had, in the spirit and power of Elijah, why has He not commissioned Elijah's chariot of fire and horses of fire to bear me away from hence, and set me once more by my loved rocky home in the Jordan Valley? If He had even sent me some kind words, it would have comforted me; but for a whole year I have heard nothing from Him, and that, too, though He be only two days' journey from me :—not one message of mercy or of heart-cheer has reached me. The roar of the lion in the Jordan jungles, the fiercer roar of the human lion in his den of sin at Tiberias, has no terror to me compared to the terror and sadness of this strange silence. It is worse than death! If He had really been, as I had fondly thought, 'the True Light which lighteth every man that cometh into the world,' would he not have sent a needed ray into this thick darkness?"

I have no doubt that besides these, there were other misgivings which crossed and troubled the mind of the good Baptist. Like most of his countrymen, he had imagined that the Messiah, when He came, would all at once set up a great Kingdom in Palestine. But, as yet, what had Jesus done? The Roman power and yoke were as galling as ever. Then, too, Jesus was not the strict and stern Reformer John had expected Him to be. He had heard of Him joining in the mirth of a marriage-feast at Cana, and dining in the Pharisees' houses by the Lake-side. Where in all this was "the fan" that was to be in His hand, with which he was "thoroughly to purge the floor, and burn up the chaff"?

These, and such-like agitating reflections, had taken possession of the brave man's soul. I believe they came into the minds of John's disciples too. I believe it was as much for their sakes, as for his own, that he resolves to take means to have his doubts set at rest.

"I cannot," he says, "remain in this sad state, not knowing whether I have been all the time believing a lie,—deceiving myself and deceiving others. The faith of my own disciples, too, is beginning to fail as well as my own."

One day he calls to two of these, through the grated bars of his dungeon, as you see represented in our picture.

"I know," we may imagine him saying to his trusted followers, "I know what hard thoughts you are thinking, and what hard things you are uttering. I do not blame you; for they are destroying my own peace too, and greatly troubling me. Hasten without delay to Galilee, where Jesus of Nazareth is. Tell Him of our perplexities. Tell Him how needful to have our minds calmed and our doubts removed. Ask Him the plain question,

"*John calling unto him two of his disciples sent them to Jesus*" (Luke vii. 19) . . . . *page* 194

If He really be the Christ; or if we must look for some other Messiah yet to come?"

The two disciples did as John told them. They sped away up the hot valley of the Jordan till they reached the place where Christ was sojourning.

"Rabbi! our imprisoned master has charged us to deliver this urgent message: '*Art Thou the Messiah that is coming, or do we look for another?'*"

How did Jesus answer?

He replied in the most convincing of ways. He selected from among the crowd a number of those who were lame, blind, dumb, also some who had evil spirits, and "He cured them all." Then, having still further preached His great Gospel message to the poor people who were following Him, He turned round to the messengers, and said, "*Go and tell John what things ye have seen and heard.*"

The disciples went away, doubtless, very glad and joyful. It is supposed that, in addition to this first short reply, Jesus would likely send some other kind, and perhaps more special, messages to His much-loved friend.

Might He not very possibly comfort him by telling that there was some gracious purpose in that gloomy prison life which seemed so mysterious; and that even if Herod should do his worst, and thus prevent their ever meeting again in this world, they would meet in the Father's house on high; that there, through all eternity, John would behold Him as 'the Lamb of God,' and, according to the beautiful name he gave himself, be for ever "*the Friend of the Bridegroom.*"

The sequel to this scene is interesting. The disciples of the Baptist had by this time started on their journey back, and as they were seen receding in the far distance, how lovingly does Jesus, as He turns to the crowd around, speak of the character of His beloved Forerunner, who was now lying bound with chains, and about to suffer cruel death in a very few days. Never were there more touching words than those which were now spoken by the true David over his beloved Jonathan—"*Among those that are born of women,"* said He, *" there is not a greater Prophet than John the Baptist."*

When the two messengers reached the dungeon where the doomed man was, the replies they brought back must have been to him like a rift in the clouds, bringing a gush of radiant sunshine from a lowering sky. He would be his own bold, brave self again: willing to live, willing to suffer, willing to die. And when the gloomy murderers at last stood before him with the bared sword, the sweet words of Jesus would smooth that awful death-pillow: *" Blessed is he whosoever shall not be offended in me."*

John we have already spoken of as the Morning Star of the new Gospel Dispensation. Like his type in the natural heavens, how willingly he submitted that his own light should be lost and swallowed up in that of Him who was BRIGHTER THAN THE SUN. " HE *must increase, but I must decrease."* Yet, how beautiful, too, was the saying of Jesus—as " the less was blessed of the Better "—" *He was a* BURNING AND A SHINING LIGHT; *and ye were willing for a season to rejoice in His light !"*

XXX.

He teaches by Parables, and then crosses the Lake in a storm.

JESUS has returned to the Lake. Its little bays and creeks—its fishermen's huts and peasants' hamlets, its villages with their gardens, vineyards, and palm-groves, must have had a home feeling to Him now. Again crowds gather on the shore, and from the deck of a large boat He preaches to them.

His sermon that forenoon consisted of a number of sayings called *Parables*.

A Parable, as you know, is a spiritual truth or lesson taught by means of a story: I may add, very generally too by means of a story culled from God's Great Book of outer nature; something taken from the woods or rivers or plains or mountains or skies.

People living in the East have always liked knowledge conveyed to them in this way. Indeed, who among ourselves in our earliest years did not like to be addressed in the same manner; and to have a dry lesson imparted by parent or teacher in the shape of *a story?*

Jesus knew that these simple Galilean people, gathered on the beach of Gennesaret, were children in their ways; and He, therefore, explained to them the great things about His kingdom by means of these parables. In other words, He took beautiful scenes and facts from that Great Book I have just mentioned,— the hills and fields, the corn and trees, the boats and nets, the flowers and the waters,—and made these convey thoughts about God and the soul. In the language of King Solomon they were like "*Apples of gold, in pictures of silver,*" or they have been likened to a row of lovely pearls strung together on the thread of truth by Him who was "*The Truth.*"

We have not space to take separately this famous group of parables which Jesus now spake. You will find them given in full in the thirteenth chapter of St. Matthew's Gospel. I can only allude to the first. It was about *a Sower sowing his seed.*

Jesus may have lifted up His eyes from the deck of the fishing vessel, and in the rich plains straight before Him, He may have seen a farmer busy scattering his grain upon the ground. In some places the seed lay on the hard footway, trodden by the passers-by. Birds circling above the sower's head darted down, and picking up the grains as they fell, bore them away. In some places the ground was rocky,—only a little shallow mould covered the surface of the naked stone, so that though the seed sown became speedily green, yet having no depth to take root, and no moisture, it soon withered under the hot rays of the sun. In some places (as I well remember seeing still in that same plain), there are thorns and thistles much sharper and larger than any in this country, likely the same kind of thorn which afterwards was twisted into a crown for the brow of Jesus. No wonder that any seed sown among them was speedily choked. In some places the ground was rich and good, bearing wonderful crops in its season.

Jesus made that sower a type of Himself, scattering the good seed of the Word on the soil of different hearts;—" *Behold a sower went forth to sow.*"

We have these different soils in all our churches, and in all our schools, I think I may add, in all our homes and nurseries;— the *hard* ground, the *stony* ground, the *thorny* ground, the *good* ground.

Oh happy those, whether young or old, who on the great reaping-day, when the angels put in their sickles, will be found to be part and parcel of that " honest soil" which has yielded a rich harvest to the glory of God.

At the end of this Parable-sermon the sun was going down over the rocky hills behind Magdala. The birds that had all day been twittering among the branches or soaring above the cornfields—were now winging their flight to their shelters in tree and cave and mossy dell. The eye of Christ at that moment may perhaps have seen one of these birds sink singing into its nest.

At the same instant a rich Scribe came, and said to Jesus that he would like to cast in his lot with Him, and to follow Him wherever He went.

I dare say the man may have been sincere and earnest enough in what he said. But he spoke to One who knew his heart better than he did himself. Jesus saw that he would not be so ready as he thought, to leave all his family comforts, and follow a houseless, homeless Saviour. So with that bird of the air in His eye, He answered in words thus rendered in your well-known hymn—

> " Every fox hath where to rest,
> Every little bird its nest:
> But the Great God the world who made,
> Hath not where to lay His head."

Jesus must have been very weary after so long a day's labour. The crowds are still keeping around Him. They are unwilling to go away. But His kind watchful disciples see too well that their Master needs rest. So instead of walking along the beach as they intended, and spending the night at Capernaum, they push the boat from the shore, hoist the sail, and just as darkness is coming on, they are crossing the Lake to the opposite side.

It is said in St. Mark "*They took Him even as He was:*"—"EVEN AS HE WAS." The evening meal likely was not tasted, He had no warm clothing for the chilly night—no curtains for His couch, save the rough canvas of the fishing vessel. But it mattered not. He is not unwilling to go. Among the quiet hills across the Lake He can enjoy that repose which in the busier western shore cannot be obtained.

Young readers, it is a touching picture surely we here have of Jesus! It shows us, among other things, that He was in every respect a *Man*,—partaker in all the sinless weaknesses of our frail, human nature. For so tired was He with His labours, that wrapped for warmth in a coarse fisherman's coat, He lay stretched in the hinder part of the boat. He rested His weary head either on the cushion of the helmsman, or as some think on the rough wooden rail at the stern, or perhaps with a coil of ropes, instead of a soft pillow. There He fell asleep.

It would seem that when they first started and took in their anchor, the sun had set peacefully—no cloud was in the sky, no ripple on the waves. But all of a sudden one of those storms, or squalls, which so often sweep that mountain Lake, came down upon them. The wind is howling, and the waves are running high. The rain too is coming down (as the original word implies); and the boat is pitching and tossing like a cork on the waters. Yet how calm, how deep are His slumbers! The splash of the oars, the rising wind, the spray dashing over, the noise of the crew, do not disturb Him. Yes, I repeat, when I see the Saviour who died for me so fast asleep as to require the voice of His own disciples to unseal His closed eyes, it shows that He must have had a body subject to the very same weakness and weariness as that of any one of His people.

The disciples are terrified. They were well accustomed to

sudden gusts. Many a rough night had taught them to ride fearless over the waves of the Lake, and to sing cheerily their boatman's song amid the darkness. But the present must have been no ordinary tempest. They are greatly afraid lest the fragile craft may be driven to pieces, or sunk in the watery gulphs. Cowering in terror they call to their sleeping Master. They wake Him up with the cry—"*Lord, save us: we perish!*" "*Master, carest Thou not that we perish?*"

In the draught of fishes Jesus had shown His dominion over the fish of the sea. Now He is about to show that He is Ruler of the sea itself. "*The sea is His, and He made it*" (Ps. xcv. 5). The only one in the vessel calm and fearless, He rises at once from His hard couch. By a single word, "*Peace, be still,*" the rough hurricane ceases to blow, and the sea ceases from her raging —"*There is a great calm.*" He is the true Orpheus of classic fable, whose divine music in a moment chains the winds, rocks the monster billows to sleep, and unlooses every tongue in the vessel to cry out, "*What manner of man is this?*"

How easily His will is obeyed! There is no other agency needed. He did not require to stretch out a rod like Moses over the waters? No; "*He spake, and it was done.*"

You remember the words of the Psalmist? They might have been uttered by the awe-struck, adoring disciples now—"*O Lord God of hosts, who is a strong Lord like unto Thee? or to thy faithfulness round about Thee? Thou rulest the raging of the sea: when the waves thereof arise, Thou stillest them*" (Ps. lxxxix. 8, 9).

I have just told you of Jesus discoursing to the people by means of parables. By this tempest on the Lake, and by the hushing of winds and waves, He spake a parable-story of a different kind to His fishermen disciples, and one they would never forget. Storms of human passion, prejudice, and hatred, more violent far than ever swept their native lake, would ere long have to be faced by them. "The floods of ungodly men" would "make them afraid." But in the midst of their sufferings and trials they would remember the voice of ONE "*mightier than the noise of many waters, yea than the mighty waves of the sea.*" Yes, and in a yet sadder hour and power of darkness than any of these, they would hear the Master saying, in the old familiar words, "*Peace be unto you.*" "*Peace! be still!*" (John xx. 19).

XXXI.

He goes to Gadara and cures the man with the legion of devils.

THE last remark I made was, that there are storms which Jesus can calm, wilder and more furious than the wildest tempest on lake or ocean. He is going to show that He can do this now.

He and His disciples had reached, by dawn of the next morning, the opposite shore, and cast anchor on its shingle.

I remember the first time I saw these Eastern mountains a long distance off, they were glowing with the purple light of evening. But if I had been nearer they would have appeared by no means so beautiful. This country of *Gadara* is still at this day, as it was in the time of Christ, bare and rugged. The boatful of voyagers we have been following in thought, had left behind them the smiling fields, blooming flowers, and refreshing rills of the western plain, and were now within the barren territory of Philip the Tetrarch. Jesus often went to these lonely hills to pray; but it was a bleak natural sanctuary compared to the retreats above Bethsaida and Magdala. The hills rose abrupt and naked from the water's edge, with only a few patches of green upon them. On their slopes were to be seen great herds of swine feeding; animals which, you know, the Jews were by their law forbidden to keep, being unclean.

A hideous sight here meets the eye of Jesus. A man, whose wretched soul was possessed by evil spirits, rushes along one of these hillsides, then along the border of rough pebbles and shells between the precipice and the sea. He had his dwelling among the rock-cut tombs, which may still be seen among these cliffs. No shred of clothing had been left on his body. He was the terror of every one round about. They had tried at times to tame him, but to no purpose. Sometimes, for their own protection, they bound his hands with cords and ropes and chains. But the demons within him increased his bodily strength, and he snapped these bonds asunder—tore them away as if they had been tow. In his fury he cut himself with the sharp limestone flints and spikes of shell which strewed the beach. A high road seems to have led from the nearest town or village down to the shore, but "no one now could pass that way" because of him. It was not during the day only that he roamed the neighbourhood; he continued his cries all night long; startling the fishermen in their lonely watch on the Lake. Occasionally he would rush to the deeper solitudes of nature round about, "driven by the Evil Spirit into the wilderness." Like that troubled sea which Jesus and His disciples had just left—he could not rest. It would seem as if he had been sent away as far as possible from his home, wherever it was, to this lonely place, until death would give to himself and to his friends the only terrible relief.

If there was "no man" that could tame this wild beast in human shape, there was ONE, more than man, who was able to do so.

That ONE was nigh. The poor outcast comes kneeling imploringly at the feet of the kind Prophet of Nazareth.

Oh, how Jesus always forgot Himself and His own comfort in order to do good to others!

He had just come out of the boat, after His troubled sleep, all drenched with the spray of the midnight storm, and His fast not broken. But He never thinks of His own wants. A wretched being claims His pity and His power. He could not bear to see a human frame, made as a Temple for His glory, converted into a habitation of devils.

He commands the wicked spirits to come out of the man. A whole legion of them enter into a flock of swine that were browsing on the hill-top. These rush over the precipices into the Lake below, one after another, each following its blind leader, and were drowned in the waters.

Then he, out of whom the devils were cast, who had been long the scourge and terror of the region, sat quiet as a little child, at the feet of his Great Deliverer. The raging lion became, at the word of Jesus, a gentle lamb!

What a calm after so terrible a storm!

"*The man*," we read, "*out of whom the devils were departed, besought Him that he might be with Him.*" THE BRIGHTER THAN THE SUN had dispersed the thick gloom from his soul. Need we wonder if his first earnest wish were to "show forth the praises of Him who had called him out of darkness into His MARVELLOUS LIGHT"? Need we wonder, moreover, that he should earnestly desire to leave the scene of his miseries; that he should beg to be allowed to get into the vessel with Jesus and His disciples, never to leave them again? He may well have feared lest these wicked spirits might find him out once more, and that his last state would be worse than the first.

Did Jesus grant his petition?

No; as we found in the case of the widow's son at Nain, He told him rather to go away home to his friends, and inform them of the great things that had been done for him. Obeying his Lord's command, the lately wretched being became at once a zealous missionary, proclaiming throughout the adjoining city the wondrous power of the Divine Healer.

Jesus and His disciples crossed the Lake again, and found the crowd of yesterday waiting gladly to receive Him.

A number of "little ships," we read, had sailed after Him, so far at least, the previous evening, but they had to put back owing to the sudden storm. When the friendly followers who were in these smaller craft saw Jesus once more, and heard from the lips of His disciples how it was that the waves had calmed so suddenly, they were more than ever impressed with the mighty works of the Master. How strange for that Lake of theirs, with which they were so familiar, to have its furious billows stayed at a word! No Prophet since Moses had ever so ruled the stormy sea.

And yet, too, there was much about this God-Man, this Man-God, they could not understand. So great, yet so humble,—so mighty, yet so weak,—stilling storms and tempests, and yet a weary sleeper, glad of rest in a fisherman's boat!

They had yet to learn the full meaning of that "mystery of His holy incarnation," so comforting to His Church and people in all coming ages.—" Our God, yet our Brother—our Brother, yet our God."

XXXII.

He cures the Daughter of Jairus.

WHILE Jesus was welcomed by the people lining the beach, there is one who is more anxious to get near Him than all the others. Jairus was a well-known person, what we would call "a leading man," in the town of Capernaum; for, as we have before noted, he was one of the rulers or chiefs of the synagogue. When he was observed by the crowd, there is at once an opening made to let him pass through.

From his pale face, and the tear on his cheek, it is evident that there is some great trouble oppressing him; and that he is bringing his grief, whatever it was, to the Man of Sorrows. The Saviour could not fail to be well known to him. As I previously remarked, it is not unlikely the Ruler was seated in his chair of honour in the synagogue, on the occasion of Christ casting out the devils from the man who was possessed; also that he was one of those who went to plead in behalf of the good centurion's dying servant. As a fellow-townsman he could not be ignorant of the cure wrought on the nobleman's son. In these, and perhaps other cases, he had seen what the power of Jesus could effect, when vain was the help of man.

Sickness, and alas! he much fears, death, the twin messengers which had been visiting the homes of others, have now come to his own. His daughter, doubtless one much beloved, "*lay a dying*." It must have been a sad thing to see that young life ebbing fast away. The doleful word "no hope," whispered from one to another around her bed!

The father thinks of the ONE who alone can be of any avail in that hour of extremity. He says to himself, 'Jesus, the Great and Good Physician, is alone able to save my child. I feel assured, too, He will be willing. He will not turn away from my earnest pleadings. If He has stooped to heal a humble slave—a soldier's servant—surely He will not refuse to raise up the tender drooping flower of my home, and allow it to shed its fragrance once more around us.'

There is not a moment to be lost; for, like the grains you may have seen in the sand-glass, the sands of her little life would soon be run out,—the last of these were fast falling. He speeds along to the shore, as he sees the fishing-boat nearing it wherein Jesus is. In a moment he was kneeling down in an agony of prayer at the Saviour's feet, and saying, "Oh! Master, come quickly to my house; my little daughter, who is only twelve years of age, is dying. Come, put your hands upon her that she may be healed, and live."

Jesus at once said, "I will go."

Think how glad Jairus must have been, as he felt that the footsteps of the Divine Teacher were closely following his own, and that in a very few minutes Jesus will be standing by the sickbed of his dear child!

But, in the meanwhile, the Gracious Healer is stopped on His way by another petitioner.

We are not sorry to see another poor sufferer coming to get cured; but at first we almost wish, for the sake of Jairus, that she had come at some other time than now; all the more so when we are informed that, during the pause which ensued, what the sorrowing father dreaded had really taken place,—the sands *had* run out,—the pulse of his child had ceased to beat!

You will ask, who was the needy suppliant who was now the cause of this delay?

It was a woman who stole through the crowd to try and get cured of her own disease. She had been ill for a very long time. And not only must she have been a great sufferer, but from the nature of her complaint, she may, by the Jewish Law, have been considered unclean, and strictly forbidden to join in religious ordinances. If she was a good and pious woman, as we have every reason to believe she was,—how very sad, in addition to her weakness and suffering, to be deprived for whole twelve years of the means of grace! May we not think of her in her lonely hours often breathing out the fond, earnest prayer, "*My soul thirsteth for Thee, my flesh longeth for Thee in a dry and thirsty land, where no water is; to see Thy power and Thy glory, so as I have seen Thee in the sanctuary*" (Ps. lxiii. 1, 2). She probably was in humble life, and had not much money to spare. The little she possessed had been already spent in order to try and get cured. But all the doctors on the Lake-side had failed to do her any good. She was none the better, but rather the worse.

She, too, resolves to try and bring her case to Jesus. She sees she has a chance now. It may be her only one.

The difficulty is how to get near Him in the crowd. If she had been strong and well, she might have managed to push her way through, and to have knelt at His feet, like Jairus. But this she is unable to do.

She says to herself, "Oh! if I could only get near enough to touch the fringe of His garment, I am sure I should be healed."

The Saviour knew all about her. He had noted her present earnest desires. He admired much the beautiful simplicity of her faith. He pitied alike her poverty and her helplessness. The Ruler of the synagogue was rich and well known, but Jesus wished to show that in doing good to people He gives no preference to rank or station. So, before going to the house of Jairus, He imparts healing to this other sufferer. Her longing to touch the border of the robe is effected. With a thankful heart she feels that the cure is complete.

She tries to slip away unnoticed through the crowd. But Jesus, who felt the unseen touch, calls her back. He wished her to know that it was not the putting of her finger to the hem of His garment which had restored her, but her simple trust in His Divine power and mercy. He sends her away with His own loving blessing, "Daughter, go in peace."

He proceeded then to the house of Jairus.

I think I hear one of you repeat the remark already made, "What a pity Jesus had been thus stopped on the road! How sad to think that during these moments of interruption death had done its work! He might have reached the sickbed in time, had it not been for this new suppliant." And in truth during what seems the unfortunate delay, a message reached Jairus from his own house that his saddest fears were fulfilled. His tender child, perhaps his only one (like the one ewe lamb of the prophet's parable), had slept the sleep of death!

What a moment this must have been to that poor father! the blessing of his home and his life cut down; just at the age, too, most dear and attractive. How he would think of all he had lost! How his heart would be like to break as he called to mind all her little ways—the sound of her joyful footstep, the music of her cheerful voice, her gentle hand often smoothing the wrinkles of care from his brow; the pride of the present and the hope of his future! He never dreamt of such a blow as this!

Yet how beautiful is his conduct. He does not speak of the lost time which had been caused by the cure of the other. He does not say, "Oh! why did Jesus not come with me at once? If He had done so, my child might have still lived, and been spared to be the comfort of my old age." No; not a fretful word comes from his lips.

The messenger sent speaks harshly to the bereaved man. "Trouble not," he says, (fatigue not) "the Master; save Him this needless coming to the house of death. It is too late for anything to be done now."

Jairus seems to have been too afflicted to tell out his thoughts. But Jesus knew and noted the sore struggle in his heart. So, we read, He answered, "Hush, hush, *do not be afraid: only* BELIEVE. I shall raise your dear one to life again. You have just seen My power on a suffering woman—ONLY BELIEVE—and I will show you greater things than these!"

This case was different from that of the widow's son at Nain. *He* was raised up to life, you will remember, in the presence of two crowds that met outside the gate of the village. Now Jesus acts differently. He found already, according to Jewish custom, that the hired minstrels and players on funeral pipes had come to the house of the dead, making their pretended grief. They were crying aloud and beating their breasts, thus imitating a sorrow they did not feel.

"*The maid is not dead, but sleepeth,*" said the Saviour.

The paid weepers laughed at Him when He said so, and tried to scorn Him, for they knew she was dead,—that hers was the sleep from which there is no waking.

Jesus never liked pretences of any kind; so He first put out all these hired minstrels, and made the crowd remain outside too. Then He took with Him into the room His three favoured disciples,—Peter, James, and John,—also the father and mother of the child.

He stooped over the bed where she lay. Taking her hand, white with the chill of death, into His, He said, as the words tenderly mean, "*Arise, my child!*"

Instantly her spirit came back from the regions of the departed. She got up and walked.

Oh, what a happy home that house of sorrow was in a moment made! He had taken off their sackcloth, and girded them with gladness.

Though we are not told, may we not hope and believe that the Ruler's beloved daughter became from that hour a Lamb in the fold of the Good Shepherd? May we not think of her now in His presence, one of the redeemed flock reposing amid the pastures of the Blessed, and led by Him to the living fountains of waters?

XXXIII.

He hears of John the Baptist's Death.

JESUS, at this time, sent away His Apostles, two and two together, on their first missionary journey. As there were twelve of them, they would be able to visit a good number of towns and villages in a very short time. These lay all near one another round about the Lake. The Apostles had power specially given them to "heal the sick," and they were commanded to "*preach the Kingdom of God.*" Doubtless the message they carried from place to place would be mainly this: that the true Messiah had, in the person of their Divine Master, at last appeared; and they wrought miracles in support of what they affirmed.

They would go to the *Gentiles* in future years, and bear the same declaration to the vast heathen world. But now they were to go no further than the *Jews*—"*the lost sheep of the house of Israel.*"

Jesus told them, before setting out, of the trials they would have to endure. He said He sent them forth "*like sheep in the midst of wolves.*" He spoke comforting words too. He assured them that confessing Him before men, He would at last confess them before His Father which is in heaven.

He wished to teach them, as a special lesson, to trust God's gracious care and providence. Accordingly, they seem to have made little or no provision for their journey. They had not even the scrip or bag which was usually taken by travellers to carry necessaries. They had nothing but pilgrim staves; and, best of all, their Master's blessing.

After a few days they returned with joy, and gave an account of "*what they had done, and what they had taught.*" They had reaped the first sheaves of a great future harvest.

But an event of a very different kind had taken place.

Some who read this book may know, by painful experience, what a very sad thing it is to have lost one of their dearest and kindest earthly friends and companions.

Jesus had this heart-sorrow now. The mournful news of the Baptist's death had just reached Him. That death was a cruel and dreadful one. A base woman, Herodias, who called herself the wife of Herod Antipas, though she was the wife of his brother Philip, hated John with all her heart; and the cause of her hatred was as follows.

John, as we well know, was a brave, faithful man, who had the fear of God, and no other fear. One day Herod, out of curiosity, had sent to see the strange Preacher of the desert. The spare, sunburnt man appeared in the Tetrarch's palace and presence. More than likely, Herodias, as was the custom, sat on a purple throne of state by the Tetrarch's side. She had no thought or shame about her own wicked conduct. Many, perhaps most, would have been afraid to speak out honestly before all these gay, proud courtiers and rulers. Not so the Baptist.

It mattered little to him that he was not attired in 'king's clothing.' I daresay some of the officers of the court smiled at his bronzed face and camel's-hair cloak and leathern girdle. He heeded not. Just as the great Elijah, many hundred years before, wearing a similar dress, had reproved Ahab and Jezebel; so John, who had much of Elijah's spirit in him, felt that he was God's minister alike to rich and poor, kings and peasants; and he boldly said to Herod, before all his lords and servants, "You do very wrong in having Herodias for your wife. She is the wife of another; and your own lawful one, the daughter of King Aretas, is still alive."

How angry you may suppose Herodias was, to hear a poor Jewish preacher speaking thus! From that hour she resolved to have her revenge. She watched her opportunity, day after day and week after week, to secure John's murder.

Her wicked design is accomplished at last, with the help of her own equally wicked daughter Salome.

It was Herod's birthday; and a great gathering of his lords, courtiers, and soldiers, took place to celebrate the occasion. The table was laden with a sumptuous feast;—golden platters filled with meats and fruits, and golden goblets brimming with choicest wines. The banquet is over; and the drunken guests remain in the dining-hall to finish the day's boisterous hilarity with music and dancing. The young princess, who seems to have inherited the early beauty and grace of her grandfather Herod the Great, entered among the revellers, and danced before them. The weak and wicked king was greatly pleased; and, in a rash moment, he promised to give her anything she desired of him.

Salome instantly went out to her mother, and asked her advice what she should demand of Herod.

Herodias did not hesitate a moment. She was not content with saying merely that she wished John the Baptist to be killed secretly, and nothing said about it; but she told her daughter to make the king promise to send an executioner with an axe to cut off his head, and bring it back on one of the golden dishes or platters to the banquet-hall.

It has been thought probable that this feasting and dancing took place within the very castle (of Macherus) where John was confined. It seems to have been a building like many of the old "keeps" in our own country in former times, where the barons lived and feasted in splendour, while there were gloomy dungeons below in which they kept their prisoners.

I need not add that the king *did* give the fatal order. Herodias, who may well be called a tigress in human form, only made too sure of her prey.

You can imagine these last few terrible moments of John. The sound of suspected footsteps on the flight of steps leading to his gloomy cell: the heroic submission of the innocent prisoner: the flash of the sword in the darkness, and the hurrying up again amid the garish lights of the banquet-hall with the hideous gift for a Herodian princess! It was the foulest murder of that age of crimes.

We have reason to mourn over John's dreadful death; but in another sense no cause to do so, when we think of the exchange he made from his dark dungeon to the bright mansions of heaven. He was among the first on earth to bask under the radiance of THE GREATER SUN :—foremost among the privileged number who, in those Messianic times, "turned many to righteousness," and who are to shine as the stars for ever and ever.

When the murder had taken place, Jewish writers say that the Tetrarch's wife gave orders to have the mangled corpse cast outside the fortress walls, that it might be devoured by dogs. No wonder that that palace with its frightful dungeon was called by the Jews "The Black Castle!"

But John's sacred remains fell into more loving hands. A few of his select friends went to the dungeon, and "took his body and buried it." Where? Perhaps in some rocky vault or cave near the scene of his preaching by the river banks. Perhaps near the spot where he had uttered the most joyous words of his life, "*Behold the Lamb of God!*" Then they hastened away as fast as they could along the Jordan Valley, to get comfort from One who, I think, I may well call "*The Chief Mourner*" of their murdered master. In the few touching words of the Gospel narrative, "*The disciples took up the body, and buried it, and went and told Jesus.*"

When Jesus heard what had taken place, what did He do? Just as I have known youthful mourners, who, when in great sorrow, like to be alone, save, perhaps, with their brothers and sisters,—so Jesus, with His human heart deeply wounded, desires to be at a distance from the crowds on the busy western shore.

There is no spot all around where He can be so quiet as among the green hills on the north-eastern side of the Lake. So we read that, after meeting John's disciples and listening to the story of their tears, "*When Jesus heard of it, He departed thence by ship into a desert place apart.*" His own disciples were with Him, but they would not intrude upon His grief. Rather would they tenderly mingle their tears with His; for many of them loved the good Baptist almost as much as their Master did.

There was another who might well be pitied; but in a very different way. You know, I daresay, who I mean?

I verily believe Herod could never, till his dying hour, get the thought of John's cruel end out of his mind. Shortly after this, he was living in a palace in Tiberias which was called "The Golden House." The sacred writer tells us his conscience smote him, and he was visited with horrible fears. He dreaded much lest Jesus might turn out to be none other than the great and good Baptist he had slain, come to life again. He would tremble, perhaps, lest at any moment the risen John might appear before him and say in the stern words of the old law—" *With what measure ye mete, it shall be measured to you again.*"

The Greeks had a fabled female deity, the supposed daughter of 'Night,' called *Nemesis*. She was said to be the avenger of wrong and the punisher of evil-doers, bearing a drawn sword in either hand. The Pagan fable had its own stern reality in the life and conscience of Herod. The memory of John's murder was in his case the 'Nemesis' with flashing weapon, pursuing him wherever he went. The day indeed came at last, when the merited punishment he so much dreaded overtook him. "*Vengeance is mine, I will recompense, saith the Lord.*" In a few years he was banished from his throne, and died poor and detested in a foreign land; while tradition says that Salome, the daughter of Herodias, who had done her mother's cruel bidding, fell into a lake in winter, and had her head torn from her body by the sharp blocks of ice.

"*Though hand join in hand, the wicked shall not be unpunished*" (Prov. xi. 21). "*But the transgressors shall be destroyed together, the end of the wicked shall be cut off*" (Ps. xxxvii. 38).

XXXIV.

He feeds a Crowd of Five Thousand.

JESUS was not allowed to enjoy the rest He so much needed, both for his weary body and His saddened spirit. Nor was He able, as He wished, to hear from the disciples in some peaceful nook on that quieter side of the Lake, an account of their mission. He felt that after their labours they required repose as much as He did.

The vessel in which He and they were crossing was kept back by a head-wind, and after beating about, they landed near the spot where the Jordan enters the Sea of Tiberias. The mountains of Golan rose behind them.

Though the place is called "a desert," we must not picture it as a wilderness of dry sand, for it abounded in rich pastures on which cattle were feeding under the shade of oaks, terebinths, and olives; even a few peasants' and shepherds' cottages were seen on the hillsides with their little patches of garden. Only it was not peopled in the way the western shore was; nor had many cultivated fields.

Some have thought that it was still several days before the Passover. But if others are right in supposing rather that it was the very day before the Passover was kept in Jerusalem, then it was held as a holiday all around. The fishers would have moored their boats and stored their nets; the doors would be closed in the tanneries at Capernaum—the farm-servants would have left their fields, and the vine-dressers their vineyards; the women their distaffs, the very schools would be emptied of their children. "There were many," we read, "coming and going." Whatever the occasion might be, these crowds of young and old from the western shore seemed to have thought they could not spend the day better than in going to meet the vessel that was bearing Jesus across the Lake. So we read that they went in haste by foot round the beach, along by the fringe of sand or by the camel-track;—other cottagers and villagers joined them on the way, swelling the number.

You may imagine how anxiously the fishing-boat was kept in view as it fought its way through the waves. When the anchor was at last cast, a vast multitude had collected; indeed as many as five thousand men, besides women and children. Those of them who had come from Capernaum must have walked upwards of four or five miles; some had come further distances.

Instead, then, of quiet, Jesus found Himself in the midst of a great crowd.

We are told "*when He saw them He was moved with compassion.*" He likened them to a flock of sheep that had no shepherd. So He resolved to act a shepherd's part to them;—to lead them to "green pastures and still waters," and give them "meat which the world knows not of." In the words of St. Mark, "*He taught them many things.*"

We are not told what these things were. Since it was the eve of the Passover, He very possibly might unfold to them something about Himself, the true Paschal Lamb.

I think, too, He could hardly help specially adverting to John the Baptist;—His own kind heart was so full of His dear friend. He knew that very many of them loved John, and mourned sadly his cruel fate. It would be a relief to the sorrowing Saviour to speak of this first of the "noble army of martyrs;"—to point these thousands both to his holy example, and to the bright and happy world where his martyr-spirit had gone. He evidently spoke a long time to the multitude. We may well believe how many gracious words would come out of His mouth. Never did hours pass more pleasantly.

But the night is fast coming on. The crowd are faint and weary. They have tasted nothing all day. There was no inn near, and no booths erected for the sale of loaves and fruit and wine.

What was to be done? Jesus, though He never seemed to

care about His own bodily wants;—though He refused to change stones into bread for Himself when He was hungry, always thought of others. He did not like the idea of that crowd having been there all these long hours in the burning sun of an April day, without tasting a morsel of food. I daresay He would specially feel for the children who, we are told, were present. He would hear them telling their fathers and mothers how hungry they were, while their parents could do nothing for them.

The disciples come to their Master in great concern. They urge Him without delay to send the crowd, old and young, away, before they got still more faint from want of food.

But Jesus had other thoughts in His mind.

There was one boy there, who had a basket slung on his shoulders. Its contents consisted of barley loaves and small fishes from the Lake. Some have thought this "little lad," as he is called, was going about the crowd selling his small store, and getting good prices for it: he had only five of the loaves and two small fishes left. Others think, from the way the story is told in the Gospels, that he was carrying the stock of provisions which the disciples had put up before they left Capernaum, and which they intended for their own evening meal. After the previous days of fatigue and hard work, the homely fare could not have been well spared for others. It would, moreover, be a mockery of the hungry crowd to attempt to dole out among them these few loaves and fishes.

But they were enough for what Jesus wanted.

He asked His disciples to bring what was in the boy's basket. He told them farther, to make all the men sit down in rows of fifties and hundreds. The crowd must have marvelled what all this meant. They knew there was nothing to eat. Yet the disciples were busy arranging them in lines and squares. They must have felt that something strange was going to happen, though they had no idea what it was.

It must have been a wonderful banquet-hall this in outer nature;—a far more beautiful one than Herod's, with all its gold and silver cups and dishes. The people had no seats or benches. It was on nature's own loveliest couch,—a grassy slope, on which the groups reclined.

We are told specially two things about the grass; that it was very *long* ("much"), and also "*green;*" not being yet scorched and browned with the heat of summer. Doubtless it was not only verdant with the rains of spring, but it would be sprinkled with the well-known flowers of that season.

In front of this hillock—all eyes turned towards Him, with marks of grief and weariness on His own face—stood Jesus.

He takes the contents of the lad's basket; and, after lifting up His eyes to heaven, He brake them in pieces and gave them to the disciples, and then the disciples go round and round again—back and fore through the seated rows, handing to the multitude;—for the word means they went on giving.

The weary fainting crowd are all revived. The little children who had looked so piteously a few moments before into their parents' faces, are now laughing away their tears as they receive their allotted portions.

What a miracle! That handful from the boy's basket, more than feeds these hungry thousands! And when all are satisfied, there are twelve wicker baskets gathered of the fragments of fish and crumbs that lay strewn on the ground. The remains of the feast were thus greater than the provision at the beginning of it. The loaves had grown in the hands of the great and gracious Giver!

And now we may picture to ourselves that vast company rising from their green couches and about to depart to their several homes. And yet, too, they do not seem willing to go away. Why is this lingering?

One wish seems to have seized them all. To take Jesus at once and make Him a king;—the king of the covenant nation! These five thousand would form His bodyguard. As they marched through the Lake cities, thousands on thousands more would flock after Him.

This was the Messiah these Galileans longed for. He was quite after their own hearts. Not a preacher like John, to tell them of their sins;—not a prophet, as Jesus had hitherto been, curing the sick and healing the diseased. But they liked miracles on the grand scale they had just witnessed. They would like to get bread from heaven without the trouble of baking it or buying it. It was the forty years' wonders of the Sinai desert renewed, when the people got in abundance—manna and quails and gushing water. Gladly would the Jews of the Lake-side have their food thus daily meted out to them:—corn obtained without being sown, or gathered with the sickle, or ground by the millstones:—a rich feast spread merely by a word of power. They hailed a Divine Prophet who thus made their land to be, what it was called of old, "*A land flowing with milk and honey.*" They remembered, perhaps, that the leader of the Israelites in the desert—their own great lawgiver—had said that God in after ages was to "raise up a Prophet like unto him." Surely this was **He**!

Can you not imagine the scene? The excited crowd gathering around and shouting "Crown Him! crown Him!" 'Let us crown Him first in Capernaum, and then march straight to Jerusalem! There, at this gladsome season, the festive multitude will aid us in throwing open to Him the palace gates, and the children of Zion will be joyful in their King!' "Crown Him! crown Him!" is the loud ringing cry of young and old together.

Jesus, however, steadfastly refuses the offer, and He silently withdraws from their sight. He tells His disciples not to mind Him; but to go to their ship and cross the Lake. Meanwhile, as the shadows of evening are creeping up the hillsides, He ascends all alone the mountain, at the foot of which this miracle had been performed.

As He climbs, He would see the crowd below, whom He had so recently fed, going away in companies back to their villages and farmyards and fishers' huts, singing their Paschal hymns, and praising Him who had spread a table for them in the wilderness. Most of them were walking by the road along the side of the Lake, but some had doubtless come from Tiberias, and would return there in their boats again.

The sun had now set; and, if I am right as to the time I have supposed, the full moon that would be shining so brightly in Jerusalem and over all the land, had already risen. It would have otherwise been a dark journey for these multitudes; but this great golden lamp would light them back through the winding creeks and across the rough boulder rocks which in that direction strew the shore. The same moonbeams would enable Jesus to see the little vessel below, with its Apostle-crew, bounding over the waves. I daresay they, too, would have willingly joined in the wish to put a crown on their Master's head. Doubtless it was to prevent them doing so, that He had told them at once to cross, and leave Him to go up the mountain alone. He was to be hailed at a later time (that very time next year as He rode across Mount Olivet) as "*King of the Jews*," but not at present. His hour was not yet come.

GATHERING CLOUDS.

"AND IT SHALL COME TO PASS IN THAT DAY, THAT THE LIGHT SHALL NOT BE CLEAR, NOR DARK."—ZECH. XIV. 6.

"AS THE NIGHT IN THE MIDST OF THE NOONDAY."—IS. XVI. 3.

"AND NOW MEN SEE NOT THE BRIGHT LIGHT WHICH IS IN THE CLOUDS."—JOB XXXVII. 21.

"UNTIL THE DAY BREAK, AND THE SHADOWS FLEE AWAY, I WILL GET ME TO THE MOUNTAIN OF MYRRH, AND TO THE HILL OF FRANK-INCENSE."—SOLOMON'S SONG IV. 6.

"FROM THAT TIME MANY OF HIS DISCIPLES WENT BACK, AND WALKED NO MORE WITH HIM."—JOHN VL 66.

XXXV.

He walks at night on the stormy Lake.

WE have seen how Jesus told His disciples to take their boat and go straight across to "the Land of Gennesaret." They were evidently not willing thus to embark alone without their Master; for it is said, "*He constrained them to get into the ship.*" It looks as if He had to use gentle force before they would consent to be parted. He had good reasons, however, both regarding Himself and them, for urging thus to set sail.

We have hitherto been contemplating the MERIDIAN BRIGHTNESS of the Divine SUN OF RIGHTEOUSNESS. We have marked Him dispensing light and healing and blessing to the multitudes who rejoiced in His beams. We have even heard the shouts of those who wished to acknowledge Jesus then as King; in whose lips we might put the words of the great poet quoted in our title page, as they were ready to hail Him, as "Thou Sun of this great world both eye and soul!" But ominous clouds begin from this time to gather. And though no shadow from human wickedness and unbelief could really dim and obscure His heavenly glory; moreover, though ever and anon we shall mark "the clear shining after rain;"—yet the sky of His future earthly life is never altogether without gloom. These clouds, relieved only by a few transient gleams before sunset, we shall find gradually deepening into the thick darkness of the close.

The gratitude shown by the crowds He had lately fed would doubtless be cheering to Him. But He who saw the end from the beginning knew well that His enemies were on the watch, and that great trials and great conflicts were at hand. He foresaw that on the very next day He would meet with much to make His heart sad, and that, too, even from those to whom He had just been so kind. Accordingly, with the light of moon and stars guiding His steps, He continues His way up one of the hills of Golan to be alone with His Father, and to receive a fresh baptism of the Spirit. We have already seen how the great "Captain of Salvation"—Himself about to be "made perfect through suffering"—valued, as much as any of the sons He brought to glory, the power of the weapon of "*all prayer*,"—enabling Him to "withstand in the evil day."

You can picture Him, then, gradually climbing the gentle slope. Perhaps He has reached some level spot which seems to invite alike to a sweet season of rest and divine communion, and from which, at the same time, He can watch, far below, the boat with His disciples.

The wind, which had been lulled in the afternoon, has again risen. Soon the full moon is sailing in the sky through great masses of white and black cloud; and down below, the waves and their foam, tipped with her beams, look like crests of silver.

It is evident that another of the storms I have before described has come upon the Lake. On this occasion it would seem to have swept down the rocky valley behind the village of Magdala. The vessel is tossed to and fro on the raging waters.

If the disciples had had a fair breeze, they would very soon, by hoisting their sail, have reached the other side. But the wind had shifted since the morning. It was now against them; and when midnight came they were beating about in the tempest—not more than half way across. They had to take down their useless sail, and toil as they best could with the oars. At three o'clock, long before sunrise, they were still at the mercy of the hurricane; sheets of white spray dashing over the side and prow of the boat.

How they must have missed their dear Lord! How often would they think of the last storm on the Lake, when they had Him with them "asleep in the vessel." Probably, with tears in their eyes, they would gaze in the direction of the hill up which He had gone, saying, 'Oh! that He could now see us.' Better still, 'Would that He were now with us! Would that we could wake Him as before from His pillow, and obtain His needed help.'

But had Jesus really forgotten them? Was His hand shortened that it could not save; was His ear heavy that it could not hear?

No! His loving eye was every moment upon them. He was watching every wave that swept over their boat. As He knelt on the dewy grass of the mountain, though He was not praying *with* them, He was praying *for* them, that their faith fail not.

But what is this? There is a break in the clouds, and the pale moonlight shows a figure moving calmly along the top of the water. It is approaching slowly towards them. Who, or what can it be? "*It is a spirit*," they say one to another:—'It is some evil angel walking on the waves!' As the wind roared and moaned around them, and the sea yawned beneath them, they dropped their oars and "cried out for fear."

How glad they must have been when they heard a well-known voice, amid the dash of the billows, "*Be of good cheer, it is I, be not afraid.*"

It is their gracious Master; they do not mind the storm any more. That voice is enough.

"*Bid me come unto Thee on the water*," said Peter.

"*Come*," was the reply; and the bold disciple, drenched and dripping with the spray, walked on this strange pathway to go to Jesus.

At first he was fearless; but when he heard the wind sighing, and looked at the black chasms at his feet, he took his eye off his Lord. "He was afraid and began to sink."

What did he do? Perhaps we might have thought in his terror, he would call to his brother Andrew, or to strong-minded James, or to kind-hearted John, to throw him a rope, or stretch out an oar.

No! Peter knows better. He looks to none of those with him in the boat. Having taken his eye for a moment *off* Jesus,

P

he lifts it again *towards* Jesus; and even as he was sinking he cried, " *O Master, save me! else I must perish.*"

His Lord put out the same loving hand that had healed so many with its touch. Then He gently rebuked Peter, and took him into the vessel. In a moment the wind ceased; the waves were rocked to rest. Before they reached the other side, the moon was shining on the placid Lake, and as they anchored their little boat on the strip of sand at Bethsaida, the sun was breaking in the Eastern sky. " *Truly Thou art the Son of God,*" was the saying of each one of that crew to their great and gracious Saviour.

I am sure, whatever else they might forget, they never would fail to remember that storm, and the Voice that hushed it. This very time next year, they would be tossed on a more terrible sea of trial, far from the Lake of Galilee. But at that next Passover season, when the full moon was shining on the brook Kedron and on the Mount of Olives, would they not call to mind the moonlight on Tiberias, and the kind Master who came and stilled both the tempest and their fears, and brought them safe to land?

XXXVI.

He preaches in the Synagogue at Capernaum.

It was the Jewish Sabbath morning when the disciples and their Master reached the shore. They would likely go straight to Peter's house, and there take breakfast.

How much would they need such refreshment! Call to mind, young readers, how Jesus had been occupied the last twenty-four hours. He had gone for rest, the morning before, to the other side of the Lake. In the early part of the day He preached to the crowd and healed the sick. In the afternoon He fed the five thousand. At night He climbed the mountain for prayer. But even that had to be left, in order to go to the help of His storm-tossed disciples. His eyes had never been closed in sleep all night long.

And now, after a hurried repast, He and His disciples repair at once to attend public worship in the "White Synagogue" on the hillside.

Are we not constantly reminded how untiring Jesus was in doing His Father's will! It was His one thought. The first saying of His early youth was echoed all through His life— *"Wist ye not that I must be about My Father's business?"* Shortly after entering on His public labours, His words are, *"My meat is to do the will of Him that sent Me, and to finish His work."* And near to the close of His ministry He expressed this same life-motto in another form—*"I must work the works of Him that sent Me while it is day. The night cometh wherein no man can work."*

On reaching the synagogue, it is crowded. No wonder; for the news of the great miracle of the day before has already spread far and wide.

There were numbers there who had yesterday sat on the green grass, and had ate of the loaves and fishes. There were many others from Capernaum and Bethsaida and Chorazin. Boats, too, had come in, the previous evening, from the more distant parts of the Lake. They had all gathered with one object, to see the great Wonder-worker.

Jesus Himself is already in the place of worship. He is seated in the upper end, near to the Ark. The first part of the service being ended, He addresses the congregation, as we found Him doing in the synagogue of Nazareth. He speaks to them of the subject nearest His own heart.

You may remember I previously mentioned, that when in Palestine, among the blocks of stone and marble which strew the ground at Tel Hum, matted with brambles and thorns, I saw what are supposed, with great probability, to be the very ruins of this "White Synagogue." I may add, what is remarkable, that the lintel of the main entrance to the building is also lying there, amongst other fragments of pillars and friezes, with *the pot of manna* sculptured upon it. Some have ingeniously supposed that that lintel, with its carved emblem, may have suggested to Jesus the principal subject of His present discourse—the " True Bread from Heaven "—" the meat which endureth to everlasting life;" making the contrast—" Your fathers did eat *manna* in the wilderness, and are dead." I think, however, it is more natural, rather to connect the topic of the sermon with the feeding of the five thousand on the previous day. He would lead them away from thoughts about the earthly bread which He had then given them, to Himself, the true *" Bread of Life."* He knew that many had come that forenoon, not anxious about their souls, or wishing to become good and holy, but hoping for another feast of loaves and fishes, expecting the same miracle to be repeated. *" Ye seek me,"* He said, *" because ye did eat of the loaves, and were filled."*

He tells them that would be a very poor gift indeed, apart from something greatly better. He asks them not to labour for *" the bread which perisheth, but for that which endureth to everlasting life."*

They are displeased at these sayings. They do not like to hear Him calling Himself " the Bread of heaven," and " the Giver of eternal life." When He told them, still further, that God was His Father, and that His Father gave Him power to raise up at the last day, they became more angry than ever. They did not care for these spiritual things. They wanted, above everything else, some great king, with pomp and purple, to mount the throne of Judea, and deliver them from the power of the Romans.

Among His hearers were hostile Pharisees from Jerusalem, who had come, all that long way, for the base purpose of " entangling Him in His talk." But even some, who had till now been the friends of Jesus in Galilee, were beginning also to look coldly on Him. Indeed, we are told *" from that hour, many* (He had trusted) *went back, and walked no more with Him."*

The sky was too surely gathering clouds, and the disc of the Glorious SUN obscured!

Think of Jesus that forenoon, as He went outside the synagogue, feeling that saddest of sorrows—old, warm friends threatening one by one to desert Him!

It was at this moment, when wearied after yesterday's long hours of labour, and with the sleepless night which had followed, hearing these hard words and seeing these scornful looks, that He turns with a deep sigh to the fishermen-friends at His side. He says, " *Will* YE *also go away ?* Are ye also tired of your Master, longing to get back again to your boats and nets and places of custom ? "

Peter, his eyes filled with loving tears, answers for himself and for all the others, " *Lord, to whom shall we go ? Thou hast the words of eternal life. We believe, and are sure, that Thou art* THE HOLY ONE OF GOD." [Revised Version.]

These words must have been to Him "like cold water to a thirsty soul."

There evidently, at this same hour, was a new and a very different cause of sorrow which filled much of the mind of Jesus —a new cloud, deeper, darker, sadder than any that had yet dimmed His beams; alas! a cloud that had no "silver lining." In this respect a far more terrible trial was present to Him than the death of John. John He knew was in heaven, and He would soon, very soon, again meet there His loved and lost one.

There was one of His own chosen twelve—one whom He had selected as "a friend"—who was now lifting up his heel against Him, and whose future was one of gloom and despair!

Poor *Judas!* He had helped, the day before, to feed the hungry thousands. He had been one of the crew who had witnessed the stilling of the night-storm. But awful thoughts were beginning to take possession of his soul. *Jesus knows that he will by-and-by basely betray Him!* Amid the many crushing burdens which at this time the Master's kind heart had to bear, this was by far the heaviest. He could not keep it to Himself. In tones of deepest grief He says, " *Have not I chosen you twelve, but one of you is a devil ?* "

Judas, perhaps more than any of the others, had been looking to Jesus as the Founder of a grand kingdom in Judea. He had hitherto nothing in his possession save the bag or purse which carried a few Roman and Jewish coins not worth thinking about. His love of money had led him, perhaps, to dream of great riches —bags of gold instead of a few pieces of brass and silver. But now that Jesus had spoken so slightingly of "the bread which perisheth," he seems to see all his greedy schemes fading away. That sad hatred to his Master begins, which ended so miserably in "*the Field of Blood.*"

XXXVII.

He goes to Tyre, Sidon, and Decapolis.

JESUS seems to have remained some days longer with His disciples at Capernaum, working miracles and healing the sick.

He was beloved still by many; but, alas! the hatred and opposition to which I have referred, were manifestly also on the increase. Strange indeed it seems, that so much as one unkind look or word should have been given to the great and good Physician, who had no thoughts in His heart save those of compassion, and who, during the past weeks, had turned the whole district into a "Bethesda"—a "House of Mercy!"

Satan seemed to have stirred up this enmity. His principal agents in the evil work were those same Pharisees from Judea. They were continuing to do all they could, and only too successfully, to turn the villagers and citizens of the Lake against the meek and lowly One. They hated Him for saying He could forgive sins. They hated Him for making light of their traditions and rites, such as washing their hands when sitting down to meals. They hated Him, as we previously noted, for what they thought was a breaking of the Sabbath, when He allowed His disciples, as they passed through a ripe field of grain, to pluck some ears of the yellow corn, and rub them in their hands. They hated Him for dining with publicans and sinners; and for daring to take one of these publicans and make him an Apostle and friend. Perhaps they hated Him, above all, for His plain speaking, in calling themselves "Hypocrites."

Oh, He could not bear to see these men making so much of mere outward things—adorning the tombs of their prophets, cleaning their cups, basins, and drinking vessels; plunging their arms up to the elbows in water before eating—while they neglected pureness of heart and holiness of life. Their ambition was to *seem* to be good. His desire was to bring men to *be* good.

I wish you to note particularly this sudden and sad change of feeling towards Jesus, for it forms a turning point in His life. Not long before, when the disciples had gone up to the hill near Capernaum to fetch Him down, they could give as a reason "*All men seek for thee;*" and when He did obey their request, He was followed by eager, loving, weeping crowds. Now it was painfully different. Few seemed to seek for Him or care for Him. The Pharisees were ready, if they could, to stone Him; the synagogue was shut against Him. Herod and his courtiers, too, were secretly jealous and afraid of Him. Some devoted friends, aware of the peril He was in, had advised Him, for a time at least, to leave the district altogether. He does so: and directs His footsteps towards the region in which the great Elijah found a similar refuge in times of trouble;—I mean the country of Phœnicia, a narrow strip of territory north-west of Palestine, between the ridge of Lebanon and the sea.

Crossing the mountains of East Galilee, Jesus never paused till He and His little band have reached the borders of distant Tyre.

He was the less averse to leave for a while the busy region round the Lake, as He was anxious for some leisure to instruct His Apostles in the great work they would have to carry on after He had left the world.

Such times of rest and quiet, however, would seem with Him

well-nigh impossible. Now, as on former occasions, the fame of His mighty deeds had gone before Him, so that, as the sacred writer says, "*He could not be hid.*"

There was one woman especially, whose story of faith is beautifully told us. Either in some house where Jesus was seated, or else after He had just departed from its threshold, this "woman of Syro-Phœnicia" ran after Him, and implored His aid in behalf of her child. She was a heathen. Not only a heathen, but one of the Canaanites,—sprung from the nation that had so long fought with Israel in Canaan, and inflicted so many cruelties upon them.

Yet she had evidently heard of the fame and miracles of the Prophet of Nazareth; and, from what had been reported to her, felt sure that, Canaanite as she was, He would not reject her.

She pleads with Him as "*the Son of David*" to "*have mercy upon her, and heal her daughter.*"

Jesus for a time is silent. He gives her no answer.

The disciples, wishing to get rid of her, beg that He will effect at once the cure she asks, and "send her away." They regard her presence only as a trouble.

Their Master, in His reply, does not seem to afford her much encouragement, though it is with a gentle voice He says, "*I am not sent, but to the lost sheep of the house of Israel.*"

Falling at His feet, she cried, "*Lord, help me!*"

But even still, instead of being melted with this new fervent pleading, He speaks in reply (not with His usual kindness and tenderness) of the Jews as "*children,*" and of the Gentiles as "*dogs;*" animals which, next to swine, the Hebrews abhorred. He says, "*It will not do to give to dogs the bread which belongs to the children.*"

Most people would have been grievously hurt at this. We expect to see her leaving in despair,—going home again, sick at heart, to her sad and anxious watchings. But she is not repelled by the hard saying; or rather her faith has a ready answer. She replies,

"Yes, Lord; I willingly put myself in the dogs' place. They only have the crumbs to eat which fall under the Master's table. I am a poor Gentile; I am not worthy to have the bread. But I am more than thankful if Thou wilt let me have the dogs' portion, and pick up the crumbs which fall at Thy feet."

What an example of simple trust and earnest pleading! She seems to say in the spirit of him who would not let the wrestling angel go without a blessing,—

> "Master, speak! Thy servant heareth,
> Waiting for Thy gracious word,
> Longing for Thy voice that cheereth;
> Master! let it now be heard.
> With the music of Thy voice
> Speak! and bid my child rejoice!
>
> "Master, speak! I kneel before Thee,
> Listening, longing, waiting still;
> Oh, how long shall I implore Thee
> This petition to fulfil!
> Hast Thou not one word for me,
> Must my prayer unanswered be?
>
> "Master, speak! though least and lowest,
> Let me not unheard depart;
> Master, speak! for Oh, Thou knowest
> All the yearning of my heart.
> I am listening, Lord, for Thee;
> Master, speak, Oh speak to me!"[1]

The flood of love and mercy which had long been pent up in the heart of Jesus at last breaks forth. The Master does at last speak in tones of wonted compassion,—

"*O woman,*" He says, "*great is thy faith. Be it unto thee even as thou wilt.*"

When she went home, her daughter lay on the bed with the peaceful smile of a perfect cure on her face. She was a sufferer no more.

---

[1] "Ministry of Song."

XXXVIII.

He returns to the East of the Lake.

JESUS evidently did not remain long away from the Land of Israel. Indeed I do not think it is likely that He would do more than merely cross the heathen border. He may possibly have seen at a distance the temples and shrines of Baal, Ashteroth, and Hercules, the false deities which were there worshipped. He must have felt a strange interest in being within Gentile territory. As He gazed from the heights upon the blue waters of the 'Great Sea,' could He fail to think of "the *Isles of Chittim*," and the bright and beautiful lands far beyond the distant horizon, whose inhabitants were then sunk in idolatry, bowing to false gods of wood and stone; but who, in the course of ages, would come to love His name and be ready to suffer for His sake?

Be this as it may, He and His disciples slowly retrace their steps to Galilee. I say slowly, for they could not travel far at a time, as it was now the month of May, and the heat at that season was very great.

Crossing probably through one of the valleys of the Lebanon, with its gnarled firs and hoary cedars; and skirting the base of Mount Hermon, they would come down by the eastern bank of the Jordan to a half-heathen region called Decapolis.

Decapolis is a Greek word which means "ten cities." The chief of these—Gadara, Hippo, and Pella—were principally peopled by Greeks. The district was ruled, as I have already told you, by Philip.

When Jesus was last here, you may remember the people rejected Him, and prayed Him to depart from their shores. The cure He had wrought, however, on the Gadara demoniac, doubtless gave Him now a much better reception. How could the inhabitants help being attracted to the Great and Gracious Physician, when they saw, in the perfect cure effected on the man who had been the terror of their neighbourhood, proof of His divine and wondrous power? A fierce lion had been tamed into a gentle lamb.

Notwithstanding that it was harvest-time, when the people were busy with their crops, they flocked out to see Jesus and hear Him. They seem even to have remained nigh to where He was, by night as well as by day,—not returning to their homes, but (at the season when no rain fell) sleeping under the bright stars, and making the grass their couch. Doubtless He and His disciples did the same.

He wrought many miracles among them. We are specially told by St. Matthew (xv. 30) that "Jesus went up into *a mountain.*" And then he describes the crowds who carried their sick and diseased and dying friends up the hillside. It is a striking picture. Doubtless St. Matthew himself saw it, and it had fixed itself deeply in his mind. The Saviour, he informs us, was *seated* on the green turf. Down below were seen numbers toiling up the steep ascent. Some guiding the blind, some carrying the sick and the lame on mats or on litters. He even speaks of them "casting their friends down" at Jesus' feet :—as if each new company was in haste to be the first to listen to the healing word or to receive the healing touch. He cured them all.

As the crowd had followed Him for days together, He repeated in their case a miracle, like the one of which I have already told you, by feeding four thousand on seven loaves and a few fishes. You can think, therefore, once more of a similar scene to that at Bethsaida :—the people seated in rows, with their harvest dresses on, and their faces bronzed with the sun :—the disciples, as before, going up and down the dense ranks, and giving them not only as much as they could eat, but again filling their large wicker baskets with the fragments that were over.

The inhabitants of this Eastern region had no great favour for the Jews on the other side of the Lake; but they could not withhold their astonishment at the divine power exercised by the

Prophet of Nazareth; so "*they glorified*" the God of the Jews—"*the God of Israel.*"

The last week could not fail to teach a new and startling lesson to Christ's own Apostles, though it was one they were slow to learn. Their Master had been preaching and working cures in Gentile lands. He had thereby given them their first instruction—and that too by His own example—in the great command He was afterwards to lay upon them, "*Go ye into all the world, and preach the Gospel to every creature.*"

XXXIX.

He goes to the coasts of Cesarea Philippi.

AFTER remaining some time in the region on the east of the Lake, Jesus crosses by boat along with the disciples to Magdala.

Magdala, you may remember, was a village between Capernaum and Tiberias, but much nearer Tiberias. It was situated at the south side of the chain of rocky hills which hem in the rich plain of Gennesaret: a miserable enough handful of hovels at the present day; so miserable I had no desire to enter it. But it must have been beautiful in the time of Christ, embosomed in its grove of palms. It looked right across what must have been the most fertile spot almost on earth—"*The Plain,*" as it was called by the Lake-side people—with its fields of varied grain, its flowers of varied hue, and its birds of varied plumage. Glorious Mount Hermon rose in the background.

The "clouds" I have described, which had compelled Jesus to take refuge elsewhere, were still hanging over the old scene of His labour, darkly and heavily as ever. The Pharisees, who had a few weeks before driven Him from Capernaum, were ready still to do Him all the harm they could, and to injure the effect of His miracles and teaching. They had got the Sadducees, the Scribes, and the Herodians to side with them. These belonged generally to the upper classes. They doubtless had spies to watch His movements. No sooner did they see the well-known boat crossing the Lake than they hurried round the path fringing the shore, and were at the little natural harbour of Magdala, waiting to receive Him.

We are told "they asked of Him a sign." What did they mean by such a request?

They wished Him to perform some mighty works, in evidence of His claims to be ".a Teacher sent from God."

Jesus declines to do so. He knew that they desired this, not to convince them of the truth of what He taught and what He did, but rather that they might try to discover something false and unreal in His miracles. He knew too well that the most wonderful deeds He could perform would not soften or remove their hatred. Even curing another demoniac, or raising from the dead another ruler's daughter or widow's son, might only increase their opposition. He said, on another occasion, "*If they hear not Moses and the prophets, neither will they be persuaded although one rose from the dead.*"

St. Mark tells us that, when Christ refused to give them this sign, He *heaved a sigh.* It told how deeply He felt being thus treated by these narrow minds and hard hearts, on the very shores, too, which once so befriended Him.

Seeing, then, that it would only grieve His own spirit, as well as the hearts of His disciples, were He to wait longer amid these unkind looks and angry sneers, the Master at once enters, probably towards the afternoon, the same boat which had brought Himself and His friends across the Lake. Hoisting the sail, they take a more northerly course. Passing Bethsaida, Capernaum, and Chorazin on the way, they land about sunset near the place where the first miracle of the loaves was performed.

There must have been many a pang of sorrow in the human soul of Jesus during that voyage. He was bidding farewell for ever to Galilee as the scene of His preaching. He might pay it afterwards, as He did, a passing visit, but it would never again be His *home*. A few weeks before, He was hailed as King, and might have been borne in triumph to a throne. Now He felt He was a lonely, deserted Pilgrim, escaping from those who had become cruelly faithless. You may remember an expression in one of the Psalms—"*The sun knoweth his going down.*" In another sense, and with a very different meaning in regard to the great LIGHT OF THE WORLD, was that saying now true!

There was one striking miracle (illustrated on the opposite page) which Jesus now performed on a blind man, at Bethsaida-Julias.

The frequency of cures performed on the blind, recorded in the Gospels and Acts, is not anything strange to those who have been in the East. The loss of sight is there a much more common calamity than it is here. Some attribute it to the climate; some to the glare of the sun. A writer mentions that "in Jaffa every tenth person is said to be blind." In the present case, we are told nothing whatever regarding the wretched being himself who was now brought into the presence of Jesus. We may fancy him a poor, ignorant, half-naked outcast. Yet, though unable to put the thought in words, doubtless, with all his ignorance and degradation, he could feel, and feel deeply, in common with his fellow-sufferers, the plaintive sigh the great Master of Song puts into the lips of Israel's blind Judge—

> "Total eclipse! no sun, no moon.
> All dark amidst the blaze of noon;
> O Glorious Light! no cheering ray
> To glad my eyes with welcome day!
> Why thus deprived—Thy prime decree?
> Sun, moon, and stars are dark to me!"[1]

One of the main points, if not *the* main point, of interest in the miracle, is Jesus (before performing the cure), taking the helpless creature "*by the hand,*" as He "led him out of the town,"

---

[1] Handel's "Samson."

"*He took the blind man by the hand, and led him out of the town*" (Mark viii. 23) . . . . (*opposite page* 238)

away from the hard thoughts and unkind speeches that might have been uttered aloud in the throng of street or bazaar; some of which, indeed, may have already fallen on the ear of the Gracious Healer. "*And they bring a blind man unto Him, and besought Him to touch him. And* HE TOOK THE BLIND MAN BY THE HAND" (Mark viii. 22, 23).

Oh, most touching picture! We have heard of kings and queens stooping over the couch of beggary, or fetching water to dying lips. But here is the Lord and Giver of Life and LIGHT linking His hand with that of one, alike in mind and body—inwardly as well as outwardly—in deepest DARKNESS!

The man was restored. May we not hope that his eyes were opened to nobler visions than those of lake and river and mountain around him?

Jesus and His disciples now moved further north still.

Had it not been for the sorrowful feelings I have described, this could not fail to be a very interesting journey. The road or track would lead along the banks of the river Jordan and lake Merom. They continued till they reached one of the loveliest places in the Holy Land. It is a city called in the Gospels *Cesarea Philippi*, so named by Philip, in honour of his master, Augustus Cæsar. Its ruins are now called *Banias*. I believe, at the time at which Jesus visited it, it was one of those highland or upland resorts, to which the Lake people were in the habit of going in the heat of summer, when their own shores were burning like a furnace. It was pleasant for them to be there refreshed with the breezes from Hermon, and to hear the streams, fed so copiously by the melting snows, singing their way down the dells on their way to the rushing Jordan. Above the grotto in the rock, out of which the sacred river flows, Herod had erected a temple of fine white marble.

I shall never forget the pleasant afternoon I spent there, by the side of these streams, and under the groups of old olives. The wild bean especially, among other plentiful flowers, was scenting the fields close by. Hills there are in every part of the

Holy Land, but none such as you have at Banias. You are there at the very base of what they call in Syriac, "the Kingly Mountain;" though the top is not visible, owing to the 'spurs' or bold ridges it throws out on all sides. It was pleasing to be able to trace the footsteps of Jesus in such a place! He who discoursed so often about the beautiful things in nature—the morning and evening sky, the vine, the sower, the fowls of heaven—would not be insensible to the glory and grandeur of scenes like this. After disputing with Pharisees, Sadducees, and Herodians, would not the rush of the arrowy river, as it bounded from a cave green with moss and fern, sound like music in His ear? That of which Moses had a distant view from Pisgah, He was gazing upon close by—"*that goodly mountain and Lebanon.*" The cliffs and rocks would look like the walls of a great temple "not made with hands."

I shall tell you in our next, more about what Jesus said and did in this choice region of Palestine.

XL.

He is confessed by His Apostles to be the Son of the Living God.

JESUS does not seem to have entered the town of Cesarea Philippi. Indeed, He always avoided, when He could, even the working of miracles within walled cities. Both in His mighty deeds and in His teaching He greatly preferred green fields and mountain-sides and the pure air of heaven. Tiberias was the Roman capital of the Lake, filled with splendid buildings and costly villas; but we never hear of Him going into it, or once gazing on the "Golden palace" of its proud master.

So it was now with Cesarea Philippi. He went to what is called in the Gospels its "coasts;" that is, as we explained in reference to Bethlehem, some hamlets or villages in the outskirts; perhaps pitching His tent, as travellers do still, on the mossy banks of the sacred stream, amid the terebinths and blossoming oleanders.

As the gracious Master was walking in His disciples' company, somewhere nigh this spot, thinking of the clouds of sorrow that were mustering over His head, He put the question to them— "*Who do men say that I, the Son of Man, am?*"

The Apostles would, doubtless, have dearly liked, could they have done so, to reply, "Oh, all men believe in Thee as the Messiah of the Jews."

But they felt they must speak the truth. He had asked them a simple question, and they must give Him a truthful answer.

They told Him what they knew from mingling with people on the Lake-side. Some said He was John the Baptist, whom Herod had slain, now risen from the dead. Others thought He was the great Elijah come back in his fiery chariot, with power over life and death. Others thought, from the kindness He showed to the poor and distressed and sorrowful—from His gentle ways and loving words—that He must be the tender, weeping Jeremiah. The Jews thought this latter prophet had hidden the sacred Ark and the Altar of Incense when the King of Babylon destroyed the Temple, and some of them now imagined he had risen from the grave in order to set these up again.

Jesus knew too well about all these poor human guesses with regard to Him, and how far short they came of the truth. He listens in silence. He made no remark as to what His faithful followers had now said. But He wishes above all to know what their own thoughts and feelings are. He knew well that they were personally much attached to Him. He did not need to be assured of that. But He was anxious from their own lips, to hear their opinion regarding His claims to be Messiah and the Son of God. Could it be that they entertained no nobler views and ideas than others, about His character, dignity, and destiny?

Perhaps with the tear in His eye, and fetching another heavy sigh, He adds to His former question, "*But whom say* YE *that I am?*"

Peter, in the name of all the rest, has a ready answer. What golden words they were! He does not say "we hope" or "we think," but

"THOU ART THE CHRIST, THE SON OF THE LIVING GOD."

Jesus made the well-known reply to Peter and to the Church in ever age. He points to Himself as the living Rock on which that Church was built, against which the powers and the gates of hell would never prevail.

He told Peter how specially pleased He was with his declaration. Indeed, from that hour, He gave this Apostle, hitherto called *Simon*, the new name of "*Peter*" (the Greek for the Hebrew word "*Cephas*")—the name, you may remember, Jesus, at their earliest meeting, had promised to bestow upon His ardent disciple. The noble faith which he had shown in his present confession had made him fit to be one of the foundation-*stones* of the great spiritual building. It was as if His Lord had said, 'Simon! thou hast given Me My true name and title—"*the Son of the living God;*" I will give to thee also a new designation in token of My approval, and in order that in all future years thou mayest call this hour to mind, "*Verily I say unto thee, That thou art* PETER."'

In that moment of joy, when the faith of His dear disciples was secure and strong, Jesus takes the opportunity of telling what must have been to them sad and awful tidings. Deeper clouds still were brooding in the distant horizon. The announcement He makes is none other than this:—that He, the Bright SUN of Glory, is destined to undergo an awful eclipse,—that He is ere long to be given up to cruel suffering and death! Yes, He, the "Prince of Life," is *to be* KILLED!

I say again, dear readers, what a shock would these tidings be to the faithful ones who were now walking by their Lord's side! How the gentle John would be saddened! How the thoughtful Thomas would be staggered! How would all the others be dumb with terror and amazement!

One of their number, however, cannot keep silent. Always

ready to speak out his mind, Peter, with an unbecoming boldness, tells his Master that He dislikes the thought of His going to Jerusalem thus to suffer and die. It would be contrary to all his ideas of the Messiah spoken of by Psalmists and Prophets—" the Mighty One," who was to be "set as King on His holy hill of Zion," and whose "name was to endure for ever." With this earthly throne in his eye, the Apostle gave way for the moment to his natural rashness. He said, " This, O my Master, can never happen to Thee. Forbid the thought that ' the Son of the living God ' should ever be thus cruelly treated ! "

Jesus had to deliver a severe rebuke to him for venturing to speak so " unadvisedly with his lips."

And now, as the gates of Cesarea Philippi are in view, a crowd begins to gather round Jesus. Some in this crowd may possibly have been old hearers from the Lake, whose once ardent love to Him, as in the case of others, had cooled. They had sought Him for the bread which perisheth, and imagined they might secure worldly gain to themselves by becoming His disciples.

It may have been specially to these He spake words which occur at this time, and which are among the most solemn He ever uttered—" *What shall it profit a man if he gain the whole world and lose his own soul ?* " He would, perhaps, also feel such a saying very needful to be addressed to those dwelling in a half-Greek, half-Roman city, where there were many wicked scenes witnessed and many wicked deeds done, not familiar to the simple Jewish townsmen on the Lake. The very name *Banias* (Panias) spoke of the Greek god Pan, who was thought to live with his fabled wood-nymphs close by, and was worshipped with sinful rites.

I shall speak presently of a scene of wonderful glory which took place six days later, and was a fitting close to this brief retirement to beautiful Banias.

XLI.

He ascends the Mount of Transfiguration.

It is evening. The sun is setting over the Great Sea, as four figures are seen in the dusk, going slowly, first up the wooded valley north of Cesarea Philippi, and then climbing one of the bare, grassy slopes of what St. Luke calls "*The* Mountain"—the great mountain of Palestine—in other words, MOUNT HERMON.

As they ascend higher and higher, they are gradually lost from view in the shades of night. It was Jesus, and His three favoured friends, Peter, James, and John.

Six days before, the Master had told all the Apostles about His approaching sufferings and death. He saw that they were much cast down at the sad thought. Therefore, in order to sustain their faith, He is about to give to these selected three, as representatives of the others, a glimpse of His glory.

We have named this section of our volume "GATHERING CLOUDS." Though retaining the title, we have to mark here a sudden rift in the sky, and a burst of radiance, glorious, though transient.

There is no story in all the life of Jesus more wonderful or more beautiful than this. It is the story of what is called "*The Transfiguration.*"

The word means that Jesus was *changed* in His outward appearance. As we proceed, you will hear what that change was.

Let us follow, then, in thought, these four personages. We do not know, and never can know, what spur or ridge of Hermon they ascended. I remember well, when at Banias, looking up "the Kingly Mountain," and seeing more than one round grassy shoulder of the hill which might possibly have been the spot.

We may try and picture the scene. It is now night. No human footstep is heard. The shepherds have folded their flocks; the birds have gone to their nests. No sound falls on the ear, save, perhaps, the occasional hooting of the owl, or the cry of the jackal, or the murmur of the streams swollen with the melting snows, rushing down to the Jordan. The bright stars have all come out, and are gemming the sky with their lustre.

Mount Hermon is to be made presently a palace of glory to receive its King; and these twinkling stars, like silver and golden lamps, are lighting His way to it.

I cannot tell you whether Jesus and His disciples were near the top of the mountain; but I think, from St. Mark's words, they must have been within view of the summit. At all events, they must have caught sight of the snow which lies during summer as well as winter on its higher crests. The pale moonlight was falling upon it.

I think it adds much to the grandeur of the scene I am to speak of, thus to suppose that it happened *at night*.

Perhaps you may ask me, how do I imagine it took place then, and not by day? I answer, because we are told that, overcome with fatigue, the Apostles were "*heavy with sleep;*" also that "*the next day*" (the next morning) "*they came down from the hill*" (Luke ix. 37).

I may add another reason. It was at night Jesus generally went to some solitary place to pray; and we are specially told that He was engaged in prayer now. "He went up into the mountain to pray, and *as He prayed*" (Luke ix. 29).

This last statement forms the first part of the night-picture on which our eyes fall. A lonely figure is seen bending on the dewy grass. Jesus was then and there pleading with His Father, for Himself, for the Church, for the World—for you and for me. And it was "while He was praying" that all at once His countenance became radiant with glory. He who is "Brighter" than the brightest earthly luminaries, never shone with such dazzling lustre as now. "*His face did shine* AS THE SUN." This brightness spread to His very garments. "*His raiment*," we read, "*was white and glistering;*"—" so as no fuller on earth could white them;" —whiter than yon white snow up the mountain on which the moonbeams are falling (Mark ix. 3). He was like the Angel

John saw, in the Book of Revelation, "standing in THE SUN." Perhaps all around where He was kneeling,—the thorny bushes, the green sward, the wild flowers,—would be lighted up with the same strange brilliance.

But who are these two figures who appear in the midst of the brightness? They are not the Apostles; for Peter, James, and John are all three fast asleep on the long grass close by.

It is Moses and Elijah, two of the greatest names of Old Testament Scripture. Who does not like to read the story of Moses, and the bush of flaming fire, or waving his miraculous rod, or standing amid the thunders and lightnings on the Mount with God; and of Elijah, with his ravens at the brook, or offering his sacrifice on Mount Carmel, or ascending in his fiery chariot?

But whence have they come, and for what intent?

Could they have left their bright thrones in heaven, where the one had been fifteen hundred years, and the other a thousand, to descend all the way to the earth?

Yes, they have gladly done so, in order to give glory to Jesus, and to bear witness to Him as the Son of God and Saviour of lost and fallen man.[1]

The Apostles, while sleeping, suddenly feel a strange unearthly light playing on their eyelids. Is it a dream? They suddenly start up. For a moment they are almost blinded with the lustre. When they are able to look around, on what or on whom do you think their eyes would first fall?

Yes, I am sure it would be on their dear Lord and Master.

But how changed He is! No one now would recognise His common dress, soiled with the constant journeyings, it was so brilliant. No one would know His face, with its marks of weariness and sleeplessness, care and sorrow; it was so glorious and shining. Both dress and face are not only lighted, but light seems to come from them like a Sun giving forth rays.

The astonished spectators next behold MOSES and ELIAS.

They are bright also; but not so Bright as the Figure between.

---

[1] See the picture in our frontispiece.

The ONE has the glory of the SUN, the two others have only the glory of the *stars*.

The Apostles do not require to ask the question, " *What are these arrayed in white robes, and whence came they.*" Though they had, of course, never seen these famous saints before, they appear to know at once who they were. They name both of them. How interested, surely, they must have been in gazing on the glorified persons of those whose history had been taught them from their earliest infancy!

Hitherto all seems to have been solemn silence. But the stillness of midnight is now broken; for these two bright messengers are speaking to Jesus, and Jesus is speaking to them.

What do you suppose would most likely form the subject of their converse?

Would it be the glory of the beautiful scene? The roof of that great Temple of Nature, with its thousand star-lamps, and high Hermon, like a great white altar?

Or, more likely, would it be about the bright heaven far above all these stars, from which Moses and Elias had come? Would it be concerning the great God of Heaven and His holy angels—the pastures of the blessed and the living fountains of waters?

Or, perhaps, more probably still, would it be regarding the glories of the Master's Kingdom? About His dominion being from sea to sea; the kings of Tarshish and the Isles, the kings of Sheba and Seba coming from afar to bow before Him and offer Him gifts?

It was not with reference to any one of these.

Strange to say, their converse was about DEATH.

Death ! You would think the very last thing of which citizens of heaven, where death is unknown, would *come* to speak, or *like* to speak.

Yes! but their talk was concerning "*the decease*" of Jesus, which was soon to take place. It was about His decease, too, *at Jerusalem.* Not the sweet "sleep" which He gives to His Beloved; but a violent, cruel, painful departure. He, at least, knew well what sort of a death it was they meant. He, at least, saw the crown of thorns and the awful cross!

I have no doubt the Apostles, when they awoke from their slumbers, heard all this wondrous conversation. It was meant that they should hear it.

Why do I say it was meant?

Just because they were very sad, and no wonder, at the thought of their loved Master being taken from them and killed! But when they listened to these two bright inhabitants of heaven speaking about the death of Jesus, and saying it was needful in order that the world might be saved; then the disciples would have a burden taken off their minds. They would feel, 'if saints and angels loved to meditate on that deed of dying,—if all the heavenly host were interested in it, why should they think it strange, or give way to sadness?'

Peter, as usual, was the first to break silence.

It was a natural wish, but not a wise one. Hence the sacred writer says, "*He spake, not knowing what he said.*" He was so delighted with the scene on which his eye fell,—Jesus so glorious —and Moses and Elias so glorious—that he called aloud, "O Master! it is a pleasant thing for us to be here! Let not these bright ones go away! No such happy season have we ever had before. Do not let us return to dull ordinary life again. Could we not always live on this peak of Hermon, away from the plots of the Pharisees and the wiles of Herod? Could we not go and gather boughs and branches from the valley hard by, and make three leafy booths—one for Thee, and one for Moses, and one for Elias; no angry looks would fall upon us; no unkind words would reach us. Make Hermon Thy throne, and let us reign with Thee here."

In a word, Peter would like to have the Mount on which they stood made into a second Bethel; angels travelling up and down as on Jacob's ladder between heaven and earth, bringing messages of love from the upper sanctuary. If Jesus could only remain there " BRIGHTER THAN THE SUN,"—"glorious in His apparel," he thought He could have no better residence, no better place in the kingdom.

The Master does not seem to make any reply to His bold

disciple. But just as Peter had uttered his request, there is a new feature in the scene.

Jesus, Moses, and *Elias* had hitherto been seen distinctly in the clear light which surrounded them; but now a white fleecy cloud seems to come, they known not whence.

First, the three glorified figures are lost in the cloud, as in a dense mist; and then the disciples are hidden in it too.

What think you that cloud was?

It was the SHECHINAH;—" the Divine Glory "—the token of God's special presence. It was the very same cloud which rested of old on the tabernacle, and went in the form of a pillar before Israel in the desert.

This formed the most solemn moment of all in the solemn spectacle. Jesus, Moses, and Elias had hitherto alone spoken. But now there is a Voice—a new Voice—that comes out of the cloud. It says—" *This is My beloved Son, hear ye* HIM."

It was the voice of God:—God the divine Father, witnessing to the Deity of His beloved Son.

It was specially meant, too, that the Apostles should hear this voice. For even though the converse of Moses and Elias with Jesus had so far comforted them, yet you can quite believe they would be still troubled and downcast at the thought of their Master's death. They would feel as if they required higher than saints or angels to soothe their hearts and restore their faith. They might be tempted to say to themselves, 'How can this God-man die? Can He be the Eternal Son of the Father if He is going to be slain by the hands of men?'

The voice from " the excellent Glory " would, however, quite dismiss these fears and want of faith. The great God of the Pillar-cloud had spoken, and said, 'This Jesus, whom you call your Master:—this humble Man, whom the Galileans are rejecting and despising, and who is soon to be killed in Jerusalem, is indeed My beloved Son—*hear* HIM.'

Yes, how glad they would be to listen to the assuring words! How could they have one doubting thought about their kind

Saviour, when the voice of God had said, "*in whom I am well pleased*"?

And do you imagine it would only be the disciples who were glad to hear these utterances, and who would be strengthened by them?

They were doubtless intended also to strengthen and sustain Jesus Himself in the prospect of His dreadful sufferings. We may believe at Gethsemane and Calvary, Hermon, with its bright visions and glorious utterances, would be much before Him. He would remember the voice of His Father. He would remember, too, that wondrous talk about His decease; how the eclipse of THE GREAT SUN was to prove the life and light of the world;—that like the myriads of stars above His head, would be the multitudes who by His death would shine in a brighter firmament for ever and ever!

The disciples had been able to gaze on the first part of the vision without terror. But at the second part, when the great cloud covered them, and the solemn voice was heard coming from its midst, they fell flat on their faces and hid them in the grass. Perhaps they felt, what they had not done previously, their loneliness. They were now screened from Jesus. He was lost from their sight in the canopy of glory.

They continue in this posture until a gentle hand was felt touching them. They knew the touch well. They had often experienced the same before. The voice they knew even better, "*Arise, be not afraid.*"

They looked up. It was *Jesus*. The dazzling light—the bright messengers—the awful cloud, were all gone. They were alone once more with their dear Master; who was attired again, not in garments woven with the sunbeams, but in His former lowly garb, as the Pilgrim Saviour!

They might have been afraid that Moses and Elias had come to fetch Him back to heaven. How happy they were when they found that they had their best Friend still at their side, and that they were walking in His loved company down the hill. The stars were vanished, but the "Sun of their souls" was still left.

They might possibly have to face many new trials, but they had obtained a sight of the crown, and now they return to the foot of the mountain more than ever willing to bear the cross.

The early rays of morning were breaking in the Eastern sky and tipping the snowy brow of Hermon; the birds were again singing their matin song; the sheep were sprinkling themselves in the lower valley, or wending up the hill with their shepherd before them, as the three disciples and their Lord descend the grassy steps of that high altar.

On their way down, Jesus expressly told them not to tell any one of what they had seen. He also foretold His rising from the dead. They wondered very much what this could mean. They spoke to each other, but did not like to question their Master about it.

Some other scenes might by them be forgotten, but I am sure Mount Hermon never was. St. John, many long years afterwards, when he wrote his Gospel, says, " *We beheld His glory, the glory as of the only begotten of the Father, full of grace and truth.*" And Peter, in his old age, when he was writing a beautiful letter to his converts, speaks of one place and spectacle which seemed to have fastened itself above all others in his memory. It was not the first look he got of Jesus on the banks of the Jordan; nor some incident in His home at Capernaum; nor the walk on the sea; nor the Temple at Jerusalem; nor Gethsemane; nor Calvary. What, then, was it? " *We were eye-witnesses of His Majesty . . . when we were with Him in the* HOLY MOUNT!" (1 Pet. i. 16, 18).

XLII.

He goes to the Feast of Tabernacles.

Jesus, having cured a demoniac boy at the foot of the Mountain, went for a little while again to the Lake-side.

It was still very hot there. Those who had gone for coolness from its cities to the mountains, had not yet returned. So the Master and His disciples were able to have a time of greater quiet. As they had no other way of obtaining a living, it is probable that the Apostle-fishermen would go out with their boats and nets at night, and pursue their old calling. They would rest within doors in the fierce heat of the sun during the day, and listen to the teachings of their gracious Lord.

This must have been with them a season of somewhat mingled happiness. All farewell meetings are sorrowful. The last gathering in the family cannot be a joyful one, just before the circle is broken, and the brother or sister go away never to come back to it, at all events, as a *home*. It was so now. Though Jesus was to return once more for a brief time, these were the last quiet home meetings He was to have on the shores of the Lake with the friends He most loved and clung to. The kind women who shared His company would doubtless, also, occasionally be present. It is not unlikely that Mary, the Mother of the Lord, may have been now with Him. Would He give her any idea of His coming conflicts and sufferings? It is more probable, I think, that, until the time came, He would spare the saddest wound of "the Sword," which old Simeon had foretold would pierce her heart. She must, however, have had her own thoughts and fears. He, at least, knew only too well all that was before Him. "The clouds" were slowly but surely "gathering." He was to have six months of weary and anxious labour and teaching, principally in Judea and on the other side of Jordan, and these months were to end in cruel pain and death. This holy rest at His own city must therefore have been something like a Sabbath to Jesus.

There is one beautiful picture given us of these hours which never fails to interest all readers, young and old.

It is evident that in the same house where He was, there were little children. How tenderly He speaks to them and deals with them! There was one of their number on whom our attention is specially centred. The Saviour first took this child and set him down in the midst of the circle of friends who were gathered in the room. Then He folded him gently and lovingly in His arms, and said such kind words about him to the disciples. As if this were not enough, He warns them against offending one of such little ones that love Him and believe in Him. He farther assured them that the bright angels in heaven, who behold the face of His Father, have the charge of these, and rejoice to watch over them.

I have at times wondered who this favoured child was! I have often thought that all his life long he would never forget these wondrous moments. No son of King or Queen was ever so honoured as he. One of the Fathers of the Church says that this privileged little one was Ignatius, who, when grown up, died a martyr for the sake of Christ. Though we may not have much ground to believe the truth of this story, let us hope, at all events, that, whoever he was, he afterwards became a disciple and follower of so gracious a Master; better still, that he is now singing the hymn of Heaven with a sweeter voice than he could sing it on earth—

"Safe in the arms of Jesus."

We shall come to find that this was not the only occasion in which the Divine Shepherd showed His love for the tender Lambs of the flock. I heard a boy at a Sunday school once speak of Christ as "the King of Children;" and that Sunday scholar said what was true. Jesus seemed to have the charm which all kind and loving natures possess, of attracting the young to His presence. Sacred art has put youth and childhood of every age and in every possible attitude clustering around Him.

securing His attention and seeking His blessing. Travellers in Palestine at the present day know how common it is, at the close of a long journey, for the women with infants in their arms or children at their side, to form a circle around the place of encampment as the tent is being pitched and the fire lighted. May we not think of the meek and lowly Saviour, at frequent similar restings by the wayside at eventide, having like gatherings around Him; the little ones from the adjoining hamlet seated on His knee or clinging to His bosom, listening with loving wonder and joy to His gracious sayings? Can you recall some words of the Prophet Isaiah which seem to bring that picture before us better than any artist ever painted it?

"*He shall feed His flock like a shepherd; He shall gather the lambs with His arm, and carry them in His bosom*" (Isa. xl. 11).

I may only add, it is thought that it was at this same time, when Jesus spoke so kindly to that young one, that He delivered also the Parable of "*The Lost Sheep.*" Oh, how He loves the weak and helpless—the timid child or the poor lost sinner—who, like the sheep of the story, has strayed from the fold!

In the month of October, many people on the shores of the Sea of Tiberias were busy preparing to go up to Jerusalem to attend *the Feast of Tabernacles.*

This Feast was what we might call the Jews' "Harvest Home." It took place when all the crops of the year were gathered in, and before the winter rains began to fall. The corn was housed, the grapes were plucked from the terraced vineyards, the olives were shaken from the olive-trees, and the olive-oil stored up in jars. It was a Feast of thanksgiving to God, who had "crowned the year with His goodness, and made all its paths drop fatness."

Nor was this its only design. It was intended also to remind the Jewish people of the long wanderings of their Fathers in the wilderness, when they dwelt in tents, and of God's gracious care of them then. It was the gladdest by far of the Jewish festivals. It was their favourite feast.

I think, my young readers, you would have liked to be in

Jerusalem that month. Our churches, schools, and houses at home, are often decked out at Christmas time with evergreens, and hollies with their red berries. But this is nothing to what took place every autumn at Jerusalem. The streets were full of booths made with boughs of trees. Ropes were slung across covered over with branches. On the square tops of their houses there were arbours erected, beautifully green and shady.

Nor was this all. So great was the crowd from every part of the land, that the inhabitants were obliged for the time to go and live outside the gates of the city. Specially was the Mount of Olives and the slopes along the Valley of the Kedron covered with these '*Succoths*,' as they called them. At the other great festivals, the people used huts made of goats' hair, similar to what the Arabs dwell in to this day; but they were not allowed to have these now. They lived in arbours made of olive and willow, pine, myrtle, and palm.

How beautiful "the Mount before the city" must have been! It was as if in a night's time it had become a vast shrubbery or wood, so thickly were these green tents planted all over it. Peter must have referred surely to these leafy "*tabernacles*," when so lately we heard him say on Mount Hermon, "*Let us make three booths.*"

For the purpose of directing the order of the observances during the Feast, also to keep the people cheerful and happy, the trumpeters of the Temple sounded the trumpets each day twenty-one times, or nearly twice in every hour.

The gathering reminds us of our own Christmas in another way; for members of families, separated during the rest of the year, now met together, in their holiday dresses, within these verdant walls—parents and children, brothers and sisters.

You must not think, however, that the people remained in their tents. No; they kept up a procession, nearly all day long, through the streets and the Courts of the Temple. Each carried some branches in their hands; some held in their left hand a peach or citron; but all had in their right, twigs of palm, willow, and myrtle, fastened sometimes with gold and silver strings.

These they waved as they passed through the Courts of the Temple, and shouted "*Hosanna!*"

I must tell you more. Not only was it the hills and valleys round about that were thus beautified. At night, on the Temple platform, there were eight very large lamps erected; or rather two high stands with four lamps on each of them. They were richly gilded and were fifty cubits high. They shed a ruddy glow on the pillars and cloisters, and even lighted up the Mount of Olives opposite with the glare.

Instead of waving palm branches, as they did by day, the festive crowd at night bore in their hands blazing torches, amid the clashing of cymbals and the blast of trumpets. The Levites sat on the fifteen steps leading to the altar and sang the "*Songs of Degrees;*" while the women thronged the galleries (for it was in the Court of the Women these illuminations took place), and looked down on the torch-light dances. The night was well-nigh turned into day.

Some have thought that if the festal multitudes were reminded in the forenoon part of the service of the "Pillar of Cloud" which led their Fathers of old, these blazing torches and lamps would call to mind "the Pillar of fire by night" which lit up the camp of Israel as they journeyed through the desert.

It is evident Jesus was not present at the beginning of the Feast. He did not come up with the ordinary caravan from Galilee, but purposely waited till the crowd of Pilgrims had left, and then He and His disciples came quietly by themselves to Jerusalem.

His hour was not yet come. He did not wish, before the appointed time, to hasten the gathering tempest.

On reaching the Holy City, He seems to have gone straight to the Temple, and to have entered its crowded courts.

He knew well He had many enemies among these multitudes, and that it would take little to draw down the lightning from the threatening clouds. But He had vast numbers, too, of interested friends:—not a few also there were from a distance, who though they had never met Him, were curious to see with

"*With joy shall ye draw water out of the wells of salvation*" (Is. xii. 3) page 257

their own eyes the Great Wonder-Worker of Nazareth, and to witness His miracles. Accordingly, on His appearance, a stir was made; for we are told the question had been asked again and again by the anxious throng—" *Where is He?* "

" *This is Jesus!* " was whispered from lip to lip; as they gazed on a countenance 'Brighter than the Sun,' yet wan with present and coming sorrow.

He soon began to address the assembled crowd. He would be glad to have this new opportunity of acting the part of the Good Shepherd, and of speaking to the lost sheep of the House of Israel then collected in such numbers.

As was to be expected from what I have just said, there was a division among His hearers: some liked Him, some disliked Him; some said He was "a good man," others said He was "a deceiver of the people," and would have used instant violence against Him. Ah, well might the meek and lowly, the guileless and innocent One, ask the touching question, as He listened to the mutterings of the storm, " *Why go ye about to kill Me?* "

The joyous festival lasted seven days. On the morning of each day, as the smoke of the early sacrifice rose from the altar (which was wreathed with sprigs of willow) a procession, headed by a priest, went down the steep pathway from the Temple to the Pool of Siloam.

The pool is situated in a quiet recess at the base of Mount Moriah at the mouth of the Tyropœon Valley. It had very little water when I saw it, and was much disfigured with stones and mud. But it must have been beautiful at the time of Christ; with blooming gardens around, and the sparkling pool itself nestling in the rocks. Isaiah speaks of " the waters of Siloah that go softly " (viii. 6). These would be all the more peaceful, in contrast with the noisy torrent of the Kidron rushing close by.

On the occasion which I am describing, the officiating priest filled a golden bowl from the spring, and carried it, as seen in the accompanying picture, with music and song to the Temple court above. It must have indeed been a striking and picturesque

R

scene;—the groups in their holiday dresses,—blue and white, red and yellow, as Easterns like to have them,—lining the flight of winding steps leading up the rocky ridge;—each holding in the hand a festal branch, of which the palm was the favourite. Whenever the procession came in sight, the trumpets sounded, and the vast crowd took up the words of the Prophet, " *With joy shall ye draw water out of the wells of salvation!*"

On entering the Southern Gate, the Levites, in their white garments, were gathered on either side, singing joyful festive Psalms. They chanted what is called 'the Great Hallel;' and the people, old and young, round about, waved their palm branches and cried again " HOSANNA!" Specially loud were their voices when they came to the verse " *Oh give thanks unto the Lord, for He is good, because His mercy endureth for ever.*" The procession then paused, and the water was poured into a silver basin at the base of the altar.

The eighth was the last, and the greatest day of the Feast. The joy was greater then than on any of the other days. Seven times the priests walked round the altar singing their Psalms.

Yes, it was an imposing sight. But Jesus well knew that, with all the seeming joy and happiness, there were many sad hearts too in the dense throng. Hearts broken with sorrow; hearts crushed with sin. The pure waters of Siloam could do little in washing out dark stains from sinful souls, or in quenching the thirst of weary parched spirits. That golden goblet to such, would only be a " broken cistern that could hold no water."

But He also knew what alone would do them good, and give them peace. By coming to Him and believing on Him—resting their guilty troubled souls on Him—they would be safe and happy for ever.

So, standing perhaps on one of the high steps in order to be better seen and heard, the Divine Redeemer cried with a loud voice " *If any man thirst, let him come unto* ME *and drink.*"

Do the words remind you of anything He ever said before? Do they not recall what He spoke to the woman of Samaria at Jacob's well? only now, the gracious invitation was given not to one, but to thousands on thousands.

I have dwelt both in this and the former chapter, on the bright scene of the Feast of Tabernacles, because is it not interesting to think and to know that *Jesus was there?*

He mingled with the crowds. He heard the blast of the trumpets. He beheld the waving of the palm branches by day; He saw the blazing torches and fires by night. He witnessed the golden goblet carried up from Siloam, and heard the words loudly shouted again and again which really and truly referred to Himself, "*Hosanna!*" (come, Saviour), "*Blessed is He that cometh in the name of the Lord!*" How strange, these dense multitudes all praying for that Saviour to appear, who was then standing in their midst!

You may naturally be led to ask, what the result was of that visit of Jesus to the courts of the Temple on that "great day of the Feast?" Did any listen to His gracious invitation, and accept the offer of this free salvation?

Some, we are told, heard His teaching with joy, and received Him as the promised Christ. "*This*," said they, "*is* THE *Prophet.*" Others were too proud to own so humble a Galilean as their Messiah.

The chief Jews were very angry. They met in their great hall on the Temple hill, and sent out some guards, or officers, to seize Jesus.

Why are these officers so long in coming back?

They had gone to the Temple court, where they found the Saviour speaking. But before laying hold on Him, they could not resist pausing for a few moments to hear some of the gracious things He said. So good, so gentle, so kind; yes, and so divine is He,—they felt as if they could not dare to go up and close these holy lips, or bind these gracious hands.

They return all alone without fulfilling the command of their masters.

"*Why have ye not brought Him?*" the members of the angry council asked.

"We could not," was the reply. "We have heard many religious teachers, but '*never man spake like this man.*'"

Jesus went on preaching. He proclaimed Himself to be the Son of God, sent by His Father to redeem mankind. He warned His hearers that the time He would be with them was short, and that soon He would be taken away.

The Feast of Tabernacles being over, the blazing torches and fires which had been seen for seven nights were extinguished. All was once more darkness in the Temple court and on the Mount, except the light which the moon and stars might afford. Perhaps it was in allusion to this, or rather in contrast with it, that Jesus said to the crowd before they separated, regarding Himself;—"I am better than all other *Lights*. I am the only *true Light*. 'Brighter than the Sun itself.' "*I am* THE LIGHT OF THE WORLD!" (John viii. 12.)

That last evening, on the dispersing of the crowd, the Saviour appears to have gone and taken up His abode for the night somewhere on the Mount of Olives. We are not told where this place of sojourn was. Was it with the keeper of the olive garden I have before referred to, at "a place called Gethsemane"? or did He sleep in the open air, with the bright stars, like ministering angels, looking down upon Him?

We cannot tell. But His heavenly Father, in a better and diviner sense than in the case of any others, would "*give His Beloved sleep.*"

XLIII.

He cures a blind man, and delivers the Parable of the Good Shepherd.

ON the Sabbath following the autumn festival, Jesus seems to have cured a blind man somewhere outside the Temple gate.

We are not told that this blind person had asked Jesus to restore his sight. The disciples seem rather to have pointed him out to their Master, who at once proceeded to work a new miracle of mercy. He anointed the sufferer's eyes with clay, and then told him to go and wash in the pool of Siloam, the fountain at which they had so lately filled the Golden Pitcher.

It must have been a trying thing for the poor man to grope his way through the narrow alleys and streets of Jerusalem leading to the pool. Those he met, many or most of whom must have known him, would think it strange to see him with his eyes covered over with the moist clay. But he cared not what people thought or said. He did simply what Jesus told him to do. He believed the good Physician's word, and obeyed His directions. What was the result? He came back from the pool with his eyes opened. "*He went his way, and washed, and came seeing.*"

The Pharisees were, as usual, very angry. They called Christ "a sinner." They returned to the old charge, that He had broken the law, because He had wrought this cure on the Sabbath. The wonted clouds of enmity and unbelief were again gathering. We can infer, from one sentence, the strength of their scornful hatred: —"*As for this fellow, we know not whence he is.*" The blind man, however, stood up boldly for his Deliverer. The Pharisees wished him to deny Jesus, and, as they said, to "*give God the praise*" of his recovery. But he would not tell a lie against his own conscience. He had an upright as well as a grateful heart. He would not denounce the kind Healer who had wrought such a cure upon him. "Whether He be a sinner," said he, "or no, *I know not; this one thing I know, that whereas I was blind, now I see.*"

The Pharisees for the moment turned their rage from Jesus on the restored man. They did the most cruel wrong which could be inflicted on a Jew. The sacred writer tells us, "*They cast him out.*" Yes, I repeat, that was a terrible deed of vengeance. Do you ask me why? A man "cast out" was considered unclean. He was, for the time that sentence was on him, not deemed worthy to be called an Israelite. He was not allowed to go to the Temple or synagogue. He was shunned and avoided by his nearest friends. His very parents and brothers and sisters were not allowed to speak to him!

But this object of the Saviour's mercy had now a Better than the best of human friends. That Friend found him out, and spoke kindly to him, when others had no words or looks but those of harshness. "*Jesus heard that they had cast him out; and when He had found him, He said unto him, Dost thou believe on the Son of God? He answered and said, Who is He, Lord, that I might believe on Him? And Jesus said unto him, Thou hast both seen Him, and it is He that talketh with thee. And he said, Lord, I believe. And he worshipped Him.*"

It may seem, at first, strange, that immediately after Jesus had performed this cure, He delivered the striking discourse, related in the tenth chapter of St. John, about *The Shepherd and the Sheep.* You will naturally ask, Had the healing of this blind man anything to do with such a subject?

While I answer, No, I may tell you what I think may possibly have suggested it.

I remember, one Sunday I spent on the Mount of Olives, being much struck and interested in meeting, half-way across the hill, a shepherd and his fleecy charge. The shepherd was going before, and the sheep were following. May not Jesus have noted a similar flock just at that moment, as He looked across to the green pastures of the Mount? And not the flock only, and their leader; but up the hill-slope He may have seen one of the many sheepfolds that were there, with the wicket-gate and the rough wall or enclosure round about, either formed of stones or of wattled boughs of olive and willow.

If so, need I say the sight would abundantly supply Him with thoughts for this instructive parable; enabling Him to speak words of rebuke and warning to the hostile Pharisees, as well as of comfort to His own disciples and to His people in all ages.

The same beautiful image is often used in the New Testament: Jesus "finding" His sheep, "keeping" His sheep, "feeding" His sheep, "watching" His sheep, and finally "folding" His sheep amid the verdant meadows of heaven.

In the present parable He reproves the false shepherds,—those whom He calls the "hirelings,"—those who had no care or love for the flock, who were ready to flee when the wolf was near. He speaks of Himself as "*the Good Shepherd,*" who "*lays down His life for the sheep.*" Towards the close of the parable, He describes the gate of the sheepfold (for long ages entered only by Jews) as thrown open to all. He beholds people of every nation entering in, and becoming part of the Great Flock redeemed with His blood. "*Other sheep I have,*" said He, "*which are not of this fold: them also I must bring, and they shall hear My voice; and there shall be one fold, and one Shepherd.*"

Some of His hearers were evidently impressed. Not so, however, the majority. What He had declared about the "other sheep" being welcomed into the fold, as well as regarding His relations to the Father, only seemed the more to stir up their enmity and hatred :—"*Many of them said, He hath a devil and is mad. . . . Then the Jews took up stones again to stone Him*" (John x. 20, 31).

It is evident that the sky was becoming more and more charged with the coming storm. Every day "the floods of ungodly men" were increasing. But He, around whose head these clouds were gathering, had One on His side Greater than all that were against Him, and of whom it was sublimely said, "*The clouds are the dust of His feet*" (Nahum i. 3).

XLIV.

He goes to Galilee, and sends out Seventy Disciples.

SHORTLY after this, Jesus seems to have returned for a brief season to the north of Palestine.

Space will not allow me to tell you about a number of events which happened at this time in the story of His life. It was doubtless, His last visit to Galilee before His death. But it was not, like the former one, a quiet, happy meeting with friends. It must have been in many ways full of sadness. His enemies here, too, as in Judea, were lying in wait for the Innocent Lamb of God:—nay, not a few of them thirsting for His blood. These enemies were composed of all ranks: from the highest to the lowest; from jealous Herod Antipas, to the fickle multitude; that same multitude many of whom used, in former times, to hang with earnest attention on His lips.

No wonder that He no longer speaks to these ungrateful people as He was wont to do (as He loved to do), in the still small voice of mercy and compassion. His words now rather remind us of what John the Baptist said of Him:—"*Whose fan is in His hand, and He will thoroughly purge His floor.*"

He cried "*Woe! woe! woe!*" over these guilty men and guilty cities, that had returned hatred for His kindness. He told them they were more sinful and ungrateful even than the inhabitants of wicked Sodom on which God had rained fire and brimstone. For if He had trodden the streets and done for the cities of the plain what He had done for the cities of the Lake, "they would have repented long ago in dust and in ashes."

Sorrowful as the heart of Jesus was, He still bravely went on with His work of preaching and healing, till the time had arrived when He must set out on *His last journey*.

He did not flinch or hesitate, on leaving the spot He had known so long and loved so dearly. Even though He knew all the dark days that were at hand, "*He steadfastly set His face to go up to Jerusalem.*" He seems not to have taken the road by the Jordan valleys, which was pleasantest in winter, but went round by Samaria.

In the course of the journey, which occupied some weeks, He spoke some of His most striking parables, such as that of the Unjust Judge and the Good Samaritan. Besides parables, He uttered many other solemn words and warnings.

It would seem to have been about this time, and before leaving the shores of the Lake, that Jesus gathered His more faithful followers around Him, and from their number chose seventy disciples to go before Him from place to place, preaching the doctrines of the Gospel, and preparing the people to welcome Him in the different hamlets and towns through which He was to pass.

We are not told the names of any of these seventy. They were doubtless plain humble men, gathered from the localities where Jesus was best known. They were not learned or wise. They had the love of the Master in their hearts, and that was better than all head learning.

The Jews had divided the world into seventy nations, just as they themselves were divided into twelve tribes. By thus sending out seventy preachers, might not Jesus announce the great purpose He had in view, of conveying the message of salvation to "*all the ends of the earth*"?

These good men started on their mission in pairs, or two and two together. They had no change of clothes, no bag to carry provisions, and no money in their purses. Nothing but their pilgrim staves, and simple faith in Him who had sent them.

Picture their going from village to village and city to city, boldly proclaiming the coming King and kingdom, and working miracles in the name of their great Lord. Their experience was similar to His own; and similar to that of His faithful ministers in every age of the Church. In some cases they found teachable minds; in others, hard hearts. Some whom they addressed believed, others rejected the message.

After a little time of absence, they returned to Jesus with an account of their work. They seem to have been astonished at their own success, and especially at their power in casting out devils. Perhaps He saw that they were inclined to be boastful and proud about this. He therefore says to them, "Do not so rejoice about the devils being subject to you. There is a matter which ought to make you far more joyful: rather rejoice that your names are written in God's Book of Life."

The great and good Shepherd of the parable, however, Himself "rejoiced in spirit!" Not only did He rejoice that, by means of these under shepherds, stray sheep had been brought back to the fold; but He was happy to think that, if proud Pharisees and Scribes rejected His Gospel, the humble, the suffering, the poor, the lowly, had welcomed the "glad tidings." Lifting up His eyes to heaven, He uttered this beautiful prayer—"*I thank Thee, O Father, Lord of heaven and earth, that Thou hast hid these things from the wise and prudent, and hast revealed them unto babes. Even so, Father! for so it seemed good in Thy sight!*"

Shortly after this time, Jesus seems to have crossed to a district on the other side of the Jordan called Perea.

Perea was part of the highlands of East Palestine. David, I mentioned before, wrote and sang some of his most plaintive psalms there, when he was obliged to flee an exile from his throne; and now the Son of David, like His royal ancestor, makes it a place of refuge from the wiles of His foes.

Jesus, I need not observe, would not have gone away unnecessarily from danger. He was not afraid. But His time—the time appointed for Him to suffer and to die—was not yet come. Clouds have still farther to gather, and evening shadows to fall, ere THE GREAT SUN sets in darkness and blood.

XLV.

He delivers the most beautiful of all His Parables.

SOME have thought that it was among these wild mountain scenes, with their streams and pasture lands, that the divine Saviour spake the beautiful parable of "*the Lost Sheep.*" He brings before us the wanderer first straying on the mountains; then brought back on the shoulders of the shepherd; the shepherd, on reaching his home—some quiet pastoral hamlet in the valley—calling together his neighbours, and saying, "*Rejoice with me, for I have found my sheep which was lost.*"

No image of Jesus seems to have been so much a favourite in the early Church as this. In the place where the first Christians used to bury in Rome—"the Catacombs"—the figure of the Shepherd, with His crook in His hand, and carrying the lost sheep, is frequently seen cut in slabs of stone. Religious painters of all ages have loved the same subject. Varied has been its treatment; from that in the works of the early centuries and the middle ages down to the latest great picture in our own country, where the gracious Shepherd is represented with the feeble lamb which had strayed from the fold, nestling in His bosom,—a fragment of prickly thorn still clinging to its fleece, the mute evidence of its wanderings.

If Perea be the scene of this parable, it would also most likely be that of the story which immediately follows in St. Luke's Gospel, and which, I think, I may well call the most wondrous and touching description of grace and forgiveness to be found in all the Bible.

I refer to what is known as "*the Parable of the Prodigal Son.*"

Who does not love that parable? Grown up men and women, over and over again, have read it. Old men and women have their Bibles often soiled and worn at that place, as if to mark how frequently they have turned to gaze on the picture that never tires. The young love to read it, because it is a story—though a very sad one—of youth. Even children are never weary of sitting on their mother's knee when that parable of all parables is told to them.

You know it well. The happy home—the kind father and his two sons. The younger son wishing, like many foolish boys, to have his own way, thinking it would be nice and pleasant to do just as he liked.

That son leaves his parents' dwelling, and goes off with his portion of money in his pocket to the '*far country.*' I need not remind you of his misery. Once so happy, now so wretched. Once the hand of innocence linked in his father's, with servants to wait upon him, and a bed of down to sleep upon—the kiss of a father's love the last thing at night and the first to welcome him in the morning. Now all these things gone! He soon had "*spent his all.*" In some desolate, far-off wild,—perhaps amid the mud and mire of winter and the cold of biting winds, he is feeding swine. So greatly was he in want, that he would have been glad to have, for his own food, the hollow husks which the swine were eating. "*But no man gave unto him.*" No kind voice was there to speak to him; no pillow for his aching head but the withered leaves or the grassy sod. He was free once; now he is a slave.

Though no ear can hear him in that lonely place, and no hand can help him; yet, in his misery, he lifts up his eyes, streaming with tears, and cries—"*I perish with hunger!*"

Suddenly, as if he awoke from a troubled dream, "*he came to himself.*" As if a ray of light had flashed in the midnight darkness, he recalls the old, loved, happy home, with its scenes of mirth,—the halls where the banquet used to be held, the gardens where, amid the beauty and fragrance of flowers, childhood played; oh, above all, the bright faces that used to smile upon him, and chief among these his kind *father's*—yes, the smile of the father he had forsaken, and whose heart he had well-nigh broken!

'Can I ever dare to return there again? Can I dream of HIS ever receiving me back again? No; impossible. I never, at least, can be his son. But glad, oh, how glad, should I be, if he would only take me in as a servant! The meanest drudgery in the house would be happiness and freedom to me compared to this!'

He says to himself, "I will try." "*I will arise, and go to my father, and will say unto him, Father, I have sinned against heaven, and before thee, and am no more worthy to be called thy son: make me as one of thy hired servants.*"

After saying so, he did not put off time. "*Then he arose,*" and, just as he was, in his ragged dress and faint with hunger, he grasps his staff, and commences the long, weary journey.

What is taking place all this time in his old home? Has the

father he has so wronged forgotten him? or, more likely, does he hate him? and if ever they met again would he have only words of harshness and cruelty to say to him? Has he given orders to his servants that if ever the ungrateful boy comes to the gate, or knocks at the door, he is to be driven away with angry words, and told never to show his face there in future?

Oh no! it is quite the reverse. That wronged and injured father, during the sad, weary weeks and months (or it may be years) of his son's absence, was always thinking about him, and had nothing all the while but *love*—a FATHER'S love—in his heart. The old man, it may be, had gone, time after time, to the top of the hill, that he might look eagerly along the far-stretching plain or valley, to see if there was any appearance of his lost child!

One day—one evening—he was thus standing on the hill-ridge, gazing wistfully, with his hand screening his eyes. He looks and looks again.

At last he sees a black speck on the horizon. It comes nearer and nearer—nearer and nearer still. "Oh!" he cries, with a gush of tears, "can it be?—yes, it is!—my son! my long-lost, my dearly-loved son!"

He cannot wait a moment. Though the youth is yet a great way off, he descends at once down the slope. On—on—he still hastens, till at last the two meet, and are locked in each other's arms.

For a few moments they cannot speak for weeping.

The son is the first to stammer out some words. What are they?

We can only catch the broken utterances, "*Sinned! sinned!*" "*Not worthy! not worthy!*" "Have you the poorest servant's place to give? even that is too good for me!"

The father does not give an answer to the speaker. But he turns round to some of the servants of the household, who had joined them, and says to them, "The very best robe in all my wardrobe, bring it for my boy, to put in place of these tattered rags. The best ring in my jewel-case, bring it for his finger, and sandals to cover his bleeding, blistered feet. Go and prepare a great banquet in my house. Kill the fatted calf; gather the minstrels into the hall for music and dancing and song. Invite all you can, to make it the gladdest feast I ever had—'*For this my son was dead, and is alive again; he was lost, and is found.*'"

I have elsewhere put the touching story into the following lines :—

"Return, return, the way is long and dreary ;
Return, return, O wand'rer sad and weary ;
   Why so with sin beguiled ?
Thy father's heart is breaking,
With this cruel long forsaking,
   Come back, come back, my child !"

"Gladly I would, for with hunger I am perishing,
The memories of home still fondly I am cherishing,
   I'm weary in the wild :
No Sabbath bells now ringing,
No loving voices bringing
   Peace to this heart defiled !"

"Return, return, why any longer linger ?
There are sandals for your feet, and a ring to deck your finger ;
   Your father reconciled,
With pity will behold you,
In his arms he will enfold you ;
   Come back, come back, my child !"

"I come, I come, my heart with joy is beating ;
I come, I come, as I hear thee thus entreating
   With accents fond and mild ;
I thought myself forsaken,
But to-morrow I'll awaken,
   Waken, once more, thy child !"

"Oh joyful sight ! at last he is appearing ;
Light up the festal-hall—the wand'rer is nearing ;
   Go let the board be piled,
Let fatted calf be killed for him,
And golden goblets filled for him
   I've found, I've found, my child !"

XLVI.

He goes up by Jericho to Bethany.

AFTER an abode of some weeks in Perea, Jesus returns to Jerusalem.

He was always longing to call more wanderers into His fold; and knowing that many would be in the capital city at *the Feast of Dedication*, He undertakes this fresh journey.

In going from Perea, there is only one way He could select. He must have come up the steep road leading from Jericho; a road dreary in itself, and which then, as now, was the haunt of thieves or wild Arabs from the desert. I remember when journeying there, it was necessary, in order to secure safety, to pay "robbers' money," and to have a son of the chief shiekh as an escort. The first part of the rugged track is full of rough stones, and the ascent is fatiguing till the traveller reaches the Mount of Olives.

Jesus would likely pause for the night at Jericho. If so, it would take between five or six hours next day to reach the heights around Jerusalem. It would not be so hot as in the previous months, for it was now the beginning of the Palestine winter (December). The country, and specially this part of Judea, would at that season be very bleak and bare. The pasture on the limestone hills would still be faded and bleached with the summer's sun. The "early rain" had fallen; but it was the "latter rain" which refreshed the land.

I have spoken of Jesus going to the neighbourhood of Jerusalem, and not to Jerusalem itself. For I think it most likely to have been on this very occasion that a glimpse is given of a family circle, who are new to us and whose names have not yet occurred.

We have already in earlier pages spoken of two *Homes of Jesus*.

NAZARETH was His *early*, and CAPERNAUM was His *second*, principal abode. But towards the end of the Gospel story, we are introduced to a *third* home, which in many ways shines out the brightest and loveliest of them all;—BETHANY.

The former two, as you know, were far away from Jerusalem: —*Bethany* was very near it. I can truly say no place in the Holy Land did I visit with more interest, or indeed with such interest as this.

I think you would like to hear an account of it, because it was the house of all others to which the Son of Man and Son of God seems to have gone most frequently, in the closing weeks of His life. When His heart was bowed down with sorrows greater than He had felt before, and the last closing terrible hour was nigh, oh how much He must have enjoyed the kind words and welcome which always greeted Him in that village! How the Dove of Heaven must have rejoiced often to fold His weary wings in this peaceful "cleft of the rock!"

If you ask me what Bethany is like now, I could only tell you it is one of the most wretched villages in all Palestine, I might almost add in all the world. You can hardly picture the misery and filth of the poor creatures who live or herd together in these stony hovels. The hovels themselves, I am not wrong in saying, are worse than the worst Irish cabins.

But this filth and wretchedness cannot rob Bethany of its outward beauty, and its abiding interest.

I never can forget the first time I went to it by the steep path across the Mount of Olives. How often Jesus must have crossed by that very same footroad! for the roads of Palestine cannot be much changed from what they were; this one hardly could at all. On coming to the summit of the little 'pass,' I thought how *His* eye, which always so delighted in the loveliness of His own lovely world, must have rested on the wonderful view which there breaks on the sight. There are wooded knolls and clumps of olive, almond, and fig, close by;—then the strange white wilderness beyond, going down, down, far below, in a succession of natural terraces, to the deep valley of the Jordan.

Then the gleam of the Dead Sea, sleeping in the hollow, like a huge mass of quicksilver;—and behind all this, the great giant wall of the Moab Mountains. Jesus, when He was carrying on His ministry in Jerusalem, generally took that pathway in the evening, just before sunset, when He had left His labours in the Temple, and ere the gates of the city were shut. I like to recall Him, who at another time spoke of the red glow of the sky, pausing to gaze on the glory of these Moab hills lighted up with the last fires of day;—a mass of purple and gold, crimson and violet—colours never to be seen on our hills at home.

The village of Bethany, though quite near Jerusalem, is entirely screened from it by the eastern slope of the Mount of Olives. It stands at the head of the steep road I have just spoken of, which leads down to Jericho and the Jordan. It may probably always have been the site of one of the watch-towers of Jerusalem, guarding the valleys which lead to the East from hostile armies. I have spoken of the trees which at the present day mingle with the white rocks and green sward around. But, in the time of Jesus, clusters of palms, which gave the village its name ("*House of Dates*"), with their tall stems and hanging leaves, must have lent an additional loveliness to the quiet retreat.

The house, which the Saviour so often made His home there, had three inmates—a brother and two sisters—Martha, Mary, and Lazarus. They all three loved Jesus, and Jesus loved them. They do not appear to have been poor. Some references in the Gospel story would seem, on the contrary, to show that they were well off, and had rather a better house than the other villagers.

Even now, in the rude hamlets of Palestine, there is a chief man called "*Sheikh*," who lives in a higher class dwelling than his fellow-villagers, and is known by his peculiar dress. Possibly Lazarus may have been this head villager or *Sheikh* in "the town of Bethany." To this day, among its ruined houses, there is a larger one than the others, pointed out as "the Castle of Lazarus." Whether these fragments of ruined wall really formed the home of the family of Bethany, we cannot tell. I did not go inside;—but travellers, if they choose to listen to idle tales, are still taken down by taper-light to a gloomy cellar below, which is shown as the room where Jesus sat at meat with the favoured household. We can be quite sure of this, however, that somewhere at least among that cluster of stone and mud habitations, the Lord of Glory sojourned again and again when He was on earth; that often, when very sad and downcast, it must have been to Him like a gush of sunshine in a dark day—when turning the corner of the Mount of Olives, His eye fell on three figures looking eagerly, either from their little garden or from the flat roof of their dwelling, for the coming of their Divine Guest.

The first of these visits, I repeat, would seem to have taken place now. We may think of Jesus, tired and travel-worn after that long weary journey on foot up "the Robber's Way," reaching the home of His friends.

He had, perhaps, come upon the inmates unexpectedly, which may account for Martha being bustled while putting the house in order, preparing the supper, and spreading the table. She was evidently the active member of the family, and took all the household cares upon herself. She was a true disciple of Christ, and from the reverence she had, she wished to show Him every kindness.

But it would appear on the occasion of this visit, she was needlessly concerned as to getting ready the evening meal, and was rushing hither and thither about the house. It was altogether an unnecessary anxiety on her part. Bread and fruit, and a jar of water from the village well, would have satisfied all His desires. In the words of Jesus she was "troubled about many of these things" which to Him were indifferent.

Mary, her gentle younger sister, on the other hand, remained at the feet of her Lord, drinking in heavenly lessons from His lips. There she sat on, hour after hour, as if she could never tire. For the meaning of the word is, she "kept on sitting."

While He gently rebukes Martha for her well-meant bustling ways, and for a hasty speech about her sister; He says of the latter—"*Mary hath chosen that good part which shall not be taken away from her.*"

This is our first glimpse into the Bethany home, but we shall come very soon to speak more about Jesus there, as well as about Martha and Mary and Lazarus.

XLVII.

He attends the Feast of Dedication, and returns to Perea.

JESUS would cross the Mount of Olives from Bethany to be present at "the Feast of Dedication."

This, like that of Purim, was not one of the great or ancient feasts of the Jews. It had not been instituted for more than two hundred years. It was appointed to keep in mind the expulsion from the Temple, of wicked and profane Antiochus Epiphanes, by Judas the Maccabee with his few brave soldiers. Being connected strictly with these sacred courts in Jerusalem, it was not attended by many people from Galilee, so that the crowd assembled was by no means large.

I have told you the feast took place in winter. It began a few days only before our Christmas, and lasted eight days. It was kept a good deal in the same way as the Feast of Tabernacles, especially by the carrying of palm branches, and, when the inclement season did not prevent, by having lights in the Temple court. Indeed, it was known by the other name of "the Feast of Lights." As in the case of most of the Jewish high days too, there was introduced the music of the lute and cymbal, and the blowing of trumpets.

During the Feast of Tabernacles, in October, the weather was always bright and beautiful. But now the heavy early rains of Palestine had generally set in; so that those who had assembled in the Temple were glad often to get under the shelter of the cloisters, and specially under the largest one, called '*Solomon's Porch.*' This porch was a furlong in length. It received its name owing to fragments of Solomon's great Building still being preserved amid the stones and cedar-wood of which it was composed. It was the first cloister which was entered from *the Gate Shushan*, and its lofty arches protected the worshippers both from the burning sun of summer and the heavy rains of winter and spring. I have told you before of the trophies of war that were hung in public view. These beautiful cloisters would seem, on the occasion of this feast, to have been decorated with the shields and banners, the swords and spears, which the brave Judas had taken from the enemy.

The sacred writer informs us that, in accordance with the custom I have just explained, "*Jesus walked in Solomon's Porch.*"

As He did so, groups of interested and excited worshippers and pilgrims gather round Him. The Pharisees, as before, form part of His hearers. They ask Him to declare plainly whether He were Christ or not.

Jesus does not wish to be considered the Warrior-Messiah whom the Jews desired. He knew that they were longing for "a Prince of this world"—some hero with sword and shield, like that same Judas whose name was on every lip at the Feast of Dedication.

No! He wished to claim for Himself a far higher and nobler kingdom. As the Son of God, sent down by the Father to save the world, He claimed to be Divine. He tells these questioning Pharisees, "*I and My Father are One.*"

That word fell like a spark. The flame of their anger burst instantly and wildly forth. "He speaks blasphemy!" is the shout of many voices. Heaps of rubbish and fragments of stone, from repairs going on in the Temple, were lying about. These were picked up by the Pharisees, just as they had been, nine months before, at the Feast of Purim; and, with eyes gleaming with vengeance, they would have murdered Jesus on the spot. But they were too cowardly to put their threats into execution;

or rather, a Power not their own prevented them from doing so. Perhaps Christ's divine presence and majesty put a restraint on their wicked purpose, and caused the stones to drop from their hands.

At all events, He passed through the crowd unharmed, as He had done before at Nazareth. Probably crossing the little bridge over the Kedron, and going up by David's foot-road among the olive-trees, He would feel happy once more in the peaceful home of Bethany.

Having spoken His solemn message at this winter feast, He sees that it would be well not further to rouse the passions of His Jerusalem enemies. He therefore does not return to the Temple again. He thinks it better not even to remain at Bethany. Those who desired His death might soon have found Him out in the house of Lazarus, and have raised a new tumult against Him. He goes down, therefore, the steep Jericho road with His disciples, and, crossing the Jordan, takes up His abode again in Perea.

EVENING SHADOWS.

"BEHOLD NOW THE DAY DRAWETH TOWARD EVENING."—JUDGES XIX. 9.

"THE WATCHMAN SAID, 'THE MORNING COMETH, AND ALSO THE NIGHT.'"—IS. XXI. 12.

"I MUST WORK THE WORKS OF HIM THAT SENT ME, WHILE IT IS DAY; THE NIGHT COMETH, WHEN NO MAN CAN WORK."—JOHN IX. 4.

"THEN JESUS SAID UNTO THEM, 'YET A LITTLE WHILE IS THE LIGHT WITH YOU: WALK WHILE YE HAVE THE LIGHT, LEST DARKNESS COME UPON YOU: FOR HE THAT WALKETH IN DARKNESS KNOWETH NOT WHITHER HE GOETH. WHILE YE HAVE LIGHT, BELIEVE IN THE LIGHT, THAT YE MAY BE THE CHILDREN OF LIGHT.'"—JOHN XII. 35, 36.

"AND THEY WERE IN THE WAY GOING UP TO JERUSALEM; AND JESUS WENT BEFORE THEM: AND THEY WERE AMAZED; AND AS THEY FOLLOWED, THEY WERE AFRAID."—MARK X. 32.

XLVIII.

Before He leaves Peræa He blesses Little Children.

THE "*Gathering Clouds*" are deepening into "EVENING SHADOWS."

> " The sunny morning-glimpse is gone,
> That morning note is still ;
> The dun, dark eve comes lowering on,
> The spoilers roam at will." [1]

It was now the middle of a Palestine winter. The winds that howled around the Divine Pilgrim in these uplands, and the rain which fell from the gloomy skies, reflected the increasing gloom and sorrow of His own spirit. Except the inmates of that kind Bethany home, now far off, and the handful of faithful disciples at His side, He could count on few real friends. He could not forget that what He last saw in the courts of His Father's House were eyes flashing with fire, murderous stones clenched in cruel hands, and fierce words, worse than all to bear. There was the ever-present thought, too, to which I have already referred, and which at this time must have been surely sadder than any other, that among those who were His daily and hourly companions, there was ONE His future *Betrayer!*

The very neighbourhood where He was, could not fail to make Him sorrowful. He must have had many sacred remembrances of John the Baptist, whose bold tones so often rang in the Jordan Valley hard by. John's eyes had for a whole year been closed in death, as His own would ere long be. The country people in these secluded highland valleys had known the Baptist well, and loved him much. They knew, too, the reverence John had for "the Lamb of God ;" and many of them followed the footsteps of Jesus,

---

[1] Keble's Miscellaneous Poems.

and believed on Him, for John's sake. This was one 'rift in the cloud'—one gleam in the darkening sky.

Though I must pass over, without mention, several occurrences at this time in the life of Jesus, I cannot omit *one* of His sayings and doings specially interesting: all the more so, because it is put down as the last act and the last word of the Holy Son of God during His visit to Perea. It shows how the longer He was among the people, the more they loved Him.

It was a repetition of the touching picture we have gazed upon before—Jesus folding in His arms some tender infants that were now brought to Him. The mothers of the district had seen how loving He was to all—healing the sick, patiently teaching the ignorant, binding up the broken-hearted, entering the very houses of publicans and sinners, and inviting them to share His salvation. They thought to themselves, just as many other mothers in Judea and Galilee had done, 'If He be thus gentle and merciful to grown-up people, will He have no kind word to speak to our little ones?'

Knowing that He was on the point of leaving their district, perhaps never to return, they came crowding around Him, bringing their children, that they might receive His blessing.

The disciples might have known, from former experience, how glad their Master would be to welcome and embrace these tender lambs of the flock. But they were not so loving or kind as He. They thought that with His long journey before Him, and with the heavy burdens that were weighing Him down, these mothers, on the present occasion, at least, would only trouble Him. They wished to turn them away. They may have had their own ideas, too, as formerly, that the little children were not fit disciples and subjects for such a Kingdom as His. Why seek needlessly to engross His attention and occupy His time?

But the thoughts and wishes of the gracious Saviour were very different. He was far from being pleased with His disciples. He first "rebuked them;" and then beckoning the crowd of mothers to His side, and taking the little ones, one after another in His arms (yes, the very youngest, too, in all the crowd), He repeated those dear words which most of you have been taught to learn by heart as your first Gospel verse—" *Suffer the little children to come unto Me, and forbid them not, for of such is the kingdom of heaven.*"

It is a beautiful incident this, surely, in the Divine life-story. Look at it! It is the meek and lowly Jesus, not only repeating the encouraging saying just quoted, but as the little ones smiled fearless in His bosom, " *He laid his hands upon them,*" in the ancient way of bestowing a special blessing.

Ah, neither these Perean mothers nor children would ever, all their lives, forget that day! Out of the mouths of many of these babes and sucklings praise would be perfected to Him on earth. May we not farther think of some of them, or all of them, now, as among the holy, happy band around the Throne of Heaven, who are singing ' *Glory! glory! glory!* ' ?

XLIX.

He hears of the Death of Lazarus, and goes to Bethany.

WHAT messenger is this coming in great haste to where Jesus was?

It is a man from Bethany, probably one of the villagers. He has come expressly all that long way, and has evidently something very urgent to tell.

It is a message informing Jesus that his friend Lazarus is very ill. It must have been a sudden sickness that had overtaken the brother of Martha and Mary, for we heard nothing about it when Jesus was so lately with them.

Let us go in imagination to that home on the slope of Olivet. The two sisters have begun to feel uneasy about the one of all earthly relatives who was most dear to them. At first they never dreamt of danger. But as in many cases of illness, the ailment which at first seemed slight, got more severe. His cheeks became more sunk, his eyes duller, his pulse weaker. Their hearts now failed within them. Seated by his bedside, they look anxiously at one another, and scarcely like to whisper or avow what they both are beginning to fear.

In their agony of mind they turn their longing thoughts to HIM who is now at a distance,—the Great and Good Physician; —"the Meek and Lowly," yet the Mighty and the All-powerful Saviour.

But is it not strange that HE has not thought of *them?* He knew, doubtless, all about the illness of His friend:—and *such* a friend. For I believe I am right in saying, that not even His own Apostles did Jesus love more than Lazarus. Why, then, has He not come? Why has His footstep and gentle knock not been heard at their door? And if He did not Himself hasten to that sickbed, they knew that He who could cure the nobleman's son at a distance, had only to speak the word, where He now was, and their brother would be restored.

They cannot endure this silence — the anguish of delay. What do they resolve upon?

They send a messenger down the Jericho road to Perea. The message he bears is a very short one, "*Lord, behold, he whom Thou lovest is sick.*" They do not ask Jesus to hasten personally to their relief. They leave to Himself what is best to be done. But I think we may gather from the story, that they either expect or hope to be gladdened and comforted by His own presence.

Lazarus becomes worse and worse. Death was evidently near at hand: a few hours more, and all will be over. You can think of Martha stealing again and again out of the darkened chamber to the roof of the house. She looks wistfully down the steep valley, longing either for the return of the person sent, or, what would be better still, for her Lord Himself. She knows that every hour, every moment was valuable. "Why," she is ever inwardly asking, "oh, why does He thus tarry?"

The messenger at last comes back. But he has come all alone, and Jesus has sent no message!

'What!' the heart-broken sisters would exclaim in sorrow and amazement, 'have you brought with you no word of healing nor even of sympathy to us from His own mouth?'

Their grief is now at its height. The worst has taken place. The lips and eyes of the dear brother are closed in death.

The neighbours in the village, as was the custom, gathered in their house to sympathise with the bereaved. Friends from Jerusalem, some of these among the upper classes (priests and scribes), came also. There would be the hired minstrels, besides, wailing and beating their breasts in mock sorrow. That sweet, peaceful dwelling has become suddenly a house of lamentation and woe.

Nor is this all. For after the shadows of death had fallen, these sisters, who must have known the touching story of the widow of Nain, may have had a gleam of hope. But now even that is past. The last sad duty of all is discharged. In these hot countries the funeral takes place very soon after the death; indeed, as I noted in speaking of the widow's son, the burial is completed, if possible, the very same day at sunset. Accordingly, the family cave or vault in the graveyard at Bethany had been opened; the body of Lazarus was laid in its rocky-resting place, and the bereaved sisters had returned, bowed with sorrow, to their once happy, but now desolate home.

At a time of bereavement and death, there are often some special words which dwell on the lips of the mourners, regarding those that have been taken from them; words which, in their grief, have got hold of them, they know not how, and which they repeat over and over again almost without knowing it. What were these in the case of Martha and Mary?

"*Oh, if* HE *had been here, our brother had not died.*"

And where, you may well ask, *was* Jesus? Where was He who loved Lazarus so much, and had such frequent joy in being his guest? Can He have forgotten him at the very time when His presence and friendship would have been most needed and prized? Was it like His kind heart still to be away? Surely, you will say, if He sent no message, He will at all events start immediately after being told of the illness. What could have delayed Him on the road?

It *does* seem, at first, very strange, when we read as follows:— " *When He had heard therefore that he was sick, He abode two days still in the same place where He was.*"

What! Lazarus sick, and Jesus not apparently caring! A messenger specially sent to tell Him of the illness, yet Jesus not apparently caring! Saddest of all, Lazarus dead—Lazarus in his grave, and yet the kind, loving Master, who with a word could have healed him, still far away! For two whole days He remained in Perea, as if nothing had taken place!

But Jesus has ever wisdom and love in all that He does. He wished to teach Martha and Mary, He wished to teach His suffering people in all ages, the lesson—" *Trust Me in the dark.* If I do not all at once remove your trials from you, you may be sure there is some good reason for it."

At last He tells His disciples that He is going up again to Judea to visit the home at Bethany.

They say 'No: the Jews will stone Thee: it will be certain death to venture.'

The Master replied, and His answer is a beautiful one, 'If a man walks under the light of God, with the sunshine of God's love upon him, feeling that he is doing his duty, he has never any cause to fear. It is only if he walks in the darkness of sin and unbelief and distrust, that he need be frightened and afraid of stumbling.' I should like you to read the very words of Jesus, —" *Are there not twelve hours in the day? If any man walk in the day, he stumbleth not, because he seeth the light of this world. But if a man walk in the night, he stumbleth, because there is no light in him.*"

Thomas, one of the Apostles, was a cool, cautious man, more so than any of the rest; but when he heard the brave words of his beloved Lord, he threw aside his natural calmness and restraint and expressed himself willing to share every danger to

"*But Mary sat still in the house*" (John xii. 20)

page 287

which his Master might be exposed. 'If they stone Him,' he said, 'I am ready for His sake to be stoned too. Let us all be willing to give our lives for Him, if need be:' *"Let us also go that we may die with Him."*

Jesus had broken the sad news about His friend to the disciples. First He had told them that Lazarus *"sleepeth;"* then more plainly, *"Lazarus is dead."*

In awe and silence the little band proceed on their journey. Though little more than twenty miles from Perea to the Mount of Olives, they took four days to it. On the last of these they would likely rest for the night at the Good Samaritan's inn, halfway between Jericho and Jerusalem, and reach Bethany on the afternoon of the fourth day.

Let us now return in thought to the scene of death.

I think I see Mary, the younger sister, as in the accompanying picture, seated on the ground, barefoot and in tears, with rent dress and dishevelled hair—her sandals and muffled harp lying close by. The empty bed is at her side, with the now unowned *abbáh*, so familiar to her eyes, hung above. The well-known pilgrim-staff, needed no more, rests on the vacant chair. The unused scrolls lie mute on the table, just as he left them. The jars with fragrant flowers and sweet herbs he loved to tend, now stand unheeded at the entrance-door. The sacred names of JEHOVAH, painted, as was often the custom, in Hebrew letters on the wall (*Jehovah Jireh: Jehovah Nissi: Jehovah Shalom*), can speak to the wounded one at present no silent word of comfort. Even the presence of sympathisers from village and city is hardly known to her. They seem to sit apart from the young mourner, as if afraid to intrude on the sacredness of her sorrow. She hears the hired wailers as though she heard them not. She sits—no jewel on her arm, no sandal on her feet—absorbed in the deeps of her own speechless grief. Nor does she seek to change her posture, unless it may be to rush for a moment to the window looking towards the Moab mountains,—lifting her eyes to the hills, from whence, alas, cometh no help!

Martha, on the other hand, cannot rest. She rises every now and then from her sister's side, and hastens up to the house-top, or it may be to some quiet nook in the garden, which overlooks the Jericho road, to see if she can descry anything of Jesus. Hearken to her. She is still repeating, half-aloud through her tears, "*Oh, if He had been here, our brother would not have died!*"

At last the well-known little company are seen in the distance. Soon they have reached the outskirts of the village, where you may think of them pausing after the fatiguing ascent under the shade of some olive and carob trees.

Martha goes out by the wicket-gate to meet them, and perhaps to prevent them at present coming nearer the house: for she knew well the great danger Jesus was in from the Jews in Jerusalem. She knew all about the stones they had so recently taken up to stone Him; and as many Jews from the city were now in her home of sorrow, she might think it better to receive Christ alone outside the town, and there unburden to Him her grief.

When she reaches the Master's presence, the familiar words are the first she utters—perhaps some unkind thought of blame mingles with them—"*Lord, if Thou hadst been here, our brother had not died.*"

Jesus, however, has no ungracious saying in His reply. He comforts her. He tells her that "her brother would rise again." She says she knows that,—that he will rise at the last day. But that is not the comfort she desired now. If the grave had not closed over him, she would have dearly liked him back to be a living brother to her still on earth.

Her Lord then utters one of those beautiful sayings which may well be written in golden letters—"I AM THE RESURRECTION AND THE LIFE. *He that believeth on Me, though he were dead, yet shall he live.*"

But Martha feels that she must not have all these words of comfort to herself. She hurries back to the room where Mary is still sitting, and whispers secretly to her the glad message—"*The Master is come, and calleth for thee!*"

Mary is not so prudent and cautious as her sister; her grief has made her forget all about the Jews wishing to stone Jesus. With haste she rushes out of the house to meet her Lord. In a moment she is at His feet, while the same words which, like a strain of mournful music, had been ringing in both their ears, come also to her lips—"*Lord, if Thou hadst been here, my brother had not died.*"

In the meantime, the Jews and the hired mourners who were in the house followed Mary outside. They did not hear what Martha had said to her. They thought she had followed her sister in order to weep at the side of her brother's grave. When they had reached the spot to which she had gone, to their amazement Jesus of Nazareth was standing there!

I wonder what His disciples were thinking all this time? They, too, could hardly fail to recall the scene at the gate of Nain, when the dead son was raised up. What was to hinder their Master now, from raising up a dead brother?

Yes; but the cases were very different. The widow's son had only died that forenoon. Lazarus had been dead four days: the grave had closed over him, and corruption had begun.

It is very touching to read of the grief of these two weeping sisters. But what is most touching of all is when we are told that "JESUS WEPT!"

His human eyes were filled with human tears as He stood by His friend's grave and heard the sobs and heart-breakings around Him: thinking perhaps also of the miseries and sorrows which death and sin together had caused to the world. Surely these tears revealed alike how great was His grief, and how kind His heart.

I need not dwell on the rest of the well-known, touching story, —the gathering round the rocky grave, the prayer of Jesus to His Father, and the rolling away of the large stone at the entrance. Then, how, not as man, but as the great God, He cried with a loud voice, "*Lazarus, come forth.*"

Imagine the stillness of the crowd. Will the dead man hear? Is his not rather a sleep far too deep to be disturbed—a sleep from which there is no awaking?

T

There is a noise and a stir inside the vault. Oh, wonder of wonders! Lazarus was dead, but Lazarus now *lives!* "*And he that was dead came forth, bound hand and foot with grave-clothes; and his face was bound about with a napkin. Jesus saith unto them, Loose him, and let him go.*"

You can only picture that happy return to the home close by, which is desolate no more: the risen man, with the flush of life on his cheek, restored to the embrace of his loved sisters; and they with joyful hearts exclaiming, "*This our brother was dead, and is alive again; he was lost, and is found.*"

> "From every house the neighbours met,
> The streets were filled with joyful sound;
> A solemn gladness even crowned
> The purple brows of Olivet."[1]

That delay of two whole days in coming to Bethany, at the time so strange,—Martha understands it all now. The words of Jesus make everything plain—"*Said I not unto thee that if thou wouldst* BELIEVE, *thou shouldst* SEE *the glory of God?*"

If He had cured Lazarus at once, or by merely sending a message (as He had done in the case of the nobleman's son and the Phœnician woman's daughter), how many lessons of comfort would have been lost to these sisters; to those that stood by; to the Church in every age; and specially to all sad and broken hearts? Think what a blank would have been in your Bibles if this story of sickness and death had not been there;—Jesus coming, and weeping, and comforting!

Oh, when my young readers are brought to their first hour of grief, they will know what a precious chapter this is, about the saddened, and yet gladdened, HOME OF BETHANY!

---

[1] In Memoriam.

L.

He goes to the town of Ephraim, and thence to Jericho.

WHAT a stir is caused in Jerusalem! Two miles from the city, a dead man—a man for four days in his grave—has come to life again! And it is Jesus of Nazareth (who had been so nearly Himself stoned a few weeks ago), that has raised him up!

"Jesus must be the Messiah:—Jesus must be the Promised King," shout many.

Others are only more enraged against Him than ever. Some of these very Jews who had beheld with their own eyes the miracle at Bethany, instead, as they might well have done, of falling at His feet, and crying out 'My Lord and my God,' went straight from the house of Lazarus to plot His murder.

That murder, indeed, was already secretly resolved upon by the great Jewish council; at the head of which was Caiaphas, the High Priest, and his son-in-law, Annas. "*If we let Him alone*," they said, "*all men will believe on Him.*"

The Sadducees joined with the Pharisees in their dreadful purpose. The sect of the Sadducees did not believe in a resurrection. They were, therefore, very angry at the alleged miracle of Lazarus being raised to life.

The leaders of the council wished the dark deed done if possible before the Passover. If they waited till the feast had begun, there might be many friends of Jesus present, who would take His part, and, perhaps, rescue Him from their vengeance.

The Saviour would not have shrunk needlessly from danger. If it had been the Divine will, He would at once have bowed His head to the storm and said, as He did soon after, "Even so, Father, for so it seemed good in Thy sight!" But "the hour" of which He had so often spoken, had still "not yet come." So He once more leaves Bethany, and goes to a small town or village on the hills at Bethel, near where Jacob slept and dreamed his dream. The name of the town was Ephraim. It was about twenty miles distant from Jerusalem. It looked down on the valley of the Jordan, and had a view of the grand Moab mountains, with which Jesus was now so familiar.

The Master and His disciples remained in the breezy uplands of that district for some weeks. They had great need to turn aside and "rest awhile." And though ONE at least too well knew that the clouds were rapidly gathering for the last awful tempest, —here they enjoyed, brief and transient as it was, a season of perfect retirement.

Doubtless, He who so much loved prayer, had many quiet hours of communion with His Father on these lone desolate hills. It would be a fitting time, too, away from the din of the city and the plots of His enemies, still farther to instruct His Apostles, in the near prospect of being taken from them, and of their being left to fight the battle alone.

At last the appointed *hour* really has arrived. He must turn His steps towards the city and scene of His death. On leaving the place of their present sojourn, the sacred writer tells us specially, that Jesus walked in front of His disciples.

They followed at a little distance; and as they followed Him "*they were afraid.*" It was a new feeling to them; for they had never before any cause of dread in the presence of so loving a Master. They knew, however, from His look of pensive sadness and His strange silence, that there was something, more than common, brooding in that great heart of His.

The crowds are beginning to throng the green valley below, on their way to the Passover; some on mules, camels, and asses; some on foot, carrying branches of palm and myrrh, their voices tuned to the Paschal songs. It was again that season of the year we have more than once noted, when the corn was ripening, the birds singing, and the flowers gaily fringing every crag of white limestone. As The Twelve were still walking on by themselves, separated a few paces from their Master, Jesus stops, and calls them near to Him. He has something very solemn to say.

He had told them often before of His coming sufferings, even of His approaching death. But He had kept from them till now the most startling part of the revelation. What was that?

It was, not only that He was to be betrayed and scourged, mocked, and insulted; but, oh, most dreadful and shameful of all, He was to be CRUCIFIED! It was the death reserved for the meanest slave. They all knew too well the horror of the words *" Cursed is every one that hangeth on a tree!"*

Yet, too, how little did those disciples seem really to understand the full force of His announcement! His own thoughts were about deep sorrow and humiliation—His anguish and bloody sweat, His Cross and Passion. They, poor, frail men, were dreaming still of some grand empire with crowns and thrones: about their Lord and Master being King, and they His "satraps" or courtiers. They began the old strife, as to "which of them should be the greatest;" which should have the chief seats of honour nearest Him in the new kingdom.

Alas! they would ere long discover, that it was a far different crown and sceptre which were to be placed on the head and in the hands of their suffering Redeemer. They thought they would be quite able to drink of His cup. We shall come soon to find how hollow their boast was, and how sadly their ability failed them!

It was in all likelihood on a Thursday, that they had thus joined one of the bands of worshippers on one of the great roads of Palestine north of Jericho. There would probably be a number of their old Galilean acquaintances in the same caravan: they may have made previously some agreement to meet, and complete the rest of the journey in one another's company. We like to have beloved relatives with us or near us in a season of sore anxiety and trouble: it would be a comforting thought to the lone sad heart of Jesus, that so many of His dearest friends would be in Jerusalem at the time of His sufferings. Among the friends they had now joined would very possibly be the Mother of the Saviour; His cousins; and the holy women who ministered to Him, and who were ere long to minister more lovingly than ever at His cross and at His grave. We are specially told that Salome, the mother of James and John, was there.

In many former years, that Passover journey had been a peculiarly joyous occasion to *one* of that pilgrim band to whom I have just referred:—going up with her dear Son, first from Nazareth and afterwards from the Lake. But His manner, His appearance, His words, all tell her too faithfully now, as they had already done His disciples, that there is an hour of darkness and mystery at hand. She would still, however, as before, keep all these fears locked up in her heart.

The caravan is coming near the famous city of Jericho.

LI.

He passes through Jericho, and cures Blind Bartimeus.

JERICHO is now, like Bethany, a cluster of ruins. When there, a fellow-traveller and myself were asked by some of the wild-looking people to go and visit an old dying man in the middle of their village. We were in that way better able to see the wretchedness of their hovels, and to get a glimpse of their savage looks and life. In the present aspect of the place there is a sad change indeed from the City of balsam and palm-trees, orange and olive groves. A whole forest of palms used to stretch from the outer walls to the Jordan, and for miles on every side. Now no tree is left to give a trace of the ancient name; nor one relic of the balsam plantations, yielding the 'Balm of Gilead,' whose perfume had a reputation among all the bazaars and luxurious cities of the East, in the time of the Jewish historian. I could see little in the shape of vegetation, excepting the thorny nabk, and some dwarf bushes bearing beautiful little fruit of a red waxy colour ("Apples of Sodom?"). The only green shady spot left near it, is the Fountain of Elisha, with its unusually clear gushing water. No remains are to be found of the vast buildings; —the walls with their massive gates, and corner forts,—the temples and theatres and circus, with which Herod the Great had strengthened and adorned his favourite city, and upon which the eyes in that gathering of Paschal worshippers must now have fallen, as they were approaching its northern entrance.

Jesus, we read, and the pilgrim company, "passed through" the city. The crowd was becoming gradually larger. They would seem to have been leaving the western gate fronting the Valley of Achor, when, amid the noise and turmoil, a voice is heard calling aloud. Who is this?

It is one of the row of beggars that were wont to sit, as they still do, outside the gates of cities in the East. His name is given to us,—*Bartimeus the son of Timæus.*

That poor man's case was a very sad one. He was not only a beggar, covered with rags, and thankful for the smallest pittance from the passers-by; but he was smitten with the blindness we have already found to be so common in the Holy Land. He had sat there for years in the brightest noonday, but that noon was all darkness to him. There was now the blue sky of April above him, but he saw it not. There was the green flush of spring on that great garden of South Palestine—a gorgeous carpet of daisies and anemones, yet he saw them not. There were the deep glorious shadows and crimson tints on the near mountains of Moab and Gilead, yet he saw them not. The very stars which glanced and gleamed like diamonds in the midnight heavens were all a dream to him; he had heard about them—no more. Oh, how he longed like others, his fellow-sufferers, of whom we have previously spoken, to have his eyes opened to enjoy God's best gift in outer nature—the sweet, blessed, cheerful light of day! His rags and his beggary were bad enough; but it was the life of perpetual darkness that was worst of all to bear:—every day groping his way to the same place; the same hum of voices passing and repassing; the same tramp of feet;—soldiers from Herod's palace and barracks; priests from this Levite city on their way to Jerusalem; Essenes from the desert, unsandalled and unshorn, muttering their prayers as they flitted by; pedlars hawking their wares; workmen hastening to their work; the women with their pitchers going to Elisha's fountain for water; the merry laugh of children running by their side;—he heard all this, but he saw nothing!

For days together, at this particular time of which I speak, there has been more of a noise and bustle, owing to the eager multitude flocking up to the greatest of the annual feasts.

Blind men are very quick in hearing. Bartimeus hears it whispered among the crowd—"*Jesus of Nazareth is coming!*"

He is all eager to listen. The name and fame and miracles of Christ could not be strange to him. He, doubtless, had heard how that gracious Wonder-worker had already cured blind people, and given them sight, both in Judea and Galilee.

There is no time to hesitate. "*Jesus of Nazareth is passing by.*" If he does not speak to Him and plead with Him at once, he may lose the opportunity. It may be his one chance. It *would* have been his one, his last chance; for we do not read of Jesus ever again coming or going that way.

As the crowd are surging by, the blind man cries in the loudest tones he can, "*Jesus, thou Son of David, have mercy on me!*"

Not only the general throng, but even the friends and followers of the Saviour, are displeased with the suppliant. They speak some angry words to him. They tell him to "hold his peace"—to cease his pleadings; there was no time for the caravan to halt for such as he!

Does Bartimeus give heed to these silencing voices, and resign all hope?

No; they may say what things they choose, they cannot hush the cry of faith. He only raises the accents of his voice higher and louder amid the buzz of the crowd, and shouts, "*Jesus, thou Son of David, have mercy upon me!*"

The Master, who had showed so lately His love for helpless babes and prattling children, now shows His love and pity for this friendless, stricken sufferer. He heard the voice:—*that voice stopped Him.* It is a wonderful instance, surely, of what the cry and prayer of faith can do. *Jesus stood still !*

This was not all. He told those around Him to bring the suppliant near.

Some of the kinder amongst them hastened to the blind man with the joyful words, "*Be of good cheer; rise, He calleth thee.*"

Bartimeus throws aside His ragged cloak, and comes to Jesus. The Saviour looks upon him with divine pity, and puts forth on his behalf divine power. His sight is restored !

> " Mourning, I sat beside the way,
>   In sightless gloom apart ;
> And sadness heavy on me lay,
>   And longing gnawed my heart.
> I heard the music of the psalms
>   Thy people sang to Thee ;
> I felt the waving of their palms,
>   And yet I could not see.
>
> " But words of Thine can never fail ;
>   My fears are past and o'er :
> My soul is glad with light,—the veil
>   Is on my heart no more.
> A sudden answer stilled my fear,
>   For it was said to me—
> ' O sightless one ! be of good cheer ;
>   Arise ! He calleth thee.'" [1]

All the wonderful beauties of nature in a moment burst upon him—the sky, the clouds, the hills, the streams !

But I think there is *One* Object, above all others, his eye would most fondly rest upon.

Yes, it would surely be JESUS Himself, his kind Deliverer. He cannot leave Him. He follows the footsteps of the gracious Physician, up the steep road, with songs of praise ; and many others

---

[1] Lyra Germanica.

in the crowd, who had seen the miracle, break forth into thanksgivings also. I like the idea in a great picture I saw lately, of Christ entering Jerusalem in triumph, three days after. Bartimeus is there, waving his palm branch, and shouting his Hosanna to One BRIGHTER than that bright sun his eyes had so recently for the first time beheld!

> "I will praise Thee, *Sun of Glory!*
> For thy beams have gladness brought.
> I will praise Thee and adore Thee
> For the light I vainly sought;
> Thou didst come my soul to cheer,
> Shine, ETERNAL SUNBEAM, here!"[1]

It was on this same interesting occasion that Jesus called Zaccheus the publican, and added him also to the number of His disciples.

I remarked before, in speaking about St. Matthew, upon the usual greed and extortion of these publicans. The sight of them was most hateful to the Jews. Zaccheus would not likely be an exception to the general rule. No city in Palestine, indeed, gave a better opportunity for levying tax-money than Jericho. Fruits and perfumes alone (from its miles of tropical gardens) would yield to a greedy exactor an enormous revenue. But Christ once more shows what the power of His grace can do.

You know the story well. The little man (for he was small of stature) climbing up among the thick branches of the avenue of sycamore-trees ("fig mulberries") which lined the road: Jesus seeing him—calling him down—calling him by name—speaking kindly to him;—yes, so kindly to a man who was thus hated by all others for his mean trade and mean ways;—"*Make haste and come down, Zaccheus, for to-day I must abide at thy house.*" Then the narrative further tells, how the once grasping publican received the gracious Prophet and Healer as a guest at his table:

---

[1] Hymns from the Land of Luther.

how, touched by the loving heart and loving ways of Jesus, he resolved, from that .day henceforth, to end his base, cheating, covetous practices;—to give the half of all he had to the poor, and to pay back, four times over, his past unfair and dishonest gains.

Oh, what a happy word that was the Saviour of the guilty and the lost addressed to him—" *This day is salvation come to this house.*"

Jesus proceeds on His way from Jericho.

It is along the same road He had now so often travelled, and which I have already described,—beginning with one of the grandest valleys in the south of Palestine, now called *Wády Kelt.* Rugged precipices are overhead, where eagles build their eyries, and splintered rocks are down below, where the winter torrent, fringed with oleander and thorn, rushes to the plain of Jericho: then the same treeless, dreary ascent for miles together, with not even so much as a tuft of grass, up " The Robbers' Valley," to Olivet and Zion.

Though steep, King Herod had made this road a good one. I daresay he had often himself driven by it in his chariot to and from Jerusalem. Pieces of the solid Roman pavement still remain.

There would only be two pausing places then, as now, for the refreshment of travellers. In these dry and thirsty lands, as you know, it is always where a well is to be found that the camels and asses are unladen and the tents are pitched. There happen to be only two such fountains in all that wild and burning stretch. The one at the Good Samaritan's Inn, of which I previously told you, three hours from Jericho; the other, just as beautiful Bethany begins to peep out from its nest of olives. This latter has the touching name given to it of " The Fountain of the Apostles." I have called it the 'touching name,' because it seems to recall the picture of a tired and weary company of disciples and their Master thankfully resting on its rim of stone under the dripping rock. What was said of another Well, with whose interesting story you are familiar, was doubtless often equally true of this one, "*Jesus being weary with His journey, sat thus on the well:*"—asking, perhaps, some chance Bethany villagers, who had come to draw water, to let down their pitchers and allow Him and His travel-worn friends to quench their thirst. As we dismounted at that sacred stone-trough, under the ruined arch, could we help thinking of HIM? Fatiguing enough every traveller finds the hot journey even on horseback:—what must it have been to climb, as we know the Pilgrim of Pilgrims did, that sultry ascent *on foot!*

It was probably on Friday afternoon that Jesus reached Bethany, and next day was the Jewish Sabbath. The vast caravan, with which He had travelled for two days, would now leave Him. Instead of turning (as *He* did) by the path to the right, which led to the village, the other festal worshippers would continue their way across the shoulder of the Mount of Olives. On the backs of their asses, mules, and camels, there would be slung a number of tent-poles and rolls of canvas. Before sunset (at which time the Jewish Sabbath began) these wooden poles and bundles would be taken down, and the Paschal tents would be pitched somewhere on the green grass of the mountain, or along the gorge of the Kedron. Many other similar huts would already be erected by those of the travellers who had arrived. Indeed at this sacred season there was quite a little pilgrim city outside the walls of Jerusalem, besides the vast multitude of strangers who were lodged in the houses within.

The disciples would, doubtless, accompany Jesus to Bethany.

How pleasant it would be for Martha, Mary, and Lazarus to welcome their kind Friend again! How much they would have to speak about! If He were loved before in that home, He would now be loved more than ever.

And yet the hearts of the sisters could not fail to be oppressed with new and peculiar anxieties; not only because of the danger to which their gracious Lord was exposed from the Jews in Jerusalem, but they knew that these same Jews were already plotting the death of their own dear brother also. The miracle of his resurrection had led many to believe on Jesus, and the chief rulers disliked the thought of the most important witness to that deed of divine power being allowed to live.

How lamentable was the wilful, wayward unbelief of these leaders of the nation! They were, alas! shutting their eyes against the Light of the Glorious SUN! Again, how sadly did their case illustrate the words, we have more than once quoted, spoken to Nicodemus:—"*This is the condemnation, that* LIGHT *has come into the world, and men loved* DARKNESS *rather than* LIGHT*!*"

GLEAMS BEFORE SUNSET.

"AT EVENING TIME IT SHALL BE LIGHT."—ZECH. XIV. 7.

"JESUS SAID, NOW IS THE SON OF MAN GLORIFIED, AND GOD IS GLORIFIED IN HIM. IF GOD BE GLORIFIED IN HIM, GOD SHALL ALSO GLORIFY HIM IN HIMSELF, AND SHALL STRAIGHTWAY GLORIFY HIM."—JOHN XIII. 31, 32.

"LET NOT YOUR HEART BE TROUBLED: YE BELIEVE IN GOD, BELIEVE ALSO IN ME. IN MY FATHER'S HOUSE ARE MANY MANSIONS: IF IT WERE NOT SO, I WOULD HAVE TOLD YOU. I GO TO PREPARE A PLACE FOR YOU. AND IF I GO AND PREPARE A PLACE FOR YOU, I WILL COME AGAIN, AND RECEIVE YOU UNTO MYSELF; THAT WHERE I AM, THERE YE MAY BE ALSO."—JOHN XIV. 1-3.

"A LITTLE WHILE, AND YE SHALL NOT SEE ME: AND AGAIN A LITTLE WHILE, AND YE SHALL SEE ME; BECAUSE I GO TO THE FATHER."—JOHN XVI. 16.

LII.

He is entertained at a Feast in Bethany.

THE Evening Shadows in the life of Jesus, as we have seen, were fast falling. He—the Divine *Sun of Righteousness*—was wading through storm-clouds :—these, too, increasing and deepening all over the horizon. But as bright rays, like parting smiles in death, are often observed, in outer nature, breaking through the gloomiest western sky ;—so it was in the closing scenes of the Great "*Light of the world.*" One of these farewell gleams—" GLEAMS BEFORE SUNSET "—we are to speak of now; and others will follow.

On the Sabbath evening (the day after the Saviour's arrival) there was a feast given in the Bethany Home, evidently in honour of the Divine Guest. It would seem as if the family had expected His coming, for many Jews had crossed the hill in order to meet Jesus as well as to see Lazarus.

Though this supper was given by Martha, Mary, and their Brother, it is said to have taken place in "*the house of Simon the leper.*"

I have no doubt you will ask, who was Simon ?

I cannot positively tell you. It has been thought (and the idea is an interesting one, and not certainly improbable) that he may have been the father of the household ;—that being a leper, he had been obliged, hitherto, like all such sufferers, to live by himself ;—but that Jesus—the leper's Friend, as we have already seen Him to be in far-off Galilee—had mercifully cured him.

Simon's heart was full of gratitude to the Great Physician. If it were indeed the case that he was the head of the family, the good and gracious Prophet of Nazareth had restored to him also his own, his only son, the pride and joy of his home. A touching picture would thus be brought before us ; the healed father and the living son seated at the same table together, gazing with fond love and wonder on their Great Deliverer;—the voice of rejoicing and of salvation in that tabernacle of the righteous!

Jesus was reclining on a couch by the side of the table. All the rest of the family seem to have been present to the close of the entertainment, except Mary. Where has she gone?

By-and-by we see her coming behind her divine Lord. Kneeling down, she breaks a box filled with precious ointment; so precious, as to be worth £10 of our English money; then she pours its contents first on His head and then on His feet. Not content with this, she takes the long tresses of her hair, and wipes His feet with them.

Even could the deed have been done in silence, it would soon have made itself known; for the ointment was fragrant, and the whole house was filled with the odour.

What a beautiful token this was of her devotion and love! That alabaster casket was likely the most valued thing she had in her possession; perhaps some gift she had received long ago, and which she had been treasuring up to use on some fitting occasion. That occasion has now come. On whom can her grateful heart more joyously bestow it than on Him she had such cause to adore and reverence. She felt nothing could be too good or too costly to offer so kind and gracious a Saviour and Friend. In addition to what He had done for her own soul, she owed to Him what was to her the most valued life (or lives) in all the world. We shall presently see how gratefully that deed of love was accepted and acknowledged by Him who was the Object of it!

While, however, Mary was busy bestowing her costly offering, the disciples looked at one another.

They were poor men, and did not like to see valuable things thrown away. Their Master had taught them to be kind, and to give alms to the needy. He had praised a poor widow for putting her little mite into the Temple treasury-box. He had spoken severely about a rich man, who had neglected the poor at his gate, and spent all upon himself,—on his dress, and his table. Only three days before, He had been pleased at hearing Zaccheus say that he would give the half of his goods to feed the poor. It may have seemed strange, then, when they saw Mary breaking her beautiful white casket, that Jesus should allow such waste. Might not the money have been better employed?

One of their number spoke his thoughts aloud. He was very angry about the matter, although his anger, as we shall presently find, proceeded from the basest motives. 'If I only had possessed this alabaster box,' said Judas, 'I might have sold it for a large sum.' "Not that he cared for the poor." If the box had really fallen into his hands, doubtless he would have managed to take for his own use a goodly portion, at least, of the money obtained for it.

Jesus knew well the greedy purposes of that wicked man. He saw, too, that Mary was troubled about such ungenerous thoughts regarding her ointment. She, meek and lowly like her Master, is silent under these cutting sayings. But He who loved to see her gratitude and devotion, and who was cheered with this little gleam of light in His own "cloudy and dark day," is *not* silent. He speaks kindly words about her; and at once puts an end to these captious objections. He said, "Do not trouble her; she has done a good work in putting this ointment on My head and feet. It is as if she were anointing My body for My coming death and burial. *The poor ye have always with you, but Me ye have not always.*"

Alas! this incident was, as I have called it, but "a little gleam of light." The clouds speedily close again.

Judas had hitherto appeared, like his brother Apostles, to love his Master. But what had now taken place, while it fatally crossed his hopes, revealed at the same time the hollowness of his affection. The vile purpose in his heart gets the better of him. Till shortly before this period, as we have seen, he had clung to the thought, in common with the others, of Jesus founding a temporal kingdom. He would seem, moreover, to have had deeper and more selfish designs, in the prospect of such a kingdom, known only to himself. He had evidently, with cunning forethought, laid his plans to become its royal treasurer. By having charge of the King's money, he would have ample scope to satisfy his own avarice. But now all these covetous dreams and longings are at an end. He whom he had hoped thus to hail as a great Sovereign, had just spoken of His "dead body" and His "burial." Judas wished no such Lord and Ruler as this. He was soon to show how poor and insincere the attachment was, that could be tampered with (yes, and *bought*), for a few glittering silver coins!

He left the feast in the house of Simon, and plunged out into the dark night.

Going straight to Jerusalem, he has his first secret interview with the priestly leaders of the nation—entering into a shameful compact with them to betray his Lord for far less than the worth of Mary's alabaster box. For thirty Jewish shekels the ungrateful, mean-souled man, has agreed to deliver up the kindest and best of Masters. The paltry bribe was the price at which a slave could be ransomed; or, to put it in another shape, if a slave had been accidentally gored by an animal, it was the sum which the master of the slave got as "compensation" from the animal's owner! (Exodus xxi. 32). We shall come, farther on, to find how the base bargain was carried to completion.

Such an act as that of Judas stands alone in the world's history. And yet, let my young readers remember, that this miserable traitor was at one time an innocent child playing at his mother's feet, with no thought of a future so dark with guilt and despair. His black crime reads, surely, a terrible lesson as to what *one* sin in the heart, if indulged, may lead. Judas loved money; and see what were the results of his greedy thoughts and greedy deeds. The two texts resound over his grave with an awful warning—"*Hardened through the deceitfulness of sin*"—-" IT WERE BETTER FOR THAT MAN IF HE HAD NEVER BEEN BORN!"

LIII.

He crosses in triumph the Mount of Olives.

THE first time I went to Bethany, I took the steep path which goes straight across the Mount of Olives from Jerusalem. This is the shortest way to it. But the principal road—what must have been in former days the great highway—winds along by the south side of the mountain.

In coming from Jericho, after passing Bethany, this same road suddenly turns to the right, and the first glimpse of the Holy City is obtained. It there continues down a steep slope, at the foot of which there is a sharp angle, and then a gradual ascent. The opposite summit being gained, a wonderful view reveals itself. Though the gorge of the Kedron is between, the whole of Jerusalem rises up all at once like a beautiful vision, with its walls and towers and domes.

The sight is striking, even now, and one never to be forgotten. What then must it have been in the time of which I am now speaking, when the glorious Temple was there in its full grandeur, with its gilded roofs and marble colonnades; beyond it the great towers of Herod; also Herod's palace, standing conspicuous, on the heights of Mount Zion! Truly, in the words of the prophet, it must have looked "a crown of glory in the hand of the Lord, and a royal diadem in the hand of our God."

Think with what pride these crowds I have recently described must have gazed on all this; think specially with what joy and wonder the youths, who had come up for the first time to attend the Feast, must have looked across to that "Jerusalem," whose name they had been taught to lisp and love on their mother's knee! It must have been far more splendid than their best thoughts could have pictured it to be. How would the words of one of their favourite psalms come to mind, and perhaps be repeated aloud by many lips—"*Beautiful for situation, the joy of the whole earth is Mount Zion, on the sides of the north, the city of the Great King!*"

It is now the first day of the Passover week (corresponding with our Sunday). Many pilgrim bands and caravans are coming across at sunrise by this same road. They have been travelling all night by the light of the stars and of the Passover moon. Droves of lambs also, for Passover offerings, are occasionally seen. Some of these are on the highway; others are resting beside their shepherds close by, and nibbling the young grass on the hillside. Many of them would be set apart that same afternoon for sacrifice.

The early morning hours are now past. But what is this? The crowds from the direction of Bethany seem all at once to have increased. It is not one group of travellers that is now seen; many of them appear to have mingled, and are joining in loud exclamations as they come slowly along.

There is some one in the midst, seated on an animal, numbers pressing around Him. Those who are leading the colt or foal have put their upper cloaks on its back, as a cushion or saddle-cloth; others of the pilgrims are strewing their garments on the road to form a sort of carpet for this Rider. Their cry becomes more distinct as they come nearer. It is the shout of many voices—*Hosanna! Hosanna! Hosanna!*

What can this mean? "*Hosanna,*" though but one word, was, as I formerly told you in speaking of the Feast of Tabernacles, the nation's brief prayer for its coming Messiah, and the nation's shout of welcome to Him.

Need I tell you who it is who is thus riding along in royal state?

It is the Redeemer coming in triumph from Bethany to Jerusalem!

An old prophet, called Zechariah, had thus, many hundred years before, written about Him, and about this very day— "*Rejoice greatly, O daughter of Zion; shout, O daughter of Jerusalem: behold, thy King cometh unto thee: He is just, and having salvation; lowly and riding upon an ass, and upon a colt the foal of an ass."*

The prophet's words are now fulfilled. It is Jesus, and still " the meek and lowly Jesus." But He is coming as KING to His own Zion.

Lately, we spoke of Him as a weary, tired traveller, walking up the hot stifling valleys from Jericho on foot. Now He is mounted on the animal which the old princes and prophets, the rulers and judges of Israel, were wont to ride upon rare and public occasions. Horses were used in the chariots of war; asses were used as symbols of peace. I should tell you that these latter are not the despised animals in Eastern countries which they often are with us. I was much struck with the beauty, and even grace, of some I saw in Palestine and Syria.

Why, you may perhaps ask, did Jesus make use of one of these now? He was not in the habit of having such help in His journeys. And, surely, there never was an occasion when He less needed it than the present, for He had enjoyed a whole Sabbath-day's rest at Bethany; and Jerusalem, where He was going, was only the short distance of two miles. Nor, need I add, did He ever care about 'show' or 'appearance.' You will remember one time, when they wished very much to make Him a King, He positively refused. Why then, at this particular season, does He ride in royal majesty, and be willing to receive the hosannas of the crowd?

I answer, first; He wished, for once, to tell the Jews, who had rejected Him and tried to stone Him, that He was really the Son of God, and the Great Messiah.

Nor was this His only or His chief reason. He was to suffer death that week,—to die for the sins of the world. He desired by this public entry into Jerusalem *to attract attention to His Great Sacrifice, and to Himself the great Victim.* He wished to show who the true Paschal Lamb really was, and to whom all these thousands on thousands of innocent animals which were to be killed, pointed.

I may add another reason,—as He was in a few days to be

stripped of robe and mantle and to be nailed to a cross of shame, He wishes, once at least, to give His own Apostles, and all His faithful disciples then gathered at the Feast, a glimpse of His royalty and glory. He permits mantles to be spread in homage on His royal pathway: He allows the crowd to indulge in shouts of royal welcome!

Just after the procession had left Bethany, they obtained that view, I have already described, of a part of the hill of Zion. It embraced the site of King David's palace, and also of his tomb. The rest of the city is meanwhile hidden by the shoulder of the Mount of Olives. But that glimpse is enough to remind them that Messiah was to be "King David's kingly Son,"—the Son who was to "reign in righteousness;" and they add, therefore, to their shout of *Hosanna*,—"*Hosanna to the Son of* DAVID! *Blessed is He that cometh in the name of the Lord. Blessed is the kingdom that cometh of our father* DAVID!"

Perhaps the disciples might once more be led to think in their simplicity that the doom of the Roman has come,—that, after all, their dreams are yet to be made true, and their lowly Master is to become King of Judea.

The crowd was gradually becoming larger. Those who, the evening before, had seen Jesus at Bethany, had returned to Jerusalem and spread the news of His arrival there. Many of the pilgrims inside the city, including a number of His own disciples, went forth to meet Him and to join the triumphal procession. As they flocked up the side of the Mount of Olives, they cut down branches of the fig and olive and palm from the groves and gardens all along the slope;—trees which fell by the axes of the Romans many years afterwards, and which have never grown again. These branches were spread alongside the Rider's way; while the long fronds of the palm are waved before Him. Thousands of new voices swell the same cry, "*Blessed is He that cometh in the name of the Lord.*"

You know, doubtless, of what palm-branches were the symbols?

They were a double emblem of *gladness* and of *triumph*. You remember the beautiful passage in Revelation (written by one who was with his Master now on Olivet and witnessed the present scene),—where the happy white-robed company in heaven are spoken of as having the palms of *joy* and *victory* in their hands? (Rev. vii. 9).

The two processions, the one coming from Bethany, the other from Jerusalem, would probably meet down in that hollow at the angle of the road of which I have just told you. Those from Jerusalem would then turn round and precede the Redeemer: while those I have first spoken of would come after Him. St. Mark alludes to this when he says—"*They that went before, and they that followed, cried Hosanna.*" The two streams thus uniting, a shout, loud as the noise of many waters, went up. It would be heard among the Paschal tents pitched on the Mount, and echoed in the courts of the Temple.

The words of the Angels' Hymn, sung at the birth of Jesus over the plains of Bethlehem, would beautifully mingle with David's *name*, and David's *Psalm*, "*Hosanna to the Son of* DAVID. PEACE *in Heaven and* GLORY IN THE HIGHEST!"

> "Ride on! ride on in majesty!
> Hark! all the tribes Hosanna cry:
> O Saviour, meek, pursue Thy road
> With palms and scattered garments strewed.
>
> "Ride on! ride on in majesty!
> In lowly pomp ride on to die:
> O Christ, Thy triumphs now begin
> O'er captive death and conquered sin."

The procession advances, and the shouts get louder and louder as they reach that spot where Jerusalem comes in sight.

LIV.

He weeps over Jerusalem, and then enters the City.

But something startling here takes place.

When all the others are singing their loud songs and waving their emblems of triumph; while every other eye is beaming with gladness, there is One filled with tears.

It is the triumphant Saviour Himself. He reins in the animal on which He is mounted; and gazing across on the walls and palaces, the Temple and towers, which have just risen in view, the tears flow down His cheeks;—" *When He came near, He beheld the city, and wept over it!* "

Yes, how strange seem these tears! We did not so much wonder at His weeping at Bethany, for that was a scene of sorrow and death, and He was the tender, sympathising man, as well as the Great God. But strange, in the midst of loud shouts of joy,—He, too, the hero of the hour, that we should read— "Jesus wept!"

Do you ask why He wept?

It is not difficult to answer. He knew, what none of these eager multitudes did, that, not many years hence, all that splendid vision would melt away; that at a future Paschal feast the Roman armies would be encamped on the very spot where the palm-branches were now strewn; that millions would perish in the devoted city on which He now gazed: while of that snow-white Temple and these great walls whose stones look as if giants had raised them, it would be too truthfully said—" *There shall not be left one stone upon another that shall not be thrown down.*" Perhaps, more than all, He weeps because He thinks of the sin that will cause this misery, and bring about the entire ruin of the nation!

These tears Christ shed were not ordinary ones. It is worth

noting, that the word used about His weeping at the grave of Lazarus, is a different one from what is used about His weeping over Jerusalem. The one speaks of silent tears, the other of a loud lament, a bitter weeping as if His heart would break. If you read the passage for yourselves, you will see that the sorrow of Jesus was so great that it choked His words. He could not, for the sobs of grief, say all that He intended to say. "*If thou*," are His words, "*hadst known, even thou in this thy day, the things that belong to thy peace*"—then there is a stop, a pause, as if unable to finish the sentence—"*but now*," He adds, "*they are hid from thine eyes!*"

When I stood on that spot in early spring, I remember well it was sprinkled thick with red anemones. The Christian pilgrims in Palestine call these flowers by the touching name of "the Saviour's blood-drops." He shed His tears on this spot, and He could almost see from it the olive grove, where, in a few days more, blood would fall in sacred drops from His brow and stain the green sward at His feet.

After this affecting pause, the "King of the Jews"—for King He was—moves on. The procession descends the road to the right, past the Garden of Gethsemane. Crossing the brook Kidron, they enter the streets of the city.

All there is noise and excitement. The people are leaning out of their windows, or stooping over the ledge of their flat roofs. As they hear the shouts, and see the waving of the palm branches, they cry, "*Who is this?*"

Then the Temple-gate is reached. Jesus dismounts and enters it.

For the second time He drives out the money-changers who, with their noise and shameless bargaining and traffic, had made His Father's house like a robber's den.

When order was restored, He soon got a crowd of hearers gathered round about Him. But what delighted Him most of all, were the Hosannas, which had ceased for the time on the lips of others, but which still arose from the lips of children in the Temple.

The chief priests said nothing about the praise which had been uttered by grown-up Jews; but when they heard the tender voices of the little ones take up the Hosanna-song, we are told "they were sore displeased."

Jesus was *not* displeased. We may believe no garlands cast at His feet that day on the road from Bethany were half so beautiful as those thrown by the hands of young worshippers. No music that He heard that day was half so sweet to Him as when "the children of Zion were joyful in their King!" He answered, "*Have ye never read, Out of the mouth of babes and sucklings, Thou hast perfected praise.*"[1]

What a beautiful incident this triumphant entrance of Jesus was! How worthy of the Prince of Peace! At that very time, Rome often had her great processions too, from her Capitol up to what she called 'The Sacred Mount.' But they were the processions of war-horses and war-chariots,—of weeping men and women,—of chained slaves, and wailing captives. How different from the present! Who were some among the rejoicing multitudes that followed in the train of Jesus? There were the cripples He had healed; the blind whose eyes He had opened; the lepers He had restored to health and home and friends; the dumb whose lips He had unsealed. Each was bearing his palm-branch in this march of peace! Yes, and as we have seen, children, too, are there, lining the royal procession with their tiny branches and flower-wreaths, attracted by the gentleness of the Divine Rider's ways and the sweetness of His voice.

Alas! Jesus too well knew, that before these strewn palm-leaves were withered, some of the voices which were now shouting *Hosanna*, would be crying "*Crucify Him! crucify Him!*"

In the evening of the day He and His disciples went out to beloved Bethany.

---

[1] In the accompanying illustration, the Mount of Olives covered with tents, and the Hosanna road which the Redeemer had just crossed, are in the distance. The steep footpath leading to Bethany (that generally taken by Him and His disciples), is seen on the left, with the Garden of Gethsemane below.

"The children crying in the Temple and saying, Hosanna to the Son of David" (Matt. xxi. 15)

page 316

LV.

He foretells the Destruction of the Temple, and is further betrayed by Judas.

IN the early morning, both of Monday and Tuesday, Jesus went into Jerusalem from Bethany, and taught in the Temple. On these two days He delivered some of His most solemn discourses and parables.

He left the sacred courts on Tuesday afternoon never again to return. Can you remember the words which He said on thus leaving?

They were the most touching (I should rather say, the most awful) spoken during the whole course of His ministry. How different from the winning and tender sayings with which He began His teaching in the synagogue of Nazareth, when He spoke of Himself as being anointed by His Father to proclaim a gracious message to the poor, the broken-hearted, the captive, the blind, the bruised!

These proud Jews in Jerusalem would not listen to His pleadings. They had turned a deaf ear alike to His earnest warnings and His loving invitations. He tells them that the hour of mercy, long offered to their guilty nation, is past and gone. They had despised all His counsel, and would none of His reproof. His heart is burning with grief and holy anger:—His eyes are filled with tears. And as He thought of the terrible woes He had done all He could to prevent, but which they had brought upon themselves—the famine, the siege, the cruelties and tortures—He bursts out in these most mournful accents—" *O Jerusalem, Jerusalem, thou that killest the prophets, and stonest them which are sent unto thee, how often would I have gathered thy children together, even as a hen gathereth her chickens under her wings, and ye would not ! Behold, your house is left unto you desolate.*"

Jesus then crossed the brook Kedron with His disciples.

They sat down to rest a-while on the sward of the Mount of Olives. The hum of busy tents would be all round; but they would choose one of the many green knolls, where, in the cool of the evening, they might converse without being disturbed. The Temple, of which every Jew was so proud, and whose ruin the Saviour had just foretold, was immediately opposite. He loved it much, as His Father's House. In its courts, thirty-three years previously, He got His first and earliest welcome from old age; and, only two days ago, He received His last from infancy and youth—the children who cried '*Hosanna.*'

He must have felt sad, indeed, as He gazed on these huge towers and battlements of white marble; on these beautiful gates and pillars; on that golden roof, now gleaming in the setting sun, and thought of all being soon levelled with the dust!

The disciples could hardly believe His words. As they, too, looked across the valley to the huge stones of the Temple wall, they said, '*Master, see what manner of stones and what buildings are here.*" (They might well be struck with the "manner" or size of the stones, for many of them were from twenty to thirty feet long.)

"*There shall not be left one stone upon another that shall not be thrown down!*"

In a few years, all that Jesus had said came quite true.

It must, on the other hand, have been a joy to Him at this time—one of the brightest "gleams" towards the close of His earthly days—to go, evening after evening, to the peaceful home of Lazarus and his sisters. It was the place that most recalled His happy early years, when He used to pluck the spring flowers on the hills of Nazareth, and watch the sun going down over the distant sea. The affection of the family would remind him, too, more than anything since, of His mother's tender love. Though we are not told, it is, I think, more than likely she may have been herself now living in the home at Bethany. We know from the sacred writers that she was in Jerusalem on the Passover week. Having her own sad thoughts of what was going to happen, she would surely try to be with her loved Son as long and as much as she could. May we not think of her thus, each afternoon, watching His coming across the "olive-bordered way," and joining in the welcome to the simple evening meal? He had read the words and known the truth of them (they would be dearer to Him than ever now)—"*As one whom His mother comforteth*" (Isaiah lxvi. 13).

On the Wednesday, He does not appear to have gone to Jerusalem, but remained during the day and night at Bethany.

We are not told anything as to how He spent these closing hours. He needed rest after all He had gone through the last three days. But it was more than rest He desired. He would, doubtless, seek out one of the many quiet nooks near the village, where he could, by prayer and communion with His Father, prepare Himself for His sufferings. When He lay down on His couch that night, it would be His last sleep; at all events, His eyes would not close again till they closed in the sleep of death on the cross and in the tomb!

All the Apostles were either with or near their Master that day. There was one exception:—that was Judas. He had left Bethany and gone to Jerusalem. You can readily conjecture the reason of his sad journey there. Satan, we have already seen, had "entered into him," and filled his heart with gloomy, dreadful thoughts. You can follow him in imagination as he hurries along with his eyes bent on the ground.

He goes straight to a building with a massive gate. On being admitted, he finds himself in a large pillared hall, where the seventy-one chiefs of the nation are assembled. They are looking very angry, and speaking very loud. It was a meeting of the Sanhedrim in the palace of the High Priest. The palace was on the south side of the valley of Hinnom, on a rising ground, still called "the hill of evil counsel."

Judas was just the person whose help was now required, and whose appearance was welcomed. They had resolved on putting

Jesus to death. But they wondered how they could succeed in getting hold of Him. They dare not attempt to seize Him openly in the midst of the Feast, for there were many there who loved the Saviour, and who would have tried to rescue Him from their cruel hands. They would thus have created "an uproar among the people." Besides, even had there been no such danger, it might be difficult for them to find Him out among the great Passover crowds without some one to help them.

Judas knew well the places where Jesus would most likely be discovered. He knew, above all, where He went to pray. He knew of one such favourite place near a garden on the Mount of Olives. In the stillness and darkness of night, and after the crowds of pilgrims had gone to rest in their tents and houses, he could easily contrive to have Him seized, and delivered into the hands of His foes.

The great Council had already, four days before, as we have previously noted, entered into a nefarious bargain with the traitor. Of his own accord he now appears a second time before them, and by the offer of his base services relieves their perplexities.

They agreed to pay him down the money whenever he surrendered the Saviour into their hands.

There was a piece of ground which this covetous man wished very much to have. It was situated above the valley of Hinnom. His eyes would often fall upon it as he crossed the Mount of Olives with his Master:—he could see it at present from the High Priest's palace:—he had, perhaps, so far bought it with the money he had already stolen out of the disciples' purse. But that purse was now empty; and he might fear that he would lose the field altogether. The shekels he received for betraying his Lord, and some more he would hope to obtain by-and-by from the same heads of the nation, would enable him to make sure of it. These, and other unlawful longings, lured him too sadly on to his soul's ruin!

I cannot tell you anything more about Judas that night— where he went, or where he slept.

Would he dare go back to Bethany with the horrible secret in his gloomy soul? He may have done so; for, as we shall soon see, he had the baseness next day to take his seat at the Paschal table, just as if nothing had happened. Perhaps, too, he might think that, by going to the house of Lazarus, he would find out with certainty where Jesus was to resort the following night. Jesus might speak about going, as the betrayer expected, to Gethsemane, and he would lay his plans to arrest Him there.

LVI.

He sends two of His Disciples to make ready the Passover.

It is now Thursday, probably the same day of the month on which the Hebrews killed their Passover lamb in Egypt, and sprinkled the lintels and door-posts of their houses with its blood.

The previous evening had been a busy one in Jerusalem. Every head of a family,—husband, wife, and children,—were employed in sweeping their dwellings, in order that no leaven might be found in any of them. They even lighted wax candles or torches, and searched every dark corner of their rooms (cupboards and presses), in case any particle might remain. The leaven was regarded as the type of sin, and the putting it away pointed to the necessity of purity of heart and life. The father of the household carried a vessel in his left hand and a brush in his right, to collect any stray portions of what was so strictly forbidden. After the search was over, the vessel was put under lock and key, and its contents, soon after, carefully destroyed by fire. Then they got ready the holiday clothes which were to be worn at the Paschal supper.

On the morning of Thursday the disciples had come to Jesus

and asked Him, "*Where wilt Thou that we prepare for Thee to eat the Passover?*"[1]

There were 'family gatherings' during the Passover week, and specially on the night of the Paschal supper. Parents and children, brothers and sisters, cousins and friends from a distance, all met under the same roof.

You will probably, therefore, expect to hear Jesus saying in reply, "I should wish our feast to take place where I am, in Bethany, among those I so dearly love." [Bethany was within the allowed distance from Jerusalem, for celebrating the Festival.]

He did not, however, say so. He evidently had a strong wish to eat that supper all alone with His own disciples. Not even was His mother to be there, or the brother and sisters of Bethany, or His cousins, or any of His most intimate friends from the Lake-side. His words are very decided—"*With desire, I have desired to eat this Passover* WITH MY DISCIPLES, *before I suffer.*"

Accordingly, He called two of them, and said, 'Go together into the city of Jerusalem, and you will be directed there to the house where we shall keep the feast.'

The two disciples thus sent were Peter and John.

When they entered the gate of Jerusalem, the city was all stir and bustle. Crowds were hurrying hither and thither. They met fathers with their boys, who had just been at the sheep-market, or at one of the folds on Mount Olivet, to purchase their Paschal lamb.

---

[1] I may mention in this note, that I have not thought it necessary or desirable to perplex the minds of my young readers with any reference to the much-debated question as to the time of this last supper of Christ with His disciples—though undoubtedly a Paschal supper, whether it were *the* great annual one, or whether, rather, it occurred in the evening preceding, and partook more of the nature of a private Passover-feast, celebrated twenty-four hours earlier than that of the nation. Though purposely abstaining from indicating any decided opinion, my leanings here, and as expressed elsewhere, are in favour of regarding the scene described as the ordinary Paschal supper. Any older readers who may feel interested, will find the question fully discussed by all the leading commentators.

You will not wonder at the turmoil, when I tell you that nearly a quarter of a million of lambs are supposed to have been killed at this one Passover. The lambs were taken up to the Temple, and sacrificed there. The priests stood in a row in the Court of Israel, holding gold and silver basins, into which the blood was poured after the animals were slain. What a strange mixture of sounds there must have been! The babble of the crowd, the bleating of the innocent lambs, the songs of the worshippers, the sacred music of the Levites, and the blast of the silver trumpets.

The two disciples have hardly entered the East Gate, when they meet a man bearing on his shoulder a vessel of water. The man was a servant. Perhaps he had just come with his pitcher from the pool of Siloam.

It is an earthenware jar he is carrying. Its contents may be intended partly for the purposes of the supper, and partly for filling the basin or laver in which the feet of the guests were washed.

The Saviour had told Peter and John that they would be sure to meet this person, and when they met him they were to follow him to his master's dwelling.

It is not likely that the master was a stranger; more probably a friend and disciple. Jesus calls him "the good man of the house." Some think that in that same abode Christ may have eaten many Paschal suppers in former years, when He came up from Nazareth with Mary, His mother. Also that it may have been the same room where we shall find Him appearing to the Apostles, when He rose from the dead three days after.

Peter and John followed the steps of this water-carrier as they had been directed, perhaps up one street and down another, till they saw him pausing before a door. They ask to see the owner of the dwelling; and when he comes, they say, "The Master (your Master and ours) has this message—'*My time is at hand; where is the guest-chamber where I shall eat the Passover with My disciples?*'"

Did the owner make any objection? No. He seems at once to bid them and their Lord a kind welcome.

The two disciples enter, and are led to a room by a flight of steps. There is a table in the apartment, and seats with cushions all round the table. The room seems quite prepared. The servant would likely put down his pitcher of water near the door, where there was the bath, and linen towels for drying the feet.

The two disciples hasten either to Bethany to tell the Master that the supper is ready; or possibly Jesus might be waiting with the others at some appointed meeting-place on the Mount of Olives, so as to save Peter and John going all that distance back.

The most of the pilgrims would be busy in their several dwellings preparing for their own Passover, so that Jesus would be able to enter the city, as He wished to do, quietly and without notice in the twilight.

Judas had, however, found out where the supper was to be held, and he came as one of the guests.

LVII.

He eats the Passover with His Disciples.

WHEN the shadows of night had fallen, and the stars were shining in the sky, we see Jesus at the table of the Jerusalem householder, with His twelve disciples. They are reclining on the couches placed around.

The supper is ready.[1] But why does the Saviour rise suddenly and go towards the door of the guest-chamber, at which they had left their sandals on entering?

---

[1] Not as in our English version, "Supper being ended," . . . but "Supper being prepared."—*Alford.*

The Apostles have omitted the usual Jewish custom after a journey, of having the feet washed before sitting down to meals. Alas! it is the same sad story again! They were jealous of one another; and disputed, like spoilt children, about the best places at the table! The man to whom the house belonged was probably engaged at a specially busy time:—he had left no servant to attend to this humble office for the refreshment of the guests; while none of the disciples seem willing to take the servant's place, and fetch the water and towels. How is the omission rectified?

Does Jesus simply rebuke them for their pride, telling them how foolish they are, and ordering them to perform the required office?

No. He gives them the severest, and yet the tenderest, rebuke He could. He felt the sadness of these envious quarrels at all times; but specially now in the prospect of His Sorrows. With His own hands he fetches that basin with the water. He takes off His loose festive garment, and ties the towel, lying beside the basin, round His waist.

The Apostles, doubtless, wonder very much what He intends to do.

He brings the brazen laver, and sets it down by the couch on which they were lying. He then Himself stoops to wash their feet, and wipes them dry with the girded towel, going round to one after the other. I believe, too, among the number, he included him who was in a few minutes to hurry away from that meeting to arrange final plans for his Master's death!

Oh, what a beautiful picture of humility! What a GLEAM of holy love and condescension immediately before the great *Sunset!* Immanuel—" God with us "—doing the meanest work of a slave, and teaching these foolish disciples the needed lesson of self-denial!

And now He has gone back to His place. He has untied the towel from His waist; and having put on His white garment again, the supper begins.

We only know the position of one of the disciples at the

sacred meal. It is that of the loving John. He was reclining at Jesus' right hand. His head was leaning on Jesus' bosom.

Never was there a holier yet sadder feast on earth than this. While they are eating it, as we shall immediately find, the Master speaks many tender, loving words. He who is "BRIGHTER THAN THE SUN" leaves behind Him never to be forgotten parting rays of blessing. They resemble the last streaks of vermilion and gold seen in the western sky—

> "Bright clouds are gathering one by one,
> And sweeping in pomp round the dying sun,
> With crimson banner, and golden pall,
> Like a host to their chieftain's funeral." [1]

The disciples could never have been fonder of their Lord than now.

Meanwhile, however, before we speak of this "golden vista," the clouds seem to gather: gradually a shade of sadness is seen creeping over the Heavenly face.

Jesus had wept recently over Jerusalem; but the present is a grief of a different kind. It seems as if it were too deep for tears. How could He bear the look of the false man who was reclining with Him at the same table? How harshly must the voice of the traitor have grated on the ear of Sinless Purity! The Divine Master of the feast knew that "the poison of asps was under his lips." He was "troubled in spirit," and with a heart full of anguish, He makes the announcement to the guests around Him—"*Verily, verily, I say unto you, that one of you shall betray Me.*"

The loving company are shocked and amazed. They are for a moment dumb. They are sure, however, that all they have heard must sooner or later take place, when their Lord has prefaced His words with "*Verily, verily.*"

---

[1] Sigourney.

At last, not suspecting each other, but each suspecting himself, they ask, "*Lord, is it I?*" They never seem to have thought of Judas being the guilty one. Like many wicked men, he was clever and cunning, and kept them from supposing him to be a cheat and a deceiver;—one who often took out of the joint-purse money that was not his own.

Jesus answers, that He will indicate who the unhappy man is, by a sign. He takes a piece of the cake of bread from the table, and dips it in the dish before Him; then He lifts the dripping morsel and gives it to Judas.

Judas stretches out his hand, and receives " the sop." Every eye of the company is now turned on him. The awful secret is out. It is he who is the Betrayer!

The wicked disciple can endure no longer the looks, and above all the ONE *look*, cast upon him ! He leaves the supper-table and the glare of the lighted room, and hurries out to the dark streets with a deeper darkness in his soul.

Terrible, truly, it is to think that this is a man who had received nothing but kindness from Jesus ; who had, during years of close intimacy, seen the holiness and tenderness of his Master's life; who had shared His daily meals, who had heard His daily prayers, who had listened to His daily teachings, who had been dealt with as a dear friend and brother. To him, Jesus had in vain spoken that parable, among others,—of " the Fool " who had sacrificed his never-dying soul for the sake of amassing some poor earthly riches !

He is on the way to earn his awful bribe—the bribe of innocent blood. The last words of Christ to him were—"*Do it quickly.*" He has made up his mind to act thus promptly. Oh, one might have hoped that the tender voice of his old Master might even yet have melted his hard heart;—that, bathed in tears, he would have rushed in agony to the feet of Jesus, confessed all, and begged to be forgiven. Alas! he has become the slave of sin ! He has "sold himself to work iniquity!"

We all know the discomfort and restraint that is felt, even

when we are among friends, if there is one false or unkind person present! Whenever the traitor Apostle had gone away from the upper room, there seemed a burden lifted off the spirit of Jesus. He even seems to contemplate with calmness and composure the thought of His own death being so near; that death which was to procure the life of the world. Indeed, His tones of sadness are changed into those of subdued joy. The first of those bright parting "gleams" of which I have just spoken breaks through the surrounding clouds, as He exclaims—" *Now is the Son of man glorified, and God is glorified in Him. If God be glorified in Him, God shall also glorify Him in Himself, and shall straightway glorify Him*" (John xiii. 31, 32).

Jesus now takes a portion of the bread on the table and some wine, and institutes the sacred rite called *the Lord's Supper.*

He said to His disciples that He wished them, and His people in all ages, to keep His dying love in remembrance. He asked them to meet often with one another in the same way as He had done that night, and to break the bread and drink the wine. The broken bread would remind them of His broken, crucified body; the wine would remind them of His poured out, precious blood. "*Do this,*" were His words, "*in remembrance of Me.*" He said over again, what He had done at the beginning of the supper, "*I shall drink no more of the fruit of the vine, until I drink it new with you in My Father's kingdom.*"

Then follow the many kind and gracious words of comfort.

The sayings of a fond father at the hour of his death are always specially remembered by his children. Jesus was about to die. These, therefore, were *His* dying words. Yes, it seems exactly as if He were gathering His dear ones around Him and giving them His last benediction!

How subdued and hushed that little company must have been, when the announcement was made, "*Hereafter I will not talk much with you!*" How doubly attentive would they be, lest any one farewell utterance or counsel should be lost!

He tells them not to allow their hearts to be troubled;—to think of the many bright mansions where they would all at last meet in the Great Father's House in heaven. How loving and tender are the very names He gives them! He calls them not 'servants,' nor 'Apostles;'—but "little children" and "friends." After commanding them over and over to "love one another," He speaks of a blessed Comforter who would come down and fill the blank in their hearts after He was taken away. Many earthly fathers when they die leave gifts to their children—money, or houses, or lands. Jesus leaves His disciples something far better than any of these. "PEACE *I leave with you*, MY PEACE *I give unto you!*"

The beautiful thing is, that though He has much greater cause for sadness, and much greater need of comfort, He thinks nothing about His own sorrows. All His thoughts are about consoling them.

But suddenly the Divine Speaker pauses, as if He had heard some warning bell.

The hour *has* come at last! He gets up from His couch. "*Arise,*" says He, "*let us go hence.*"

So, after singing a Paschal hymn, the Apostle-guests silently obey the Master's call. They descend the stair to the streets, which are still filled with busy hurrying crowds. Then, going out by the East Gate, they would take the path along the Temple-wall above the brook Kidron. In the bright moonlight the eye of Jesus may possibly have fallen on a vine, in one of the many vineyards close by, with its tender early leaves. This may have led Him to speak of Himself as "the true Vine," and His people as "the branches."

He reminds His disciples that He will soon be taken from them: but adds, that though for "a little while" they would not see Him, yet they would meet in "a little while" again. He seems to carry His thoughts forward to a happier meeting still, not on earth but in Heaven, when their joy no one would take from them.

With these and many other precious words, He sustains and comforts their distressed hearts and His own, till they have crossed the brook, and reached the entrance to a garden.

The moon is now fully up, and shining beautifully on the olive-trees and on the great Temple rock.

NIGHT WATCHES.

"THE DAY OF THE LORD COMETH, FOR IT IS NIGH AT HAND; A DAY OF DARKNESS AND OF GLOOMINESS, A DAY OF CLOUDS AND OF THICK DARKNESS."—JOEL II. 1, 2.

"I WILL COVER THE HEAVEN, AND MAKE THE STARS THEREOF DARK; I WILL COVER THE SUN WITH A CLOUD."—EZEK. XXXII. 7.

"O MY GOD, I CRY IN THE DAY-TIME, BUT THOU HEAREST NOT; AND IN THE NIGHT-SEASON, AND AM NOT SILENT."—PS. XXII. 2.

"YOUR LAMB SHALL BE WITHOUT BLEMISH . . . AND THE WHOLE ASSEMBLY OF THE CONGREGATION OF ISRAEL SHALL KILL IT IN THE EVENING" (AS THE SUN GOES DOWN).—EXOD. XII. 5, 6

"AND IT WAS ABOUT THE SIXTH HOUR, AND THERE WAS DARKNESS OVER ALL THE LAND UNTIL THE NINTH HOUR. AND THE SUN WAS DARKENED."—LUKE XXIII. 44, 45.

LVIII.

He suffers in the Garden of Gethsemane.

IN our last, we pictured the moon shining brightly on the Master's path as He passed along the Kidron valley.

In the figurative sense of the words, however, it was the Valley of the Shadow of Death through which He was now walking ;—" *This is the hour and power of darkness.*" The clouds have finally closed in. The NIGHT-WATCH of the Divine Sufferer has begun!

If you were to ask me what is the most sacred ground in all the world, I would answer, THE GARDEN OF GETHSEMANE.

It may be the longing of many of my young readers—(I know it was mine)—to see this hallowed place with their own eyes, —to look upon the very spot where the Blessed Jesus had to endure so much for our sakes.

You may, perhaps, have pictured to yourselves in thinking about it, a quiet, retired hollow, close to the brook Kidron, filled with rugged old olives; sitting under the solemn shade of which, you would be able to read the touching story of the Agony.

In this you would be disappointed. The traditional Gethsemane is not in itself interesting. It has been made very much into a modern garden, with a white-washed wall around it. Eight aged trees are the only things about the place which recall the past. Though they cannot date to the time of Christ, yet they serve to bring that night of all nights vividly before the thoughts of all who have seen them. I gazed on them from the opposite side of the valley, silvered with the light of the moon. This latter feature is at all events unchanged. These calm Eastern moonlit heavens, so truthfully described by the poet, are the very

same as, eighteen and a half centuries ago, looked down on the
Suffering Redeemer—

> " How beautiful is night
> A dewy freshness fills the silent air :
> No mist obscures, no cloud, nor spec, nor stain,
> Breaks the serene of heaven.
> In full-orbed glory yonder moon divine
> Rolls through the dark blue depths ;
> . . . .
> How beautiful is night ! "[1]

Though, therefore, no one can make quite sure that what is now pointed out *was* really the Garden of Gethsemane, we know at all events that somewhere near that very place, olive-trees hanging thick with dew silently beheld the mysterious anguish of Jesus !

The disciples, as I have already told you, have reached the entrance to the Garden along with their Master.

It was now far on in the night, probably between eleven and twelve o'clock. All was quiet and still after the stir of that busy evening. Most of the lights in the houses and tents had been put out. The one great lamp of nature, of which I have just spoken, alone illumined the valley, with its rocks and trees and the white sepulchres crowning its cliffs—almost turning night into day.

Jesus seems to have known the place well. Some think that it was an orchard or plantation belonging to one of His friends and followers ; and that this friend joyfully gave the use of it to the Saviour whenever He chose, for rest and prayer. He must have much missed, in Jerusalem, the silent hills around Bethsaida and Capernaum, where He so often bent His knees in devotion.

There may have even been some house within the Garden, in which He sometimes lodged :—or, perhaps, the Homeless One, who once slept on the plank of a fishing-boat on the Lake,

---

[1] Southey.

may have more frequently made the sod His pillow, under the shade of the olives—the great stars gleaming through their branches.

Jesus had His eleven disciples with Him. He told eight of them to tarry outside the gate, where it was more open.
See how kindly He breaks what could not fail to make them sad. He does not wish to distress them by disclosing plainly all about the scene before Him. He speaks as gently as He could. He tells them only of His prayers, not of His sore anguish. "*Wait here*," He said, "*till I go and pray yonder.*"
The other three disciples He took farther into the olive-garden along with Himself, and instructs them also to remain where He has placed them. They are to sit on the grass and keep watch there.
You doubtless know who these three were. They are Peter, James, and John. The same who were so lately with Him on the Mount, and who saw the Transfiguration.
They would wonder much what was about to happen. Was their Master once more to be glorified on Mount Olivet, as He had been on Mount Hermon? Had they not heard Him, only a few moments before, praying, "*Father*, GLORIFY *Thy Son*"? Yet they had listened to other very different words also. "*All ye shall be offended because of Me this night, for it is written, 'I will smite the Shepherd, and the sheep of the flock shall be scattered abroad!'*"
They ask Him no questions, but wait on in silence. He Himself goes further into the dense shade. The distance He withdrew from them was about as far as one could cast a stone. He seems comforted with thinking that He has His three chief and most devoted friends so near.
We surely see, my young readers, in this, the human heart of Jesus. A child when ill, and lying in the dark unable to sleep, likes to feel that its father or mother are by its bedside. Or the same child feels comforted during a storm of thunder when it buries its face in its mother's lap, or clasps its father's hands. So

it was with Jesus now. As a Brother in our nature, it helped to lift the heavy burden off His spirit, the thought of having loved ones so close at hand, who would think of Him and feel for Him in His sore struggle.

The Three seat themselves as He has told them. However brightly the moon may have been shining, the thick branches and foliage would screen the Divine Sufferer from view. He is all alone. No radiant cloud is around Him, as on Mount Hermon; no "raiment white and glistering." As He kneels on the grass, He becomes very sad and sorrowful—"*Sorrowful even unto death;*" as if this sorrow were so great, that if it had gone much further it must have ended in death. It was "a horror of great darkness:" He cannot even keep in a kneeling posture, He falls on His face—His forehead touches the bare ground. A great load seems to press upon Him. It was evidently anguish unlike any the world had ever seen.

How very strange! He who had hushed the winds and waves, cast out devils, and brought the dead to life, was now stretched helpless on the earth with "strong crying and tears!"

He entreats, in tones of earnest prayer, that God, His Father, would take that fearful load off Him.

He speaks as if a cup of awful woe had been put into His hands to drink; and His prayer is, "O My Father, if it be possible, take this cup away!" Though the night was chill and frosty, drops of perspiration, like blood, stood on His forehead, and fell on the sod at His feet!

Strange, mysterious spectacle! He who was "BRIGHTER THAN THE SUN," crying out in a midnight of gloom—

> "The way is dark, My Father! cloud on cloud
> Is gathering thickly o'er My head, and loud
> The thunders roar above Me. See, I stand
> Like one bewildered! FATHER! take My hand!"

What do you think was that load and that cup?

There was no visible threat or violence:—there was no hand of man upon Him now, as afterwards on the cross of Calvary.

No cruel spear, or iron nail, or thorny crown pierced Him. We can discern nothing around, but the silvery olive-trees rustling in the nightly breeze. The bright starry heavens were above; and His own disciples quite near.

What pain, then, is this, from which He so shrinks as to wring anguish from His whole frame?

It was the sins of all His people that were then weighing Him down: "*He was wounded for our transgressions, He was bruised for our iniquities.*" "*The Lord hath laid on Him the iniquities of us all.*"

The Ancients had a fabled Atlas, who was said to bear the world on his shoulders. Jesus was the true Atlas. He was in an awful sense bearing on His soul the burden of the world's guilt!

After some time of sore agony He rises from the ground, and goes to where His disciples are, under the trees. Perhaps, when He reaches the spot, He expects to hear them talking about Him with pity and tenderness; saying to one another, 'How can we best, in this hour of darkness, comfort Him who so lately spake such kind words of consolation to us?'

Alas! He finds them "*sleeping!*" Even Peter, who had declared brave resolves about "*never* forsaking," had his eyes closed too. The sword he had taken with him to the garden to defend his Master is lying carelessly at his side.

Jesus rose from His knees, and went, in the same manner, no less than three times to these faithless watchers. But on each occasion He finds them thus asleep. "*What!*" He says, with a trembling voice, "*could ye not watch with* ME?" 'You promised to *die* for me, can you not *watch* with Me, your Master; and that, too, even "*one hour?*"'

"*Simon*," He said, "*sleepest* THOU? *John*, who, two hours ago, leant thy head on My breast, *sleepest thou? James*, who saidst thou wast able to drink of My cup of woe, *sleepest thou?*"

He might well say, "I looked for pity, and found none, and for comforters, and I found none!"

Y

How strange they should have been so careless and cold-hearted! They had often seen their Master sorrowful, but never in such profound sorrow as now. And yet, too, how kindly He pities His poor tired followers, and makes allowance for their frailties! Hear the merciful excuse He offers for them:—"They have the heart and the wish," He said, "to be kind to Me, and to watch with Me. But they are weary." "*The spirit, indeed, is willing, but the flesh is weak.*" Most would have called it thoughtless and ungrateful slumber, He calls it "*sleeping for sorrow!*"

But if the best of *earthly* friends have failed Him, not so is it with *heavenly* Friends.

All at once there is a sudden gleam among the olive-trees. What is this? Is it only a brighter ray of moonshine that has struggled through the branches, and is lighting up the worn face of the Man of Sorrows?

No. It is a glorious Angel sent from above to strengthen Him. One of that bright band who sang His cradle-song over the plains of Bethlehem has come to support Him in His agony.

What the Angel said to Jesus we are not told. He would, doubtless, tell Him that all Heaven was watching His hour of conflict. He might, perhaps, bring some special message of love from His Father, and encourage Him to do His Father's will. He would, perhaps, remind Him of the need there was of these sufferings "to bring many sons unto glory." He would speak to Him of the millions on millions who, by the drinking of that cup of anguish, would be saved for ever and ever.

Mightier than any angel in this hour of lonely sorrow, was the support He obtained from His God and Father. He could say, in a truer sense than the afflicted Psalmist:—"*I meditate on* THEE *in the* NIGHT WATCHES. *Because Thou hast been my help, therefore in the shadow of Thy wings will I rejoice*" (Ps. lxiii. 6, 7).

The greater His agony was, He only prayed the more earnestly for strength from *Him*. An Apostle tells us He prayed "*unto Him that was able to save Him from death, and was heard in that He feared.*"

Light breaks amid the thick darkness. That hour of prayer

has so soothed the spirit of Jesus, that, on going the third time to His disciples, with a calm, brave voice He says—"*The hour is come, Rise, let us be going.*"

He had yet fifteen hours of suffering before Him ere He cried, "*It is finished!*" but in some respects the worst suffering of all was in that garden, and it was now over.

When its gloomy hours were past, the Good Shepherd goes submissively forth to lay down His life for the sheep!

LIX.

He is seized by a troop of Soldiers.

VOICES, and the tramp of hurrying feet, are heard in the distance.

Not only so, but flashing lights, too, are seen coming down the same steep path Jesus and His disciples had themselves taken a little while before.

It looks as if a band of men were approaching, holding torches and lanterns in their hands. Some seem to be soldiers, some priests, some the common rabble of the city.

The red glare reveals a figure in front, leading them on and telling them where to go.

It seems strange to see lanterns and torches in the bright moonlight. It is evident they have taken these, in order that they may make all the surer that the person or persons, of whom they are in search, may not escape among the darker corners of the garden, or into the caves of the mountain.

The band of captors have crossed the Kidron. They approach nearer and nearer till their faces are visible. There is new proof that they are not come on a peaceable errand, for some have swords, and some have clubs or sticks in their hands.

There is one there we all know too well—the dark figure in

front. It is Judas. He leaves the others, and hurries up to Jesus. He kisses the cheek that is still stained with the red drops of the agony, and says in doing so, "*Hail, Master!*"

Does he use this expression, think you, because he has repented of his crime—wishing his injured Lord to forgive him, and take him back again among the disciples?

Oh no! It is only the sign that had been agreed upon, to let the troop know which among the little company was the doomed innocent Victim. It was the basest thing the heartless traitor had yet done.

Do you remember what Jesus said to Judas?

"*Judas, betrayest thou the Son of Man with a kiss?*"

You may believe that when, in a few hours after, the meek face of the Sufferer was struck with the hands of the ruffian soldiers, He did not feel these blows half so much as the mocking kiss of His old disciple. The pain of an enemy He could bear; but "*it was not an enemy that did this!*"

The rest of the band are about to seize hold of Christ, and bind Him. The Divine Saviour comes out in the moonlight, and says, "*Whom seek ye?*"

They replied, "*Jesus of Nazareth.*"

"I am He."

There must have been tones of heavenly majesty in His voice; for these men, at the sound of it (and Judas among them), reel back with fright and fall to the ground, as if smitten down with a flash of lightning.

What an opportunity for Jesus now to escape if He had willed so to do, when the band of assassins are lying helpless on the earth! How easily He might have withdrawn Himself to a distance, as He had done more than once before; and taken refuge, either in one of the quiet valleys where He had lately been, near Bethel, or further off in the glens of Perea!

But instead of doing so, He at once surrenders Himself. He has His hands tied together with ropes, and is made a prisoner. They show Him no more mercy than if He had been a common thief.

"They went backward and fell to the ground" (John xviii. 6)   page 340

Peter is no longer asleep now. He has His sword firmly grasped in his hand, and seems resolved to sell his life dearly for his Master's sake.

He attacks one of the band. He aims a blow at the man's head, and in doing so cuts off his right ear. Jesus heals it in a moment. He would show how kind He is in the hour of greatest unkindness—kind, not to a friend, but to an enemy. He then says to the too ardent Apostle, "*Put up thy sword into its sheath;*" 'I could get myriads of angels to rescue me, if I chose now to ask My Father to send them. But I do not wish to escape. It is My Father who has mixed for me this cup of woe, and I am resolved to drink it to the dregs.'

Again we are reminded how the loving, kind heart of the Saviour never fails Him. He seeks no boon for Himself. He does not ask His murderers to untie His hands, spare His life, and let Him free. No; but He has one request to make for His disciples. "*Let these go away!*"

You will be ready to remark, 'Oh, surely, even though He wished them to escape and ensure their own safety, the disciples would never do so: they will never leave their Master thus in the hands of cruel men!' You expect, rather, to see them faithfully keeping by His side, and trying to whisper words of comfort in His ear.

Alas! *all of them have forsaken Him and fled!* Some, perhaps, have hidden among the thickets and olive-groves of the Mount; some may have hastened across to Bethany to tell the anxious inmates there of what had taken place; but not one of them remains at his post of honour and duty. No Apostle has the Lord near Him, but the false, hollow-hearted Judas!

It was just as He had foretold, a few hours before, on the way from the Paschal table—the Shepherd was smitten, and the sheep were scattered. "*Behold, the hour cometh, yea, is now come, that ye shall be scattered every man to his own, and shall leave Me alone, and yet I am not alone, because the Father is with Me!*"

Behold, then, the meek, patient, suffering, forsaken Lamb of God, without a friend on earth to cheer Him, led on to the slaughter: His hands bound behind His back;—perhaps the crimson drops of the Garden still on His dress. He could not be murdered on the spot. There were some there who were ready to stone Him to death, as they did in the case of Stephen afterwards, nigh the same place. But the Roman soldiers will see that He is first taken to be tried at a Court of Justice (or what was *called* a Court of Justice), and prevent this summary vengeance.

Their torches and lanterns would now be put out; so as not to attract attention as they convey their Victim to the palace of the High Priest.

It is now late at night.

LX.

He is brought before Annas and Caiaphas.

THE meek and lowly Jesus, wearied and exhausted with the awful conflict in Gethsemane, is hurried along by the troop of soldiers. The streets of the city would now be silent.

Any stray people they met, would wonder what so large a band of armed men were doing at that hour.

They take their bound prisoner to the house of Annas; which seems to be open, and lighted in readiness for their coming.

Annas was the father-in-law of Caiaphas the High Priest. He was seventy years of age, and venerable in appearance. But he was neither a good nor a happy man. He was a cunning covetous Sadducee; and had more power than any other Jew in Jerusalem at that time. It does not appear why they took Jesus to his dwelling, unless it was that they were anxious to get his name and support in commencing their cruel purpose,—perhaps too, they may have required his authority to hold the Council of the Sanhedrim.

The meeting was called, though it was still the dead of night. It could not, however, lawfully assemble before the morning.

The band of men who had seized Jesus do not seem to have been long at the house of Annas. Annas sent them on to the residence or palace of Caiaphas.

This latter was a large building with a wall round it, and gates in front. A portress had charge of the gates. She opened them whenever the troop of soldiers appeared.

Inside was a square court. The Divine Saviour was first brought into this open space, and then He was taken into a side room or hall. Most of those who had arrested Him waited in the court; and as the night was cold, coming as they had done from the sharp air and drenching dews of the Kidron Valley, they gathered round a charcoal fire to warm themselves.

A number of Jewish priests and rulers had hastily met together in Caiaphas' house to examine the guiltless prisoner before the Great Council met. They tried to get some admissions from His own lips, so as to make sure of a sentence of death against Him.

Jesus, I need not say, is now quite separated from His friends and followers. The sheep are scattered. And the Good Shepherd is standing all alone in the midst of fierce wolves, ready to tear Him to pieces if they can. Caiaphas, early morning though it still was, is present. He questions Him about His disciples and His doctrine.

The Blessed Redeemer answers, that He had never concealed anything; that He had always spoken openly before the world, and kept His teaching no secret. "*Why askest thou Me?*" He said to Caiaphas, "*ask them which heard Me.*"

One of the servants got very angry at this reply, and said, "Dare you speak thus to the High Priest?" and then struck Jesus a cruel blow on the cheek.

It was a cowardly act, for the hands of the Divine Prisoner were tied with cords; but even had they been free, He would not have struck the man back again. He remains calm and placid. There is no trace of "the strong crying and tears" to which He gave vent a few hours ago in the Garden. "*He was oppressed and He was afflicted, yet He opened not His mouth.*" All He says is, *If I have spoken evil, bear witness of the evil; but if well, why smitest thou Me?* (John xviii. 23).

There were false witnesses brought in to testify against Him;—shameless men who put no value on speaking the truth, and who could easily be bribed to tell lies and swear falsely. The accusers got them to say things about Jesus which were not true. Oh if Caiaphas had asked not for *false*, but for *true* witnesses, how different would have been their testimony!

Who, let me ask, would many of these true witnesses have been?

There would be the blind who had been made to see—the lepers that were cleansed—the wretched beings who had devils cast out from their bodies—the sorrowful who had been comforted—the dead who had been brought to life.

He who had done all these kind things, and who never did or said an *unkind* thing, does not attempt to answer the wicked falsehoods now spoken against Him. In accordance with the words of ancient prophecy, "He was as a lamb dumb before his shearers!"

Caiaphas was much displeased because Jesus was thus silent. Leaving his seat in a passion, and looking on the meek Prisoner, he says with a loud voice,—"Dost thou make no answer to these witnesses?"

Still Jesus holds His peace. Then in a voice of smothered rage, the High Priest says, "*I adjure thee by the living God, that Thou tell me whether Thou be the Christ, the Son of God?*"

The Accused can be silent no longer. At last He speaks, and with calm dignity says, "*I AM the Son of God.*" And He added, "*Hereafter shall ye see the Son of Man sitting on the right hand of power, and coming in the clouds of heaven*" (Matt. xxvi. 64).

Yes, He tells them plainly that He who is now standing with His hands bound behind His back, as if He were a base criminal, will then be seated on His great white throne. His accusers will then change places with Him, and be prisoners at His bar!

The whole assembly is in an uproar. Caiaphas pretends to be horrified at the blasphemy Jesus has just spoken. He takes hold of his white priestly garment, and tears it from the neck downwards. It is the sign of grief and anger. " *Ye have heard,*" he exclaims aloud, " *Ye have heard what He says, what do you resolve upon ?* "

All the judges reply, " He is guilty of death "—' Worthy of death ! Worthy of death !'

It was the first wild shout that told the nearness of the dreadful end.

Little did Caiaphas think that, forty years after this, his own children and grandchildren would miserably perish in the siege of Jerusalem. And that God in his case, as in the case of all wicked men, would make true His own solemn word—" *Be sure your sin will find you out.*"

LXI.

He is cruelly treated in the house of Caiaphas, and denied by Peter.

I HAVE told you it was still early morning, and that some hours must pass before the Sanhedrim can meet. What does the heartless Caiaphas meanwhile do ?

He himself goes away from the assemblage, and leaves the meek and gentle Jesus in the hands of these rude, unfeeling soldiers and servants, to be tormented as they please.

We have known, in the recent history of the world, what dreadful cruelties base and barbarous men delight to inflict on their fellow-creatures. It is bad enough to be cruel to the cruel ; but it is worse by far to be cruel to the good, the helpless, and the innocent.

I am reluctant to describe all that was now inflicted on the sinless Redeemer. They led Him either into the open court, or into the guard-room. There they strike Him on the face, they jostle against Him; they pull out the hairs of His beard;—they put a bandage round His eyes; and when thus blind-folded they asked in mockery, "*Who smote thee?*" They load Him with savage scoffs and jeers—they *spit* upon Him—the greatest of insults among Eastern people. To every indignity their base minds and wicked thoughts can suggest He is subjected!

Little did they think in all this, they were fulfilling the words of prophecy: "*I gave my back to the smiters, and my cheeks to them that plucked off the hair: I hid not my face from shame and spitting*" (Isa. 1. 6).

Do you wonder where some of the disciples of the Blessed Sufferer are now?

I can only tell you about two of them. John seemed to follow close in his Master's steps. For immediately after the soldiers and their prisoner entered the gate of Caiaphas' palace, the portress allowed him to pass in along with them. He must have been a spectator of the foul and cruel affront when one of the officers of Caiaphas smote Jesus on the cheek with the palm of his hand. He had wished, not long before, for a much smaller offence to bring down lightning from heaven and consume a Samaritan village. It must surely, in the case of one whose soul was all fire, have been no small effort to remain silent under so base an outrage on the Being he regarded with an adoring love!

There was another who timidly hovered on the outskirts of the crowd a far way off, and who at last, through the influence of his brother Apostle, also got inside the gate. This was Peter. He is trembling with fear at what is taking place. His conduct reminds us of the old scene on the Lake of Gennesaret, when, frightened at the stormy waves, he began to sink.

We see him seated by that same brazier I have mentioned in the middle of the court. He looks pale and agitated, and seems listening to every sound that comes from the inner room, where his Lord is. The soldiers and servants, who are gathered round this open fire, suspect, from his way of speaking, that he is one of Jesus' disciples. Specially the young woman who kept the gate—holding up her lighted lamp to Peter's face, makes quite sure that he was one of Christ's friends from Galilee: "*Thou also wast with Jesus of Nazareth.*"

Then began Peter's sad fall. I shall leave you to read the mournful story for yourselves. He denied his beloved Master three times, and the last of the three times with oaths and curses. Yes! *swearing;* uttering language we should expect to hear only on the lips of the roughest of the Roman soldiers among whom He is seated.

A cock crowing outside in the early morning, recalled to his mind the words of his Lord—"*The cock shall not crow twice, before thou hast denied Me thrice.*"

But there was something that spoke far more loudly to Peter than the crowing of that bird. As Jesus Himself, with His hands bound, was crossing over the open court, His ear heard these awful oaths, His eye fell on the poor erring Apostle.

"*The Lord turned and looked upon Peter.*"

What a look was that! A look of righteous anger; but far more a look of sorrow and pity and love. It went like an arrow to the guilty man's heart. In a moment he was stricken down, humbled and saddened. He rushed away outside the porch, in the chill early dawn, weeping very bitterly.

He never forgot those tears to his dying day. Better still, we know that he never forgot that look of pitying love. One of the old Fathers tells of him, that every time afterwards he listened to the crowing of a cock, he fell on his knees and wept.

But six o'clock in the morning has now come; so the cruel tormentors desist, for a while, at least, from their savage sport, and lead the Blessed Jesus, faint and bleeding, along the streets to the "Paved Hall" in the Temple, where the Sanhedrim has now fully met. It was called 'the Paved Hall' (*Gazith*) from being paved with square blocks of hewn stone.

The judges, chief priests, and elders are seated on high benches around a circular chamber. Caiaphas, the spiritual head of the nation and the president of the Council, is seated in the central place. The Prisoner is brought to stand immediately opposite him.

I need not describe what takes place. Very much the same questions are put, and the same answers given, as in the palace of the High Priest. Again, in meek majesty, Jesus declares Himself to be *the Son of God.*

A shout goes up, "*What need to ask farther, or to seek additional witnesses? we have heard from His own mouth.*"

So, delivering Him once more up to the guard, He is conducted across the Temple Court to another judgment seat.

LXII.

He is taken to the palace of Pilate.

WHO is this we see rushing up the Temple stairs? His face is pale; his eyes are flashing wildly, as if he had committed some fearful deed, and knew not what to do.

He goes to where a number of the chief priests are assembled, who have just been at the Council, and are now come to attend the morning sacrifice. The man shrieks out in great terror— "Oh I have sinned dreadfully! I have betrayed the Innocent; and shed innocent blood!"

I do not require to tell you who this was. Satan had till now blinded the heart of Judas. But when the unhappy traitor saw the grievous tortures to which his kind and holy Master had been subjected, conscience smote him;—his eyes were opened. He felt, when it was too late, how terrible was his ingratitude and guilt. The thirty pieces of silver—the price of his baseness—had been paid down to him. But now he could not endure the sight of these coins. So he hastens to those who had bribed him to commit the crime, and wishes them to take the money back.

He receives poor comfort from these heartless priests and elders. They were annoyed at his intruding upon them at present. They were tired after a sleepless night : besides doubtless being ill at ease about the iniquity they were in the act of committing.

"*What have we to do with that ?*" was the only answer the wretched man received.

When he sees they only mock and sneer, after all he had done to help them in their dark deed, he opens a leathern bag at his side, and taking out the money, dashes it down at their feet on the pavement floor.

His anguish of mind seems only to become worse. Descending quickly by the Temple gate, he goes to the brink of the hill above the Valley of Hinnom. There fastening a rope round the branch of a tree, in his utter despair he hanged himself. The halter broke; his body fell over the rocks into the valley beneath: there was a pool of blood where the mangled remains lay. I do not think it likely that any one buried him. Like wicked Jezebel of old, his corpse would be left to the dogs of the city to devour!

Do you ask what became of the thirty silver shekels he flung from him ?

The priests would not allow them to lie on the pavement; neither would they allow them to be put in the Treasury-chest, because they were "the price of blood." So they completed the purchase of the field which Judas had coveted. They made it into a burial-place: and ever after, it bore the terrible name of ACELDAMA, "*the Field of blood.*"

This is truly one of the saddest stories in the Bible, perhaps I should say it is the very saddest story of all.

Pontius Pilate was at this time Roman Governor of Judea.

He generally lived at Cesarea, a city built on the sea shore in the plain of Sharon. But he always came up, during the Passover, to Jerusalem with a troop of soldiers, in case of any disturbance when so many people were gathered together. On these occasions he lived in a splendid palace erected by Herod the Great. From the description given by Josephus this must have been one of the most beautiful buildings in the world; with vast walls and towers, porticoes of white marble, lovely gardens with shady alcoves, fountains, and fish-ponds; its windows looking across to the Mount of Olives, whose slopes were not, as now, bare and treeless, but rich with varied foliage as any English park. The inside was as grand as the out. It had cedar roofs like the Palace of Solomon; the floors and pavements were inlaid with precious stones. There were many vases of gold and silver seen all about the rooms and galleries.

I do not think Pilate was a cruel man naturally; but he was weak and selfish, and never scrupled about doing a bad action if he believed it would better himself or add to his power. Though he lived, as I have just said, chiefly at Cesarea (a place to which Jesus never went), I cannot think he could be ignorant about One whose fame had spread through all the land. He must have heard of Christ's miracles: His deeds of power and love and mercy. Though he would not trouble his mind on the matter, he could scarcely help knowing about the recent triumphal entry across the Mount of Olives; for it had taken place since he came on his yearly visit.

To this palace the meek and lowly Saviour is led through the streets of Jerusalem. The Jewish Council had no power of itself to kill Him. He must be tried by a Roman court, and they must get His death-warrant signed by the Roman Governor.

On leaving the Sanhedrim, His accusers would conduct Him by the short way to Mount Zion, or "the Upper City," where this magnificent residence was. They would cross over the Valley of the Tyropean by the famous bridge, which ever since the reign of

Solomon had connected Mount Moriah and the Temple with the adjoining hill of Zion.

Though now full daylight, it was still, in the truest sense, a dark 'Night Watch' in the soul of the worn, faint, yet divine Sufferer. Many people are already gathered in the streets at that hour of the morning, and when it became known who the Prisoner was, the crowd quickly increased.

We have reason to suppose that all the leaders of the Council were there, Caiaphas at their head. They would encourage the mob to follow. They knew well how easily they could manage to rouse the fierce passions of the multitude, against the Man who had dared to say that He would destroy their beautiful Temple in three days.

Indeed the crowd are even now ready to vent their wild rage against the Blessed Jesus. They would, I believe, have torn Him to pieces, had he not been guarded by the Roman soldiers: or rather, as we formerly found, protected and shielded by ONE mightier than all the legions and cohorts of the Roman Cæsar.

LXIII.

He appears before Pilate and Herod.

THEY have reached the palace gates.

Pilate would likely be asleep when they arrived. On being roused, he went at once to a balcony in front of his splendid mansion. This balcony we shall hear about more than once. It was called in Hebrew *Gabbatha*: a raised pavement composed of coloured stones and marbles. In the centre was the *bema* or Seat of Justice, from which the Roman Judge delivered his sentence.

Seeing so large a crowd on one of the days of the sacred feast, with the head men of the city, too, surrounding a Prisoner, Pilate at once knew it must be something very serious. He was aware how easily riots were created, and how difficult it was to put them down. He had done so more than once before; but only after shedding the blood of the rioters and that of his own soldiers.

He is told who the Prisoner was.

Although he well knew how fickle the Jewish people were, I think surely his first thought must have been, how singular this sudden change in their feelings towards Jesus;—the very person they had so lately welcomed and worshipped with royal honours! Perhaps he had himself seen the carpet of palm-leaves over which the Saviour rode in triumph, still lying green on the highway across the Mount of Olives.

The divine Son of God—the Lord of Glory—who had thus "made Himself of no reputation"—who had become for our sakes "a worm and no man, a reproach of men and despised of the people"—is now inside the Governor's palace.

A few of His accusers likely go in with Him; but the bulk of them remain outside the gate. Why is this? You would think they would be desirous not to lose sight of their Victim, but would wish rather to hear all that took place at His trial.

The reason is told us. It is because Pilate is a Gentile. If these Jews entered the house of a Gentile during the Passover they would be regarded as defiled, and would in this way be prevented taking further part in the Paschal Feast, which lasted seven days.

The Governor, therefore, to save their scruples, goes out to the balcony I have spoken of, and speaks to the priests, rulers, and crowd, gathered in the street below.

Till now they had been noisy, as all crowds are; but when he appears in his toga (the Governor's robe of office), there is a hush to hear what he has to say.

He asks them what they want, and what are the charges they have to prefer against Jesus.

Their answer does not satisfy him. They do not bring against the Prisoner any particular accusation. Pilate haughtily answers—

"Be it so. If you do not choose to tell me His crime, then, as a Roman judge, I shall not consider the case. You had better take Him, and judge Him according to your own laws."

Their passion is roused at his reply, and they proceed to accuse the Blessed Redeemer of being "an evil-doer," of "calling Himself a King," of "perverting the nation" (that is, of trying to break loose from the power and authority of Rome), and forbidding others to pay tribute-money to Cæsar.

Pilate returns, meanwhile, from the balcony, and goes to the Judgment Hall, into which Christ had been led. This hall would, doubtless, be one of the great public chambers of the palace. Its cedar walls would be covered with the emblems of Roman power and Roman justice. There would be, as on the raised pavement, a chair or seat for the presiding magistrate, and a guard of soldiers at the entrance.

The Roman Governor and the holy Jesus stand here face to face, and, probably, are well-nigh alone.

The only charge brought by the accusers which Pilate cares to sift is the last one. Accordingly he asks the meek Prisoner, in a half-compassionate, half-scornful tone, "*Art* THOU *the King of the Jews?*"—" THOU, with Thy mangled face and bleeding brows and tattered raiment; art THOU foolish enough to call thyself a Jewish *King*, and to claim a right to this splendid palace where now Thou standest so helpless?"

The suffering Son of Man answered him, that He *was* a king, and that He *had* a kingdom; but it was "*not of this world.*" It did not consist in crowns and jewels, in sceptres and palaces, in armies and chariots. It was a kingdom over the hearts of men.

The Roman knew nothing about such a kingdom as that—a kingdom which had no sword to protect it. He would, doubtless, say to himself, "There can, at all events, be no possible danger to my rule in the harmless dream of this mild, simple peasant-Prophet."

Although, however, he did not own it, Pilate must have been impressed (how could it be otherwise?) with the strange words and the noble bearing of this mysterious Person before him. How superior in loftiness of soul to the very best among those who were clamouring for His life!

You can imagine to yourselves the dense mob still surging round the palace gate. In that multitude, doubtless, there must have been not a few friends and loving followers of Jesus. John may have been there. Perhaps even Peter may have been hovering nigh, with his miserable broken heart; yet yearning with love, too, towards the kind Master he had denied. A gleam of hope may have shot through their breasts when they heard Pilate say, " I FIND IN HIM NO FAULT AT ALL."

But it was a gleam: no more.

The chief accusers were more fierce than ever. They answered Pilate that this Man was a leader of sedition. He had stirred up strife and tumult all the way from Galilee to Jerusalem.

GALILEE!

That word was at once seized by the Governor. *Galilee!* " Is He a Galilean?" he asks.

They reply that He is so—Jesus from Nazareth.

This at once leads to a new turn in the trial. Pilate has nothing to do with Galilee, and the ruler or tetrarch of that northern division of the land happened to be now himself in Jerusalem. He had come upon the pretence of keeping the Passover; more likely, however, only to enjoy the festive season, —not in the sacred sense of the word, but as a change from the gay and wicked life he led at the Golden House at Tiberias.

Pilate is very glad of any excuse to get rid of so puzzling a case, which aimed at the death of an innocent individual. So he resolves to send Jesus, *as a Galilean,* to be tried by Herod.

Both priests and crowd would be vexed at this delay. They had thought that the Governor of Judea would make short work of the matter; and by at once issuing an order have gratified their vengeance. Sadder still must have been the thought of this new scene of suffering to Christ Himself. Picture Him again led along the public streets amid the taunts of the unfeeling crowd!

He is taken to Herod's mansion, in a part of the city called *Bezetha*, and He there stands in Herod's presence.
You will remember having already heard of Herod in the previous story of Jesus' life. He was the same base man (Herod Antipas) who had beheaded John the Baptist. It was the first time the Holy and the Just One had ever seen the murderer of His beloved friend. It must have been a trial, indeed, to Jesus even to look on this wicked prince. Perhaps He refused to cast His eyes upon him. At all events, we know He declined to answer any of the questions which Herod put from idle curiosity. He had answered Pilate's questions; but now He remained speechless and silent. The music of that voice which had stilled wind and waves—which had spoken healing and life and peace to the poorest and most degraded of the people—never broke upon the ear of this blood-stained tyrant.

Herod proved now that he was a coward as well as a murderer. He refused to condemn Jesus and put Him to death. Why? Because he knew how many at the Lake-side still loved the Prophet of Nazareth; and if he were to kill Him, his own life would be in danger when he went back to his palace in Tiberias. All he does, then, is only to indulge the passions of his savage nature, by joining his "men of war" in mocking and "setting at nought" the Heavenly Saviour.

I cannot think that among these men of war were any truly great Romans. No really brave men would have been guilty of such cruelties. Herod himself, had he been worthy of the name of king, would have scorned such treatment. But, I repeat, he, too, jeered at the Blessed Jesus, and encouraged his unfeeling soldiers to cover Him with insult.

You can picture this divine Son of Man, clad in a robe of mockery, led back again to Pilate's palace. It would seem to have been not the Judgment Hall but "the Pavement" to which on this occasion Jesus is conducted. The Governor seats himself on the tribunal. He is evidently troubled about the Prisoner being returned on his hands from Herod. Again he tells the chief priests, elders, and people that, after sifting their charges, he could find no fault in Him; that he had sent Him to the Tetrarch of Galilee, who had dismissed Him (just as he was disposed to do) as innocent, and not worthy of death.

Pilate seems more wishful than ever to release Jesus. If that excited crowd had been made up of priests and rulers alone, he knew that he would have little chance of succeeding. But he is in hopes that "the common people," who used to hear the Prophet of Nazareth "gladly," and who had lately given Him so kingly a welcome on the Hosanna road, would support his efforts in another attempt to save a guiltless life.

He was met still with the shout, "*Away with this Man!*"

Would it be about this time that a servant of the palace comes in haste to the tribunal? He has an urgent message to deliver into the ear of his master.

It is a message from Claudia, the wife of Pilate, who has had a strange dream that morning. She dreamt of this very crowd that was now surging before the palace gates. She had seen in vision that same gentle Prisoner. Her urgent request is, "*Beware thou do nothing to that holy and just person!*"

Pilate's own sense of justice, his wife's dream, perhaps the very look of meek majesty before him—all these make him shrink from the dreadful wrong he was urged to commit.

LXIV.

He is given up by Pilate to be crucified.

PILATE makes yet one other bold attempt to rescue the Sufferer from His cruel foes.

It had been the Governor's custom, in order to please the Jews, to bestow a free pardon on some prisoner at the time of the Passover. The selection of the prisoner to be thus released rested with the people.

He makes a similar offer now.

He had just said to the mob in front of his palace regarding the Accused, "*I find no fault in Him at all;*" when, therefore, he asks, "*Whom will ye that I release to you?*" he is in hopes their hearts will be melted; and that in pity for the Man he has again and again pronounced to be innocent, they will at once petition for the discharge of Jesus of Nazareth.

In order to make quite sure they would select Him, he names another—a well-known criminal—called Barabbas. They will surely not hesitate between that meek and harmless Galilean and a foul robber and murderer, who had broken the laws both of God and man. To spare a notorious criminal—one taken red-handed in crime—and give one so kind and gracious up to the doom and death of a slave, is surely quite impossible.

Alas! the priests and elders had too easily turned the tide of popular feeling. They had stirred up the worst passions of the Jewish rabble. All cry out, "*Not Jesus, but Barabbas!*"

In a few moments the prisons of Antonia have opened their gates. The soldiers have struck off the heavy chains from the hands and limbs of the convicted murderer and set him free; while the mob still continues to cry out regarding the innocent Jesus, "*Crucify Him, Crucify Him!*"

"*Why, what evil hath He done?*" asked Pilate, shocked at their unfairness and fanatical rage.

Louder still rose the shout, "*Crucify Him, crucify Him!*"

"*I am innocent, then,*" he said, adopting the words used by his wife, "*of the blood of this just Person; see ye to it.*"

"*His blood,*" was their reply, "*be on us, and on our children!*"

Pilate comes into his Judgment Hall again. He asks his servant to bring him a small laver filled with water, in which he washes his hands. It was a sign that he would have no share in an unjust sentence.

Alas! his hands were not clean; for he proceeded to do a very base, wicked, and cruel thing. Though he had told the Jews he had found nothing in the Prisoner worthy of death, he yet "*took Jesus and* SCOURGED *Him;*"—yes, *scourged* the Man he felt and pronounced to be innocent!

Nor was this all. He delivered Him for sport up to his band of soldiers in the barrack-room. They throw a purple or scarlet robe (probably a cast-off military cloak) over His bleeding shoulders:—they cut some branches from the hard, prickly thornbushes that are so familiar still to the traveller in Palestine;—which we have seen, indeed, on the rugged sides of Mount Zion. With these they make something resembling a crown, which they put on His head;—the thorns piercing the meek brows. They further mock Him by putting a reed in His hand to serve for a sceptre, and then, in derision, they bow their knees and call Him King.

> "See Him stand! while cruel fetters
> Bind the hands that framed the world;
> While around Him bitter mocking,
> Laughter, and contempt are hurled.
> Heathen rage and Jewish scorn,
> Meekly for our sins are borne!"

But I draw the veil over the dreadful scene. If devils wickedly triumphed, it was enough to make angels weep.

What did Jesus do all this time? I shall answer again in His own words, which we have already quoted. "*I was not rebellious, neither turned away back. I gave My back to the smiters, and My cheeks to them that plucked off the hair: I hid not My face from shame and spitting.*"

Even Pilate's cruel heart is touched. He brings out to the people the pale, bruised, insulted Saviour, wearing His robe and crown of thorns. He is in hopes, even yet, that spectacle of woe will make them relent. So, conducting Him once more to the steps in sight of the crowd, he says, "BEHOLD THE MAN!" '*Behold the Man* of your own race and nation,' 'the Man,' he must have felt too, who has been alike so patient and Godlike; so different from every other prisoner that had ever stood at his bar. Oh, it might have melted the hardest, to see this kind and gracious Being—this Lamb of God—who had *spoken* nothing all His life long but loving words, and *done* all his life long nothing but loving deeds, now standing faint with loss of blood, and quivering with pain!

But the fiendish frantic cry goes up louder than ever, "*Crucify Him, Crucify Him!*"

Pilate feels it hopeless to try and pacify their clamours—so he says, "*Take* YE *Him and crucify Him, for I find no fault in Him.*"

These coward priests and rulers, however, do not wish to bear the blame of the death they so desired. They wish still to get the authority of Pilate. So they return to the charge:—"*He made Himself the Son of God, and by our law He ought to die.*"

This having no effect, and seeing that the Governor was bent on releasing Him, they try yet another artifice. Pilate had just said to them, "*Behold your King.*" Their reply had been the miserably insincere one, "*We have no King but* CÆSAR." They knew well how the Governor dreaded giving any offence to the wicked Roman Emperor Tiberius. "*If thou let this Man go,*" was their final, knowing, fatal retort, "*thou art not Cæsar's friend: whosoever maketh himself a king speaketh against* CÆSAR."

That appeal was too much for the selfish man:—a charge uttered in presence of his own soldiers!

"*No friend to Cæsar!!*" If a whisper reached the length of Rome, and the ears of the Emperor, that Pilate refused to punish a usurper; chains and fetters like these he had seen taken off Barabbas might be put upon himself.

What ought he now to have done? If he had been a truly brave, noble, high-minded man, he would have shielded innocence at any price, even though it had lost him his place and his palace.

But he basely truckles to the shouts and fury of the multitude: and after three hours' torture, both of mind and body, JESUS is given up, and led away to be crucified!

> "Now the heavy doom is spoken,
> Pilate's feeble pleading ceased;
> Jesus for the cross is chosen,
> And Barabbas is released!
> Ah! there is no loving word
> Not one voice of pity heard!
> But the loud and frenzied cry,
> 'Crucify Him,—crucify!'"

MIDNIGHT.

"THE SUN WAS SET."—GEN. XXVIII. 11.

"THE SUN AND MOON SHALL BE DARK, AND THE STARS SHALL WITHDRAW THEIR SHINING."—JOEL II. 10.

"THOU HAST LAID ME IN THE LOWEST PIT, IN DARKNESS, IN THE DEEPS."—PS. LXXXVIII. 6.

"A LAND OF DARKNESS, AS DARKNESS ITSELF; AND OF THE SHADOW OF DEATH."—JOB X. 22.

"AND WHEN JOSEPH HAD TAKEN THE BODY, HE WRAPPED IT IN A CLEAN LINEN CLOTH, AND LAID IT IN HIS OWN NEW TOMB, WHICH HE HAD HEWN OUT IN THE ROCK: AND HE ROLLED A GREAT STONE TO THE DOOR OF THE SEPULCHRE."—MATT. XXVII. 59, 60.

LXV.

He is taken to Calvary.

WE pass from the *Night Watches* of Gethsemane, with their after hours of mockery and torture, to the MIDNIGHT of deepest darkness which gathers round the cross of Calvary. Not only do we watch THE GREAT SUN going down; but in the words of one of the later prophets, the very stars seem to have "withdrawn their shining."

Let it be with devout and adoring reverence that we gaze on this closing scene :—Jesus, the patient Lamb of God, *nailed to the accursed tree!*

In a picture of the Crucifixion by one of the pious painters of the Middle Ages, the front of the cross on which the meek and lowly Saviour suffered is not seen. The artist wisely felt that it was a subject too awful to attempt. He has, therefore, hidden from view altogether the pale, drooping face and the tortured frame. Nothing is visible but the back part of the cross, and the dark shadow it casts on the ground. A great modern French painter (Gerôme) has carried this idea even farther. In his treatment of the same subject, no Sufferer is presented to view. The eye is first and chiefly arrested by the shadow of three crosses falling on the hill slope,—the centre shadow being the deepest and broadest of the three. But the faces of those passing by or standing near, as they gaze upwards on some countenance not seen, tell truly and effectively the awful story—more effectively and touchingly, indeed, than if he had loaded his canvas with all that is often so ghastly in the works of Italian painters. He helps the spectator farther to read his meaning—to understand this eclipse of *the all-Glorious* SUN—by the unearthly gloom which drapes the landscape, and the pale sickly hue which covers the very buildings of Jerusalem. Nothing else claims attention in the picture, save some streaks in the distant Eastern horizon. Bars of lovely roseate-cloud help to remind those gazing on the scene of anguish and horror, that that mysterious darkness is not to last for ever—but that ere long "the shadow of death will be turned into the morning;" and "a new enlightened world" will be able to sing the well-known lines of Wesley,—

> "Love's redeeming work is done;
> Fought the fight—the battle won:
> Lo! our Sun's eclipse is o'er;
> Lo! He sets in blood no more!"[1]

If it were not needful, in a life of Jesus, to include the story of "His Cross and Passion," I would willingly, like these painters, leave it entirely out. I shall, however, try at least to dwell as little as possible on the details of bodily pain.

The spectacle is both so awful and so humbling, that before I speak of the closing hours of Him who endured all this grief and woe that we might live for ever, let me, in a word, recall to your minds who that pale, weary, tortured, dying Sufferer really was. He *seems* nothing more than a helpless cruelly-used *man*. But it makes the scene all the *more* mysterious, when you carry in your thoughts the name given to Him in the great hymn so dear to old and young—

> "Thou art the King of Glory, O Christ,
> Thou art the everlasting Son of the Father."

Or rather, to give the words on which these and all "Passion hymns" are founded—"*Who, being in the form of God, thought it not robbery to be equal with God; but made Himself of no reputation, and took upon Him the form of a servant, and was made in the likeness of men; and being found in fashion as a man, He*

---

[1] A similar reverential treatment has suggested itself to our artist, in the accompanying illustration, altogether apart from the above remarks. The three crosses are seen, but they are "afar off."

"*There were also women looking on afar off*" (Mark xv. 40) . (*opposite page* 364)

humbled Himself, and BECAME OBEDIENT UNTO DEATH, EVEN THE DEATH OF THE CROSS!"

About nine o'clock in the morning, a crowd is seen coming out of Pilate's palace. He has given the fatal order. The news soon spreads abroad that Jesus is about to be killed. The death inflicted by the Jews on their criminals was by stoning. But the Son of Man and Lord of Glory, as He Himself had foretold His disciples, is to be *crucified*.

Crucifixion, as I have previously remarked, was deemed the death of greatest shame. It was a punishment only inflicted on the meanest of the people,—on slaves, or on captives taken in battle. No Roman citizen, however great his crime, could be sentenced to so degrading an end. It was called " the accursed death of the cross."

It soon became evident that the report regarding the doom of the meek and lowly Saviour is true. The noisy crowd is coming along the narrow street crying out, " *Crucify Him!* " A band of soldiers is headed by an officer on horseback, followed by the chief priests and rulers; and in the midst is God's own innocent Son, the loving Christ of Nazareth.

How He has "laid all His glory by!" The Prince of the kings of the earth carries on His shoulder a beam of wood;— the rough portion of a tree on which He is presently to be nailed.

I think you will say, " Is it possible?" Even though He were no more than a mere man—" is it possible? Can this be the very same, who, five days before, was welcomed into the city with shoutings and rejoicing? Where are now the crowds who spread their leafy carpets on the Hosanna road, and called Him King?"

The weight of the wooden cross is too much for Him, after all the torture of mind He had endured; the night-watch of agony— the sleeplessness and scourgings. He falls exhausted on the hard street pavement with the cross above Him!

The soldiers seem to shrink from touching that hateful beam, or helping to ease the Sufferer of the burden. What do they do?

A sable-coloured man from Africa, a native of Cyrene, attending the Passover, happens to be coming in from the country just as the procession has made its way outside the city gate. The soldiers seize hold of him, and compel him to bear the cross of Jesus.

Was this, do you suppose, out of kindness or pity?

No; I rather think it was only prompted by cruelty. They were afraid Christ might die from very weakness before He reached Calvary; and they would lose the base gratification of watching His slow sufferings.

This Cyrenian was honoured in being made to share the shame of Jesus. It was said that from that day and hour he joined himself to the sinless Lamb of God, by whose side he walked, and that his two sons became members of the early Christian Church.

You can follow then, in thought, the gathering crowd along what well might be called the "Dolorous" or "Sad Way." Released from the heavy weight, Jesus walks on, surrounded with taunts and jeers. Probably, as was the custom also—though not mentioned in the story of the Gospels—a Roman soldier went before Him with a trumpet, proclaiming the crime for which He was going to die.

Amid the noise of the rabble, and the tread of feet, His ear caught the sound of something like people weeping. On turning round, who does He see?

It was the first drop of comfort in His bitter cup. Some of the women of Jerusalem, who had been led to own Him as their Master, Saviour, and divine Friend, are close behind. They dare say nothing: but He knows all that they are feeling towards Him by the tears they shed. When He fell under the burden of the cross, He may first have heard their bitter sobs. It was a proof not to be mistaken of tender, holy love and sympathy.

He turns round His pale, blood-stained face, and speaks to them calmly and gently, yet in tones of intense sadness—

"*Daughters of Jerusalem,*" says He, "*do not weep for Me, rather weep for yourselves and for your children.*" 'Rather weep over the sorrows and sufferings your nation will have to endure for all their sins; and specially for the crowning crime of My death.'

Ah, how terribly fulfilled, in less than forty years, were His words of pity and woe! The day did come, when thousands on thousands of Jews ("themselves and their children") were crucified by order of Titus the Roman general. The historian tells us, indeed, that so vast were the numbers of these poor sufferers, that there was scarce room for the crosses to stand where they were planted on the slopes around the city. Then, surely, the prayer of Christ's enemies was answered in a way they never thought of when they uttered it, " *His blood be on us, and on our children!* "

LXVI.

His sufferings on the Cross begin.

JESUS is not the only Victim who is to be crucified that memorable Friday.

In order, perhaps, to attract a dense crowd, so as to make His death as widely known as possible, two other criminals are also brought from their cells. They are bound with ropes, and are walking in the same dismal procession. They are supposed by some to have belonged to the fierce robber-band of which Barabbas was captain. One who has vividly pictured the scene, has thus represented Barabbas following his unhappy fellow-bandits to Calvary:—

> " I joined the crowd, that streaming through the gate
> Passed on to Golgotha. I stood and watched
> The three led forth to death. All faint and weak,
> And sinking 'neath the burden of His cross,

> The Prophet Teacher came. The other two
> Were sharers with me in my outlaw life;
> With me had plundered, revelled, dwelt in caves;
> Or in the forest depths of Gilead's hills,
> With me had dared defy our Roman lords." [1]

It was still early—about the time of the morning sacrifice. The procession must have been some little distance from the Temple; but in the pauses of the noise and babble of the crowd, the ear of Jesus may have caught the blast of the silver trumpets, reminding of the sacred Paschal season.

At last a halt is made. They have reached a bare gloomy place, outside the walls of the city, named *Golgotha*. It was called so because, probably, it was a low hill of rounded shape, something in the form of a skull. It was the 'Tyburn' of Jerusalem; the place where thieves and robbers and murderers were executed.

I repeat, that I shall not pain you by describing minutely all that now took place. Enough to say, that the body of the Blessed Jesus was nailed to the cross. The cross was then inserted, with a cruel jerk, into a pit or socket dug in the ground.

The hours of intense suffering have begun, and the glaring sun is beating on His unsheltered head!

The four soldiers on duty while away the time by dividing the clothes that had been worn by Jesus amongst them. There are two garments. His upper vestment they tear into four parts; "to each soldier a part." But the one beneath, worn by the poor of Galilee, and which was "woven without seam," they do not divide. There may possibly, unknown to them, have been a sacred value and interest attached to this seamless garment. Who knows but it may have been one woven for Him by His own mother in the evening hours in the humble home of Nazareth, or in some dwelling by the Lake-side? For this the soldiers cast lots. Little did they think that even in this small matter they were fulfilling a prophecy contained in the 22d

---

[1] Professor Plumptre's "Jesus Bar-abbas."

Psalm—" *They pierced my hands and my feet. I may tell all my bones; they look and stare upon me. They part my garments among them, and cast lots upon my vesture*" (ver. 16, 17, 18).

Then these heartless guards resume the stern duties assigned to them. A crucifixion was nothing new to men who were accustomed to shed blood like water.

Meanwhile, the lips of Jesus are heard to breathe an earnest prayer in the midst of His anguish. What are the words of it? Is it a prayer like that He poured forth in the Garden of Gethsemane, that if possible the cup might pass from Him? Is it a petition that His Father would send a legion of angels to smite down His cruel murderers and deliver Him from lingering torture?

No, it is a prayer, indeed, for His enemies; but it is a prayer for mercy on their souls;—a prayer of kindness and compassion, uttered, too, at the very moment when the nails were cruelly tearing His hands and feet. How the language must have struck these Roman soldiers! Not bitter curses, as they were wont to hear from the lips of those they crucified; but an earnest entreaty on their behalf. No wonder that tradition speaks of some of them becoming afterwards Christians—brought to use very different words from those they once would have uttered:—" God forbid that we should glory save in the Cross of our Lord Jesus Christ!"

The custom was to place over the cross the name and the crime for which the criminal suffered. These were generally printed, too, on a wooden label. This label was, sometimes, previously fixed round the prisoner's neck on the way to the place of execution. Large words are inscribed in black letters on a board above the sacred head of Jesus. Pilate had ordered them to be put in three languages, so that all might be able to read them:—

"THIS IS THE KING OF THE JEWS."

In all the sad scene there is only one touch of pity mentioned on the part of His crucifiers. It seems to have been usual, during a crucifixion, to dull the sense of pain by giving some drops of myrrh, mixed with vinegar (or the sour wine of Palestine). This was offered to the suffering Lamb of God. He merely put it to his lips,—no more. Why, do you suppose, did He thus refuse?

It was because He did not wish to deaden suffering. He resolved to drink the bitter cup, put into His hands for the world's redemption, to its dregs. The two thieves beside Him would likely accept gratefully the mixture, and thus have the severity of their death-pangs materially diminished. Not so with Jesus. He heard every cruel jest, every mocking word. He saw the crowd making light of his tortures. He desired no relief till He had paid the fullest wages of sin. The Captain of our Salvation was "made *perfect* through suffering:"—" He *endured*, as seeing Him who is invisible." How exactly the words, spoken 1500 years before, in the same Psalm from which I have already quoted, were fulfilled:—" *All they that see me laugh me to scorn: they shoot out the lip, they shake the head, saying, He trusted on the Lord that he would deliver him: let him deliver him, seeing he delighted in him*" (ver. 7, 8).

And so we read in the story of the Gospels, how the unfeeling passers-by only wagged their heads in derision, saying, "*Come down! Come down!* Thou who didst say Thou wouldst destroy our beautiful Temple and build it in three days, show us that Thou hast the power by now saving Thyself, and descending from Thy cross!"

Even the chief priests and elders joined in the taunt,—" *He saved others, Himself He cannot save!*"

Nor was it the coarse crowd, the savage soldiers, and the enraged priests and elders alone, who were thus loading Him with jeers and insults. Even the two thieves at His side added their unpitying challenge—" *If thou be the Messiah, save thyself and us.*" Listen once more to the prophetic words of Jesus in the 22d Psalm. How it describes the scene! "*Many bulls have compassed me: strong bulls of Bashan have beset me round. They gaped upon me with their mouths, as a ravening and a roaring lion. I am poured out like water, and all my bones are out of joint: my heart is like wax; it is melted in the midst of my bowels*" (ver. 12, 13, 14).

Yes, wherever His eye turns He can see nothing but these "roaring lions." On either side of Him is a dying, blaspheming felon. Beneath him are the rude soldiers. Before Him the mocking crowd. And, worst of all, unseen by mortal eye, is *the* 'roaring lion,' Satan himself—assailing the meek, sinless Saviour.

Yet all this time not a word of anger or complaint escapes His lips!

We are told that at such scenes of crucifixion the poor victims were often heard, either shrieking out with pain, or, as I have already said, cursing their tyrants and crucifiers as they implored in vain for mercy; but the gentle Lamb of God is still, as we found Him in the Garden, " dumb before His shearers." " He opened not His mouth."

> " Still pours along the multitude;
> Still rends the heavens the shout of blood;
> Hands clenched with rage—their vestures torn,
> The curse, the taunt, the laugh of scorn,
> All that the dying hour can sting
> Are round Thee now, thou thorn-crowned King!
>
> " Yet cursed and tortured, taunted, spurned,
> No wrath is for the wrath returned,
> No vengeance flashes from His eye,
> The Sufferer calmly waits to die;
> What say those lips by anguish riven?
> 'God, be my murderers forgiven!' "[1]

---

[1] Croly.

LXVII.

He pardons the penitent Thief, and commends His Mother to the care of John.

PERHAPS it may have been this Godlike silence and holy calm, this meekness and patience of the Blessed Jesus, which led to the next incident in these awful moments.

One of the two thieves continues railing at the sinless One by his side. But the other has ceased to do so. He has come rather to pity Him;—to pity Him, because he knows He is innocent, and is suffering wrongfully.

He first addresses and reproves his wicked comrade. "*We receive,*" he says, "*the due reward of our deeds, but this Man hath done nothing amiss.*"

But he more than pities Jesus. In that hour, when every other voice is raised against Him, that dying thief pleads *for* Him!

He may probably have heard often before of the name—"*Jesus of Nazareth.*" Who knows but that from some den or cave, where he and his robber band were lurking for their prey—perhaps the black caverned crags in the dell of Arbela; perhaps the brigand haunts in "the Bloody way" on the road to Jericho—he may have mingled with the crowd where Jesus was! Who knows but that, unknown to his comrades in crime, he may have listened to one or more of the gracious words which came out of the mouth of the Holy Teacher, and witnessed one or more of His mighty deeds? Now, as he turns his dying eye towards the sacred face on the centre cross, he reads the title—"JESUS OF NAZARETH, THE KING OF THE JEWS." He trembles. He believes! He calls that dying One "*Lord.*" He speaks of His "kingdom;" the kingdom Pilate had smiled at. He prays to Him; he asks Jesus to "*remember*" him!

Jesus had not spoken up to this time. But He speaks now. All the jibes and taunts of His foes He has heard in silence. But when the prayer of a poor hell-deserving outcast reaches His dying ear—the lips of love are unsealed. In words which have proved like a gleam of light to many in the thickest gloom of the dark Valley, he says, " *Verily I say unto thee, To-day shalt thou be with me in Paradise!*"

Is it not a beautiful thought, Jesus and the dying thief He had saved, entering Paradise together? The pierced hands of Jesus opened the golden gate of mercy to the chief of sinners!

But what all this time of the Saviour's disciples and friends? How dreadful for them to think of their dear Lord thus suffering! Not a few of them, too, beheld Him thus hanging between heaven and earth—a spectacle to devils and angels and men—dying in slow agony!

Some of these kept at a distance—" beholding afar off "—not venturing, either by sign or by word, to show how deeply they felt. Chief among them were some women from the Lake-side, the same, perhaps, I have already spoken of, whom He had joined in the pilgrim caravan at Jericho that very day week. Others were nearer. They had gradually made their way through the crowd till they stood as close as they could under the cross. Their presence must have been as comforting as that of the Angel who was sent to strengthen Jesus in Gethsemane the night before.

There was one female in that crowd who surely to Him had a deeper interest than all the rest. It was Mary, His own mother. She was there along with her sister and Mary Magdalene.

Ah, now, surely, had come at last to her the sad hour, of which aged Simeon had spoken thirty-three years before! She is near the foot of the cross, gazing on her pale, bleeding Son. One of the very oldest Christian hymns, called the '*Stabat Mater*,' the English translation of which may be familiar to some of you, thus recalls the touching scene and moment—

> " At the cross, her station keeping,
> Stood the mournful mother weeping,
> Where He hung—her dying Lord ;
> For her soul, of joy bereaved,
> Bowed with anguish, deeply grieved,
> *Felt the sharp and piercing sword.*"

How she would think of all He had been to her in the past! How different this hour from those sunny days at Nazareth, when in His sacred boyhood He roamed the flowery hills, or sat pensive by her side in the evening twilight, or wrought with His own hands the livelong day to supply her wants and repay her early love!

Jesus sees her. He gazes upon her in silent compassion and tenderness. In the midst of His dying agonies His filial love is deep as ever. What does He do? What does He say?

He unburdens His heart of His one earthly wish—His one earthly anxiety. It is that she, His beloved mother, would be specially cared for. He desires to spare her more suffering. He cannot bear to think of her remaining where she is—a spectator of still deeper anguish—knowing, as He does, that His own darkest hour of woe had yet to come.

At Mary's side there is another friend very dear to Jesus. It is the Apostle John.

" *Woman*," said He, with a faint but most tender voice, as He points to the loving disciple, " *behold thy son.*"

And then He makes over to John this most precious earthly charge—" *Son, behold thy mother.*"

They both understood His wish that they should leave together the scene of sorrow. Yet it must have been hard, too, for Mary to take at such a moment her last farewell. What a look of anguish that must have been when she raised her eyes, hitherto bent on the ground, and gazed for the last time on the ghastly face that strove in its agony to give a parting fond look, if not smile, of affection! How HE would think, too, of all she had been and done to Him—the hours of earliest infancy in Bethlehem; the days at Nazareth; the nights when she had ofttimes

"*And from that hour, that disciple took her unto his own home*" (John xix. 27.) . . . . *page* 375

sung over His slumbers her holy temple-song; the hours of sickness in which she had soothed his aching head; the thirty blissful years they had spent together, each one of which had added to her claims on His filial love!

Obedient to His silent wish, the beloved disciple takes the sorrowful mother of Jesus away from the scene. Her bent form and slow step and pale cheek tell how deeply the sword had pierced. How different does she look now from what she was when we first knew her as the young maiden in her village home! John gently supports her, and, with her arm linked in his, he took her from that hour to his own home in Jerusalem. You see them in the accompanying picture reaching the portals, whose side-stones were still red with the sprinkled blood of yesterday's Paschal lamb.

LXVIII.

He suffers amid the darkness, and at last bows His head in death.

ALTHOUGH now truly MIDNIGHT to the Soul of Jesus, the fierce sun of noon is pouring down his rays on the three victims on the three crosses.

But suddenly the bright blue sky becomes dim and cloudy. A thick darkness settles all round Jerusalem. It looks almost as if that glorious orb in the outer world had hid his face, ashamed to gaze on the sufferings of his Almighty Maker!

You remember the strange brilliance of the nightly heavens at the birth of Jesus; when shining hosts of angels seemed to have fetched down lamps from the upper sanctuary to light up the plains of Bethlehem? Now it is the reverse. Nature, which then put on her white vestal garments, clothes herself at mid-day in sackcloth and mourning. No wonder! That sun had witnessed many dreadful scenes since he first shone on the beautiful earth, but never a scene like this.

> "The sun paled in a fearful hour,
> The stars might well grow dim,
> When this mortality had power
> So to o'ershadow HIM."

The darkness continues for three hours. During the time it lasted, all was still. The crowd seemed awed, and the Divine Sufferer, too, remained in speechless agony. Silence and gloom brooded over the scene.

At the end of these three hours, there is a loud wail heard rising from the central cross. It is Jesus uttering the bitterest cry that ever arose from earth to heaven—"MY GOD, MY GOD, WHY HAST THOU FORSAKEN ME?"

The awful soul-sorrow of Gethsemane has come back to Him. We never can know all the mental anguish of those three hours of darkness which ended in that wail of woe!

The assaults of Satan were terrible, but most terrible of all was the hiding of His Father's countenance. The cruel tortures of man were bad enough. These He could bear:—these He *had* borne without a word of complaint. But when the Father's loving face appears to be veiled, we seem to hear Him say, in the words of the old Patriarch, "*Have pity upon Me, have pity upon Me, O ye my friends; for* THE HAND OF GOD HATH TOUCHED ME!"

Oh deepest of all deep mysteries! The "*Light of Lights*"—"BRIGHTER THAN THE SUN"—"*dwelling in the light which no man can approach unto*"—undergoing such an *eclipse* as this!—exclaiming, not of human foes or hostile devils, but bemoaning to His own Divine Father—"*Thou hast laid Me in the lowest pit, in darkness, in the deeps. Thy wrath lieth hard upon Me, and thou hast afflicted Me with all Thy waves*" (Ps. lxxxviii. 6, 7).

We never can explain—we never can fathom—the full meaning of that desertion. Doubtless He speaks as our Sin-bearer. He felt the burden of the world's guilt laid upon Him—"*He bare our sins in His own body on the tree.*" In such a sense, but in no other, could it be that God had "forsaken Him." Never for a moment could the Father cease to love His dear Son. Hence, in the very thickest darkness, Jesus clings to the joyful assurance— "MY GOD!"

It is now drawing towards afternoon. The crosses had been erected nearly six hours.

"*I thirst,*" feebly exclaimed the dying Redeemer. It was the only boon which, during all that long time, He had asked for Himself.

A jar was standing close by, filled with the sour wine I have already mentioned which was taken by the Roman soldiers. One of these, touched more than his fellows with pity at seeing such goodness along with such suffering, ran and put a sponge on the end of a reed, and, dipping it into this vessel, raised it to the parched lips of Jesus.

Immediately after that, the dying Saviour utters just one word. It is three words in our Bible. It was only *one* in the language He used:—" IT IS FINISHED !" The Great Sun of Righteousness is just setting amid the shadows of death!

> "Thou noble Countenance!
> All earthly suns are pale
> Before the BRIGHTNESS of that glance
> At which a world shall quail;
> How is it quenched and gone!
> Those gracious eyes grow dim!
> Whence grew that cheek so pale and wan?
> Who dared to scoff at *Him?*"[1]

"*It is finished!*" Yes; but it was the shout of victory! It was proclaiming that Satan was overthrown—that the Great Redemption of the world was completed—that peace had been made through the blood of His cross—that, "having overcome

---

[1] Paul Gerhardt.

the sharpness of death, He had opened the kingdom of heaven to all believers!"

Then, having commended His spirit into the hands of His Father, He bowed His head on His breast.

You sometimes hear of people who, from very great grief, are said to "die of a broken heart." It is thought by many able writers this was really true of Jesus:—that owing to His awful mental sorrow—far more killing than bodily pain—His heart was actually *ruptured.*

Did He not Himself say, in the words of the 69th Psalm, "*Reproach hath* BROKEN *my heart*"?

Though all is quiet and silent now on that cross, Nature is not silent.

Does she not seem to say, in her own dumb language;—'That dying, that dead Man, is THE GREAT GOD'?

While the heavens are still darkened, the whole of the city of Jerusalem is shaken with an earthquake; the solid rocks are split in twain, and the graves are opened.

The High Priest, too, was startled in the midst of his devotions in the Temple by the effects of this earthquake. The rocky hill of Moriah, on which the Temple was built, quivered under it. Just at the time of the evening sacrifice, when the smoke was going up from the altar of incense, the curtain which hung down in front of the Holy of Holies was rent in twain, torn from top to bottom. It was the sign and signal that the earthly priesthood was at an end: that "the way" was now open "into the Holiest of all by the blood of Jesus."

But to return to the scene on Calvary.

Those who hitherto had only mocked, now look up to that meek head drooping on the cross, and as they beat their breasts, exclaim, "*Truly, this was the Son of God!*"

One of those who uttered this confession was the officer, or Centurion, commanding the troop of soldiers. He had seen the darkness, and felt the earthquake shock. These two things alone must have greatly startled and astonished him. But he had seen something more amazing still. He had watched, for six long hours, the words and actions of that central Sufferer. He had often seen soldiers die as heroes amid the horrors of war. He had at times seen the gladiators or miserable captives, who were torn by wild beasts in the Roman amphitheatre, bearing themselves bravely in the midst of cruel pain; but he had never seen so holy a death as this;—such patience, such gentleness, such submission! There were indeed no outer rays of brightness;—no halo, or radiant circlet, such as the Christian painters make around the sacred head, to assert or indicate His Deity. But there was a brightness and halo more wondrous still. It was "the beauty of holiness." The divine glory shone in His every look and word through that suffering flesh. It compelled a stern warrior to own Him first as a "righteous man;" and then to add, "Surely he must be" (what I have heard them call Him in mockery) "THE SON OF GOD!"

Even some of the vulgar mob, who had waited during all these dreadful hours, returned to the city smiting on their breasts, awed by the look and bearing of the crucified Jesus: not a few of them, we may well believe, shocked at the inhuman cruelty of His murderers.

LXIX.

He is taken down from the Cross and laid in a Tomb.

THREE o'clock was past, and the Jewish Sabbath began at sunset. As the law would not allow of dead bodies being taken down from the cross during Sabbath hours, the Jews asked as a favour of Pilate, that the soldiers should hasten the deaths of the prisoners, so that their corpses might be removed at once, and not be left to pollute the sacred day.

The two thieves were still alive. Crucified criminals were known indeed to linger on in their agony for days together; so the soldiers take iron hammers or clubs, and break *their* legs first. When they come to the centre cross, they find Jesus is dead already; His eyes are quite closed. Accordingly, they do not mar His sacred body. They thus fulfilled a prophecy about Him as the true Paschal Lamb: that though His blood was to be shed, and His flesh pierced and torn, yet " *a bone of Him should not be broken.*"

But one of the soldiers takes a spear and plunges it into His side, reaching the heart. It was to make quite sure that life was gone. A stream of blood and water flows out of the gash which the spear has made.

The remainder of the story is shortly told. Joseph of Arimathea, a rich man, and a secret disciple, makes offer of a new tomb which he had built in his own garden. He went himself to Pilate, and got leave to convey the dead body of Jesus to this sepulchre. The Jews then, like the Jews in Jerusalem at this day, had their places of burial adjoining the city. Nothing struck me more than the thousands of white grave-stones, mingling with old mouldering ones, all along the Valley of Jehoshaphat, on both sides of the Brook Kidron up close to the Eastern wall.

Although the tomb was prepared by Joseph for himself, he felt it an honour indeed to give it as a royal chamber for "the King of the Jews." The name of this pious man will always be loved and honoured for what he did. The disciples and friends of Jesus, so helpless at this trying hour, must have been solaced by knowing that the lifeless body of their dear Lord had been tenderly cared and provided for. Pilate, I daresay, would only have scorned a request from *them;* but he was not loath to grant a favour to this wealthy citizen.

The bodies of the two thieves would likely be thrown into some pit in the Valley of Hinnom, there to be devoured by the dogs that prowled about the city. This was the usual fate of those who suffered death for their crimes. The grave of Jesus was in the peaceful retirement of a private garden, amid the sweet fragrance of the flowers He loved so well.

Both Joseph and Nicodemus were members of the very council that condemned Christ. They not only refused, however, to consent to the wicked act of the Sanhedrim; but they thus openly told, by a deed as kind and generous as the other was base, how strongly opposed they were to the cruel death of a just and innocent Prophet, and would have no share in the crime. It was a bold thing for them to do. Perhaps had either Joseph or Nicodemus been alone, they would have felt unequal to the task. But the one brave-hearted and truth-loving man would help on and encourage the other. When the disciples are scattered like timid sheep, the body of their dead Shepherd is rescued from devouring wolves by those we should have least expected to interfere—two wealthy Jewish strangers: " *He made His grave with the wicked, and with* THE RICH *in His death!* "

You can, doubtless, recall the only other time we have heard the name of Nicodemus. It was when he came to see Jesus timidly by night. Now he comes boldly and without fear in the open light of day. There is a beautiful candour and love of truth in this " man of the Pharisees." Unlike most of those of his class, he had the fear of doing wrong, and the wish to do what was fair and just and right. Tradition says, that shortly after this, he became himself a disciple of Jesus, and was baptized by the hands of Peter and John. Christ had told him in that midnight converse how God had " so loved the world " as to " give His only Begotten Son." He had seen and learnt surely on the Cross of Calvary what that " so " meant. " As Moses had lifted up the serpent in the wilderness " (other words of Jesus to him that same night), so had he seen the Son of Man " lifted up." It is pleasant for us to think of him as one of those of whom Jesus speaks when He said—" *And I, if I be lifted up on the cross, will draw all men unto Me.*" Mary of Bethany, with the contents of her alabaster-box, anointed her Lord for His burying. What Jesus said of her on that occasion may at all events be said with equal truth alike of the good and kind Joseph, and of his brother Jew—

that "Wheresoever this Gospel shall be preached in the whole world, there shall this deed be told for a memorial" (Matt. xxvi. 13).

The soldiers take out the iron nails which, eight hours before, had been driven into the hands and feet of Jesus; and Joseph, along with Nicodemus, wrap the Body in a roll of fine linen, and embalm it with sweet spices. The fragrant myrrh and pounded aloes, brought by Nicodemus, are placed all through the folds of the shroud. It was a costly offering, for its weight was a hundred pounds. The Head was wrapped round with a separate linen napkin pure white.

It is now soft evening light. The darkness of three hours ago has passed. The sun is nearing the western horizon as the precious burden is laid in its tomb. That tomb, I need hardly tell you, was not, like our graves, dug in the ground. It was a cave or small cavern hewn out of the solid rock. The sepulchre was new; no body had ever been laid there before. It would seem also to have been very near the place of crucifixion. They rolled a great stone to the opening to keep all secure.

Two sorrowful women from the Lake-side are watching at a little distance. If the body had been cast, like that of other criminals, into a common pit or grave in the open field, they could not bear to have been thus near. But in the quiet of that garden, away from public traffic, they can sit in pensive sorrow, and gaze on the spot which holds their 'loved and lost.' They have their own purposes of coming, after the Sabbath is over, with other fragrant spices to complete the embalming. Meanwhile they are too tearful and sad to be of any help; and they feel they may well leave this first hasty burial in the hands of others.

The darkness was already gathering as these two sorrowing friends, perhaps others with them, left the hallowed spot, and went, with little thought of rest or sleep, to their various homes. The other women had already gone into the city to buy spices before the shops were closed. They would thus be in readiness.

after the Sabbath's forced rest was ended, to return to their holy labours at the tomb.

I may well end by saying, Oh marvellous story! We noted, at the beginning of this volume, the condescension of Jesus in coming into the world, not as a full-grown man, but as a feeble, helpless Babe—laid in a manger, and hanging on His mother's breasts. We have to note the same, regarding the manner of His death as that of His birth. If it was needful for Him to die as a great sacrifice for sin, He might have died in solitude. He might have ascended the heights of Hermon, as Moses did those of Nebo, and with no ruffian taunts or cruel jests sounding in His ear, but with His own disciples around Him, He might have yielded up His spirit to His Great Father in heaven.

But He wishes here, also, to show the marvels of His condescension. He submits, not to a hero's, but to a felon's end. He dies the most cruel and shameful of deaths.

> " Bound upon the accursèd tree,
> Faint and bleeding, who is He?
> By the eyes so pale and dim,
> Streaming blood and writhing limb,
>   *   *   *   *
> " By the last and bitter cry,
> The Ghost given up in agony;
> By the lifeless body laid
> In the chamber of the dead.
>   *   *   *   *
> " Lord! our suppliant knees we bow,
> SON OF GOD! 'tis Thou, 'tis Thou!"[1]

" *Ye know the grace of our Lord Jesus Christ, who, though He was rich, yet for our sakes He became* POOR (stooped to the lowest depths of shame and suffering), *that we through His poverty might be rich!*"

---

[1] Milman.

LXX.

His Tomb is watched by a Guard of Soldiers.

JESUS was laid in Joseph's rock-hewn sepulchre, on Friday, before sunset.

The Jewish Sabbath has now passed, on which day all "rested, according to the commandment." It was the saddest Sabbath in the world's history. Think what must have been the feelings of the disciples of Jesus during its long hours—*their Lord lying dead!* Think of the sorrow of His many other devoted friends— those from the Lake-side—those at Bethany and elsewhere! Think, above all, of His loved mother's anguish of soul. She could say, in sadder tones than those of the aged Patriarch, "*I* AM *bereaved!*"

It must have been sorrow, too, in the midst of much outer joy. In Jerusalem that Sabbath day was an high day. Not only was it the Passover Sabbath, but it was the day before the Festival of "First Fruits." A vast number of people, old and young, went out in the evening to some field near the city, where priests, appointed by the Sanhedrim, gathered a sheaf of new corn. This sheaf was taken next morning, with the sound of music and amid crowded streets, to the Temple, and there waved before the altar: an ox with gilded horns and an olive-wreath on his head going in front of the priestly band.

But the blast of the trumpets, and the singing of Paschal and harvest hymns, must, in the case of all the followers of Jesus, have been music and songs to "heavy hearts." The city was bright with the glorious sun of a Palestine spring, but the true "Sun of their souls" had set in darkness and death. So stupified were His disciples with sorrow, that they seem to have forgotten all about the saying of their dear Lord, that He was to rise again from the grave.

It is not unlikely that on this Sabbath,—to them of gloom and woe, these trembling ones had shut themselves in the same upper chamber where they had so lately listened to their Master's tender farewell words of comfort—the gracious voice they feared they would never listen to again. How they would talk through their tears about yesterday's awful scene! how they would dwell on the happy, holy past—the days of loving friendship and sacred joy never more to return!

At the close of that Sabbath, while the streets of Jerusalem would be ringing with the festal mirth I have just described, a watch, not of Jewish, but of Roman soldiers, clad in armour, have been placed at the tomb where Jesus was laid. Possibly they may have been the same soldiers who, the day before, were set on guard at the cross, and who witnessed so heartlessly the scene of agony. They pace by turns up and down all night in the silent garden.

Why have these soldiers been sent there?

It was owing to a request made to Pilate by the chief priests and rulers, to prevent the possibility of friendly hands, in the dark, stealing the body of Christ. They were afraid, if the disciples effected this, they might try to make the people believe that their Master had actually come to life again, as He had predicted.

You will remember that Jesus, more than once, told His Apostles about His rising from the dead the third day: specially in the course of that memorable journey when, for the last time, they were on their way to Jerusalem.

Nor was it to His own immediate followers alone He had spoken of that event. When the Scribes and Pharisees came, asking Him to give them "a sign," He replied that "no sign would be given to them but that of the prophet Jonas"—"*For as Jonas was three days and three nights in the whale's belly, so shall the Son of Man be three days and three nights in the heart of the earth.*"

The Pharisees remembered these words well, and were now uneasy about them. Hence all the pains and precautions they take to make the sepulchre sure.

2 B

The guard of soldiers, along with the priestly enemies of Jesus, put a seal upon the stone which covered the mouth of the tomb. They probably attached to both tomb and stone a strip of parchment or leather, and fastened it to either end with a seal. This seal, I may add, was generally not of wax, but of baked clay; and after it was affixed it would be quite impossible for any one either to enter the sepulchre or to go out of it, unless the stone were violently displaced.

With this sealed stone, and these watchful sentinels, then, at the grave's mouth, the enemies of Jesus can keep their minds at rest. The seal could not be tampered with; and it would be certain death to any Roman soldier to sleep at His post.

We must not suppose that all the interest about that tomb was confined to a handful of disciples and friends. The name of Jesus must have been on many thousand lips that Sabbath in Jerusalem. He was well known now through all the land. Some believed Him to be a Teacher sent from God; others, a Prophet; others hailed Him as "Son of David," and Heir to the throne of Israel; others believed that He who could still the sea, and cure the sick, and cleanse the leper, and raise the dead, must be nothing short of Divine. Very many more than all of these, knew Him, whether He were man or God, to be good, and holy, and loving, and tender-hearted. Could they fail to be indignant at the shameful fate to which He had been subjected yesterday and the day before? His seizure by soldiers at night; His three-fold trial, with all its wrongs; first His fainting under the beam of the cross, and then His being nailed to it in anguish? Could they fail to have heard of the rocks being rent, or to have seen the darkening of the sun? These things were not done in a corner.

Yes, we may be sure that for the dead Saviour there was many a pitying, sympathising thought among the Paschal crowds that memorable Sabbath.

LXXI.

His Tomb is found empty by the Holy Women, and visited by Peter and John.

It is not yet the dawn of the third morning. The stars are still shining. I daresay the soldiers, chilled and weary with their long night-watch, are longing for daylight.

Something suddenly takes place. These sentinels—yes, the brave Roman soldiers—are seen rushing into the city! Men that never turned their back on any foe in the field of battle are frightened now?

What has caused this fear?

They have felt another earthquake similar to that which occurred two days before. As the ground shook on which they were keeping watch, the large stone at the mouth of the tomb of Jesus snapped the seals with which it had been bound. An angel in snow-white raiment, and whose face was bright as the lightning, rolls it back from the entrance, and seats himself upon it.

The heathen soldiers, in superstitious terror, fall in a faint to the earth. They become "as dead men," when they see this glorious being in "armour of light" seated on that slab of rock. So soon as their senses recover, they hurry away, as I have just told you, in the dark, to give the alarm.

But daybreak is now drawing nigh. There is a faint streak of light in the Eastern sky : the top of the Mount of Olives is just tipped, and no more, by the first rays of the rising sun. In this grey of morning-dawn, when the birds had hardly wakened up to their early song; when the dew was lying thick on the grass of the garden, and diamond-drops were hanging on every bush and tree, three figures are seen approaching with timid yet eager steps. They are carrying in their hands small jars or caskets; also some rolls of linen cloth.

They are the women of Galilee, who had been last at their dear Lord's cross; they are now first and earliest at His tomb.

They had been waiting anxiously for the dawn of the morn after the Sabbath, that they might come to complete what had been done in haste two nights before—anointing the body of Jesus. In one sense there was no need of any more embalming, after the costly offering of Joseph and Nicodemus. But "many waters cannot quench love." These devoted female disciples wished to show that theirs was no common affection; and this was all they could do to testify how deeply they mourned their loss. They have brought with them the ointments which they had prepared in the failing light of Friday.

It is evident that they had no dream of ever seeing their Beloved Master alive again.

The names of these pious women are Salome, the mother of the Apostle John, and, perhaps, Joanna; Mary Cleophas and Mary Magdalene. The mother of Jesus was not among them. We may well suppose she was too weary and overcome with sorrow, to be able for this new effort of strength. It was to them a holy, but a most mournful errand:—I daresay their sleepless eyes were dim and red with weeping. If they were never to see Jesus in life, they had come to take a last view of the face that had looked so often and so tenderly upon them; and to lay their ointments on the torn but sacred brow. Then, after swathing the body, they would return home to feel more than ever their loneliness and desolation.

They are conversing with one another as they enter the garden gate and draw near to the sepulchre. Although there are four of them, they begin to remember that they have not the strength of men. They begin to think of the difficulty of getting the huge stone removed which they had seen on the Friday night rolled against the door. They do not appear to have known anything about the guard of soldiers which had been placed there by Pilate.

But what is this? Dim dawn of morning though it be, their eyes cannot deceive them. The work is already done which they had desired. The stone is already rolled aside. The sepulchre is open!

Mary Magdalene is overcome with fright. She thinks at once of the tomb having been entered and pillaged, and of the sacred body having, perhaps, been hurried away to the common grave of criminals. She rushes at once back to the city. On finding Peter and John, she tells them what her eyes have seen—" *They have taken away,*" she says, " *the Lord out of the sepulchre, and we know not where they have laid Him.*"

She feels her weakness as a woman to do anything to recover the stolen body; but, with their ready help, it may not be too late to find out the robber-band who have committed the daring deed.

Meanwhile the other women, whom Mary had left in the garden, are braver than the soldiers. They go forward with anxious beating hearts to the open tomb.

They look in. It is not in one sense empty. There is some one there. But it is not the voice they are wishful to hear which greets them. It is that of an angel. He looks like a young man, and is clothed in a long robe of white—the emblem of gladness.

He quiets their minds. He uses the very word which was wont to be so often on the lips of their loving Master—" FEAR NOT;" adding, "*for I know that ye seek Jesus, which was crucified. He is not here; He is risen, as He said. Come, see the place where the Lord lay!*" Then he farther bids them go as fast as they can, and not only tell the joyful news to the disciples, but also that, as a good and kind Shepherd, Jesus is to "go before them into Galilee" (the pleasant and much-loved Lake-side again), where He will once more meet them.

There is one name in the angel's message which surely speaks very lovingly of the unchanged heart of the Master. He sends that message to all the disciples, but there is only *one* He specially singles out among them. Unless you had previously known the selection, would you not have been disposed to say, 'Surely it must be John;—John His best beloved friend;—John who has had the privilege of being intrusted with the most hallowed of charges!'

But it is not so. Of all the scattered sheep of the fold, it is to the truant wanderer a message of forgiveness is sent:—" *Go and tell* PETER!"

The three females, whom the angel addressed, sped back as he had bidden them to the city. They are full of joy, as well as awe, and are in such breathless haste that they speak to no one they meet.

Can we wonder that when they enter the upper room, the gathered disciples refuse to credit so strange, so wondrous a story? That the poor trembling sheep, scattered in " the dark and cloudy day," would not believe that the Shepherd they had seen torn by ravening wolves had come to life again! It seemed like a foolish and idle tale.

Our attention is next directed to two men hastening in the direction of Joseph's garden. One is in front of the other; for he is younger and fleeter of foot. I think I need not ask you who these are.

No sooner had Mary Magdalene found Peter and John, than they started off in haste to know for themselves what had taken place.

John reaches the tomb first. He pauses at the entrance, and seems afraid to do more than look in. He gazes with mingled wonder and alarm.

But the other, the brave and now penitent Peter, cannot be content with resting outside. As a Jew, he will become unclean by touching the place where the dead has been laid. But what is that to him? He at once enters,—John following. And what do they see?

They observe, first, that the body of their buried Master is evidently not there: the tomb is empty. Then the same thought naturally occurs to them as it did to Mary; robbers must have entered it at night and stolen Him away; perhaps for the sake of getting possession of Joseph's costly myrrh and aloes.

But, on looking round, this supposition cannot be correct. Robbers would never have taken the pains to fold up so carefully the grave-clothes. The swathing-bands were in one part of the cavity:—the linen napkin that had been bound around His thorn-crowned head was carefully folded up and laid by itself in another part. There was no sign of haste or confusion, which would have been the case had thieves forced their way in and made off with the body.

The Beloved Apostle was the first of the two to entertain the thought of Jesus having indeed Himself risen. "*He saw and believed.*"

" And the disciples," we read, "*went away again to their own home.*"

I have often thought of that morning walk of these two chief friends;—their strange bewildering joy! 'He must be alive!' 'Shall we indeed see Him then once more?' 'He told us that we would.' 'The "little while and ye shall not see Me," is past; and did He not add, "a little while and ye SHALL see Me?" That little while is surely come now! Oh, that we only knew where we could find Him! Oh, that we could see Him coming to us as He did of old on the stormy Lake, and hear the sweet accents of His own voice—" Fear not, it is I, be not afraid !"'

THE GREAT SUNRISE.

"WEEPING MAY ENDURE FOR A NIGHT, BUT JOY COMETH IN THE MORNING."—PS. XXX. 5.

"AND HE SHALL BE AS THE LIGHT OF THE MORNING WHEN THE SUN RISETH, EVEN A MORNING WITHOUT CLOUDS."—2 SAM. XXIII. 4.

"THE LIGHT OF THE SUN SHALL BE SEVENFOLD, AS THE LIGHT OF SEVEN DAYS, IN THE DAY THAT THE LORD BINDETH UP THE BREACH OF HIS PEOPLE, AND HEALETH THE STROKE OF THEIR WOUND."—IS. XXX. 26.

"AND VERY EARLY IN THE MORNING, THE FIRST DAY OF THE WEEK, THEY CAME UNTO THE SEPULCHRE AT THE RISING OF THE SUN. AND THEY SAID AMONG THEMSELVES, WHO SHALL ROLL US AWAY THE STONE FROM THE DOOR OF THE SEPULCHRE? AND WHEN THEY LOOKED, THEY SAW THAT THE STONE WAS ROLLED AWAY; FOR IT WAS VERY GREAT."—MARK XVI. 2-4.

"FEAR NOT YE: FOR I KNOW THAT YE SEEK JESUS, WHICH WAS CRUCIFIED. HE IS NOT HERE: FOR HE IS RISEN, AS HE SAID. COME, SEE THE PLACE WHERE THE LORD LAY."—MATT. XXVIII. 5, 6.

"WHO HATH ABOLISHED DEATH, AND HATH BROUGHT LIFE AND IMMORTALITY TO LIGHT."—2 TIM. I. 10.

LXXII.

He reveals Himself to Mary Magdalene, and to Peter.

ONCE more we may return to the words—"*Watchman! what of
THE NIGHT? Watchman! what of THE NIGHT?*"
"*The Watchman said,* THE MORNING COMETH!"
Oh happy day for a benighted world! The BRIGHTER than the
brightest earthly sun has come forth from His chamber of death,
rejoicing more than ever "as a giant to run his course." He
has "turned the shadow of death into the morning." "*The
darkness is past and the true* LIGHT *now shineth!*"
In the golden radiance of the first Easter, let us go in thought
and contemplate—THE GREAT SUNRISE!

Mary Magdalene, the most faithful and devoted of the female
followers of Jesus, has returned to the tomb after all the others
have left.
It was surely a brave thing for her to do: to go back by herself to that garden with its lonely grave. But she cannot bear
to be away. Her tear-dimmed eyes tell how deeply concerned
she is. "*Mary stood without, at the sepulchre, weeping.*"
Gaining courage, she stoops down, and looks in to the hollow
cavern. If He be indeed taken away,—if rude hands have stolen
the dear remains, she will at least be permitted the mournful
satisfaction of beholding the spot which so lately contained what
she loved most in the world. She will see the stony pillow
whereon lay the pale face she expected to have bathed with her
tears!
All is stillness.
The angel forms, I have already spoken of, had not been seen
by Peter and John. But they appear again to Mary. There are

two of them. They are clothed in white. One is seated where the head of Jesus had rested, and the other at His feet, as if still keeping watch over the Lord of men and angels. The Roman soldiers were terrified at the vision of *one* angel:—Mary is not afraid at the sight of these *two*. Sorrow will not permit fear to get the better of her. She seems scarcely conscious of their presence. Her mind was quite taken up with the one thought—" Where her Blessed Lord could be."

They speak to her. They say, in compassion for her great grief—" *Why weepest thou ?* "

She replies in the very same words she spake to Peter and John—" They have taken away my Master out of His grave. Oh ! tell me where they have laid Him ? "

Angels could not comfort her—Angels could not heal her wounded spirit. But THERE WAS ONE NEAR AT HAND WHO COULD !

At that moment Mary seems to feel as if a third person were nigh. On hearing a footfall, she turns round and sees a solitary Figure standing close by the tomb.

Half-blinded by her weeping, she can think only of Joseph's gardener come to begin his morning's work.

She speaks to the Stranger of the one anxiety that was burdening her heart. *He* must know surely something about that tomb being empty, and of its having become no longer the grave of her Lord but the haunt of angels !

He, too, gently asks the cause of her tears.

" *If thou have borne Him hence*," she replies, " *tell me where thou hast laid Him, that I may take Him away.*" Yes, her love was so great, she feels that she would have power for anything; that even a woman's arm would be strong enough to bear the dead body.

She little knew to whom she was speaking. Her tears were like a veil that hid the reality from her sight.

One word, spoken by the supposed gardener, reveals the well-known Voice and Presence !

THE GREAT SUNRISE.

> " Weeper ! to thee how bright a morn was given,
> After thy long, long vigil of despair ;
> When that high Voice which burial rocks had riven,
> Thrilled with immortal tones the silent air.
> Never did trumpet royal blast declare
> Such tale of victory to a breathless crowd,
> As the deep sweetness of one word could bear—
> MARY !"

She at once replies in an ecstasy of joy,
RABBONI !

Rab was the Chaldean word for 'great.' *Rabbi* was a stronger form of the same word, 'greater,' 'dearer.' But RABBONI was the intensest form of all. It expressed strong devotion and love. It was the name which naturally gushed from Mary's trembling lips—" My great One ;—*my greatest ;—my best ;—my fondest Master !* "

It was the voice of her Beloved ! The same voice that first spoke peace to her troubled soul, and cast out the seven devils that had long ruled her wretched body. He now "calleth His own sheep by name, and leadeth her out." He is fulfilling His own sweet promise, contained in the prophecy about the smitten Shepherd and the scattered sheep—" *I will turn mine hand upon the little ones.*"

And how kind the manner in which He reveals Himself to her! Not in dazzling, terrifying glory, as the Great Conqueror of death ; but as " *that same Jesus,*"—the Brother-man—the old Friend of the Galilean shores :—so humble in appearance that she mistakes Him for the servant or keeper of the garden !

But could she possibly after all be deceived? Might it not be a mere vision in her fevered brain,—not a reality ? She will at all events make sure of this.

She rushed forward ;—putting forth her hand to touch Him. She will clasp in adoring reverence the feet she had so often followed by the Lake-side, and from her humble home at Magdala, but which she had last seen pierced on the cross.

With calm, divine majesty, Jesus tells her *not* to touch Him !

The body she gazed upon was the same as ever; and yet it was *not* the same. It was a spiritual body;—glorified by His victory over death. "*Touch Me not,*" He says.

At the same time He commands her to "go to *His Brethren,*" and to tell them not only of His having risen from the tomb, but that He is soon to ascend to Heaven, to "*His Father and their Father, to His God and their God.*"

How beautiful is the name Jesus here gives to His disciples! He had just risen victorious over the grave. No earthly conqueror had ever gained such a triumph as this. But to show that His love and affection are unchanged,—that He is the meek and lowly Saviour still,—He calls them not even 'disciples,'—not even 'friends,'—but '*brethren*':—"MY *brethren.*"

Mary is not slow to do what her blessed Master had told her. She, too, hastens to the city with the joyous tidings, "*I have seen the Lord!*"

What a privilege was hers! to be the first preacher of that gladdest truth a lost world has heard, "THE LORD IS RISEN INDEED!" God rewarded her watchful love. She had "waited on Him and been of good courage," and He had "strengthened her heart."

The other women, shortly after this interview with Mary Magdalene, were similarly honoured. Jesus met them, and said, "ALL HAIL!"

What a glad morning that must have been to all these varied friends and disciples! Yes, and, I repeat, for the Church of Christ to the latest ages of time! That divine "SUN," who had so lately gone down in the darkness of the tomb, has risen never again to set!

> "Oh! Day of days! Shall hearts set free
> No minstrel rapture find for Thee?
> Thou art the Sun of other days,
> They shine by giving back Thy rays."

Need I say, there surely must have been one among the number, that Resurrection day, happier than all the rest? It was the loving mother of Jesus. What must have been John's joy, to whom she had been so affectionately committed from the cross, when he reached his own house that early morning, and brought her the thrice glad news—" *Your Beloved Son was dead and is alive again!*" Salome, John's own mother, was one of the three women who had gone early to the sepulchre. She would also confirm the wondrous tidings which her son had brought. Weeping had endured for the past two nights, but joy came in the morning. The Psalmist's words would have a new meaning to all of them on this great Christian Sunday ;—" *This is the day which the Lord hath made, we will rejoice and be glad in it.*"

Some time during these memorable hours, but we are not told when or where, Jesus met the Apostle Peter. How kind, thus so soon to speak with the guilty one who had so basely denied His Master, and to assure him that his risen Lord had been "patient with him, and forgiven him all!"

What, it may occur to you to ask, are the chief priests and rulers doing now? Has the resurrection of Christ convinced them, too, of their guilt and crime? Do they also come, and, falling at His feet, " own Him as the divine Son of God?"

No: they try basely to bribe these Roman soldiers, just as they had done Judas. They gave them money to circulate the shameful falsehood—that they had slept on guard; and that the disciples of the buried Jesus of Nazareth had really come by night and stolen His dead body!

LXXIII.

He joins the two Disciples on the way to Emmaus.

Towards the afternoon of that same eventful day, two men are seen passing out of the Joppa gate on the west side of Jerusalem.

Probably they have just been with the company of Apostles and other friends gathered in the upper room, and are now returning at the close of the Passover feast, to their own house in the country.

We see at once, as they are walking slowly along, engaged in earnest talk with one another, that they are dejected and sad. Their sadness would be in striking contrast with the mirth and joy of others. They would likely be overtaken by not a few who had been, that morning, in what was called the procession of the "*Biccurim*," at the gathering of the first-fruits in the valley of Rephaim;—Paschal groups, carrying their osier baskets, full of the gladness of that glad season, "joying according to the joy in harvest." But there is no brightness in the faces of the two travellers.

I need hardly ask you what they are talking about, and what is the cause of their heavy sorrow?

There was just one theme—one thought—in the hearts and lips of the friends of Jesus this day. "*They talked together of all these things which had happened.*"

Can we wonder at their dejection? If any one of us had a dear friend, the news of whose death we had just heard, how grieved we should be! Even if that friend had loving relatives gathered round his bed to smooth his dying pillow, still we should feel sad. But if that same friend had been made to suffer cruel pain and torture, how deep and intense our heart-sorrow would be!

It was thus with these two wayfarers that afternoon. The

kindest Friend they ever had, had been seized by murderers, and nailed to the cross. They may probably have watched the dreadful scene with their own eyes: they may have gazed for hours on that pale suffering face on Calvary, and felt how powerless they were to render any relief. The whole was fresh on their minds and memories, for only two nights had since passed. What else could they do, but deeply mourn?

While they are proceeding on their journey, a Stranger joins them, and takes part in the conversation. He asks them what they are musing upon, and why they look so sorrowful during the days of a feast at which all were wont to be joyful?

He inquires of them so kindly, that they tell Him frankly about the burden of woe pressing on their hearts.

They tell Him in simple language the entire story of the shameful death and crucifixion of Jesus of Nazareth. They add, what to them, perhaps, was the saddest of all, that they had hoped at one time this crucified Man of Calvary was the Messiah Redeemer, they had so often and so earnestly longed for; who was to deliver the nation of Israel and reign as King in Zion.

Their hopes had vanished with His death. They wonder now how they could have allowed themselves to be deceived as they had been. And yet, they had heard a strange story too about His empty tomb. Some female acquaintances of theirs had gone that morning early to embalm His body. They not only found His sepulchre deserted, but angels were within it, who told them, most astonishing of all, that Jesus was alive.

The Stranger, in reply, talks to them at great length. In doing so, He purposely veiled their sight, that they might not at first know Him. He gently rebuked them for their want of belief, and for their slowness of heart. He showed them out of the writings of their own prophets, beginning with Moses, that it was necessary for the promised Christ (in order to redeem the world) to submit to death, just as Jesus had done.

Though Cleopas and his fellow-villager were doubtless well acquainted with the Old Testament Scriptures, the unknown Wayfarer gave what was to them quite a new explanation of text

2 C

after text, and passage after passage, with reference to the sufferings and glory of Messiah. He specially showed how it was necessary that His glory should be preceded by suffering. "Why," He seems to say to them, "have you such thoughts in your hearts, because Jesus of Nazareth was subjected to anguish and humiliation? Did you expect that He would come as a mighty warrior with helmet and sword, shield and banner? or did you expect Him to appear as a king with a sceptre in His hand and a crown on His head, and the palace of Zion for a home? If you did, you have mis-read your own prophets. They told you beforehand that He was to have none of these things, but the very reverse. They told you, that in order to save your souls, He was to come, a Man of sorrows—a slain Lamb—a smitten Shepherd:—to be wounded—bruised—chastised;—to have stripes laid upon Him—and finally to die and be laid in the grave. Instead of surrendering all hope, and giving way to sadness and despondency because of His cross and sufferings; that lowly and despised One is the very Messiah you ought to have expected."—"*Ought not Christ to have suffered these things, and to enter into His glory? And beginning at Moses and all the prophets, He expounded unto them in all the Scriptures the things concerning Himself*" (Luke xxiv. 26, 27).

I do not suppose these disciples had so much as a thought about the road they were travelling, and the beauties of nature all around them, even though it was the bright season of the Palestine year:—that same season which has now often been referred to in the preceding pages, when the Spring flowers were at their best and loveliest. Some of the trees were in full leaf,—others, like the hawthorn, were loaded with blossom and fragrance; the valleys were covered with corn; every grove was filled with song, from the trill of the finch to the sweet notes of the cuckoo. They had far different themes, however, to engross their attention than budding vines and fig-trees, or the little hills rejoicing on every side. Mile after mile is passed, new valleys open upon them, sprinkled with blue flax and campanula, crimson anemones and white daisies. But they walk with their eyes, now bent on the ground, now turned to the earnest Stranger. Who can He possibly be? They have just come, as I have supposed, from the gathering in the upper room. But all that the desponding disciples there said, had tended rather to chill their hearts; —while this fellow-Traveller has cheered, comforted, refreshed them. From no lips, save those of ONE, had they ever heard such sweet and precious words. It was that ONE who was now talking with them, though they knew it not!

And now they have reached the village to which they are going. It was called *Emmaus*—a word which is supposed to mean "a warm bath useful for healing."

If you ask me 'where Emmaus was?' I can only reply that its situation has hitherto been, and still is, a matter of great uncertainty. The party of able men who are now exploring Palestine, have lately brought to light the most probable site yet suggested, in a valley eight miles south-west of Jerusalem. If this turns out to be the right position, the road these two disciples now pursued would be out by the Bethlehem Gate, passing the very walls within which their Lord was born, and along the Roman highway, which then skirted the famous pools of Solomon. The enormous roots of oak-trees discovered, would seem to indicate that the now comparatively barren hills around were then clothed with timber. After the Stranger joined them, the mouth of a valley would be passed, likely then, as it is described now, "well watered and filled with lovely shady gardens of orange and lemon." By-and-by they would come to a wall of limestone where there is a clear spring; nigh to which, at the present day, are the ruins of a village called Khamesa.

This may or may not be the true site of Emmaus. But at all events Cleopas and his friend pause at a humble door in some such retired village, bearing the latter name.

It is evening light, with the beautiful sunset-glow on the hill-tops around.

The Stranger seems about to part with them, and to make as if He would go on farther. They are grieved to lose His company;

His words had greatly comforted their hearts, and revived their dying hopes.

They said to Him—" Oh do not leave us! Do not go away! *Abide with us, for it is toward evening, and the day is far spent.*"

The unknown Friend obeys their request, and enters the house with them. They are happy He has done so; for it would seem to indicate His purpose to tarry with them till the morning; and thus they would be enabled to prolong their converse together till midnight, on these holy themes which had made their walk of eight miles appear so short.

The table is spread for refreshment, or perhaps for the usual evening meal; and as was the wont among the Jews, they gave the Stranger the place of honour.

There was some Paschal unleavened bread on the board. In the course of the simple repast, He took the bread in His hands, and, before they began to eat, He blessed it, and divided it in two pieces, and gave to each of His fellow-travellers a piece.

In a moment they perceived who He was. Strange they had been so long in making the discovery! But something about Him;—perhaps the tones of His voice;—perhaps the wound-marks on His hands as He breaks the bread;—perhaps some radiant *light* on His SUN-LIKE countenance—reveal that it was none other than JESUS *Himself!*

Yes—all that the women had told them is true,—more than true; for they only could inform them that the sepulchre was empty; but Cleopas and his companion have *seen* the risen One, and conversed with Him.

They have scarce had time, however, to recover from their wonder and joy when He has left them. The couch on which He had blessed the bread is empty. He has vanished out of their sight!

This only was a fresh evidence and assurance as to who their mysterious Guest was. They looked at one another and said— "*Did not our heart burn within us while He talked with us by the way, and while He opened to us the Scriptures?*"

LXXIV.

He appears twice to those gathered in the Upper Room.

WHAT do these two disciples do?
They had just had a journey of seven or eight miles. They must have been tired and weary, not only with the walk, but with their longer hours of grief and sorrow. They doubtless had intended to spend the night at Emmaus. But they are so glad at heart, they cannot rest until they have gone back all the long distance to Jerusalem after sunset, that they may confirm the news to the anxious friends of Jesus.

You can imagine that if they had travelled slowly out to their village home, how speedily they would hurry over hill and dale in returning, till they reached the Joppa Gate again. The same road they had pursued, had, in long years gone by, been often traversed by the most splendid of all the Kings of Judah. Black blocks of basalt are still there, over which his chariot, with magnificent white horses, was driven almost daily to his favourite gardens at Urtas. It had been trodden that day by One who, though in lowly garb and surrounded with no royal retinue, was really and truly 'Brighter' and more illustrious than even "Solomon in all his glory!"

It was now late in the evening. The Paschal crowd the travellers had met in the afternoon were all dispersed: the road was quiet and deserted.

On reaching the upper room the door was locked; for the timid disciples were afraid of what the Jews might do. But it would be quickly opened when Cleopas and his companion made known who they were, and what their errand was.

You can picture the scene which followed. Not only were the Apostles present, but we are told also a number of other disciples—"they that were with them." We can only guess who these others might be. Doubtless there were some men and women from the Lake-side;—perhaps the family of Bethany—the risen Lazarus and his two sisters. Who knows but Zaccheus and Bartimeus, from Jericho, may have been drawn thus far from their own homes by gratitude and pity. It may be also, Nicodemus, and Joseph of Arimathea, who had both been getting braver every hour. And if her grief allowed her, might not John have brought thither his most sacred charge? Might not the mother of Jesus have been there to listen in a gladder form to His own words from the cross, "*Woman, behold thy Son!*" Would she not perchance remember how long, long ago (no less than twenty-one years since), she had "*for three days* sought Him sorrowing;"—three days in great trouble and torture of mind, thinking she would never see Him again; when lo! on the *third* day, she and Joseph were gladdened by finding Him alive;—hearing His voice in one of the Temple courts, telling that He was about His "Father's business." Now this early picture and experience is repeated. Three days of sadness and gloom are turned, like the other, into wondrous joy. It is the Father's business which has again hidden Him from her sight for three days in the grave. But the third day has now come. That business is completed. He could say, "*I have glorified Thee on the earth; I have finished the work Thou gavest me to do.*"

When the two men first enter the little assembly, they find that many present are in fear and doubt and wonder; knowing not what to think or believe amid the varied, strange, conflicting reports.

With glad hearts they must listen now to the news, "*We have seen the Lord!* We have spoken to Him. He appeared to us as a traveller, and we have walked with Him along a country road. We have sat at meat with Him in our own village, and received bread broken by His own blessed hands!"

If any, notwithstanding what they have just heard, still

continue to doubt :—these doubts will be immediately set at rest. For, all at once, Jesus Himself—the Risen One—the Lamb of God so lately sacrificed—appears to them! The door of the chamber where they were assembled was fastened ; but his glorified body could not be shut out by any locks or bolts. With no sign or sound ;—no apparently undoing of latch or opening of door, He stands in the midst of the little gathering, and utters His old, well-known word, " *Peace be unto you.*" It must have recalled, at least to the ten Apostles, the special blessing which, four days previously, He had given them at the last Supper. That " PEACE " had since then been finally secured—"*peace through the blood of His cross.*"

When Jesus thus suddenly presented Himself they were at first fearful. They thought he was a spirit,—just as some of them had done on the midnight waves of the Lake a year before.

But He calmed their fears—" *Why,*" said He, " *are ye troubled, and why do thoughts arise in your hearts?* " He showed them His wounded hands and feet, still fresh with the prints of the nails. He showed the open spear-wound in His side. He tells them to touch Him, in order to satisfy themselves that He was possessed of a real body of flesh and bones, though a glorified one: " *Behold My hands and My feet,*" He says, " *that it is I Myself.*" For the same purpose He eats a piece of broiled fish and some honeycomb before them ; and then finishes some earnest words by giving the twofold message they were to deliver :—" *that repentance and remission of sins should be preached in His name among all nations.*" That great mission was to " begin at Jerusalem." They were to make the first offer of His pardon and salvation to the people of the very city that had slain Him!

He repeats His blessing, "*Peace be unto you,*" and then breathed on them, and said—" *Receive ye the Holy Ghost.*" Having done all this, He seems to have suddenly vanished out of sight again, just as He had entered the room.

Oh what a happy meeting! Hesitation and unbelief have now given way to a gush of holy joy and full faith. All questionings and doubts are at an end. They could say, as St. Paul said soon after, "*It is Christ that died, yea rather that is risen again.*" Then truly were the disciples "GLAD *when they saw the Lord.*" Do you not think that through their tears they would sing Psalms of praise,—praise to the great and gracious Father in heaven, who had fulfilled His own promise, spoken in one of these Psalms regarding His Son, that He would not "*leave His soul in hell, nor suffer His Holy One to see corruption*"? The peace which for days had fled from their hearts, and, I may add, the rest needed for their weary bodies, would now return. They could have had little repose since that terrible Thursday evening.—But He, whose voice and presence has allayed their misgivings, would anew give to "His beloved, sleep." Surely even Mary could that night lay down her head tranquilly on her pillow. She might sing her old song once more, with a new and more glorious meaning—"*My soul doth magnify the Lord, and my spirit hath rejoiced in God, my Saviour!*"

Thomas, one of the disciples, was not present along with the others. He would not credit the news that Jesus was risen. On the contrary, he had given up all hope, and had remained for seven days in this unhappy state of mind—his brother Apostles doing their best, in vain, to convince him. He sadly and gloomily said to them, "*Except I shall see in His hands the print of the nails, and put my finger into the print of the nails, and thrust my hand into His side, I will not believe*" (John xx. 25).

The following Sunday evening, Christ again suddenly appeared to the disciples, and Thomas was of the number. The same kind words were repeated by Divine lips as on the evening of the Resurrection.

Jesus knew that Thomas was upright, honest, and brave. Was it not this disciple who, devoted to His Master, had said once, when others were trembling and fearful, "*Let us also go, that we may die with Him*"? The Risen One asks him to reach forth his finger, and touch the wounds in His hands and side. Thomas at once surrenders his unbelieving thoughts. He did not even wait to touch the body of Jesus—his old Master's presence and voice were enough: he exclaimed, "MY LORD, AND MY GOD!"

Jesus wished, by the offer He made of touching Him, to convince the doubting Apostle, and any others who might share his misgivings, of the reality of His human nature—that He had risen with an actual human body. Thomas not only now believes this, but, in doing so, he avows his belief in the still higher truth of the Saviour's *Deity*. He calls Him, in devout reverence, not only "My *Master*," but "my GOD." For you must observe that his exclamation is not the mere cry of wonder and astonishment. It was a confession of his faith. The words were, in his lips, the same as those of the "Apostles' Creed" are in our own—"*I believe . . . in Jesus Christ, His only Son, our Lord.*"

In after years, not one of the disciples were said to be more faithful than Thomas. Ever after that hour of the second Sunday evening, he became "strong in faith, giving glory to God." There is a tradition of his having gone to some countries far east of Palestine, and of his suffering martyrdom for the sake of Jesus either in India or Persia.

Christ, on the present occasion, very gently rebuked him. But His rebuke contains for us, and for all who love the Saviour's name, one of the most precious utterances that ever came out of His mouth: "*Thomas, because thou hast seen Me, thou hast believed,* BLESSED ARE THEY THAT HAVE NOT SEEN, AND YET HAVE BELIEVED!"

The bustle of the Passover Feast was now over. The Apostles and friends of Jesus soon returned to their distant homes. They must have carried with them there a wondrous tale of love and suffering and triumph!

The crowds of modern pilgrims to the Holy Sepulchre, prize, above all, the sight of the miraculous flame which superstition kindles every Easter day on the Saviour's tomb. The tapers they light with this "holy fire" are speedily extinguished, in order that they may retain them as precious relics. They are sacredly preserved on their persons or in their dwellings till their last hour arrives. Then they are kindled afresh, and burned beside their death-pillow, irradiating, as they suppose, the dark journey when they pass through the Valley of the Shadow of Death.

The disciples had now, in a nobler and better sense, carried away with them from their Lord's tomb "the holy flame." The old prophetic voice had been joyously fulfilled—"*Arise, shine, for thy* LIGHT *has come, and the glory of the Lord is risen upon thee!*" and with a different meaning from that which the same prophet's words, in another passage, convey—"*The Light of Israel shall be for a fire, and His Holy One for a flame*" (Is. x. 17). With the gladdening assurance that He who was to them 'Brighter than the Sun' had dispelled all their doubts and darkness, they might well cheer their homeward way with the words of the Hallel, sung so lately in very different circumstances—

> "*God is the Lord, which hath showed us* LIGHT :
> [or "kindled for us the flame."]
> *Bind the sacrifice with cords, even unto the horns of the altar.*
> *Thou art my God, and I will praise Thee :*
> *Thou art my God, I will exalt Thee.*
> *O give thanks unto the Lord; for He is good :*
> *For His mercy endureth for ever.*"

LXXV.

He shows Himself to His Disciples on the Lake-shore.

WE need not wonder at the Apostles directing their footsteps to the Lake-side. For, you will remember, a message had been sent to them by their Divine Master, as well as by the angels who appeared in His empty tomb, that He was to "*go before them into* GALILEE."

On their return, they take up their old employment as fishermen. They have now no longer a common purse, and they must toil for their daily bread.

They would be glad of the change from the awful and exciting scenes so lately witnessed in Jerusalem. It must have been a relief to be away from a city whose very gates and streets seemed stained with innocent blood—to find themselves by day treading once more the quiet pebbly beach, and at night, under the starry sky, watching the ripple of the familiar waves, or letting their nets down for a draught.

Gennesaret must have been dearer to them than ever. Besides being their home, it was the place in all Palestine they connected most with their loving Lord. It was there He had summoned them first to leave all, and follow Him. Every hill, from Mount Hattin with its double top, to Mount Hermon with its crown of snow—every nook of the winding shore, from the palm-groves of Magdala to the grassy slopes of Bethsaida, recalled His name and presence. The flowers which bloomed on the wayside and on the mountain slopes, the very birds which sang and twittered among the branches, or winged their flight over the Lake, brought to mind His sacred words. Here is the spot where He wrought a mighty miracle. There is the field of corn which suggested the parable-story of the sower sowing the seed. Here are the silent hills, with their thorny glades, where He went to pray. There is the turn in the road or the street where He invited the weary and the heavy-laden to come and have rest. There, where their fishing-boat is just crossing, He came to them in the midst of the howling wind and storm, and said, "*Fear not, it is I.*"

We must not think that the Apostles, by taking thus to their craft and nets again, had their hopes clouded and enfeebled as to Jesus being the Messiah, or that they had abandoned thoughts of going as His missionaries to spread the good news. No; they would only continue their toil till He met them, in accordance with His gracious promise, and until they received from His own lips further directions as to the future.

One evening seven of them set out " a-fishing " on their inland sea: Peter and John, James, Thomas, Nathaniel, and two others whose names are not given—possibly Andrew and Philip. They seem to have taken their large fishing-boat, towing a small one behind.

We can well imagine where their thoughts were, and what their converse was in these night-watches. "Shall we see Him soon? or may some weeks probably still elapse ere we have the joy of welcoming Him? and when He does appear to us, where or what will be the place of our meeting? Will it not likely occur in some quiet resort, where He may speak to us all alone? Will He not possibly come, too, on the 'first day of the week,' as He did in the upper room in Jerusalem, and breathe upon us His blessing? Or, as we saw Him glorified on Mount Hermon, is it improbable that it may be on the same beautiful hill, perhaps on the same spot, we shall see His glorified body once more, glowing with snow-white lustre, His face 'shining as THE SUN?'"

They have not dreamt of the likelihood of His coming to them in their every-day ordinary work and toil.

These seven fishermen had a disappointing night of it. They had let down their net during these long hours with no result. They had not so much as one fish in the hold of the boat. They are tired and sleepy and hungry. Doubtless, all they had gone through during the past weeks would make them feel more than usually fatigued and downcast.

In the grey dawn of morning, when nature was still slumbering; when no bird was on the wing, and no light in the hamlets; when the dull mist was still hanging on the mountain tops; they pull their boat towards the nearest shore. It was likely to a part not far from Bethsaida, having a rim of broad and pearly sand.

There is only one solitary Figure standing on the beach. The Stranger can scarcely at first be discerned in the glimmering dusk. As they draw closer, there seems a fire of "charcoal" burning, aided, perhaps, with the leaves and driftwood strewn on the shingle. They would probably imagine that this was only some other fisherman like themselves, who had finished his night-work on the Lake, and was now in the act of preparing his breakfast. Or, as there was no boat apparently near, he may possibly be some stray traveller who has been benighted; who, when he heard the near splash of oars, waits to obtain direction for his journey; or, perhaps, after a long fast, expects, when the boat is moored, to share some of the spoil they have taken in the Lake.

The way He speaks to the approaching boatmen seems to confirm their suspicion. After the manner which Eastern people have of addressing one another, He says—

"*Children, have ye any meat?*" "Have you caught any fish?"

They were likely still a good way out from land. But in the quiet morning air, His voice sounded clear and distinct. They answer "*No.*"

"*Cast,*" He says, as if He had seen a shoal of fish going in that direction, "*cast your net on the right side of your boat, and ye shall find.*"

It may have seemed a useless thing to do: but they thought they might as well take the Stranger's advice, and attempt this last venture. On letting down their net, a great number of fishes are immediately enclosed. The net is so heavy they cannot pull it up again into the boat.

All this was the work of a few moments. But even a few minutes in the East make a rapid change in the light. The sun had now topped the Gadara hills. The Figure, up to this time dimly visible, is now plainly revealed.

John's quick ear had been the first to catch the music of the Master's voice.

"*It is the Lord!*" says he to Peter, with trembling joy. He not only knew the voice, but, doubtless, he remembered another full net and "draught of fishes" two years and a half before. Some have supposed that he was first assured of the glad truth by observing a miraculous radiance around the face on which he gazed;—something akin to the glorified aspect he had last witnessed in the upper room in Jerusalem; something feebly resembling, what he afterwards, in far more dazzling vision, beheld in Patmos, "a Countenance like THE SUN shining in its strength." As it is, however, expressly stated in the inspired narrative, that "Jesus stood on the shore, *but the disciples knew not that it was Jesus;*" is it not sufficient to imagine, that the light of early day falling direct on the Divine-human countenance, along with the tones of the voice, were made, without any supernatural agency, the joint revealers of the glad surprise? Nature's morning-lamp, lit in her own great Temple, disclosing to these early worshippers the Person and glory of her Great High Priest!

Peter had his loose fisher's coat thrown aside; but in a moment he took it from the deck of the boat, and girt it about him. The strong man, with his brawny arms, is seen cleaving his way through the gentle swell of the wave towards the beach. He swam a hundred yards. There, wet and dripping as he was, he cast himself at Jesus' feet. The other six disciples land in the little boat, dragging behind them the net with its ample contents. The larger vessel could not be brought to shore, owing to the water being shallow.

They have all now landed, and the captured fishes are pulled up the shelving bank. They are even counted,—153 of them. But though they were so many and so large in size, not a mesh of the net is broken.

"*Come to your morning meal,*" said the Risen Redeemer.

They did not require to prepare on "the fire of coals" any of their own newly-caught fish. Some were there already, broiling on the hot embers along with cakes of bread.

Do you ask where Jesus had got these things? It seems enough to reply, that He, who on the banks of that lake could feed five thousand men on a few loaves and some small fishes, had only to speak the word, and land and sea would furnish the needful provision for such a repast.

Oh how like the old loving ways of the Master! watching them afar off in the midnight darkness, and having this gracious supply quite ready for them; so that they had no fuel to collect,

"When the morning was now come, Jesus stood on the shore." (opposite page 414)

or fire to kindle, or bread and fish to prepare. It was all waiting for these weary men !

Jesus, with His own hands, gives to each a portion. In tearful silence they must have looked on the Hands with the deep gashes of the nails still upon them. How they must have been reminded of a recent very different spectacle from that quiet sunrise on the Lake! How it must have recalled, too, many holy and sacred occasions when they had sat with their Lord at similar wayside meals in days gone by; when He had called them "*children:*" when He had shared their frugal fare, in the early morning, before they began the labours and fatigue of the day, or in the hush of the evening, after a hot day's travel among the hills and dusty roads of Galilee! How often had they reclined, as they were doing now,—boulder or grassy turf serving alike for couch and table!

There was something, however, at present different from any of these former times;—something about Him that awed them with reverence; for not a word seems to have been spoken. They appear for the time dumb in His presence; none of them durst ask, " *Who art Thou?* "

Breakfast is over. The sun will by this time have risen high above the eastern hills, and flooded the Lake with molten gold. The first breeze of morning may have begun to stir the waters, and the little rippling waves are making their soft, gentle music on the beach. As they gather around the ashes of the fire, Jesus begins to speak; and there is one of the number whom the Master very specially addresses. It is he who had plunged into the water, and swam first ashore. Three times over He puts the question to Peter—" *Simon, son of Jonas, lovest thou Me?* "

I need hardly ask the reason of that question being thus repeated ? You remember well the threefold denial of this once faithless, but yet loving and beloved Apostle. The Saviour, in His kind way, does not mention the denial in words; but He takes this significant method of recalling it.

Peter felt the rebuke. He was peculiarly grieved when, for the *third* time (bringing to mind the saddest of his three denials),

Jesus said unto him, "*Lovest thou Me?*" With all his heart and soul he makes answer, "*Lord, Thou knowest all things, Thou knowest that I love Thee.*"

Jesus tells him, as the best proof of his love, to go, in all time to come, and act the part of a shepherd of souls. "*Feed,*" He says, in the tender words of the original,—"Feed *My little lambs, feed My sheep.*"

Peter's risen Lord lifts, too, the veil from the future; and warns him that he will be called, in after years, to suffer and die for His sake. Indeed, He foretells the very manner of his death; that when he became "old," he would "stretch out his hands" on the cruel cross.

Peter wished much to know what would afterwards happen to his oldest friend—his dearest life-companion—John. "*What shall he do? What shall his lot be?*" Will he have a hard and rough path to tread, and a death of suffering to die? or will his be "a taking of rest in sleep;" will he be borne gently to heaven on the wings of loving angels?

"*What is that to thee?*" said Jesus: "leave that to Myself;—*Follow thou Me.*" Thou didst once before say, "*I am ready to follow Thee to death;*"—'Do so now.'

Peter from that hour was true to his Master's bidding. He lived ever after a brave and noble life, and died a hero's death.

This is surely a beautiful story, my young friends, of Jesus meeting His disciples in the early morn! It seems a picture of what He will do in the case of all His dear followers, whether young or old. After the long night of death is over, and the dawn of glory breaks, He will meet them on the heavenly shore; call them "children;" spread a glorious banquet for them; and make them happy for ever in His own presence and love!

LXXVI.

He meets Five Hundred Brethren on a Mountain in Galilee.

DOES Jesus converse with any of His other disciples and friends again in Galilee after His resurrection? or was this, which I have just described, His only meeting with them?

No. On some mountain He had appointed, a large farewell gathering takes place of all His dear followers.

I cannot tell you where the mountain was. It may have been on one of the wooded glades of Tabor. It may have been at the scene of the Transfiguration on Hermon. More likely still, it might be either on Mount Hattin—"the Mount of Beatitudes," or on one of the nearer green hills surrounding the inland sea, and which looked down upon the chief sphere of His labours. It would, at all events, doubtless, be some quiet spot, where (as we found on the similar, but more private occasion of His eating the Passover) He could best gather around Him, like a kind father, the children He loved, and address to them solemn parting words.

We are not told any particulars about this assemblage. We can only picture in our minds what it would be, and who came to it. There were five hundred people there, young and old (1 Cor. xv. 6).

With what glad hearts they would obey the invitation! Most of those present would likely be from the towns, villages, and hamlets on the Lake; but some, too, would come from a distance. They would willingly undergo any amount of fatigue or toil to behold and hear their dear Lord again.

You can imagine them gradually gathering. The lame He had healed, the sick He had restored, the blind He had made to see,

2 D

the sorrowing ones whose broken hearts He had bound up. We can even venture to think of a few special names with which we are now familiar. There might be Jairus, with his loved daughter gently leaning on his arm. There might be the maniac of Gadara, clothed and in his right mind, now a calm and loving believer. There might be the good centurion, with his restored servant; the widow of Nain, with her son walking by her side; sympathising adherents and followers even from "The Golden House." There might, moreover, be the holy female disciples from Magdala and Capernaum—Mary, Joanna, and Susanna; also the sinful woman from the city, who washed the Lord's feet with her tears. All these, with many others, might be assembled that memorable morning on this new *Gerizim*—"the hill of blessing," conscious that they were for the last time in their divine Master's presence.

It must, indeed, have been with mingled feelings that they repaired to this quiet temple of nature, to receive a farewell benediction from the Great High Priest before He left the court of the earthly sanctuary for "the Holiest of all." Perhaps a truer comparison of this gathering, would be to the closing scene in the Temple of Jerusalem on the Day of Atonement. Jesus, having entered within the veil with the offering of His own blood, now comes forth to bless His waiting people.

The five hundred may have been seated in rows on "the green grass," just like the five thousand at Bethsaida on the occasion of the miracle of the loaves. As they are waiting eagerly for His appearance, all at once the Saviour manifests Himself. It was after the same manner as He had done in the upper room in Jerusalem on the evening of the first Christian Sunday,—in glorified human form. We are not told how these vast crowds received Him. But we know that His own chosen Apostles went down on their knees before Him in silent adoration: although doubt still lingered in the minds of some of them (Matt. xxviii. 17).

He does not refuse their reverence and worship. He does not say, with the angel in the Book of Revelation, when John fell at his feet to worship him, "*See thou do it not, for I am thy fellow-servant; worship God.*" No; Jesus, as GOD, accepted the homage of those in that mountain assembly by whom He was best beloved!

With what breathless attention they would listen to the tones of the voice they knew so well!

We are not told all the gracious words He spake to them. We have only a very few of these recorded; but they are most precious and comforting.

"ALL POWER," saith He, "*is given unto Me in heaven and in earth.*"

Many there, had seen Him not long before—"the Man of sorrows"—undergoing grief and cruelty and pain—dying on a cross. But now He is the "*Captain of Salvation,*" who has been "made perfect through sufferings." Being invested with this '*All-power*' as the reward of these sufferings, He turns to His Apostles,—the chief officers of His great army, and gives them what an old writer calls their "marching orders"—"*Go and teach all nations, baptizing them in the name of the Father, and of the Son, and of the Holy Ghost.*"

The first use the Risen Jesus makes of His kingly rule is to break down the wall between Jew and Gentile. The tidings of salvation are to be borne to every land and every shore. Pilate had written above the cross—"KING OF THE JEWS;" but He had put the title in the three great languages of the world—Latin and Greek, as well as in Hebrew. "All kings" were to fall down before Him—"all nations" were to serve Him. To revert to one of the earliest sayings of this volume in connection with the Divine infancy, that BRIGHT SUN was to be "a *Light* to lighten the *Gentiles*," as well as "the glory of His people Israel." The commission, moreover, was not, 'Go and subdue with the sword;'—not 'Go and conquer with armies;'—but "Go and *teach.*" They were to tell these nations the good news He had spoken, and the glorious doctrines He had taught. Like David in his combat with Goliath, they were to take nothing in their hands but the simple sling of faith, and the smooth pebbles from the running stream of *truth*. " Out of weakness they would be made strong."

Beautiful, above all, are the very last words spoken on this occasion by Him who was still "the meek and lowly Jesus." They contained the best and kindest promise He could have given. It was the promise of His own *presence, love, and blessing*. As if He had said, ' I am soon to leave you ; and yet, in the best sense, I shall *never* leave you.' It was a promise to the Church He had purchased with His blood, embracing remotest ages— " *Lo, I am with you always, even to the end of the world.*"

Having uttered these sayings, He withdraws from sight, and the crowds disperse to their different homes again. It was a day and a scene not one there would ever forget.

There was one private interview after this, which took place between Christ and one of His apostles. It is mentioned twenty years after by St. Paul. It was a meeting, not with John, nor with Peter, but with his cousin *James*, the son of Mary Cleophas. Often, at the close of life, people have a great fondness for the friends of youth. They cling to old attachments ; and, sometimes, as the best proof of friendship, they send for such companions of their early years, not only to take a sacred farewell, but perhaps also to tender some kind parting advice or counsel, which they would not think of giving to others.

May it not have been with something of these feelings that Jesus met James all alone ? He was the last we read of, who saw the Lord *quite* alone. He had been His associate in childhood and youth. He had known Him far longer than any of the other disciples.

It seems to give us a new and beautiful glimpse as to how real the human nature of the Saviour was, that He appears, last of all, to the old school companion and boy-friend He had at Nazareth. It has been supposed, that possibly a very different object in such a meeting, may have been to prepare James for the post he was soon to take, of Chief Pastor of the Church at Jerusalem. Could another desire in the heart of the Risen

Redeemer also be, to ask His human relative to share with John a tender interest in His dear mother's well-being? We are not informed. It may have been so. We may feel assured that interview would always form a sunny spot for the good apostle to look back upon. This we know, that he afterwards lived a very holy life. He wrote the Epistle in our Bibles which bears his name. He was, some years after, cruelly stoned to death. Who can tell but Jesus may have said something at this private conference which may have made him brave and courageous in that trying hour?

I have just alluded, for the last time, to an honoured name which has frequently occurred in these pages:—that of the blessed mother of our Lord. Did she die in Jerusalem? or in more distant Ephesus? We cannot be certain. There is a touching tradition of the Early Church, though no more than a tradition, that she was buried, at her own request, by the loving hands to whom she had been committed, in the Garden of Gethsemane.

DAWN OF ETERNAL DAY.

"THY SUN SHALL NO MORE GO DOWN."—IS. LX. 20.

"SO THEN, AFTER THE LORD HAD SPOKEN UNTO THEM, HE WAS RECEIVED UP INTO HEAVEN, AND SAT ON THE RIGHT HAND OF GOD."—MARK XVI. 19.

"LIFT UP YOUR HEADS, O YE GATES; EVEN LIFT THEM UP, YE EVERLASTING DOORS; AND THE KING OF GLORY SHALL COME IN. WHO IS THIS KING OF GLORY? THE LORD OF HOSTS, HE IS THE KING OF GLORY."—PS. XXIV. 9, 10.

"THE CITY HAD NO NEED OF THE SUN, NEITHER OF THE MOON, TO SHINE IN IT; FOR THE GLORY OF GOD DID LIGHTEN IT, AND THE LAMB IS THE LIGHT THEREOF."—REV. XXI. 23.

LXXVII.

He is taken up to Heaven in a Cloud.

IN the preceding section, we have stood in thought by the sepulchre in the garden, and watched THE GREAT SUNRISE. We are told in one of the Jewish sacred writings, that the priests on duty in the Temple, during the last watch of the night, looked eagerly, morning after morning, for the sun's earliest ray tipping Mount Hebron—a conspicuous hill south-east of Jerusalem. When its summit caught the longed-for beam, the cry burst forth—"*Barkäi ad Chebron!*"—" The light of day appears on Hebron!" This was followed by a blast of trumpets, answered in the distance with a peal of bells. The rising sun was the signal for the commencement of the services within the sacred courts.

The true LIGHT OF DAY,—"*above the brightness of the sun*"—has risen from the gloom of the grave and of death. But His rising, too, is only the signal for the commencement of the loftier services of the Temple above, in the New Jerusalem—"the house not made with hands, eternal in the heavens." With a higher than earthly meaning may it be said, "*In them hath He set a tabernacle for the* SUN; ... *His going forth is from the end of the heaven, and His circuit unto the ends of it*" (Ps. xix. 5). "*For Christ is not entered into the holy places made with hands, which are the figures of the true; but into heaven itself, now to appear in the presence of God for us*" (Heb. ix. 24). Our last glimpse of that All Glorious SUN, whose course we have sought reverently to trace, will be as He vanishes from sight within the Golden Gates. His ascension to Heaven was truly, to His glorified Church, the DAWN OF EVERLASTING DAY!

"The sweet Story of old," then, is drawing to a close. Forty days have passed since Jesus rose from the dead, and He is about to return to His Father.

A little while before the Feast of Pentecost, the disciples seem to have gone back from Galilee to Jerusalem. We find them once more with their Master; probably they are in "the upper room"—the same chamber which had so many memories of gloom and doubt, as well as of peace and joy.

They leave it for the last time in His company. On frequent occasions before, had they journeyed together. They have their final walk now. It is along the same footpath they knew and loved so well. Their risen Shepherd, we read, "*led* them out." They knew not where He was going; but they followed Him trustfully; although, in doing so, they may have had at the same time their own strange sad thoughts as to what was about to happen.

They cross the brook Kidron, and climb the steep road leading across the Mount of Olives to Bethany. They do not enter the village, but apparently strike off the beaten track to one of the quiet heights near it, and where the noise and din of the neighbouring city could not be heard.

I remember well when there, looking around and wondering where that most sacred place could be on which the human footsteps of Jesus last rested! No one can tell. I sat down with a friend on a grassy knoll, which might possibly answer to it, and read the story of the Ascension. I shall, at all events, ever think of that spot in connection with the great closing scene in the life of the Divine Saviour. It was a short way from the road, on the side or ridge of a little valley. There were fragments of worn limestone rocks scattered about with heath growing upon them, and numbers of olive, fig, and almond-trees,—the last in full blossom. Bethany was hid in the hollow to the right. There was a grand view in the far distance, deep, deep down, of the Jordan Valley and the Dead Sea. Above was a sky of unclouded blue.

The Blessed Lord and His followers, as they walk across the hill, are engaged in earnest conversation.

"*Master*," say they, "*wilt Thou at this time restore again the kingdom to Israel?*"

Perhaps the question was suggested as they stood for a moment near the top of Olivet and gazed on the glorious Temple, with Herod's towers and palaces behind it. Notwithstanding all they had heard from Jesus' lips, to the last they still seem to have clung to the hope of His driving away the hated Roman, and reigning on the ancient throne of David!

He replied to them—"Do not inquire about the times and seasons." He told them He had nobler and better work for them meanwhile to do. They are not to expect an earthly kingdom: they are rather to prepare others for a heavenly and eternal one. And so He renews the great commission He had previously given, that they are to "*Preach the Gospel to every creature.*" He enjoins them to "begin at Jerusalem;" then to go to Judea; then to Samaria; then to "the uttermost parts of the earth." He told them, further, not to return at present to the Lake-side; nor yet to start at once on their great work of teaching and preaching; but to wait at Jerusalem till Pentecost; when the Holy Spirit would be poured out upon them, and they would have new power given them from on high.

All His directions being completed, the gates of Heaven are thrown open to receive Him back.

The songs of angels are already floating in His ear, yet still His loving thoughts are with those He is to leave behind!

He lifts up His hands (the hands with the print of the nails still upon them), and blesses His Apostles. While in the act of blessing, His glorious and glorified body begins to move from the earth.

Slowly He ascends in the deep, calm blue of that hot summer sky. A cloud, similar to the one we saw on Hermon, comes down to meet Him. Without wing or chariot-wheel, He is borne up in that bright white covering. Higher and higher it mounts, till it becomes a speck, and is lost from view.

In this glorious vanishing of THE GREAT SUN to shine in

brighter worlds, I am reminded of a poet's description of His type in the heavens—

> "And then, in glorious pomp, the SUN retired
> Behind that solemn curtain, and His train
> Of crimson and of azure and of gold
> Went floating up the zenith, tint on tint,
> And ray on ray, till all the concave caught
> His parting benediction!"

Or in the similar words of another—

> "Then the cloud rose sunward
> Ever brighter, higher,
> Ever floated onward
> Towards the Gates of Fire.
>
> "All its being belted
> With a glory bright,
> Into heaven it melted
> In a dream of light.
>
> "And when earth was covered
> With its twilight shroud,
> Still a radiance hovered
> Nigh the vanished cloud."

The disciples feel for the first time that they are orphans. They gaze steadfastly upwards, dumb with silence. No trace of their dear Master is to be seen. There was nothing but the still silent air above and around them. The last glimpse they had was that of His hands extended in blessing. But it was enough to tell them that no distance, no space, no time could ever separate them from His love!

When they turn their straining eyes back, however, to the green mountain-slopes around, they feel they are not alone as they had imagined. Two angels are standing behind them. They speak some comforting words. They address them as "*Men of* GALILEE." These bright messengers may, perhaps, before this time, have sped on 'angel-visits' to Jesus on some of the silent mountains of *Galilee,* where He was wont to pray.

What is the consoling message which these two shining ones deliver?

It was that this same Jesus—the meek and the lowly Saviour—who was now taken to Heaven, would "so come again in like manner;" when He would say to His Church and people—" *Come, ye blessed of My Father, inherit the kingdom prepared for you from the foundation of the world.*"

All the eleven fell down on the green turf, not to worship the angels, but to worship Him who had been received up into glory!

It was a wondrous moment. When these eleven men were lying dumb and speechless on the grass of an earthly hill, all Heaven was stirred to receive back her crowned Mediator. The adoring ranks of angels made way for Him as He passed up the golden streets to sit down for ever at the right hand of God! On this same Mount of Olives, a few weeks before, there had been a triumphal procession, amid the waving of palm branches, into the earthly city;—but what was it to this glorious entry of the Divine Conqueror within the heavenly portals, among a multitude "clothed in white robes, and *palms* in their hands."

The Apostles rose from their knees to go back again across the Mount. With what feelings do you suppose they will return?

Oh, I am certain you will think and say, 'It will be with eyes filled with tears, and with hearts ready to break. It will surely be with them as with those who have come from seeing the vessel sail with their eldest and best-loved brother to a far distant land; or like those who are returning to their desolate home after laying the head of an honoured parent in the grave.'

Yet, strange to say, that was not the case. We read, " *They returned to Jerusalem* WITH GREAT JOY!" We look for tears and we hear songs. We look for them daily in the sacred courts, doing little else than mourn their unspeakable loss; but we read, " *They are continually in the Temple,* PRAISING AND BLESSING GOD!"

How was this? Birds sing in sunshine. Now that "the Sun of their souls" had vanished from their sight, how could they thus wake their tongues to melody?

I answer—The many promises of Jesus; the parting blessing of Jesus; along with the saying of the angels, had all greatly comforted them. They would think, doubtless, with grateful joy over the three happy years they had spent in the service of their Master, and enjoyed His gracious love. They would think of the Divine Spirit He had pledged to send when He went away; whose presence was to atone for His own loss and absence, and who was to "abide with them for ever." Above all, they would dwell on what the shining messengers had told them, that He himself would come again as a *Brother-man:* or, as in His own tender words a few weeks before—"*I will come again and receive you unto Myself, that where I am there ye may be also!*"

In many a future day and future year, how often would these disciples think of that farewell hour, that farewell look:—the extended hands—the loving blessing—the ascending cloud—the angel promise!

They would say to one another, not in the words, but in the thought of the poet—

> "No fear but we shall soon behold,
>   Faster than now it fades, that gleam revive;
> When issuing from His cloud of fiery gold
>   Our wasted frames feel THE TRUE SUN and live!"[1]

One of these devout gazers thus speaks of "that blessed hope" with holy joy, and prays about it with earnest longings, many years after. It was the one glad thought of his life. It took all the gloom away from his prison home. "*Behold, He cometh with clouds!*" . . . "*Even so, come, Lord Jesus, come quickly!*"

---

[1] Keble.

Young readers! who have followed me in the foregoing chapters, I would seek, ere closing, to remind you yet once more (as I have sought to do frequently) of the golden thread running all through this wondrous Story of the most wondrous of lives,— that this meek and lowly Jesus, who was born at Bethlehem; who lived in the village of Nazareth, and toiled at daily labour there; who agonised in Gethsemane, who was crowned with thorns, who bled on Calvary, who was laid, pale and silent, in Joseph's garden-tomb—was none other than THE MIGHTY GOD! He was not, as some unworthily speak of Him and think of Him, merely a good and holy Prophet—one of the illustrious teachers or sages of humanity, like Socrates or Solon, Seneca or Solomon;—one of many bright and glorious *stars* which have appeared from age to age. No; He is the great central SUN, around whom these stars all revolve. "*His goings forth have been from of old, from everlasting.*" His name is what the ablest and noblest of human teachers never dared to assume—"IMMANUEL, GOD WITH US."

"GREAT IS THE MYSTERY OF GODLINESS: GOD WAS MANIFEST IN THE FLESH, JUSTIFIED IN THE SPIRIT, SEEN OF ANGELS, PREACHED UNTO THE GENTILES, BELIEVED ON IN THE WORLD, RECEIVED UP INTO GLORY!"

As you take a yet parting gaze on this Divine Vision, are you able to say, "*We beheld* HIS GLORY, *the glory as of the Only-Begotten of the Father,* FULL OF GRACE AND TRUTH"? The famous statue of Memnon, on the plain of Thebes, was said, under the influence of the sun's morning rays, to emit strains of music. Happy for you if, in life's young morning, you have been made the subjects of a grander, diviner reality—if, shone upon by One "BRIGHTER THAN THE SUN," you give out from your earliest years the tuneful melody of a holy, pure, devoted life, saying, "*My voice shalt thou hear in* THE MORNING, *O Lord!* IN THE MORNING *will I direct my prayer unto Thee!*" Thus paying your "*morning* sacrifice," you will be able to look forward with joyful hope to that better world, where the happy myriads who bask under unsetting beams are said to shine "as the brightness of the firmament" and (in the reflected light of the True SUN) "as the stars, for ever and ever."

> " No cloud upon its radiant joy,
> No shadow o'er its bright employ,
> No sleep—no night,
> But perfect sight,
> THE LORD OUR EVERLASTING LIGHT!"

" *And the* LAMB *is the* LIGHT *thereof !* "—Does not this assertion seem to intimate (what was already said in the beginning of this section), that Jesus will never cease to be the SUN of His Redeemed Church in Heaven ? Yea, more! that the glories of the Godhead will, during the ages of eternity, be seen and gazed upon through the softening light and lustre of His glorified humanity ?—

> " Oh who shall bear
> The blinding glare
> Of the peerless LIGHT that shall meet us there !
> If without a screen
> At one burst be seen
> The Presence in which we have ever been ?
> What eye can gaze
> On the unveiled blaze
> Of the lustrous throne of the Ancient of Days !

> " Arm of the Lord !
> Creating WORD ;
> Whose glory the silent skies record,
> Who hast set Thy name
> In scrolls of fame,
> On the firmament's all-encircling flame !

> " I gaze o'erhead
> Where Thy hand hath spread
> For the waters of heaven, their crystal bed ;
> And stored the dew
> In its depths of blue,
> Which the fires of the *sun* come tempered through.

> "As soft they shine
> Through that pure shrine,
> *So beneath the veil of Thy flesh divine,*
> Will beam the LIGHT
> That were else too bright,
> To fall on a ransom'd mortal's sight!"

Be this, meanwhile, the closing petition of all whose eyes have traced the preceding pages. They are words specially befitting the lips of those still breathing the air of life's early hours—

> "O LIGHT! whose beams illumine all,
> From twilight dawn to perfect day,
> Shine THOU before the shadows fall
> That lead our wandering feet astray;
> At morn and eve Thy radiance pour,
> That youth may love and age adore!"

" THEN SHALL THE RIGHTEOUS SHINE FORTH

AS THE SUN,

IN THE KINGDOM OF THEIR FATHER"

(Matt. xiii. 43).

THE END.

www.ingramcontent.com/pod-product-compliance
Lightning Source LLC
Chambersburg PA
CBHW022102300426
44117CB00007B/555